$35.00

D0723849

ᘔ005

MISSIOLOGICAL EDUCATION
FOR THE TWENTY-FIRST CENTURY

Paul and Rosemary Pierson

American Society of Missiology Series, No. 23

MISSIOLOGICAL EDUCATION FOR THE TWENTY-FIRST CENTURY

The Book, the Circle, and the Sandals

Essays in Honor of Paul E. Pierson

J. Dudley Woodberry
Charles Van Engen
Edgar J. Elliston
editors

Wipf & Stock
PUBLISHERS
Eugene, Oregon

Wipf and Stock Publishers
199 W 8th Ave, Suite 3
Eugene, OR 97401

Missiological Education for the Twenty-first Century
The Book, the Circle, and the Sandals: Essays in Honor of Paul E. Pierson
Edited by Woodberry, J. Dudley, Van Engen, Charles, and Elliston, Edgar J.
Copyright©1997 Orbis Books
ISBN: 1-59752-236-8
Publication date 6/7/2005
Previously published by Orbis Books, 1997

This volume is dedicated to
Paul E. Pierson,
missionary, pastor, and former dean of
the Fuller Theological Seminary, School of World Mission

Contents

ECUMENICAL CONTEXTS
Sandals from Other Sanctuaries

FUTURE
Toward New Books, Circles, and Sandals

The *American Society of Missiology Series*, in collaboration with Orbis Books, seeks to publish scholarly works of high merit and wide interest on numerous aspects of Missiology—the study of mission. Able presentations on new and creative approaches to the practice and understanding of mission will receive close attention.

Previously published in
The American Society of Missiology Series

Preface to the Series

The purpose of the American Society of Missiology (ASM) Series is to publish—without regard for disciplinary, national, or denominational boundaries—scholarly works of high quality and wide interest on missiological themes from the entire spectrum of scholarly pursuits relevant to Christian Mission, which is always the focus of books in the Series.

By "mission" is meant the effort to effect passage over the boundary between faith in Jesus Christ and its absence. In this understanding of mission, the basic functions of Christian proclamation, dialogue, witness, service, worship, liberation, and nurture are of special concern. And in that context questions arise, including, How does the transition from one cultural context to another influence the shape and interaction between these dynamic functions, especially in regard to the cultural and religious plurality that comprise the global context of Christian mission?

The promotion of scholarly dialogue among missiologists and among missiologists and scholars in other fields of inquiry may involve the publication of views that some missiologists cannot accept, and with which members of the Editorial Committee do not agree. Manuscripts published in the Series reflect the opinions of their authors and are not understood to represent the position of the American Society of Missiology or of the Editorial Committee. Selection is guided by such criteria as intrinsic worth, readability, and accessibility to a range of interested persons and not merely to experts or specialists.

The ASM Series Editorial Committee
James A. Scherer, Chair
Mary Motte, FMM
Charles Taber

Foreword

Richard J. Mouw

The language of the missionary movement has typically been characterized by a sense of urgency: "O Zion, haste / thy mission high fulfilling."
This should not surprise us, since the missionary movement has been caught
up in matters that are indeed urgent. The Christian community has received a
direct mandate from the Lord to carry the gospel to the nations. Eternal destinies are at stake. To such a mandate haste is a highly appropriate response.

This book is an exercise in missiology, the academic study of the church's
missionary activity. Academic discussions work best when they are not done
in haste. This book provides us with an excellent sampling of high quality
academic exchange about the missionary enterprise.

Is there a contradiction involved in engaging in non-hasty, reflective discussion about matters of extreme urgency? Not really. Hospital emergency
rooms are places where urgent activity is always occurring. Haste is typically a necessity when dealing with medical crises. But emergency rooms
need to be backed up by careful, non-hasty academic research. The medical
experts who go into action when the ambulance arrives can do their work
well only because medical researchers work patiently in laboratories and
attend scholarly conferences.

Fuller Theological Seminary's School of World Mission was founded on
the conviction that the urgent task of bringing the gospel to the lost must be
undergirded by the careful academic study of the church's life and mission.
This volume, dedicated to Paul Pierson, one of the great evangelical leaders
in missiological education, provides clear evidence of the integrity of this
academic enterprise. The scholars whose contributions are recorded here
are deeply committed to the faithful and informed fulfillment of the missionary mandate.

Richard J. Mouw is president of Fuller Theological Seminary and professor of
Christian philosophy and ethics. He served for seventeen years as professor of
philosophy at Calvin College before coming to Fuller in 1985. He is on the edito-
rial board of *The Journal of Religious Ethics*, *Word and World*, and *World Vision
Magazine*, and also serves on the board of the Institute for Ecumenical and Cultural
Research.

Indeed, one of the beauties of this volume is the manner in which it bears witness to the way in which God has rewarded the sacrificial efforts of those missionary pioneers who traveled far to bring the good news to those who had not yet heard it. The missionary movement has established a Christian international network that has made possible an exciting cross-cultural conversation intensified by a degree of spiritual bonding that is seldom available to other academic guilds. And this conversation—as is so evident in this volume—opens up wonderful new insights into the riches of redemption.

Jesus Christ, the all-sufficient Savior, is building his church by redeeming persons from every tribe and tongue and people and nation. This redemption is experienced in a rich variety of cultural contexts. It is inevitable that different people will feel the Savior's loving touch in different ways; to meet Jesus in the desperate circumstances of urban homelessness in North America is a different experience from meeting him at a mass evangelistic meeting in Mexico City or in a jungle clearing in Papua New Guinea.

To study this kind of contextualization and to explore its importance for our evangelistic and pastoral programs is an exciting and illuminating project. It requires careful research, probing minds, and a spirit of adventure. And it can only flourish as an academic activity if it is done out of a deep desire to advance the mission of that body whose supreme purpose is to bear witness to the power of the only Name under heaven that is given for our salvation. This book shows us what that kind of study can be like. May it be a blessing to all who want to see more clearly how careful missiological reflection can provide strong support for the church's urgent missionary task.

Preface

Charles Van Engen

In this Preface I want to locate this book within the larger history of the discussion of the relationship of mission studies to theological education in the West and particularly in the United States. This volume and the conference from which it emanated are part of an extended conversation among world-class thinkers, participants and shapers of missiology and missiological education concerning mission studies, mission education, and formation for mission service. It forms part of a search for self-understanding on the part of mission educators. What Darrell Whiteman has said in his chapter about the value of the study of anthropology is true also about the value of reflection about missiological education: "The greatest value . . . is not in what we learn about exotic cultures that are different from our own, but rather, in what we discover about ourselves."

Calling attention to the need for evaluative reflection, Gerald Anderson pointedly asks, "How do we account for the decline in interest and support for world mission in the main-line Protestant denominations and the Roman Catholic Church in the West—at the same time that we have more professors of mission and more studies of mission?"

This book involves evaluative reflection and careful listening on the part of mission educators. Ken Gnanakan emphasizes critical self-evaluation in his presentation. "The training of missiologists is urgent," he says, "but top priority will need to be given to evaluating what is being done in order to develop more effective people and programs for the future." This book involves careful listening as well. As Tite Tiénou says in his chapter, "In my judgment, listening before speaking is the first act of sound missiology; it must therefore be incorporated into missiological training. Listening enhances the possibility of reflection. Missiological training which includes serious reflection will prevent the practice of mission from being mere ac-

---

Charles Van Engen was born and reared in Mexico, where from 1973 to 1985 he served the National Presbyterian Church of Mexico in theological education, evangelism, youth ministries, and refugee relief. He is presently Arthur F. Glasser Professor of the Biblical Theology of Mission at Fuller Theological Seminary's School of World Mission.

tivism." So this book constitutes a search for a new future in mission education into the next century, a movement toward what Samuel Escobar calls in his chapter, "post-Enlightenment missiology."

Missiological education has a rather long history. One of the earliest Protestants to advocate mission education was Johannes Hoornbeeck (1617-1666). According to Johannes Verkuyl's description in *Contemporary Missiology: An Introduction* (1978), Hoornbeeck followed Gisbertus Voetius (1589-1676) in borrowing heavily from the Roman Catholic Congregatio de Propaganda Fide with its longer history of missionary experience and its network of missionary support and reflection. Hoornbeeck suggested that universities should keep theological students informed about mission issues, establish seminaries, and train missionaries.

Two hundred years later in Germany, in 1864, "Karl Graul, founder of the Leipzig Missionary Society, was appointed to a newly established chair in missiology at Erlangen University . . . but his death shortly after his inaugural lecture prevented him from occupying this position (Bosch 1982, 14).

Thirty-two years later, at the University of Halle in 1896, Gustav Warneck furthered the discussion with his *Evangelische Missionslehre*, a work that Johannes Verkuyl calls, "a trail-blazing effort in systematic missiology." This book would stimulate, parallel, and be followed by a host of new writings and discussions of mission during the next fifty years, particularly in Europe—not least among these being the work of Josef Schmidlin, first incumbent in the first chair of missiology at a Catholic institution, in 1910 at the University of Münster. In 1923 Schmidlin published a kind of Roman Catholic counterpart to Warneck's work entitled *Katholische Missionslehre im Grundriss*. Earlier, in 1902, Robert Speer wrote *Missionary Principles and Practice*, in which he suggested the development in the United States of a science of missions, also following the pattern of Gustav Warneck's work. In Dutch missiology one can see Warneck's influence on Johannes H. Bavinck in his *An Introduction to the Science of Missions* (1960 and 1977).

In this volume Andrew Walls describes Alexander Duff's work at New College, Edinburgh, and the establishing of "the first chair of mission studies anywhere in the Protestant world." Along with the English, Germans, and Dutch, Scandinavian Protestants thought and wrote rather extensively about mission education, particularly during the first half of this century. Olav Myklebust's magisterial two-volume study, published in 1955 and 1957, is still the touchstone for all subsequent discussion of mission studies and missionary formation as these relate to theological education.

In a survey article in *Missiology* in 1976, R. Pierce Beaver pointed out that during most of the eighteenth and nineteenth centuries:

> Seminary professors produced very little of the literature used in mission study and promotion on the campuses. Secretaries of the board

were the major writers, especially Rufus Anderson . . . and his post-humous disciple Robert E. Speer. . . . Biographies were perhaps the favorite study material [in seminary mission studies], and throughout the nineteenth century the Memoirs of David Brainerd and of Henry Martyn stimulated vocations to service abroad above all others. Works by missionaries and the periodicals of the boards were extensively used. The activity of the Student Volunteer Movement stimulated regular mission study on the [seminary] campuses (Beaver 1976).

"Meanwhile mission studies," Beaver pointed out, "had actually been creeping into the curriculum of various seminaries." For example, in 1899, William O. Carver became the first full-time professor of comparative religions and missions at the Southern Baptist Seminary in Louisville. In 1901 "the Divinity School of the University of Chicago added a Professorial Lecturer on Modern Missions, Alonzo K. Parker. The Yale chair was established in 1906 with Harlan P. Beach as professor, and the Day Missions Library was founded. The Episcopal Theological Seminary at Cambridge instituted a professorship in 1907 with Philip M. Rhinelander as incumbent." By 1910 a report on the teaching of missions given at the World Missionary Conference at Edinburgh stated that "there were four full professorships [of mission]: Southern Baptist Seminary, Yale University Divinity School, Episcopal Theological Seminary (Cambridge) and Omaha Theological Seminary" (Beaver 1976).

However, after 1920 the teaching of missions in theological seminaries further declined. Beaver reports that "the economic depression which closed the decade [of the 1920s] ended further multiplication of teaching posts, and by the mid-1930s threw the whole Protestant missionary enterprise into reverse. World War II marked the end of the old order of overseas missions" (Beaver 1976, 76).

Commenting on this period, James Scherer observed:

Missiology in the United States in the pre-1950 period, unlike its more academic European cousins, failed to develop a genuinely scientific and academic character, and was plagued by a certain immaturity with regard to definition, methodological basis and objectives. Little wonder that after 1945, with the collapse of the old colonial structure, the rise of an international Christian community on six continents, and the growth of the ecumenical movement, missiology in America had to be reestablished on a new foundation (Scherer 1985, 447-48).

The teaching of missions in Bible institutes and colleges flourished, as the reader will note in Kenneth Mulholland's chapter in this book. Beaver writes:

The [Bible college] movement began with the establishment by Dr.
A. B. Simpson in 1882 of the school which a few years later became
Nyack Missionary College . . . followed in 1886 by the foundation of
Moody Bible Institute. By 1960 there were 250 schools with 25,000
students. . . . The colleges have been sources of missionary vocation
for the nondenominational faith missions, while the institutes have
trained their candidates. Probably the great majority of North American missionaries now serving overseas are graduates of these institutions (Beaver 1976, 77).

During this same time, the professors of mission in the seminaries were
not faring very well. Beaver writes:

The Association of Professors of Missions (APM) came into existence in 1950, not as an expression of the old missionary triumphalism,
but as an attempt to construct a lifeboat for floundering brothers and
sisters. The biennial reports of the Association reveal the wrestling
done by the members over the reason of being of such a discipline,
curriculum and teaching methods during the past twenty-five years.
. . . The Association marks the beginning of a new era rather than the
climax of the old order. Hope for the rebirth and advance of academic
missiology in the seminaries and university divinity schools is kindled
by the founding and rapid development of the American Society of
Missiology (ASM), by the professional and research doctoral programs of the School of World Mission of Fuller Theological Seminary, and by the new interest in missiological research among conservative Evangelicals.

Beaver's optimism proved well-founded. As of 1995, the Association of
Professors of Mission has over 200 members, the ASM has over 350 and
the Evangelical Missiological Society (EMS) has over 300.

During the last fifteen years a number of Protestant missiologists have
reflected on the matter of missiological education. In an article entitled
"Theological Education in Missionary Perspective," David Bosch followed
Hans-Werner Gensichen's lead in suggesting that theological education needs
both a missiological dimension and a missiological intention, both the study
of God's mission and the furthering of the study of the church's missions.
Bosch affirmed:

The solution lies neither in regarding missiology as a subdivision of
one of the classical theological disciplines nor in its self-assertion as
an autonomous subject. We need a third option. . . . When [missio-
logy's] right to exist was grudgingly conceded [in theological educa-
tion] . . . a solution was attempted in either assigning to missiology a
completely separate sphere, making it a component of one of the "clas-

sical" disciplines, or hoping the other disciplines would embroider their own courses slightly by including some threads of mission. None of these attempts proved satisfactory. . . . It seems to me that we need a combination of these three solutions. . . . Mission is the action of God in which the church shares and which belongs to the essential nature and character of the church. . . . Missions are particular forms of this essential participation [by the church] in God's mission, related to specific times, places or needs. They are identifiable activities of the church—activities which flow from its missionary nature (Bosch 1982, 20-30).

Harvie Conn called this

a new collaboration between missiology and theology . . . [a recognition that] in its times of greatest glory, theology was nothing more than reflection in mission, in pilgrimage on the road among the timebound cultures of the world. It was also reflection on mission, on Jesus as the good news for the world, on the church as salt and light and leaven for the world (Conn 1983, 13).

In 1984 Harvie Conn and Samuel Rowen updated the discussion concerning missiological education by publishing a compendium of some of the best writings on the subject in a volume entitled *Missions and Theological Education in World Perspective*.

A year later James Scherer presented a study to the Association of Professors of Mission (APM) concerning "tradition and change in the teaching of missions." Scherer's presentation was based on data "obtained from 66 participating U.S. member schools of the Association of Theological Schools (ATS), out of a total of 154 schools polled, plus two additional institutions engaged in mission research or education but not ATS-related" (Scherer 1985, 445). "The survey," Scherer explained, was "broadly representative of the situation in mainline Protestant denominational, Roman Catholic, nondenominational, evangelical and independent theological seminaries" (Scherer 1985, 445).

Scherer summarized this landmark report by saying:

Responses to the . . . survey . . . seem to reflect a marked improvement in the status of mission teaching at the M.Div.-seminary level when compared to the results of the 1973/74 survey. . . . There are distinct signs of reconstruction and renewal, not least in the conciliar and denominational schools where the attrition was most keenly felt [earlier]. . . . Overall there appears to have been a fairly widespread increase in mission interest and awareness, and a decline of negativity, since about the termination of the Vietnam involvement. The new attitude is marked by an openness and willingness to deal with his-

toric claims and to face current challenges. .... Fifty-five of the 66
seminaries offered some type of course in missions; only 11 did not.
. . . A number of seminaries, such as Fuller Seminary with its School
of World Mission, and the schools of world mission and evangelism
at Trinity and Asbury have established separate professional schools
specializing in mission studies. Such schools typically offer multi-
degree programs on various levels ranging from the master's degree
to the academic and professional doctorate in missiology, and provide a wide range of courses (Scherer 1985, 452-53).

In 1987 W. Richey Hogg surveyed the teaching of missiology in the
United States by comparing five significant centers of mission education in
1950- 1953 (Southern Baptist Theological Seminary, Yale University Divinity School, Union Theological Seminary, Princeton Theological Seminary, and Hartford Seminary's Kennedy School of Missions) with five significant centers in 1986-1987 (Princeton Theological Seminary,
Southwestern Baptist Theological Seminary, Fuller Theological Seminary's
School of World Mission, Asbury Theological Seminary's E. Stanley Jones
School of World Mission, and The Overseas Ministries Study Center). Based
on his survey, Hogg remarked on the changes facing missiological education:

In those 35 years (between 1952 and 1987) of rapid change within
the world Christian scene, the whole demographic center of gravity
of the faith has shifted to Asia, the Pacific, Africa, and Latin America.
Rapid growth appears in Africa and parts of Asia, and the emergence
of millions of Christians in China with steady growth continuing brings
joyous astonishment. The number of American missionaries serving
overseas has doubled, the overwhelming majority from the "evangelical" segment of American Protestantism. . . . Three of the four
seminaries [in the 1987 survey] are . . . "independent, evangelical."
That reflects in considerable part the roughly 95 percent "evangelical" component in American missionaries overseas today (Hogg 1987,
503).

Finally, Hogg noted three other major shifts: the increasingly important
issue of the relation of mission and theology, the growing number of international students in American theological (and especially missiological)
education, and the Association of Theological Schools' recent program in
"globalization of theological education" (Hogg 1987, 504). Hogg's survey
served to raise awareness that mission education in the 1990s and into the
next century would look dramatically different from that seen thirty years
ago.

Echoing some of Hogg's concerns, Addison Soltau suggested that the mission curriculum of the future must focus its work in mission theology, seeking to address five basic motifs of a missionary theology: a biblical understanding of history and the God who directs that history; God's method of disclosing himself; the nature of the Christian life; the life of the corporate body of Christ, the people of God as a traveling, scattered community; finally, correction is needed in the church's self-understanding regarding its organizational structure.... A missionary theology must include the very nature of the gospel and the way we understand it (Soltau 1988, 11-16).

In 1990, Norman Thomas spoke to the APM concerning globalization and the teaching of mission. In his address Thomas called attention to the issues that must be faced if the "globalization" project of the ATS was to be more than a passing fad. To be more than that, Thomas felt it must respond to at least four major polarities: "parochialism or globalization?" (the relation of the Western churches to the world church); "maintenance or mission?" (the question of the ultimate purpose for which the church exists); "clericalism or shared ministry?" (the issue of the professionalization of the clergy and the missionary ministry of church members); and "analyst or catalyst?" (the role of the missiologist within a theological faculty committed to globalization) (Thomas 1990, 15-21).

The history, people, and issues mentioned above have influenced the thinking of the contributors of this volume. This book takes a special place in the history of the discussion. In terms of the broader history of missiological education, it highlights the recent development of "schools of mission," Hartford's Kennedy School of Missions being one of the earliest. Second, the volume represents the shift in North American Protestantism from conciliar influence to Evangelical and Pentecostal/Charismatic prominence in mission education—and from denominational mission to interdenominational agencies and sodality organizations.

Further, because this volume is associated with the installation of the fourth dean of the School of World Mission (SWM) at Fuller Seminary, it is important to reflect on the significance of SWM's own pilgrimage in missiological education. The first dean, Donald A. McGavran, from India, established the School of World Mission in close conjunction with the Institute of Church Growth, a relationship which I explore in one of the final chapters of this book. The second dean, Arthur F. Glasser, served in China, had been a mission executive, and is concerned about the development of mission theology as well as missiology related to Chinese and Jewish evangelization.

The third dean, Paul E. Pierson, in whose honor this volume is being published, has been a missionary in Latin America, a seminary president in Brazil, and has served as pastor of local congregations in the United States. His interest in mission history provides a springboard for reflection on the present and future of mission, missiology, and mission education. The fourth dean, at whose installation these presentations were originally offered, has been a missionary in the Middle East, is a scholar of Islam, and is concerned about the relation of the world church to people of other faiths.

Interestingly, most of the issues that have surfaced in the historical development of the teaching of missiology globally have also influenced the directions of the School of World Mission. These issues contribute to the structure of this book. The reader will notice that the major authors are not all on the faculty of Fuller's School of World Mission. Rather, the SWM faculty wanted to use this opportunity to listen to what others were saying and to reflect on the implications of that for their own approach to missiological education. Exceptions to this are found in the final section, where the editors of the volume respond to what they have heard. Finally, as a case in point that synthesizes all the matters addressed in the book, Dean Gilliland offers a tribute to Paul Pierson, in whose honor the volume has been published, and whose life and ministry epitomize the evaluative reflection and careful listening advocated herein.

I wish to add my own words of heartfelt love and admiration for Paul Pierson. As dean, he was the one who convinced me to join the faculty of the School of World Mission. Paul very carefully and patiently facilitated my introduction into the Fuller Seminary community. With his loving, cheerful, authentic, and conscientious leadership style, he has been a constant source of encouragement and vision for me both personally and professionally. When I think of someone who models for me a missionary pastor of vision and courage, I think of Paul Pierson. I praise God for Paul as my superior, mentor, colleague, pastor, and friend.

Let me also express my gratitude to Betty Ann Klebe and Nancy Thomas, whose loving, joyful, precise, and careful work has been a tremendous asset to me in compiling, typing, redesigning, and shepherding this volume toward completion. A big thank you is also well-deserved by Anne White of Fuller's word-processing office for the care and thoroughness she has shown in preparing the manuscript—especially considering the difficult task of bringing together the Bibliography.

It is my hope that these chapters will stimulate Christian leaders to think theologically and missiologically about the way we form leaders for the manifold ministries of Christ and his church in the various contexts of tomorrow's world. May we all together as the church of Jesus Christ continually seek greater proximity to our Lord and Savior, in whose mission we participate.

Abbreviations

CWME	Commission on World Mission and Evangelism, WCC
DWME	Division of World Mission and Evangelism, WCC
EFMA	Evangelical Foreign Missions Association
EMQ	*Evangelical Missions Quarterly*
EMS	Evangelical Missiological Society
ER	*Ecumenical Review*
ETS	Evangelical Theological Society
FTS	Fuller Theological Seminary
IBMR	*International Bulletin of Missionary Research*
IFMA	Interdenominational Foreign Missions Association
IMC	International Missionary Council
IRM	*International Review of Mission*
IVP	InterVarsity Press
LCWE	Lausanne Committee for World Evangelization
MARC	Missions Advanced Research and Communication Center
NCC/DOM	National Council of Churches/Division of Overseas Ministries
NCCC	National Council of Churches of Christ in the USA
NEB	New English Bible
NIV	New International Version (of the Bible)
OBMR	*Occasional Bulletin of Missionary Research*
RSV	Revised Standard Version (of the Bible)
SCM	Student Christian Movement
SIL	Summer Institute of Linguistics
SPCK	Society for the Propagation of Christian Knowledge
SWM	School of World Mission (Fuller Theological Seminary)
TDNT	*Theological Dictionary of the New Testament* (Kittel)
TEE	Theological Education by Extension
TR	Theology of Religion
UBS	United Bible Societies
WCCC	World Council of Churches of Christ
WCL	William Carey Library
WEF	World Evangelical Fellowship

INTRODUCTION

Past Symbols of Interacting Theory, Reflection, and Experience

J. Dudley Woodberry

At the threshold of the present millennium a pattern of instruction developed in al-Azhar mosque in Cairo that can be instructive to missiological educators as we approach the threshold of another millennium. A teacher sat with a book in his hand in a circle of students, all of whom had left their sandals at the door. This setting, in what became a major center for missionary education, suggests the primary components that must interact for meaningful missiological education to take place. The book *portrays the* theory, *the* study circle *the* reflection and interaction, *and the* sandals *the* experience. *Whether the book is transformed into a CD-ROM, and the study circle becomes interaction and reflection through e-mail, and the sandals are exchanged for Boeing 747 seats, the three must always go together. Hence they form the conceptual framework for these essays.*

THE DESIGN OF THE BOOK

This conceptual framework seemed fitting because these essays are offered in honor of Paul Pierson as a respected and loved dean and mission historian. They were originally presented on the occasion of the inauguration of his successor as dean of the School of World Mission at Fuller Theological Seminary, who was simultaneously installed in its new chair of Islamic studies. Thus the design of the book reflects the perspective of a dean sitting in a chair of Islamic studies. Historically the professor at academic centers like al-Azhar sat by a pillar on a chair in the circle of students. Endowments were raised to support the occupant of the chair, and this

---

After missionary experience in Pakistan, Afghanistan, and Saudi Arabia, **J. Dudley Woodberry** taught Islamics at Reformed Bible College in Grand Rapids, Michigan, and later served as director of academic affairs at the Zwemer Institute of Islamic Studies. He has been at Fuller since 1983 and is now dean of the School of World Mission and professor of Islamic studies.

Muslim educational form lent its name to all subsequent "endowed chairs," whether in Bologna, Oxford, or Fuller. The outline of this book reflects the different perspectives from such a chair.

The Heritage of Books, Circles, and Sandals: Historical Contexts

As in history, scholars and missionaries in Christian monasteries and Muslim teaching mosques learned from those before. So must we. At its best the medieval educational system here portrayed by the book, the study circle, and the sandals represented the interaction of theory, reflection, and experience, with the resultant blossoming of useful knowledge. But far too often it degenerated into merely passing on information from the book in the head or hand of the professor to the head or notebook of the student, without the creative interaction of reflection and experience.

The historical section looks at how missiological education has developed and some of the lessons learned, along with the research resources available and still needed. Global trends are identified together with the changes in education they suggest for the future. Bible colleges get special attention because they have been more successful on the whole than their seminary and university counterparts in providing accessibility, the interaction of theory and practice, and spiritual formation.

Sandals from Other Sanctuaries: Ecumenical Contexts

In our medieval model the sandals at the door gave evidence that the place of study was first of all a place of prayer, and contemporary missiological education must first be in the context of a worshiping community where spiritual formation is primary. Likewise the sandals included those of professors and students coming from other branches of the community of faith. In fact, the teaching *madrasas* that became attached to many mosques often had four sections (*iwans*) facing onto a common courtyard, one for each of the Sunni schools of sacred law.

In a similar vein this section of the book listens to the insights and concerns of Charismatic, Ecumenical-Protestant, Roman Catholic, and Orthodox missiologists. Another branch of the church that will require increased attention is comprised of the rising new apostolic paradigm (what some have called "postdenominational") megachurches which are doing their own church-based theological and missiological training. They obviously are more in touch with many current trends and needs in society than many of their main-line counterparts, but their leaders need the depth and breadth that some academic institutions can provide.

Sandals from Other Lands: Regional Contexts

Historically, professors and students traveled to Cairo from Baghdad and other centers of learning with the resultant cross-fertilization of ideas that led to the flowering of science and culture in the Abbasid Empire. Listening to others is even more necessary today in Christian missiological education as the numerical and vital centers of the global church and mission continue to move to Africa, Asia, and Latin America. At the same time post-Christian Europe looms as a major mission field. The former Eastern Bloc of Europe raises its own set of missiological challenges, with its spiritual vacuum after decades of Communist rule, the unfettering of ancient Orthodox churches, and ethnic and religious strife. Unfortunately the latter so consumed the time and energies of those equipped to write on the training of missiologists for the region that an essay on the topic will have to wait for a subsequent publication.

Variety of Books and Circles: Missiological Contexts

In the teaching mosques different pillars were identified by the subject taught there. With this analogy in mind, we need to ask, "What subject pillars should be included in a school of world mission?" At Fuller we have decided that three clusters of subject pillars are necessary—those about the *Word* (especially the theology of mission), those about the *world* (with anthropology being central), and those about the *church* (especially church growth principles and the lessons of mission history). As the pillars in a mosque are connected by arches or beams, so these subjects must be connected with each other, with the specializations increasingly demanded in today's world, and with related disciplines in theological schools and secular universities.

Certain disciplines are discussed in this section because of their special relevance or the issues they raise. The marriage of the theology of mission with the behavioral sciences has revolutionized missiological education and its effectiveness. With the explosion of urbanization in the world, urban studies need central focus. Likewise Bible translation has increasingly shifted from translating Scripture to giving local translators the skills to translate the Bible themselves. The adherents of the monotheistic faiths of Judaism and Islam are being seen by some today not as objects of mission but partners in mission. To emphasize the need of their adherents for Christ, Judaism gets special treatment in this section and Islam in the next. Finally, since much of the evangelization of the world has been and will be by lay people, training appropriate to the laity is highlighted.

Toward New Books, Circles, and Sandals: Future Contexts

To meet the needs of a changing world the "book" (or the theory) may increasingly need to be put in forms like CD-ROM or Hypertext Markup Language. The "circle" of interactive reflection may also need to be enlarged to other continents by forms of e-mail or interactive television supplemented by means for personal interaction. In this way the "sandals" of experience can remain in contexts of home ministry. At the same time the mushrooming masses of the world's poor will require means within their reach that do not distort the incarnational form of the gospel. The essays in this section integrate the insights of the previous chapters, raise some of the areas with which missiological education must deal, and suggest the forms that it can take.

Conclusion: Till the Final Book Is Opened in the Final Circle

Following reflections on Paul Pierson as a missiological educator who connected the mission, the church, and the academy, the final chapter looks to the creativity required in what may become the final chapter in salvation history. The times require the balancing of creative tensions, the forming of creative partnerships, and the developing of creative methodologies. Then those from every tribe and nation will leave their earthly sandals to join a circle with the One who knows the secrets of history as he opens the final book.

THE OCCASION OF THE ESSAYS

The essays included here were occasioned by the calendar and the events of the world and the school where they were first presented. They were delivered at a conference in conjunction with the inauguration of a new dean of the School of World Mission at Fuller Theological Seminary. Thus they represented an effort to celebrate the past and to listen to colleagues from other institutional contexts concerning what emphases should be made in the next period of missiological education.

In the Christian world calendar, these essays come at a notable time:

- two hundred years after William Carey's booklet, *An Inquiry into the Obligations of Christians to Use Means for the Conversion of the Heathens*, which launched modern Protestant missions from a Baptist church in England that is now a mosque, and launched some paternalism too;
- five hundred years after Columbus's voyage, which brought both Christianity and exploitation to the new world.

They also come in the final years before the start of the third millennium, which many, such as the international movement "A.D. 2000 and Beyond," have made a target date for the planting of churches among every major people group.

More important than the changing of the guard in a school or dates made prominent in a calendar by the decimal system are the events taking place in the world and the church that signal a new era—an era of many ambiguities, wonderful opportunities, and great rewards.

World Trends

Political trends have been made graphic by the collapse of the Berlin Wall, marking the decline of Marxism and the rise of capitalism and democracy. Yet the disappearance of the wall not only gave greater access for the gospel but also let loose powerful divisive forces such as ethnic rivalries. The increasingly porous Bamboo Wall is now wrapping itself around a Hong Kong filled with political, economic, and religious enemies of the present system. Prominent in the shifts of power have been people movements like those in Eastern Europe. Although the uncovered spiritual vacuum has given opportunities for Christian witness, it has also given similar occasion for its many rivals.

Economic trends included first an increased shift of financial resources to the OPEC nations, leading to major support of Islamic causes. Most significant is the increased economic power of the Pacific Rim nations—Japan, Korea, Taiwan, Hong Kong, Singapore, and fast-rising China. The impact of the European Economic Community has yet to be seen. The West still controls far more financial and institutional resources for mission than the developing nations where major church growth is taking place. Thus both face the challenges of responsible partnership. Yet the Pacific Rim countries are assuming and must increasingly assume the funding and training of missionaries.

Not all are sharing in the new prosperity. The gap between haves and have-nots widens as industrialization marginalizes rural masses and those who flood into the cities but are unable to enter the work force. The poorer nations have not been able to compete and have been buried beneath such large national debts that they will never be able to dig themselves out. Yet the church is growing in these areas and needs relevant education for its emerging leaders.

Secularization and religious resurgence continue. Secularization was the offspring of the Enlightenment and has led to the loss of traditional values and some of the traumas of contemporary societies. Resurgent traditional religions, especially Islam, have been the result. They in turn have often sought to bring other religious and nonreligious groups under their control. These movements call for empathetic and creative study, interaction and response.

Urbanization is growing at such a rate that by the early years of the twenty-first century a majority of the world's population will be living in cities. The resultant pressure on the infrastructure of cities and urban peoples raises challenges for missiologists to understand and train Christians to minister to their needs. Likewise the presence in cities of members of most of the world's people groups opens opportunities for creative mission strategies.

Information technology, which is mushrooming today, offers unparalleled opportunities for witness and missiological education as long as it is kept a servant rather than a master and is wedded to personal mentoring and fellowship. In like manner methods must be used that are appropriate to the growing number of the world's poor. The incarnational method as well as the message of the Master Teacher, who inaugurated the first millennium, must continue to guide us as we follow him into the third millennium.

Church and Mission Trends

The global church is experiencing a profound shift of its numerical and vital center from western and northern to eastern and southern hemispheres. At the time of this writing, missionaries sent from and supported by churches in Africa, Asia, and Latin America are becoming more numerous than Western missionaries. At "GCOWE '95" in Korea, missionaries from that majority world were increasingly in control. This phenomenon presents new challenges for missiological education in the West.

In addition, the makeup of the world church is changing, with Evangelical and Charismatic churches comprising an ever-increasing proportion. Traditionally these groups have had less concern for the formal education of their leaders than their main-line colleagues. Another phenomenon is the emergence of megachurches that train their own staff and missionaries in-house rather than in seminaries.

On the one hand we are seeing more emphasis on the local church as the mission agency and locus of missionary training. On the other there is increasing cooperation among churches, denominations, and mission agencies on the international level. These departures from traditional patterns open new doors for partnership in missiological education.

The mission task has become both less focused and more focused in different segments of the church. In a world of increased religious pluralism, many seem to be losing a sense of universal norms of right and wrong and the centrality of Jesus Christ. Theological relativism has dampened the zeal for a uniquely Christian mission. This calls for a renewed emphasis on a biblical theology of mission.

Others in the church have focused on unreached peoples and have set a goal to establish an indigenous evangelizing church movement among each people group by the beginning of the next century. Simultaneously the multifaceted nature of mission is increasingly recognized: the concerns for evangelism, peace with justice, religious liberty, and social concern for the poor are increasingly impacted by methodologies that embrace power encounter, dialogue, common witness, and spirituality.

The tide of world mission went out from the East to the West and North at the beginning of the first millennium. During the second it came crashing back to the East and South, often carried on the waves of colonialism. Now, as the tide shifts to thrust out again from the eastern and southern shores on the brink of the third millennium, missiological educators in the West must test the currents and heed the warning of Shakespeare's Brutus to launch out "at the flood" rather than be "bound in shallows."

HISTORICAL CONTEXTS

The Heritage of Books, Circles, and Sandals

1

Missiological Education in Historical Perspective

Andrew F. Walls

The building in which I work has two components. One is New College, established in 1846 for the training of the ministry of the Free Church of Scotland and now housing the Faculty of Divinity of the University of Edinburgh; the other, the General Assembly Hall of the Church of Scotland, originally that of the Free Church. Both components are properly linked with missiological education.

EDINBURGH, 1910

The General Assembly Hall was the scene of the great World Missionary Conference of 1910. That event in some ways instituted the missiological education of the Western church. There, Christians could catch a glimpse of what a truly worldwide church might be like. There the churches saw the inadequacy of their existing structures to carry the tasks laid by God upon his people. There the Western church realized the need for Christians to work across national, denominational, and confessional boundaries. There came hints of the riches about to be showered upon the church from the non-Western world. And there came that most Christian utterance from the young South Indian clergyman V. S. Azariah, pointing to the beam which must be plucked from the elder brother's eye of the Western church.[1] New international cooperative initiatives developed as a result of Edinburgh 1910, and to match them came new international cooperative developments in mission studies.

Andrew Walls is director of the Centre for the Study of Christianity in the Non-Western World at the University of Edinburgh, Scotland. He formerly worked in Sierra Leone and Nigeria, and has held posts at Aberdeen and Yale Universities.

Indeed, the conference was at the center of a minor renaissance of mission studies. The "Statistical Atlas of Christian Missions" was part of the conference preparation. A new scholarly journal, the *International Review of Missions* (now the *International Review of Mission*) was set up, containing in each issue an international bibliography of mission studies. From the same conference Samuel Marinus Zwemer got the idea for an international and interconfessional journal to further one of the most baffling of all the tasks of Christian mission, the Christian interface with Islam. That journal was the *Moslem* (or, as it now is, *Muslim*) *World*.

ALEXANDER DUFF

But the other component of the building, New College, also has a claim upon our attention; it was there that the first chair of mission studies anywhere in the Protestant world was established. It is outside our scope to trace the steps leading to this event, or to follow through the process of which it is a part, a process which led to the establishment of the discipline of missiology in the universities of Germany, the Netherlands, and Scandinavia, and the erection of chairs of missions in American universities and seminaries. Nor is it necessary to do so, for both have been magisterially chronicled by the venerable apostle of cooperative mission studies, Professor Olav Guttorm Myklebust of Oslo.[2] Instead I want to focus on a few events in Edinburgh. This focus is not on account of institutional patriotism (as will become clear, the story is institutionally double-edged), but because the story is a figure for the present time.

Central in the story is Alexander Duff, the first missionary to be formally commissioned by the Church of Scotland. He was at the time the most celebrated Indian missionary after Carey. His visit to the United States in 1854 initiated what is arguably the first international missionary conference.[3]

In June 1866 he addressed the General Assembly of the Free Church of Scotland.[4] He had retired from the mission field and was serving as convener of the church's Foreign Mission Committee. In that presentation he placed before the Assembly a scheme that he had first put forward as a young missionary thirty-five years earlier.

The burden of Duff's address was that regular theological education for the ministry of the church made no specific provision for study of the actual task of the church, for what, according to the Savior's parting commission, was "the end and object of his incarnation, life, sacrificial death, resurrection and ascension into glory."[5]

A Chair of Evangelistic Theology

To remedy this, Duff proposed the erection of a chair of evangelistic theology. Its scope would be broad, catholic, and comprehensive. Part of its responsibility would lie within the theological disciplines: to unfold from the Scriptures God's design for the redemption of the world; in other words, to display the missionary process within the total setting of biblical and dogmatic theology. Another part would be historical: to explore and explain the extent of the fulfillment of the Great Commission so far. This would include investigating the processes of evangelization in the early church and the ways by which the peoples of northern and western Europe received the Christian faith. It would also examine the history of modern missions in Asia, Africa, and the Pacific Islands. A further branch of the duties of the chair might at a later time have been described as phenomenological, involving as it did an examination of the beliefs and thought patterns of the leading branches of the human family; another would be practical, dealing with the necessary qualifications for effective missionary work. In fact, evangelistic theology, as Duff conceived it, would need to employ every discipline in the theological curriculum but also go well beyond that curriculum.

The Missionary Institute

This chair of missiology (as it would probably be called today) was only the first stage of Duff's scheme. Associated with the chair would be a "missionary institute," which would address the questions arising from the encounter with other cultures. It would develop a study of what Duff called "the geography, history, ethnology, mythology, habits, manners and practices of unevangelized peoples and nations."[6] It is noteworthy that Duff, whose personal judgment of traditional India was uncompromising, nevertheless saw that such things must be taken seriously in the evangelistic process. Nor was the missionary institute to confine its attention to the peoples of the southern continents. It would address the condition of the Scottish cities (by introducing specialists from the home missionary enterprise). It would review the religious situation of the European continent and consider how to provide for the Christian good of the families now emigrating by the hundreds to North America, the Antipodes, or South Africa. It would reflect the experience of missions to the Jews.

"If this Professorship and Institute be established and properly wrought out," Duff went on, "it may become a model to all the churches of Christendom."[7] The importance of such a model was reflected in the fact that the continued existence of those same churches was involved in the maintenance of mission. The vitality, the spiritual existence of the church itself depended on the practical maintenance of the great doctrine of Christ's headship and kingship over the whole world. Thus chair and institute would stand in affirmation of the headship of Christ, of that bedrock of Scottish covenant theology, "the Crown Rights of the Redeemer." As it was, the Scottish churches—to look no further—had very little idea that their own continued existence depended on extending that headship. They were merely playing at the margins of world mission. To blame the slightness of the current missionary effort on shortage of resources was to trifle:

> We have among us material resources enough and to spare. I must hold, with the Bible in my hand, that any one of our principal cities, Edinburgh, Glasgow, Aberdeen, or Dundee, could maintain all our existing missions, and even greatly extend them, without themselves suffering any discomfort or loss.

> (Here there were cheers from the assembled fathers and brethren.)

> What then might not the whole Church accomplish, if all gain were consecrated as holiness to the Lord?[8]

Loud and prolonged applause followed the address, says the reporter, "during which Dr. Duff was assisted out of the hall, in a state of extreme exhaustion."[9]

IMPLICATIONS FOR MISSIOLOGICAL EDUCATION

The implications of this pioneer program of missiological education are worth a moment's reflection. First, Duff's scheme assumes that the study of mission lies at the center of the theological curriculum, not at its margin, for mission is the reason for the existence of the church. Certainly Duff intended the chair of evangelistic theology to further the preparation of missionaries; he had seen too much of the waste and despair that occurred among young missionaries who could not cope with the demands of another culture. Equally, he desired an increase in the number of missionaries from Scotland. But he did not view his missiological chair as solely, or even primarily, concerned with missionaries. The branch of study that he was advocating belonged to the life of the church as a whole; it was relevant to everyone concerned with the Kingdom of God. It was not only for those who must encounter Hindu intellectuals or African monarchs, but for those whose ministry lay amid highland farms and flocks, Clydeside factory sirens, or among the fat Jeshuruns, stocked with solid comforts of the urban middle class.[10]

Second, despite the fact that Duff was making his appeal to the highest court of his own church, he saw the enterprise to which it related as essentially ecumenical. There were loud but perhaps rather embarrassed cheers when Duff announced that the necessary endowment for the chair had already been promised. Any embarrassment would arise from the fact that most of those who were providing the endowment were not members of the Free Church, which was the immediate beneficiary. They gave, said Duff, because missionary spirit superseded all denominational and ecclesiastical considerations whatsoever. It is still more striking that Duff, a Protestant of unshakable, not to say crustacean, convictions, found a model in Rome. He accepted the Catholic insight of missionary zeal as one of the marks of a true church and reflected that Rome "has, with her wonted sagacity, outstripped the languid efforts of Protestantism."[11] He was thinking here of the Urban University with its international student body and of the vast library of the Propaganda Fide, in comparison with which Protestant provision for mission studies was indeed languid. He thought also of the Feast of Languages held each year in Rome at Epiphany, when the mighty works of God were recited in languages from all over the world. This reflection of Pentecost pointed to an aspect of the church which was still hidden from most Western Christians, and from almost all Western Protestants.

Third, Duff assumed that the study of mission would be interdisciplinary. We have already seen that he envisaged his "evangelistic theology" as employing all the usual theological disciplines. But theology was not enough; Duff's vision, which incorporated the institute as well as the chair, embraced a whole array of linguistic and historical studies which would be brought to the proper understanding of the Christian mission. It included also what today we would call the history of religions, anthropology, and a range of social studies. Duff did not use these names, but he knew the areas of discourse they stood for and their essential connection with the process of declaring Christ's headship throughout the world. He saw that the study of mission would involve exercising all the theological disciplines to the full and applying them beyond their current use in conventional theological studies. It would also mean extending the human sciences, not only beyond the point of the resources of even a well-equipped theological institution, but beyond what then bounded the horizons of most of the universities of the West.

IMPLICATIONS FOR THEOLOGICAL EDUCATION

This takes us to another aspect of Duff's vision, one with momentous implications. Implied in his appeal is that the study of theology in its entirety, and the church's whole conception of itself and its place in the world, should be informed by the experience which had come from the missionary movement. The missionary movement had arisen in an environment conditioned by centuries of interaction between Christian faith and European history, culture, and conditions. Western theology, and the Western sense of theological priorities, was shaped by that experience. Not only so, it was limited by that experience. Despite the assurance that came from a long tradition of territorial identification with the Christian faith, despite the confidence that came from an inheritance of generations, the theology of Western Christendom, Catholic and Protestant alike, was essentially local, even parochial. Here was an aspect of the significance of the missionary movement which Duff saw only in part. It had brought Western Christians into situations entirely outside the previous recorded experience of Christianity, and left them without its familiar landmarks.

The essential missionary experience is to live on terms set by someone else; it involves engaging with ideas and with forms of thought and language not one's own. It is an Abrahamic journey, calling for faith to go out, not knowing where it will lead, assured of the end but not of the route. Duff, whose ministry in India had seen one burst of spectacular encouragement preceded and followed by long years of exploration, trial, and frustration, was aware of the limitations of conventional Western theology—what most of his colleagues assumed to be all the theology there was or could be—when it came to the Christian encounter with the non-Western world. In most ways he was himself quite a conventional, indeed a conservative theologian[12]; but he was aware that in India Keshub Chunder Sen and the Brahmo Samaj were posing questions with which Christian theology hitherto had not had to deal.[13] He knew less of Africa than he did of India, and he was clearly baffled by the Xhosa cattle killing in South Africa, but at least he was aware of it as a religious event without parallel in Western experience. Even by the time of Alexander Duff, the Christian encounters taking place in Asia and Africa were requiring that theological discourse be enlarged. All sorts of factors—commercial, military, strategic, colonial, imperial— were bringing the West into contact with the non-Western world, but it was the missionary movement which was to be the most important means for the education of the West, the most potent instrument for changing the mind of the West about the non-Western world. The simple reason was that the nature of the missionary task required constant engagement at the most fundamental levels of language and thought. In the course of the nineteenth and early twentieth centuries the missionary movement opened new frontiers for Western scholarship, providing sometimes the raw material, sometimes the methodology, sometimes both. Duff realized that this new corpus of learning was vital to the missionary task of the church. He seems also to have glimpsed that it had considerable implications for theology.

We have already heard that the Assembly loudly applauded the vision of the old missionary, especially when the members realized they would not have to pay for it. Within two years the chair was set up and the first professor appointed. Not surprisingly, Duff himself was given the task of translating his proposals into practice.[14]

He was now well over sixty years of age, and not a very fit man; his tenure was not a long one. He had only one successor, another old missionary, another brief tenure.[15] Before the century was over, the chair had disappeared.[16] No other British university, north or south of the border, adopted Edinburgh's abandoned child. Nor, as far as I have noticed, did anyone ever mention again the great mission studies institute. The second component of Duff's vision never took shape.

THE COLLAPSE OF MISSION STUDIES IN SCOTLAND

The collapse of mission studies in Scotland had nothing to do with any collapse of interest in overseas missions. On the contrary, the years in which provision for missiological education declined until it faded away coincided with an unprecedented expansion in the number of missionaries from Scotland and England alike, and with an exponential increase in the number of well-educated missionary candidates. Somehow the church came to believe that the prosperity of mission had little to do with the prosperity of mission studies.

There were perhaps some local causes for this anti-climax. Certainly Duff was not a very good professor. Always prolix, his wordiness increased with age, and he evidently had difficulty in bringing his course on the history of missions beyond the time of Abraham. The account of Henry Drummond, later to be D. L. Moody's intellectual troubleshooter in the student world, shows how alien Duff seemed to the eager young bloods of the 1870s.[17] They were taken up with themes like the impact of science on theology; of what relevance to them was that old patriarch forever blithering of Hindu gods whom no one cared about?

But the reasons for the loss of the vision go deeper than the failings of any individual incumbent. If we turn to the reports of the student conferences which mark the high point of the missionary movement, there is much on the value of reading as a preparation for missionary service; bibliographies, some quite extensive, are regularly supplied. But as far as the regular theological curriculum is concerned, a comment of J. H. Bernard, New Testament scholar and professor at Trinity College, Dublin, is eloquent. Addressing a conference of the Student Volunteer Mission Union, he admits that it would be highly desirable to include the study of mission in the curriculum. It is, however, impossible. There is simply not room for it, for nothing now taught could possibly be omitted. The study of mission should therefore be strongly encouraged, as extracurricular reading.[18] The implication of such a policy is clear: the study of mission will be an extra for those who expect to become missionaries or are otherwise interested in that sort of thing.

To an extent—perhaps, indeed, he had no alternative, given the circumstances of the time —Duff had laid himself open to such a response by insisting the activities of his new chair would not affect the other branches of the theological curriculum.[19] If, in a curriculum already demanding, it did not affect them, it could only mean that missiology was peripheral to the curriculum, which in turn means that at any time of pressure it would be vulnerable. If, on the other hand, it did affect the other disciplines, one can be sure that their proponents would rise up in the guise of the defenders of law and order and implement the first law of academic practice, which is that nothing may ever be done for the first time.

THE PAROCHIALISM
OF WESTERN THEOLOGICAL EDUCATION

Professor Bernard's answer to Duff, that mission studies must be an extra to the theological curriculum, has been devastating in its effects, as devastating where missiology survived as a curricular element as where (as in nineteenth-century New College) it did not. In the former case, it forced missiology to concentrate on the initiation of professionals, on inspiration and motivation, on methods and techniques. In the latter, the effect on Western theology has been that of oxygen deprivation. Conventional theology has been preserved from any breath of influence from the non-Western world and thus has been able to maintain its essentially local character and parochial relevance. Theological disability has increased with the demographic transformation of the church in the present century. Ordinary theological education has no way of coping with the fact that the majority of Christians are Africans, Asians, or Latin Americans, and that the proportion of those who are is rising daily. It has no way of coping with African or Asian Christian history, for its natural instinct is to see these as some sort of addition or extension to a "church history" already known, defined, and understood, or as a matter of strictly local interest. Any suggestion that the traditional Western model of church history has itself to be reconceived in the light of the changed realities of the church is threatening. Theologically, it reflects a set of priorities that have arisen from local Christian thinking about local Christian situations, but so secure is it in the traditions of the elders that it assumes that its own theological priorities are universal. It has no room even to recognize that there may be different sets of priorities that arise from the situations of other Christians; no machinery for coping with theology which starts at a different point; no apparatus for handling such a question as "What is Christ's relationship to our ancestors?" or for handling a theological thesis such as "Is Christ our ancestor?"

Conventional theological education too often employs pre-Columbian maps of the church. Everyone is aware, of course, that there is a New World, that there are Christians— perhaps many Christians—beyond the Western world. But the pre-Columbian theological map that they work with prevents their giving them theological space. That map no longer reflects reality. It is little use to draw new insets to put in its corners; it will have to be thrown away. And mission studies are essential for the redrawing of the theological map.

HOLY SUBVERSION

For today it is not necessary to be impaled on the horns of Duff's dilemma, of weightless addition to or ceaseless competition with the other theological disciplines. There is a third possible mode of existence for mission studies. That is to subvert the other disciplines, engage them, excite them, irritate them, force them into new channels. I believe that part of the vocation of mission studies in the West today is to just such a labor of holy subversion. Two considerations suggest its current timeliness.

One is the fact that Western theology is now belatedly striving to cope with the presence of the other faiths of the world. Of the various factors which have forced this issue on the Western theological agenda, the crucial one is probably the rising consciousness of the Asian presence in the West. In other words, the faiths of Asia have now been brought into the Western intellectual and social context, and Western theology has to meet them there. Western Christianity has a fund of experience of encounter with other faiths, a fund painfully gathered through several centuries of contact in the missionary movement. And it has an inestimable resource for the encounter in its kinship in the family of Christ with that larger portion of Christian believers who belong to the southern continents, and who themselves, for the most part, trace their Christian origins ultimately to the missionary movement. The trouble is that Western Christianity, in having to repent of the colonial past, identifies the missionary movement in terms of that lamented era. As a result, it frequently seeks to comprehend the encounter with other faiths without the benefit either of its own accumulated experience or of its richest resource. There can be no valid theology of religions that does not take responsibility for the missionary movement. There can be no responsible Western Christian approach to Hinduism that does not take account of the experience of Indian Christians.

THEOLOGICAL EDUCATION'S NEED FOR MISSION STUDIES

But there is another consideration. It is true that Western Christianity needs the studies which mediate the accumulated experience of the missionary movement and the worldwide experience of the Christian family. But, still more, it needs those resources in order to face its own quite indigenous needs. It is now too late to treat Western society as in some sort of decline from Christian standards, to be brought back to church by preaching and persuasion. Modern Western society, taken as a whole, reflects one of the great non-Christian cultures of the world. There is one department of the life of the Western church that spent centuries grappling with non-Christian cultures, and gradually learned something of the processes of comprehending, penetrating, exploring, and translating within them. That was the task of the missionary movement. Further, there is a vast store of Christian experience and energy outside the West. Perhaps the way to the new evangelization of the West is connected with the legacy of the missionary movement from the West.[20]

The distorting and debilitating effects of the separation of missiology from theology, as though it were some sort of addition to theology rather than theology itself, have gone far beyond the realm of theological education. But it will be remembered that Duff's vision for mission studies was not confined to a missiological chair. His vision of an institute of languages and cultures was not simply a dream of future grandeur; it reflected sober realism about the nature of the task of mission studies. The studies of mission involve invading humane as well as divine learning, throwing the frontiers of that learning forward, stretching its methods to the limit, and devising new ones.

During Duff's lifetime Western knowledge of the non-Western world was transformed.[21] It can be argued that the foundations of most of the study of African history, African political science and economics, African relations with the West, African linguistics, African anthropology and sociology—all the themes and resources which the student of Africa, however secularly minded and however anti-colonial in tone, has to deal with—lie in the mission studies of an earlier day.

An equally telling story comes from China and India. A look at some of the versions of Buddhist and Taoist texts promoted under the name of D. T. Suzuki reveals that they are basically reissues of translations by James Legge of the London Missionary Society, the fruit of a Christian missionary's attempt to understand the ancient wisdom of China.[22] Similarly, an Indian secular publisher has recently issued as a standard reference text an *Outline of the Religious Literature of India*. It first appeared in the early part of this century, the work of another missionary scholar, John Nicol Farquhar.[23]

Let us not fear secular learning. In the service of the Kingdom there is no secular learning; it all belongs to the Redeemer of the world. Mission studies are not simply preparation for mission; mission studies are part of mission.

Nothing illustrates this better than the story of serious Christian engagement with Islam over the last couple of centuries. From Henry Martyn to Louis Massignon the key factors in Christian encounter with Muslims have been sanctity and scholarship. If there is one statement which can be safely made of the next chapter of that interaction, it is that it will require both saints and scholars.

Let the last word, like the first, be with Alexander Duff:

> I pray God that this matter may sink into the heart of many parents, that ministers may lay it to heart, that students of theology may know what the world is thinking of them, and that professors of theology may know what the world is expecting of them.

"Dr. Duff," says the reporter, "was here compelled to solicit a healthy space to recover from his exhaustion."[24]

Notes

1. Azariah's address ("Give us FRIENDS!"), arguably the most remembered utterance of the whole conference, was in fact given at a fringe meeting. It occurs in

the first volume of the series *World Missionary Conference 1910: The History and Records of the Conference* (Edinburgh: Oliphant, Anderson and Ferrier, 1910), 306-15.

2. O. G. Myklebust, *The Study of Missions in Theological Education*, is an historical inquiry into the place of world evangelization in Western Protestant ministerial training, with particular reference to Alexander Duff's chair of Evangelistic Theology (Oslo: Egede Instituttet, Vol. 1, 1955, Vol. 2, 1956).

3. See *Proceedings of the Union Missionary Convention held in New York, May 4th and 5th, 1854* (New York: Taylor and Hogg, 1854). On its significance, see W. R. Hogg, *Ecumenical Foundations: A History of the International Missionary Council and its Nineteenth Century Background* (New York: Harper, 1952, 37f).

4. Duff, with the other serving missionaries, had adhered to the emergent Free Church of Scotland at the division of the Church of Scotland in 1843.

5. Alexander Duff, *Foreign Missions: Being the Substance of an Address Delivered Before the General Assembly of the Free Church of Scotland, on Friday Evening, June 1, 1866* (Edinburgh: Elliot, 1866, 27). See the section of the address which deals with the proposed missiological chair and which the missionary institute occupies (pp. 25-33).

6. Ibid., 28.

7. Ibid., 31.

8. Ibid.

9. Ibid., 33.

10. "It is believed that ministerial services at home would be vastly augmented in efficiency, were all pastors imbued with the principles and spirit of Christian missions," ibid., 27f.

11. Ibid., 26.

12. "We are on the eve of being overwhelmed by Essay and Reviewism, Colensoism, Mauriceism, Stanleyism, and other isms nearer home" (ibid., 31). On Duff's laments late in life about the movement of theology within the Free Church itself, see George Smith, *The Life of Alexander Duff DD, LLD* (London: Hodder and Stoughton, 1881), 449ff. The passage is missing from the earlier two-volume edition.

13. Duff had already quoted Keshub Chunder Sen at length, representative of those "half way up the hill towards the sunshiny eminences of revelation" (ibid., 18ff). In a letter to a newspaper, later published as a postscript to the report (ibid., 33), Duff drew attention to the work of the Indian minister Lal Behari Dey in this climate of ideas.

14. Duff's career as professor is little featured by his contemporary biographers, not even by his successor, Thomas Smith (*Alexander Duff, DD, LLD*, London: Hodder and Stoughton, 1883). Duff returned to the theme of his Assembly address in his inaugural lecture as professor. See "Evangelistic Theology," an inaugural address by Alexander Duff, delivered in the Common Hall of the New College, Edinburgh on Thursday, 7th November 1867 (Edinburgh: Elliot, 1868).

15. Thomas Smith, an established mathematician who had been a colleague of Duff in India, was appointed to the chair in 1880. He was already 63, even older than Duff had been at his installation.

16. It survived for a few years in attenuated form as a short-term lectureship. The (still continuing) Duff Missionary Lectureship is not part of the College framework.

17. George Adam Smith, *The Life of Henry Drummond* (London: Hodder and Stoughton, 1902), 42f.

18. "You cannot teach everything to a young clergyman any more than to a young doctor or lawyer." *Students and the Missionary Problem*, addresses delivered at the International Student Missionary Conference, London, January 2-6, 1900 (London: Student Volunteer Missionary Union, 1900, 231). Bernard's paper, entitled "The Need of Advance in Missionary Education," occupies pp. 230-39.

19. ". . . it was never intended that any such portion of the time of students should be allotted to the subject as would in any way materially interfere with existing arrangements" (Duff 1866, 27).

20. On the argument of these paragraphs cf. A. F. Walls, "Structural Problems in Mission Studies," *International Bulletin of Missionary Research* 15 (4) (1991): 147-55.

21. Cf. A. F. Walls, "The Nineteenth Century Missionary as Scholar," in N. E. Bloch-Hoell, ed. *Misjonskall og Forskerglede, Festskrift til professor Olav Guttorm Myklebust* (Oslo: Universitetsforlaget, 1975), 209-21; and "'The Best Thinking of the Best Heathen': Humane Learning and the Missionary Movement," in K. Robbins, ed., *Religion and Humanism: Studies in Church History 17* (Oxford: Blackwell, 1981), 341-53.

22. The best recent treatment of a neglected figure is L. Pfister, "The 'Failures' of James Legge's Fruitful Life for China." *Ching Feng* 31 (4) (1988), 246-71.

23. On Farquhar see E. J. Sharpe, *Not to Destroy but to Fulfill: The Contribution of J. N. Farquhar to Protestant Missionary Thought in India Before 1914* (Lund: Gleerup, 1965), p. 24.

24. Duff 1886, 23.

2

The State of Missiological Research

Gerald H. Anderson

In 1991 I published a study of developments in mission research, writing, and publishing during the last two decades (Anderson 1991). I concluded that study with several observations which I want to begin with here. Then I will comment and expand on one of them.

OBSERVATIONS CONCERNING MISSION RESEARCH

1. There has been a remarkable turnaround in the last two decades in the revitalization of research and scholarship in mission studies. In 1971, when the state of missiological education in the United States was in serious decline, no one anticipated that this remarkable revitalization was going to happen and, if told what would happen, no one may have believed it possible. Can we now anticipate what is possible over the next two decades? Can we dream dreams of what could happen and what needs to happen if the future of scholarship in missiology is to be strengthened, expanded, and enhanced? As in 1971, are we standing—unaware—on the brink of another new era of understanding, opportunity, and initiative in missiological research and education? What will it take to bring it about—or has it already begun?

2. The revitalization in mission studies has not been matched by a revitalization in mission involvement in many churches. Why? How do we account for the decline in interest and support for world mission in the mainline Protestant denominations and the Roman Catholic Church in the West—at the same time that we have more professors of mission and more

Gerald H. Anderson is editor of the *International Bulletin of Missionary Research* and director of the Overseas Ministries Study Center in New Haven, Connecticut. As a United Methodist missionary in the Philippines from 1960 to 1970, he taught church history on the faculty of Union Theological Seminary near Manila.

studies of mission? Are there signs that this problem is also beginning to affect Evangelical churches?

3. Where is the basic missiological research that guides the policy and decision-making of North American mission agencies today? While mission studies have multiplied in academic circles in the last twenty years, it is not clear that much of it finds its way into the executive offices of the typical mission agency today. Why is this the case?

4. Despite the positive developments in missiological education during the last two decades, missiology is still peripheral to the mainstream of theological studies, and even more marginal to the historical and social sciences. The very successes of the last two decades could help to perpetuate the marginality of the discipline; professionalization may contribute to isolation. To meet this challenge, missiologists should be encouraged to engage in research and teaching that involve collaborative, cooperative, and interdisciplinary opportunities.

5. Some scholars, such as Lesslie Newbigin and Wilbert Shenk, argue that the Christian mission is now in the midst of a paradigm shift toward a fundamental reorientation to an understanding that the mission of each church begins with its own culture and extends to the whole world. This is required in order to recover a genuinely missionary existence within Western culture to re-evangelize the West. It is also the biblical pattern of beginning "in Jerusalem" and then going "to the ends of the earth" (Acts 1:8).

6. As the center of ecclesiastical gravity shifts from the northern to the southern hemisphere (to use Walbert Bühlmann's phrase), it is vital for the future of missiological scholarship that greater effort be made to recognize, include, encourage, support, share, and cooperate with scholars and centers in Asia, Africa, Latin America, the Caribbean, and Oceania. This is where the greatest potential is for the future of missiological scholarship.

7. Attention needs to be given to defining and clarifying basic terms and concepts to avoid confusion in missiological studies. One illustration is the confusion over terminology of enculturation, inculturation, acculturation, inter-culturation, indigenization, contextualization, adaptation, accommodation, assimilation, vernacularization, and translation. Another cluster includes witness, evangelism, evangelization, and mission.

8. North American scholars are fortunate to have rich library and archival resources available for research. But these resources have serious limits, weaknesses, and urgent needs. Anyone concerned about the present state and future prospects of missiological research should be concerned that library and archival resources be preserved, maintained, developed, utilized, and shared (see Peterson 1991, 155-64).

9. Perhaps the most serious challenge to missiology today is the spread of a radical relativism in the theology of religions, as represented in *The Myth of Christian Uniqueness* (1987), edited by John Hick and Paul F. Knitter. Langdon Gilkey at the University of Chicago, a proponent in this theological movement, advocates a shift in Christian theology from a belief

that Christianity contains "the definitive revelation among other revelations to some sort of plurality of revelations" and a "rough parity" of religions, with "recognition of the co-validity and co-efficacy of other religions" in terms of communicating saving grace (Gilkey 1987, 37-39). Another voice representing this theological trend is Schubert M. Ogden, who teaches theology at Southern Methodist University. In *Is There Only One True Religion or Are There Many?* Ogden "claims a priori, in advance of actually encountering specific religions and validating their claims to truth, that, if the Christian religion itself is true, then any and all other religions can also be true in the very same sense, because or insofar as they give expression to substantially the same religious truth" (Ogden 1992, 103).

This virus of radical relativism is reaching epidemic proportions and poses a life-threatening condition in the Body of Christ. The danger of this to the missiological self-understanding of the church must not be underestimated or disregarded; its consequences could be far greater than were those of Hocking's *Re-thinking Missions* in the 1930s (Hocking 1932). Lutheran theologian Carl Braaten says, "The question whether there is the promise of salvation in the name of Jesus, and in no other name, is fast becoming a life-and-death issue facing contemporary Christianity. In the churches this issue will become the test of fidelity to the gospel, a matter of *status confessionis* more urgent than any other" (Braaten 1992, 89).

10. From church history we know that renewal rarely comes from the centers of power and authority in the church. Instead, renewal comes from the ecclesial fringes—from small, peripheral, dissident, despised, innovative, untidy groups and movements in the church. This has been true also in the renewal of mission studies in the last two decades. The burst of new initiatives for the advancement of scholarship in missiology has not come from the old academic centers. Rather, it has come from schools and institutes, publishers, programs, associations, networks and movements that have often been peripheral, voluntary, independent, dissident, innovative, and untidy.[1] We should not be surprised, Tracey K. Jones, Jr. reminds us, that "untidiness and confusion have characterized the great periods of missionary expansion" (Jones, *IBMR* 1986, 50).

11. Mission scholars lack many of the fundamental reference tools for research that are available in other disciplines: the large-scale reference works—encyclopedias, dictionaries, lexicons, handbooks, collections of texts, critical surveys, and bibliographical guides. Andrew Walls says, "I am sure there is no department of theological study in which the scholarly instruments are so few and so primitive as in mission studies" (Walls, *IBMR* 1991, 151). He rightly points out that the *Concise Dictionary of the Christian World Mission* (Neill, Anderson, and Goodwin 1971) is now out of date and out of print, but there is nothing to replace it as yet. The *World Christian Encyclopedia*, edited by David B. Barrett, is the only large-scale reference work of scholarship in English published in the last two decades for missiologists. It is enormously useful, but is of a different genre than the

dictionary-type project that needs to be done again on a larger scale. Andrew Walls urges that "it is a propitious time for toolmaking. . . . Modern methods of data storage and transfer make large-scale cooperative work easier to handle than ever before. Surely a renaissance of mission studies will be marked by some first-rate instrument making" (Walls, *IBMR* 1991, 151).

The good news is that this is happening, and I want to devote the rest of this essay to looking at some examples of projects that are in preparation or have recently been published.[2] Not all of these are reference tools in the sense of dictionaries and encyclopedias, but all of them are works of comprehensive scale and significance for missiological research.

ONGOING PROJECTS IN MISSION RESEARCH IN ENGLISH

First are several projects underway in the non-Western world. In Singapore a team of three scholars at Trinity Theological College—John Chew, Scott W. Sunquist, and David Wu—are editors of the *Dictionary of Asian Christianity*. They have eight regional teams in Asia that are coordinating authors and articles in their respective regions. The dictionary—an ecumenical project—will have two thousand articles, with maps, time charts showing the relationship of political/social history with Christian history, and survey articles on each country and church tradition. They hope to complete it in the mid-1990s and are negotiating with an American publisher. Most of the funding for the project is coming from Asian sources.[3]

The Church History Association of India adopted a plan in 1974 to publish a six-volume history of Christianity in India with a "new perspective." Instead of treating the history of Christianity in India as "an eastward extension of Western ecclesiastical history," this project plans to treat it as "an integral part of the socio-cultural history of the Indian people . . . [and] focus attention upon the Christian people in India; upon who they were and how they understood themselves; upon their social, religious, cultural and political encounters, upon the changes which these encounters produced in them and in the appropriation of the Christian gospel." The editorial board and the authors in the series include both Indians and expatriate missionaries.[4] So far three volumes have appeared and have been well received.

Also in India, Saphir P. Athyal, formerly at Pune Biblical Seminary, is editing the *India Christian Handbook*, which seeks to be "the most comprehensive single-reference volume on Christianity in India." The project has an ecumenical editorial council representing most of India's major denominations and Christian organizations, together with five central staff members based in Pune, thirty-one part-time researchers, and two regional coordinators. The volume, to be published in 1996, will provide a comprehensive directory of all Christian churches and organizations, including information on various ministries of hospitality, education, evangelism, justice, literature, media, missions, service, and welfare. Athyal says, "Our intent is that the *Handbook* should be detailed, inclusive, and missiological."[5]

Dr. Athyal is also editing a large volume entitled *The Church in Asia: Present Challenges and Opportunities*, a symposium sponsored by the Asia Lausanne Committee, to be published in India in 1996. Two problems, he says, are that "Christians in Asia know more about the church in the West than the church in Asia," and most studies of the church in Asia have been written by Western authors. Therefore this work will be primarily for Asians and by Asian authors (presumably Evangelical Protestants, since it is sponsored by the Lausanne Committee), with one chapter for the church in each country of Asia, together with general articles on such themes as the charismatic movement in Asia, Asian indigenous missions, and the role of women in the church in Asia. The main focus of the book, however, "will not be a historical outline of the church and present data information, though these will be included. But the distinctive character of the book is that it aims to help the reader to feel the 'heart throbs' of the church in each nation of Asia, by describing the critical issues it faces today and the challenges and opportunities before it."[6] The book will certainly be read with interest in the West as well, and it should help to facilitate better understanding of the Asian church by Christians in the West.

The Working Commission on Church History in the Third World, established by the Ecumenical Association of Third World Theologians (EATWOT) in 1983, has been coordinated by Enrique Dussel in Mexico, widely known for his study *A History of the Church in Latin America: Colonialism to Liberation (1492-1979)* (Dussel 1981). The purpose of the commission is "to promote the writing and publishing of church history of the Third World from the point of view of their struggling peoples rather than from the point of view of the [Western] missionary churches." More specifically it seeks "to formulate a methodological presupposition for a church history perceived from the point of view of oppressed peoples." At an international consultation convened by the commission in London in 1989, the outline for three volumes of church history of the Third World was planned—one each for Latin America, Asia, and Africa. The first volume to appear was *History of the Church in Latin America*, a large symposium edited by Enrique Dussel, published in 1992 by Orbis Books in the United States and by Burns and Oats in England. The volumes on Asia, edited by Teotonio R. de Souza, SJ (Goa), and Africa, edited by Ogbu Kalu (Nigeria) have been delayed and their future is uncertain.[7]

Enrique Dussel is also president of the Commission for the Study of Church History in Latin America (CEHILA), which has sponsored a vast array of publications since it was founded in 1973, all with the same goal of writing and publishing a new perspective on church history of the Third World from the point of view of oppressed peoples rather than mission history from the point of view of Western churches. Its books are published primarily in Spanish, Portuguese, and English (Orbis Books in the United States).[8] This project is a major contribution toward addressing the problem described in 1970 by Stephen Neill regarding the fact that so much about the history of Christian missions has been written by Western scholars. It has been written, said Neill, "far too much from the side of the operators and far too little from that of the victims. . . . We know fairly well what it feels like to be a missionary; we know much less of what it feels like to be the object of the missionary's attentions" (Neill in Cuming 1970, 160).

There has never been a comprehensive narrative study of Christianity in Asia from the beginnings to the twentieth century in a single work by one scholar (with the possible exception of K. S. Latourette's seven-volume *History of the Expansion of Christianity*, which was not devoted solely to Asia). Now, however, one is in process. It is *A History of Christianity in Asia* in two volumes by Samuel H. Moffett, published by Harper-SanFrancisco. Volume 1, *Beginnings to 1500*, was published in 1992, and volume 2, which brings the story to the twentieth century, should appear by 1997. This pioneering work is the product of a lifetime of missionary service and study by the distinguished Henry Luce Professor of Mission and Ecumenics, Emeritus, at Princeton Theological Seminary. Those who have worked in the field of Asian church history can appreciate the vast scope and variety of movements and literature that are involved in this monumental project covering twenty centuries in the largest geographical region of the world.

For the history of Christianity in Africa there has not been a comprehensive study available that covers the whole history of the whole church in the whole continent by a single scholar. But this is being remedied with several new works. First is the *History of Christianity in Africa* by Bengt Sundkler to be published by Cambridge University Press in 1996. Sundkler, the former Swedish Lutheran bishop of Bukoba, Tanzania, and later professor of missions at the University of Uppsala, is the author of two highly regarded earlier Africa studies: *Bantu Prophets in South Africa* (second edition 1961) and *The Christian Ministry in Africa* (1960). He had been working on this larger project for at least twenty years prior to his death in 1995, and its appearance has been eagerly anticipated by students of African church history in many parts of the world.

The *Oxford History of the Christian Church in Africa* by Adrian Hastings was published in 1995. Now professor emeritus in the department of religious studies at the University of Leeds, England, Hastings was a Catholic missionary in Africa early in his career and has written extensively on the church in Africa: *Church and Mission in Modern Africa* (1967), *Christian Marriage in Africa* (1973), *African Christianity* (1977), and *A History of African Christianity, 1950-1975* (1979). In addition, since 1985 he has edited the *Journal of Religion in Africa* (see Hastings 1992, 60-64).

Two additional works in this field are John Baur, *Two Thousand Years of Christianity in Africa: An African History 62-1992* (Nairobi, Kenya: Paulines, 1994), and Elizabeth Isichei, *A History of Christianity in Africa: From Antiquity to the Present* (Grand Rapids, Mich.: Eerdmans; London: SPCK, 1995).

Three valuable bibliographical tools for mission research have been announced. The Centre for the Study of Christianity in the Non-Western World at the University of Edinburgh, directed by Andrew F. Walls, prepared a cumulative index of the *International Review of Mission* 1912-1990 that was published by the World Council of Churches in 1993 (Walls 1993; Smith 1993). In preparation now at the center in Edinburgh is a cumulative bibliography of the *International Review of Mission* 1912-1987. The American Society of Missiology is sponsoring a bibliography project, with Norman E. Thomas as general editor; it plans to publish in 1996 an annotated bibliography of the ten thousand most important books in the field of missiology published in European languages from 1960 to 1990. These will be indexed by author, title, subject, and language of publication.

Surprisingly, a comprehensive history of Catholic missionary outreach from the United States has not yet been written, although bits and pieces of the story have been done, as some individual mission congregations in the United States have written their own histories. Therefore the United States Catholic Mission Association is sponsoring a project to produce a one-volume, scholarly history of United States Catholic missions from 1880 to 1980. Sister Angelyn Dries, OSF, who teaches at Cardinal Stritch College in Milwaukee, has been commissioned as author of the project, which aims to be published before the end of the decade.

Another lacuna for missiologists is the lack of any comprehensive study of Christian attitudes and approaches to people of other faiths, and how people of other faiths have perceived and responded to Christianity throughout the history of Christianity. Again, parts of the story have been studied but not the whole in any depth. Now a major project is underway that will make a significant contribution in this area. It is a multi-year, multi-author, eight-volume project entitled *Christianity in Its Religious Contexts*. The general editor is Frederick W. Norris from Emmanuel School of Religion in Johnson City, Tennessee.

Considering the importance of Pentecostals in world mission today, we are fortunate to have the *Dictionary of Pentecostal and Charismatic Movements*, edited by Stanley M. Burgess and Gary B. McGee (Grand Rapids, Mich.: Zondervan, 1988). Three additional dictionary projects will also be important tools for missiological research. A *Dictionary of Scottish Church History and Theology*, prepared under the auspices of Rutherford House in Edinburgh was published by T. and T. Clark and InterVarsity Press in 1993. Nigel Cameron of Rutherford House is organizing editor, with David Wright of New College, Edinburgh, Donald Meek of the Department of Celtic at Edinburgh, and David Lachman as general editors. There are over three hundred contributors. The work gives a comprehensive coverage of Scottish Christianity from the outset to the present, with special attention to the Reformed tradition. There are a large number of biographical entries. Since Scottish churches and missionaries have had such a large role in Christian missions, the dictionary is valuable for mission scholars.

The *Blackwell Dictionary of Evangelical Biography: 1730-1860*, edited
by Donald M. Lewis, Regent College, Vancouver, Canada, was published
in 1995, by Blackwell in Oxford, England. "This work seeks to provide
biographical treatment and to indicate the sources for study of figures of
historical, literary or religious significance anytime between 1730 and 1860
who were associated with the Evangelical Movement in the English-speak-
ing world," according to a prepublication announcement. The dictionary
has about thirty-five hundred entries from more than three hundred authors.
Clearly this will be a rich resource for missiological research.

Several years ago I was surprised when I realized that there had never
been published a single work devoted to biographies of persons related to
Christian missions that covered the whole history of missions and all traditions of Christianity. So I have undertaken to edit a *Biographical Dictionary of Christian Missions* that will include brief biographical articles with
bibliographies on twenty-three hundred outstanding persons in the history
of Christian missions, from the post-New Testament period down to the
present, including a few living persons who are over seventy-five years of
age. While I have been doing preliminary work on the project for several
years, it is only now, with the counsel of an international editorial advisory
board of prominent missiologists, and a grant from the Pew Charitable Trusts,
that we are able to move ahead with the project and assign articles to authors. One of the features of this project is that it will make a special effort
to have women and non-Western Christians represented more adequately
than is usually the case in such works. It will be published in 1997 by
Macmillan Library Reference U.S.A.

Also in preparation is *The Evangelical Dictionary of World Missions*,
with A. Scott Moreau as general editor, assisted by Charles Van Engen and
Hardd Netlarel as associate editors, to be published in 1998 by Baker Book
House. This comprehensive reference work will include twelve hundred
articles covering a broad spectrum of mission theology, theory, history, organizations, and practice.

Another type of reference collection, planned as a successor to the *Mission Trends* earlier series, is the *New Directions in Mission and Evangelization* series, edited by James A. Scherer and Stephen B. Bevans, SVD, published by Orbis Books.[9] Volume 1, published in 1992, is a collection of
"Basic Statements 1974-1991." These are official mission statements produced by church and associational bodies under four headings: Conciliar-
Ecumenical, Roman Catholic, Eastern Orthodox, and Evangelical Protestant. The earliest statement is the Lausanne Committee for World
Evangelization's 1974 Lausanne Covenant. The most recent are the Vatican
statement on "Dialogue and Proclamation," a message from the World Council of Churches' Seventh Assembly at Canberra, and a message on Jewish
evangelism from a consultation sponsored by the Lausanne Committee, all
1991. Volume 2 on "Theological Foundations" was published in 1994. Subsequent volumes in the series, we are told, "will deal with such subjects as

missiological foundations and problems, Gospel and culture, theology of religion and interreligious dialogue, mission and social justice, and spirituality for mission." These collections of important missiological literature are useful and important because they facilitate missiological research.

ONGOING PROJECTS IN MISSION RESEARCH IN GERMAN AND DUTCH

Until now I have mentioned only projects in the English language. There are four works in German and Dutch, however, that are of special importance for our purposes and should be included. First is the *Lexikon missionstheologischer Grundbegriffe*, with 110 articles on basic missiological concepts by ninety scholars, edited by Karl Müller and Theo Sundermeier, well-known German Catholic and Protestant missiologists (Berlin: Reimer Verlag, 1987). Hans Kasdorf in his review in the *International Bulletin of Missionary Research*, described this volume, as "a veritable curriculum in contemporary missiology," with emphasis on contemporary missiological issues (*IBMR* 1989, 140). Orbis Books will publish an English edition in 1997, titled *Dictionary of the World Church and Mission*.

Another important reference work in German is the *Lexikon der Mission* (Graz and Vienna: Styria, 1992) by Catholic scholar Horst Rzepkowski, SVD, professor of missiology at the Divine Word seminary in St. Augustin, near Bonn, and editor of *Mission Studies*, the journal of the International Association for Mission Studies. The 420-page *Lexikon der Mission* includes articles on mission history, theology, ethnology, and biographies. It is an impressive achievement.

In 1988 a team of Dutch Protestant and Catholic missiologists worked together to produce *Oecumenische Inleiding in de Missiologie: Teksten en konteksten van het wereldchristendom* (Kampen: Kok), edited by F. J. Verstraelen, et al. It is a pioneering effort by an interconfessional team to pool resources and take a new approach to teaching missiology, with chapters on definitions, foundations, theology of religion, and current theologies of mission, followed by studies on the context of mission in various countries and regions of the world. An English edition, *Missiology: An Ecumenical Introduction*, enlarged with new chapters on missiology in North America and the new situation in the former Soviet Union, was published by Eerdmans in 1995. The new work will probably become a textbook replacement for J. Verkuyl's earlier work *Contemporary Missiology*, which was published by Eerdmans in 1978.

Jan A. B. Jongeneel, professor of missiology at the University of Utrecht, is the author of *Missiologie*, a Dutch compendium of nineteenth- and twentieth-century mission studies. Originally published in two volumes (The Hague: Boekencentrum, 1986, 1991), it is now available in a single volume of six-hundred pages; part 1 is titled "Zendingswetenschap," part 2 is "Missionaire theologie." It is the sort of encyclopedic textbook for which

European scholars are famous, but which is not common in English, at least in missiological studies. Jongeneel says that his work "is not a handbook on mission(s), but on mission studies: i.e., missiology. It does not provide a comprehensive survey of mission(s), but rather a comprehensive view of the . . . study of mission(s). In other words: it is not primarily interested in the phenomenon of mission(s) . . . but in the way in which it has been studied."[10] With its thorough survey and scrutiny of the emergence and development of missiology as an academic discipline, giving careful attention to the major figures—both Protestant and Catholic—and the landmark literature, the work is a great service to missiological research. To my knowledge there is nothing comparable to it in scope and detail. An English edition of volume 1 was published by Peter Lang in 1995. Volume 2 in English will appear in 1997.

These are encouraging signs of vitality in missiological research. Yet, when considering the vast scope of Christian global outreach and the transition from Christendom to world Christianity, we recognize the inadequacy of present investment in scholarly infrastructure for the advancement of scholarship in studies of mission and non-Western Christianity.

Furthermore, Andrew Walls reminds us that a renaissance of mission studies

> will require not just rigorous scholarship, but *depth* of scholarship. . . . It will require integrated scholarship, which engages with all the existing theological disciplines and in doing so enriches them. . . . It will need to demonstrate learning and professional competence in the phenomenology and history of religion and in the historical, linguistic, and social sciences too, for those disciplines also need the renaissance of mission studies. . . . It is necessary therefore to realize that the world of learning is a mission field too. Quality, depth and range of scholarship are the marks of a vocation—and a collegial and demanding vocation, needing all the traditional missionary attributes of devotion, perseverance, and sacrifice (Walls *IBMR* 1991, 150).

This is the research agenda of missiological education for the twenty-first century.

Notes

1. I have described some of these efforts for revitalization of missiology in "American Protestants in Pursuit of Mission: 1886-1986" (1988, 112ff.), and in "Mission Research, Writing, and Publishing: 1971-1991" (1991).

2. For this brief survey I refer only to works in English, with the exception of four works in German and Dutch that I will mention later.

3. Letter to the writer from Scott W. Sunquist, April 29, 1992.

4. D. V. Singh (1982). In contrast to the "new perspective" of this series, see the

more traditional perspective represented in Stephen Neill (1984/1985), from the beginnings to 1707.

5. Letters to the writer from Saphir P. Athyal, March 31, June 6, and September 15, 1992; also press release from the project.

6. Ibid.

7. Information provided by Enrique Dussel, letter to the writer, June 25, 1992.

8. Ibid.

9. For an introduction and description of the series and the first volume, see Scherer and Bevans (1992).

10. Information provided by J. A. B. Jongeneel, letter to the writer, November 12, 1991.

3

Missiological Education for a Global Era

Paul G. Hiebert

How should we train missionaries and church leaders for the twenty-first century? This is not a question for the future. The students we now have in our classes will be the world leaders in 2030 c.e. The eight-year-olds in our Sunday Schools will be missionaries in 2050 c.e. We are like mission educators in 1945 trying to prepare missionaries for 1992: before the collapse of colonialism, the rise of the cold war, the emergence of the church around the world, and the collapse of communism.

It is easy to plan for the past. It is what we know best. Planning for the future is perilous at best, but we must do it if we want to join in what God is now doing around the world.

HISTORICAL TRENDS

To understand Christian missions in the future, we need to understand our mission history and the forces at work in the world around us.

The Rise of Colonial Missions

The modern Protestant mission movement was born with the arrival of Ziegenbalg and Plutschau at Tranquebar in 1706, and of William Carey in Serampore in 1793. The early missionaries identified closely with the people, learning their languages and translating their sacred literature into English. They often faced fierce opposition from the mercantile companies which

---

Paul Hiebert served as a missionary in India, where he also grew up. He taught anthropology and South Asian studies at Kansas State University, the University of Washington, and Fuller Theological Seminary, before coming to Trinity Evangelical Divinity School, where he is chair of the Department of Mission and Evangelism, and professor of mission and anthropology.

were expanding their rule around the world. The wedding of Christian missions with colonialism occurred largely after 1856, when the British Crown took over the rule of India. After that date European countries rushed to divide up the world into colonies.

The colonial governments were much more hospitable to missionaries. David Bosch notes,

> As it became customary for British missionaries to labor in British colonies, French missionaries in French colonies, and German missionaries in German colonies, it was only natural for these missionaries to be regarded as both vanguard and rearguard for the colonial powers. Whether they liked it or not, the missionaries became pioneers of Western imperialistic expansion (1991, 304).

John Philip, superintendent of the London Mission Society at the Cape of Good Hope, and a strong champion for oppressed peoples in the colonies, wrote,

> While our missionaries are everywhere scattering the seeds of civilization, social order, and happiness, they are, by the most unexceptionable means, extending British interests, British influence, and the British empire. Wherever the missionary places his standard among the savage tribe, their prejudices against the colonial government give way (1828, ix).

Despite its colonialism, the modern mission movement was remarkably successful. By the middle of the twentieth century small bands of missionaries had planted churches in most lands. In 1900 C.E. 95 percent of the church was in the West, and white. By 2000 C.E. an estimated 60 percent of the world's Christians will be in non-Western countries, a testimony to God who worked despite the faults of his messengers and the flaws of their methods.

Among these flaws was the tie of Christianity to Western colonial powers and Western culture. The church often turned to colonial rulers to enforce social reform, and mission converts often became cultural aliens in their own lands. Moreover, the idea of Western superiority often produced in missionaries an arrogance not befitting the gospel.

The Anti-Colonial Era

Opposition to the colonial exploitation of the people was voiced from the beginning by a few missionaries. The modern anti-colonial movement began, however, with the emergence of nationalist movements in the colonies and with the growing opposition to missions among secular humanists in the West. In recent years it has been backed by Hindu, Muslim, and Buddhist fundamentalists.

The anti-colonial critique is an important corrective to the colonial nature of modern missions. The collapse of Western Christendom (the marriage of Christianity to Western governments) and the emergence of young churches as minority communities in hostile cultures, has broken the image of Christianity wedded to political power. The church today, like the early church, must operate from a position of powerlessness and marginality.

The emergence of independent churches around the world expressing indigenous forms of Christianity is undermining the equation of Christianity with Western cultures. New and vital expressions of Christianity are emerging on the world scene. The Western church is only one among many. Lamin Sanneh notes,

> Christianity triumphs by the relinquishing of Jerusalem or any fixed universal centre, be it geographical, linguistic or cultural, with the result that we have a proliferation of centres, languages and cultures within the Church. Christian oecumenism is a pluralism of the periphery with only God at the centre (1989:232).

In the long run, however, the medicine of anti-colonialism is more dangerous than the disease of colonialism. In the first place, like the post-modernism of which it is part, anti-colonialism rejects any universal claims of truth and affirms deconstructionism and epistemological cognitive relativism. Anthony Giddens points out,

> The condition of post-modernity is distinguished by an evaporating of the "grand narrative"—the overarching "story line" by means of which humans are placed in history as beings who have a definite past and a predictable future. The post-modern outlook sees a plurality of heterogeneous claims to knowledge (1990, 182).

Today we have a growing suspicion that all belief systems—all ideas about human reality—are social constructs. Thomas Kuhn (1970) concludes that all such constructs or paradigms are incommensurable: that people in one cannot really understand or communicate with people in another. There is no way, therefore, to compare two paradigms to determine which is closer to the truth. Consequently, we cannot speak meaningfully of truth. We are left with pragmatism in which all we can say is that some paradigms are more useful than others.

One end of pragmatism is relativism and narcissism. Another is the rejection of any attempts to convert others to Christianity. In our fear of being colonial, we in the West are in danger of losing our missionary nerve. In the second place, anti-colonialism is in danger of absolutizing the historical and sociocultural contexts, and downplaying the possibility of divine revelation coming from outside our subjective human settings. Bosch writes,

This approach ends up having a low view of the importance of the *text* as coming from outside the context. The very idea that texts can judge contexts is, in fact, methodologically doubted. The message of the gospel is not viewed as something that we bring *to* the contexts, but as something that we derive *from* contexts. "You cannot incarnate good news into a situation, good news arises out of the situation," writes Nolan (1991, 430).

Owen Thomas points out that it is this emergence of "truth" from within the self that leads ultimately to "a naturalistic theism or affirmation of a cosmic soul as natural reality interacting with the world as part of the natural process" (1988, 212)—in other words to Hinduism and the New Age Movement.

Finally, anti-colonialism is essentially a reactionary movement. Its one agenda is to destroy the last vestiges of colonialism. It has no interest in and offers no solution to famines, oppression, poverty, crime, and other evils on earth. Nor is it concerned with the eternal lostness of humans apart from Christ.

The Global Era

We in the West must move beyond anti-colonialism to world thinking. We must see that the earth is being united through interlocking sociocultural systems. We must recognize that God is raising up a world church, and that we are no longer the center but partners with churches in other lands.

TRAINING MISSIONARIES FOR A GLOBAL WORLD

What implications does this all have for the content of mission training? How do we train leaders for the next half century? I suggest the following:

1. We must move from discussing theology and the social sciences to a discussion of a biblical world view.

For the most part, missionaries during the colonial era focused their attention on theology. Mission conferences and writings are full of discussions over theological issues such as the call of God, the lostness of humanity, and the nature of salvation.

In recent years, mission discussions have shifted to the contributions the social sciences have to offer. We now speak of people groups, multi-individual conversions, receptivity, and contextualization.

How do we bring theology and the social sciences together in missiology? As I listen to young seminarians in the school cafe I am struck by the duality. Here is a circle of young theologians excited about some abstract theological concept. Mission and evangelism are far from the center of their interests. There is a group of mission candidates discussing strategies for evangelism and church planting, and trying to avoid taking theology courses. Theology students avoid mission conferences, and mission students stay away from theology courses. Sadly, the two groups rarely meet. The result is a theology divorced from human realities and a missiology that lacks theological foundations.

Harvie Conn points out that one way to bridge the gap is to recognize that theology is the daughter of mission, not its mother. Most of the theology in the New Testament was worked out in response to mission problems. For instance, Acts 15 is the minutes of a mission conference. If we view theology in this light, missionaries need the help of theologians, and theologians would find their work relevant to everyday life.

But the division between theology and the social sciences runs deeper than asking different questions. They are embedded in different world views, and until these world views are brought together, no lasting integration is possible.[1] For us as Christians this must be a Christian world view. Only as we reformulate our social-science theories and our theologies in terms of a biblical world view will they become complementary maps or blueprints of reality.[2] We must, therefore, move behind the discussion of explicit beliefs to the largely implicit assumptions and categories we use to think about reality. In missiological education, this means we must reexamine the presuppositions behind our theories to determine the extent to which they are based on biblical assumptions, or on secular scientific ones.[3]

It also means that we must recognize that conversion must take place not only on the level of explicit beliefs, but also on the level of world-view assumptions. If conversion involves only the former, in two or three generations the church will face Christo-paganism, as implicit non-Christian assumptions and categories distort the explicit meanings of Christian teachings.

We must help young churches test their world views against the Scriptures. One way to do so is to reorient the theological task. Instead of looking at theology only in terms of a comparison of Christian and non-Christian beliefs, we need to examine the assumptions that lie behind each of them. For example, in India we found it important not only to teach that the God of the Bible is the only true God, but also to examine the implicit meaning of *devudu*, the Telugu word we used to translate the word *God*, and to show how our use of it is different from the ways Hindus use the term. The same is true of other key theological concepts such as *incarnation* (translated *avatar*), *salvation* (translated *moksha*), and *time* (understood in India as *samsara* or cyclical time). When we examined world views, the results were dramatic. Students with little education grasped the importance of defining Christianity in their cultural context, noting both the similarities and the differences between it and the Indian world view.

2. *We must move from indigenization and contextualization to inculturation.*

The post-modern era has made it clear to us that all human knowledge is shaped by the sociocultural and historical contexts of the knower. It is important, therefore, that we contextualize the gospel in different cultural settings so that the people understand the message clearly. Too often we have equated the gospel with our own cultural ways, and so failed to contextualize it in new cultures. Kenneth Scott Latourette notes that throughout church history the established church has wedded the gospel to its own culture.[4]

We must remember, however, that the gospel is not a message to be understood but a call to be obeyed. We must contextualize the message and the methods of evangelism for people to hear the gospel in ways they understand, but we must go beyond contextualization to an inculturation in which the prophetic call of the gospel leads to personal and corporate transformation. Contextualization without transformation leads to Christo-paganism. Transformation without contextualization lacks evangelistic outreach. In mission education we must reemphasize the absolute standards of the Kingdom of God in the middle of cultural relativities.

3. We must move from a stress on the autonomy and independence of national churches to interdependence and partnership in mission.

The colonial era saw the dependence of young churches on the older churches and their missionaries. The anti-colonial era rightly emphasized the need to recognize the independence of the young churches. Colonialism is not dead, and we must continue to guard against it. We must recognize the unity of the global church and move beyond the walls of nationalism, ethnicity, class, and gender that divide us. As Samuel Escobar points out,

> Internationalization of Christian mission means acknowledging that God has now raised up large and thriving churches in nations where sometimes the Bible was not even translated a hundred years ago. In these churches of the Southern Hemisphere, churches of the poor, churches of the Third World, God is raising up a new missionary force (1992, 7).

Such a shift calls for a radical change not only in our mission curricula, but also in the way we perceive mission training as a whole.

But we must move beyond our focus on our relationships to one another, and turn our attention again on the world and its needs. Injustice, famine, wars, oppression, and poverty reign on earth, and millions die without knowing the way of salvation. For fear of offending one another we are in danger of abandoning a lost and dying world. We need to work together under God's guidance in the mission he has given us.

4. We must move from a stress on the church and world, to God and God's Kingdom.

Most Western missionaries in the nineteenth and early twentieth centuries were largely children of the Enlightenment. They divided reality into a spiritual realm where Christianity ruled, and a natural realm where science ruled. In this context many evangelical missions saw their central task to be evangelism. By this they meant leading people to a personal, saving faith in Christ that would lead to eternal salvation. The Student Volunteer Movement, for example, had as its watchword, "the evangelization of the world in this generation."

Henry Venn and Rufus Anderson, and later Roland Allen and Donald McGavran, pointed out that evangelism by itself is incomplete. Converts must be incorporated into living churches. The strength of this view is that it ties evangelism to the planting of churches. Evangelism without the church is incomplete; the church without evangelism is ingrown.

One weakness of this approach is its human-centeredness. Mission is what we plan and do for God. Another is its failure to address the structural evils of our world. We are in danger of separating individuals from their communities, spiritual needs from material needs, the future from the present, and the gospel from its fruit.

We need to move beyond evangelism and church planting to a focus on the Kingdom of God. This reminds us that mission is first and foremost the work of God (*missio dei*). As Jürgen Moltmann notes, "It is not the church that has a mission of salvation to fulfill in the world; it is the mission of the Son and the Spirit through the Father that includes the church" (1977, 64).

There is a danger, however. If we speak of mission as *missio dei*, but do not define *dei*, we are free to equate the Kingdom with our own utopias— with Marxism, capitalism, or socialism. The Kingdom of God to which we bear witness is the Kingdom defined by Christ, its king.

Within the Kingdom the church has a central place. It is the place on earth where the Kingdom is already manifest as a sign of what is yet to come. Within the church, evangelism is central. As Bosch points out,

> Evangelism is announcing that God, Creator and Lord of the universe, has personally intervened in human history and has done so supremely through the person and ministry of Jesus of Nazareth who is the Lord of history, Savior and Liberator. In this Jesus, incarnate, crucified and risen, the reign of God has been inaugurated (1991, 412).

There is no divorce here between earthly and heavenly, between material and spiritual needs, or between salvation, righteousness and justice.

5. *We must move from positivism and instrumentalism to a critical realist epistemology.*

Modernity and its offspring, colonialism, are built on a positivist epistemology. This affirms that scientific knowledge is an accurate photograph of the world, having a one-to-one correspondence with reality.

As we have seen, post-modernity and its offspring, anti-colonialism, are based on an instrumentalist epistemology which holds that all human knowledge is captive to the subjectivity of cultural and historical contexts. Post-modernity celebrates cultural and religious diversity, and denies universals. David Harvey writes,

> I begin with what appears to be the most startling fact about post-modernism: its total acceptance of the ephemerality, fragmentation, discontinuity, and the chaotic. . . . But postmodernism . . . does not try to transcend it, contradict it, or even to define the "eternal and immutable" elements that might lie within it. Postmodernism swims, even wallows, in the fragmentary and the chaotic currents of change as if that is all there is. . . . Therefore, postmodernism typically harks back to that wing of thought, Nietzsche in particular, that emphasizes the deep chaos of modern life and its intractability before rational thought (1984, 124).

The result is subjectivism and pragmatism. Frederic Burnham comments, "The fundamental characteristic of the new post-modern era is epistemological relativism" (1989, x). This relativism destroys both missions and the gospel.

We dare not stay in relativism. Nor do we want to return to the cultural arrogance of the age of positivism. Our answer must lie in a critical realist epistemology (Barbour 1974) which holds that human knowledge is a map or blueprint that links subjective images of the world with objective realities. Such a shift will change how we view theology and mission (Hiebert 1985b, 1985c).[5] The implications of these shifts for what, how and where we teach missions are far-reaching. In the end, however, mission is not so much what we teach, but what we model.

Notes

1. For a discussion of this view of epistemology, see Larry Laudin, *Progress and Its Problems* (Berkeley: University of California Press, 1977). Laudin counters the instrumentalism posited by Thomas Kuhn in *The Structure of Scientific Revolutions*. Kuhn concludes that all knowledge is subjective, and that we cannot know if any of it is true. Consequently, we can no longer speak of truth. We can only say that certain knowledge is "useful" in certain settings. Laudin proposes a schema of human knowledge in which truth has a central place.

2. In recent years an extensive literature on the theory of complementarity has emerged. This sees different belief systems as different maps of the same reality, each of which gives true information on some specific aspect of that reality. Complementarity does not lead to relativism, for contradictions between belief systems must be resolved by changing one or the other, or both of them, or by changing the world view in which they are embedded.

3. It should not surprise us that most of the people involved in the Gospel in Our Culture Network have served in missions. Because of their cross-cultural experience, they are most aware of how much of our modern Christianity is built uncritically

on the assumptions of modernity, and how great is the need to return to a biblical world view.

4. An example of this over-contextualization of the gospel is the church in North America, which is no longer a prophetic counter-cultural community seeking to change the society around it. In recent years a number of North American Christians, most of whom have served in ministries abroad, have organized the Gospel in Our Culture Network, which is challenging the church in the United States to break from its captivity to Western cultures.

5. The shift will entail a move from Saussurian semiotics, which is built on a diadic view of symbols (form and meaning), to Piercian semiotics, which has a triadic view of symbols (form, mental image, and reality). The former leaves meaning only in the heads of people, with no real means to check the correspondence between what the speaker says and the hearer hears. The latter views symbols as the mediators between objective reality and the subjective perception of reality. In other words, meaning does not lie in human minds alone, but in the correspondence between what is in the mind with reality. We can, therefore, speak of truth, while recognizing that truth is always a subjective and limited perception of a much greater objective reality.

4

Missiological Education
in the Bible College Tradition

Kenneth Mulholland

In his *Concise History of the Christian World Mission*, the late Dr. J. Herbert Kane listed the Bible Institute Movement, the Faith Mission Movement, and the Student Volunteer Movement, as three important movements destined to have a significant bearing on the course of Christian missions in this century (Kane 1978, 101).

Although in time all three came to be predominantly North American phenomena, their impact was global. Each originated in the late nineteenth century but did not come to full fruition until the early twentieth century. Whereas by mid-century the Student Volunteer Movement had withered away, the Bible Institute Movement, gaining momentum, had evolved into the Bible College Movement.

The relationship between this movement and the Faith Mission Movement, of which the China Inland Mission, founded by J. Hudson Taylor, was the prototype, became increasingly intertwined (Frizen 1992, 30–32).[1] Significant numbers of missionaries serving under these agencies were trained in Bible institutes and Bible colleges.

For instance, between 1890 and 1976, over 5,400 alumni of Moody Bible Institute had served as missionaries under 245 mission agencies in 108 nations throughout the world. More than 2,000 of those were engaged in active missionary service at the time of the 1976 study. By the fall of 1992, a total of 6,455 alumni had served under more than 250 agencies in a total of 146 nations. Of these, 3,147 currently serve as missionaries.[2]

Kenneth B. Mulholland is dean and professor of missions at Columbia Biblical Seminary and Graduate School of Missions of Columbia International University. He served for fifteen years as a missionary in Central America.

While it is true that, historically, most of the missionaries active in the Faith Mission Movement have been trained in Bible institutes and Bible colleges, it is also true that many denominations, both large and small, have relied to varying degrees upon graduates of these institutions to fill the ranks of their missionary forces.

This chapter will focus on North American institutions. This is not to deny or downplay the contribution to missiological education of the Bible schools of continental Europe and the British Isles, many of which predate the North American schools.[3] Though neither as numerous nor as large as their North American counterparts, several of them have played a major role in the preparation of missionaries. The author also recognizes the existence of many evangelical training schools in Asia, Africa, and Latin America that are involved in missiological education. Often, the older, more established schools among them reflect the models and patterns of the schools in Europe and North America from which their founders graduated. However, with the explosion of cross cultural missionary activity in the two-thirds world, new models of training are emerging which draw from, yet move beyond, the patterns inherited from the Bible College Movement (Taylor 1991).

The purpose of this chapter is to explore the role of the North American Bible college tradition in missiological education. Today, the Bible College Movement is no longer limited to undergraduate instruction. Increasingly, it includes both graduate-level training programs and, in some cases, graduate schools, which have grown out of the Bible college tradition and partake of its evangelistic, devotional, disciplined ethos, among other distinguishing features.

DEFINITIONS AND CHARACTERISTICS

In the North American context, a Bible college is a specialized, professional school at the undergraduate level that seeks to prepare students for ministry-related vocations through biblical, professional, and general studies. In addition, most Bible colleges stress both the cultivation of the spiritual life and hands-on Christian ministry assignments.

Bible colleges can be seen as comparable to theological seminaries, except that seminaries operate on the graduate level.[4] Both Bible colleges and seminaries are single purpose institutions with a heavy concentration in biblical/theological studies. The relationship between these training institutions has tended to be complementary rather than competitive (Brereton 1990, 65). Schools in the Bible college tradition have sought to train what Dwight L. Moody called "gap men," persons who could carry out ministries requiring training beyond what local congregations could offer but not requiring seminary education. Historically, Bible colleges have offered a wider range of vocational training programs than most seminaries, which until very recently have tended to focus on training for the pastorate (Kallgren

1988, 32). Bible colleges—and the Bible institutes which preceded them—have emphasized the need for home and foreign missions, evangelism, and Bible teaching, as well as pastoral work in neglected congregations.

Like Christian liberal arts colleges, Bible colleges are undergraduate institutions. However, according to Allison (1984, 3), they can be contrasted with Christian liberal arts colleges in at least three areas: first, Bible college objectives center primarily on vocational Christian service; second, Bible college curriculum insists on a required Bible/theology core for every student and the Scripture as the integrative element in the curriculum; and third, Bible college vocational preparation requires all students to be active in some form of Christian service during their studies.

Although institutions related to the Bible college movement have evolved over the years, and although they serve a variety of sponsoring groups with diverse purposes, two clearly identifiable distinctions continue to be worthy of mention: accessibility and brevity. First, the schools which make up this movement sought to be accessible both in terms of the students they accepted and the delivery systems they employed. They aimed to train all whom God was leading into active Christian service regardless of educational level, chronological age, gender, and life circumstance.

Although most schools in this tradition now require a secondary education for admission, this was not always true. Originally, those who enrolled

> were of disparate educational backgrounds and the school leaders recognized this by providing a variety of routes for those with college, high school, or only grammar school educations. Training school graduation might mean earning a certificate, a diploma, or later on a degree. . . . No onus attached itself to those who dropped in and out (Brereton 1990, 64).

Chronologically, students in this tradition tended to be older than those entering more traditional colleges or universities. Often students were mature persons responding to the call to Christian service later in life.

Accessibility extended to women. Contrary to the practice of most seminaries, which did not admit women, the Bible college tradition opened the door of ministry training to women, usually on equal terms with men. Unlike most seminaries of the time, women were involved in teaching and other leadership positions. At one time Johnson Bible College had a woman president and at least one school, Columbia Bible College, was founded entirely by women.

Furthermore, in their attempt to make training accessible to as many as possible, regardless of life circumstance, schools in the Bible college tradition provided alternative educational delivery systems: evening courses, extension programs, correspondence schools, publications enterprises, and in some cases, even radio stations. Sometimes these alternate delivery systems developed in the direction of traditional residential education. For instance, many Bible colleges began in churches as evening Bible classes for laypersons. Often they met for an hour or two for a fifteen-week term.

As courses were added and the offerings were organized into a curriculum, the programs came to be identified as Bible training schools. The next step up was to become a day school, and eventually a fully developed Bible college. This is an ever-recurring development (Witmer 1962, 122).

However, in many cases the alternative delivery systems continued, and even expanded, alongside the development of the residential day-school programs.

Second, brevity was a hallmark of these training schools. "The student should not get entangled in what Jane Addams called the 'snare of preparation' and thus kept unduly long from the mission field until all fervor had been burned out" (Brereton 1990, 64). Allison (1984, 11) argues that the long delay required by advanced training does not serve to integrate real life with classroom studies "and may in fact be disorienting to those who may have been interested in a cross-cultural ministry." Rather than four years of university and three years of seminary, Allison advocates (1992, 1) a four-year Bible college missions program and a one-year graduate program as the preferred road of pre-field missionary training. It enables the prospective missionary to arrive on the field sooner and with less debt, "still a *learner* rather than a leader who doesn't yet speak the language."

ORIGIN AND HISTORICAL DEVELOPMENT

The Bible Institute Movement emerged in the 1880s. A. B. Simpson founded the Missionary Training Institute (now Nyack College) in 1882 in New York City. Dwight L. Moody established the Training School of the Chicago Evangelization Society (now Moody Bible Institute) in 1886 in Chicago. A. J. Gordon began the Boston Missionary Training School (now Gordon College) in 1889. Johnson Bible Institute (now Johnson Bible College) followed in 1893, Toronto Bible Institute (now Ontario Bible College) in 1894, and Providence Bible Institute (later Barrington College) in 1900. Although many of the smaller denominations and new religious groups of the time did establish Bible institutes to train persons for ministries not requiring a seminary education, most of the early schools were not under denominational control. Kallgren comments:

The early institutions offered basic training in English Bible, doctrine and Christian ministry skills, all within an ethos of personal piety and a love for the lost. Though the facilities were humble, the founders' dedication and zeal left their mark on the world (1991, 27).

Allison identifies the rise of the Bible College Movement with the shift in American education away from traditional classical studies and toward more practical vocational programs. Their development coincided with the rise of the new land grant colleges. "Bible colleges grew out of this environment, providing a practical, vocationally-oriented alternative for students whose occupational choices centered around church-related ministries" (1984, 3).

Beginning in the late 1920s, some Bible institutes began to expand their programs to four full years, adding sufficient liberal arts subjects to the curriculum to enable them to grant the baccalaureate degree. Johnson Bible College, a restorationist school founded in 1893 in Memphis, Tennessee, apparently was the first to do so. About the same time, Dr. Robert C. McQuilkin, one of the prominent pioneers in this development, desired to combine the spiritual benefits of the Bible Institute Movement with the cultural benefits of the liberal arts college. In 1929 he secured state approval for Columbia Bible College to offer a baccalaureate program centered in the Bible. Other schools soon followed suit.

In 1940 the number of Bible colleges had proliferated and their academic quality increased to the point where accreditation became an important issue. This led, in 1947, to the founding of the American Association of Bible Colleges (AABC), which more recently has linked itself globally to similar associations through the International Council of Accrediting Agencies. The first twelve schools were accredited by the AABC in 1948.

The movement continued to grow. The greatest increase in the number of new schools took place in Canada between 1931 and 1950, when 35 were founded, and in the United States between 1941 and 1960, when 106 opened their doors.

Today there are 93 colleges accredited by the AABC. Total enrollment in these schools in the fall of 1991 was 25,419, a decrease of 2,341 over the previous year. In addition to the accredited schools, there are four candidates and six applicants for accreditation. Enrollment figures are based on full-time equivalency (FTE).[5]

As the educational level of their constituency increased and the need for advanced training became apparent, a growing number of these schools added graduate programs, departments, and divisions. Columbia, in 1936, was the first to do so. Others have since developed full-fledged seminaries offering the M.A., M.Div., or Th.M. degree and in some cases even the D.Min. However, such advanced training generally partakes of many of the characteristics which historically have characterized the Bible college tradition.

MISSIONARY TRAINING

The explicit purpose of many Bible institutes and Bible colleges has been to train home and foreign missionaries. Many of the early schools even carried the word *missionary* in their names. Kallgren points out that among the objectives recommended as being normative for Bible college programs, the manual of the American Association of Bible Colleges includes "to instill a vital missionary vision and dedication for world wide service" (1988, 37).

Witmer insists that the Great Commission is the *raison d'être* for Bible institutes and colleges:

> It is the base of reference for the direction, the purpose and the subject matter of Bible college education. The founders and their successors were dominated by the conviction that the church is under a compelling obligation to make the gospel of salvation known to all mankind. This mission begins with the man next door and extends to the "uttermost part of the earth" (1962, 103).

Witmer further maintains, and I agree with him, that "Bible institutes and colleges have made their most significant contribution to evangelicalism in the preparation of Protestant missionaries." At one time 15 percent of the entire Protestant missionary force were alumni of either Moody Bible Institute or Prairie Bible Institute (Witmer 1962, 111).

From its very roots in the ministries of A. B. Simpson, D. L. Moody, and A. J. Gordon, the Bible college tradition has included a strong missionary thrust. For instance, Witmer writes of A. B. Simpson that he "had a deep concern for the peoples and nations that had never been touched by gospel light" (1962, 24). Toronto Bible Institute (now Ontario Bible College) came into existence in response to the lament of J. Hudson Taylor that out of five hundred missionary candidates, many had to be turned down for lack of adequate Bible preparation.

Among the marks which characterize missionary training in the Bible college tradition, I want to emphasize four.

Biblical

The mastery of the Bible in the vernacular language is central to the curriculum. Whatever additional fields of study the schools in this tradition may offer, a major in Bible is invariably required. This is a matter of principle. Students are taught to grasp the whole of the Scriptures and encouraged to preach and teach the Bible in the vernacular language. Courses in inductive Bible study and methodology using the vernacular are part of nearly every curriculum. While at least one or both of the original languages of the Bible may be required at the undergraduate level, they are nearly always viewed as supplementary rather than foundational to ministry. Even at the graduate level, in-depth Bible survey and Bible exposition courses occupy considerable room in the curriculum.

Practical

In the Bible college tradition, training occurs not only in the academic program, but in all those experiences which contribute to the preparation of students for effective Christian living and service. There is strong emphasis on practical training and skill development. "How to" courses on teaching and music skills, such as song leading, form curricular staples, although some schools even offer specialized courses on missionary medicine, aviation, radio broadcasting, and accounting.

Students are involved continuously in Christian service or practical work or field education. To be enrolled is to be involved in ministry. Historically, morning hours were spent in the classroom, while afternoon and evening hours were divided between study and practical work. Practical work is not just pastoral work, Sunday School teaching, or youth group leadership in a local church context. Rather, it frequently involves Christian work beyond the ecclesiastical structures with marginal, often unchurched people: Bible Club teaching, open-air preaching, prison visitation, tract distribution, personal evangelism of total strangers, and rescue mission work.

The emphasis on practical ministry is seen not only as a part of the training process, the acquisition of skills for future ministry, but also as a normal expression of the Christian life. "Christian service," says Witmer, "is not merely training for the postgraduate future; it is an outlet for the impulse to share and to serve during student days . . . glorifying God and ministering to human need, not mere practice" (1962, 138).

Contextual

The contextual nature of education in the Bible college tradition and the courses which emerged to equip students to minister practically led to unexpected pioneering innovations. Brereton captures this dynamic well when she states that these

> training schools pioneered in the field of religious education—however rudimentary a training school course in "sociology" or "pedagogy" might appear with later standards. But the pioneering grew out of judgment about the needs of new constituencies and new missionary fields, not out of any interest in curricular innovation for its own sake (1990, 64).

Interestingly enough, in contrast to liberal arts and land grant colleges, many of these training schools were located in the heart of major, often industrial cities. Training took place in a cultural mosaic and exposed students to the demands of urban ministry. "Dwight L. Moody's compassion stirred him to do something about the neglected, unevangelized masses in the urban centers of America and Britain. . . . There was a critical lack of personnel" (Witmer 1962, 24). Thus, Bible college graduates were at home in an urban world and in touch with the masses of working-class people as they sought to make relevant an old message in a new context.

Many schools in the Bible college tradition incorporate summer service on cross-cultural missionary teams as part of their training process. Often, faculty other than the missions professors are involved. N. Sanford Good, Missions Chairperson at Lancaster Bible College, writes:

> This program has grown and has had a major impact on the campus. Last year we received over eighty applications for the forty-two openings we had on the five teams. . . . Along with these teams, we still have individuals going out for the whole summer. Next year we are planning to send out seven teams. I will lead three of them and four other faculty members will lead the other ones (1992, 2).

Spiritual

The Bible college tradition emphasized spiritual formation in the form of the cultivation of personal piety. Personal godliness was stressed as indispensable to effective ministry. Many Bible colleges were influenced by the Keswick Movement. Personal devotions and corporate worship were often an enforced part of the curriculum. Classes customarily commenced with Bible reading and prayer, often for missionaries. Brereton points to an informal curriculum which coexisted with the formal one:

> They met in prayer meetings, listened to missionaries on furlough, perused letters from their peers who had preceded them to the mission fields, received support from each other during spiritual crises and regaled each other with accounts of their trials and triumphs in city mission. . . . The faculty encouraged and participated in this strenuous and dedicated atmosphere (1990, 65).

CURRICULAR DEVELOPMENT

As early as the mid-fifties, the Evangelical Foreign Missions Association (EFMA), while acknowledging the validity of wide variations in curricula and time required to train missionaries, agreed "that a missionary, apart from training for specialized ministries, needs considerable preparation in other areas to serve effectively in a foreign culture" (Witmer 1962, 113). In a pamphlet, *Preparation of Missionaries in Bible Institutes and Bible Colleges,* EFMA listed the following course areas as essential:

History of Missions, Principles and Practices (including the Indigenous Church), Bible Basis (Philosophy) of Missions, Anthropology, Non-Christian Religions, Languages (Phonetics and Linguistics), Area Study, and Hygiene and Sanitation.

While missions executives favored the inclusion of a mission major in the Bible college curriculum, "many educators, facing the problem of balancing maximum content with the limitations of time, favored a minor" (Witmer 1962, 113).

Allison, in his paper "Academic Preparation for the Missionary of the 1990s," however, strongly defends the Bible college tradition and the mission major. In response to the objection: "A missions (missiology) major doesn't prepare you to do anything specific. How can you 'mish'?" Allison explains that, among other things, "mishing" is all about a complex process involving (a) entry into a vastly different culture, (b) learning one or more new languages, (c) thinking in new thought forms, (d) working to contextualize the gospel, (e) leaving family, friends and one's own culture, and (f) coping with culture shock (1984, 6).

He goes on to compare favorably the professional training of medical doctors with the missionary training provided by an undergraduate missions major followed by subsequent graduate work which integrates academic studies with experience.

Although schools in the Bible college tradition are not liberal arts colleges, missionary educators underscore the importance of such general education courses as political science, history, sociology, and a thorough knowledge of English. Also, great emphasis is placed on training in effective communication.

SOME OBSERVATIONS AND CONCLUSIONS

First, the roots of the Bible college movement lie in the fertile soil of the evangelical awakenings of the late nineteenth century and in the increasingly pragmatic and vocationally oriented educational currents of that time. This contrasts sharply with the common view that Bible colleges were alternative educational institutions, often obscurantist in mentality, which developed at the height of the fundamentalist-modernist controversy as a refuge intending to seal youth from the corrupting influences of liberal secular culture by enveloping them in the cocoon of an evangelical sub-culture. Rather, historical investigation indicates that the Bible college movement predates the fundamentalist-modernist controversy.[6] Early schools in this movement involved many institutions from the historic denominations and those denominations themselves developed educational institutions along the same pattern for the training both of YMCA workers and of missionaries. Only at a later period in its development did the Bible college tradition become the almost exclusive educational arm of the fundamentalist and pentecostal churches.

Second, the Bible college movement produced a vast array of men and women who served to establish and nurture great Christward movements around the globe. In the judgment of Brereton (1990, 28), these persons did not generally become elite leaders, but they certainly qualified as lesser leaders and valued workers in the movements. In fact, many of those in the Bible college tradition who did go on to evangelical liberal arts colleges and evangelical graduate schools and seminaries often did emerge as international leaders.

Third, the impact of this movement on theological education around the world is unmistakable. Many of the institutions established for the training of Christian workers are patterned after schools in the Bible college tradition. At its worst this imitation has been slavish and unresponsive to contextual factors—the imposition by well-meaning missionaries who sought to clone their alma mater. In many cases, however, the imitation reflects the methodological and strategic creativity aimed at making training of leadership for the masses both practical and accessible to the whole church. Evening Bible schools, intensive courses, theological education by extension, correspondence, radio Bible classes—all of the above draw from the best of the Bible college tradition.

Fourth, the dynamic and practical training programs found among such rapidly growing younger Western-based (but rapidly internationalizing) mission agencies such as Operation Mobilization (OM) and Youth with a Mission (YWAM) bear a striking resemblance to the early Bible institutes rather than the more developed Bible colleges of North America.[7] Also, we are witnessing, particularly among large congregations, the emergence of a new church-based Bible Institute Movement, which has many parallels to earlier training models.

Finally, the jury is still out on the future shape of missiological education in the two-thirds world. Only now are missionary training institutions developing amid the burgeoning missionary movement emerging in those parts of the globe. To what extent they will adopt the patterns of missiological education as practiced in the Bible college tradition and to what extent they will navigate new courses in the uncharted waters of the next century is yet to be determined.

Notes

1. Frizen (1992) points out that the founding officers of the Interdenominational Foreign Missions Association (IFMA) were deeply involved in the Bible Institute Movement. His book provides a thorough discussion of the Nondenominational Missions Movement in the United States and Canada.

2. Telephone conversation with Dr. Ray Badgero, Moody Bible Institute, on September 16, 1992.

3. According to Brereton (1990:55), the early North American schools were

modeled after "certain European institutions that trained missionaries and other religious workers. The conservatives were not alone in their admiration of the European Schools. American Protestants of diverse persuasions—motivated by a common interest in missions—acclaimed the European schools for being fast, effective, and practical, and began establishing similar institutions in the United States."

4. Brereton (1990:55) cites A. B. Simpson, who describes missionary training colleges as "institutions less technical and elaborate than the ordinary theological seminary, and designed to afford the same wants of that large class, both men and women, who did not wish formal ministerial preparation, but an immediate equipment for usefulness as lay workers."

5. Telephone conversation with secretarial staff of the American Association of Bible Colleges (AABC) on September 11, 1992.

6. According to Brereton (1990:39), "The early Bible or religious training schools, products of the 1880's and 1890's, were not even founded by fundamentalists as such—no such designation existed then—but rather by men and women who considered themselves simply earnest and mission-minded Protestants."

7. A matter of concern among missionary educators is the apparent gradual decline in enrollment among the accredited Bible colleges in North America. This is coupled with a declining percentage of students who are specifically preparing for missionary service in these institutions. The upward mobility of the evangelical population and the economic uncertainty of the times have led many Bible colleges to move toward more diverse educational focus, similar to that offered in Christian liberal arts colleges. While continuing to insist that every student major in Bible, they have introduced into their curriculum additional majors in a variety of disciplines, often education or business administration. In a few schools missions courses are no longer required of all students but are available only as free electives.

ECUMENICAL CONTEXTS

Sandals from Other Sanctuaries

5

Pentecostal/Charismatic Perspectives on Missiological Education

L. Grant McClung, Jr.

I would like to begin my observations with the words of Luke the physician, an original Charismatic missiologist (Stronstad 1984):

> When all the people were being baptized, Jesus was baptized too. As he was praying, heaven was opened and the Holy Spirit descended on him in bodily form like a dove. And a voice came from heaven: "You are my Son, whom I love; with you I am well pleased" (3:21-22).

> Jesus, full of the Holy Spirit, returned from the Jordan and was led by the Spirit in the desert, where for forty days he was tempted by the devil (4:1).

> Jesus returned to Galilee in the power of the Spirit, and news about him spread through the whole countryside. He taught in their synagogues, and everyone praised him. He went to Nazareth, where he had been brought up, and on the Sabbath day he went into the synagogue, as was his custom. And he stood up to read. The scroll of the prophet Isaiah was handed to him. Unrolling it, he found the place where it is written: The Spirit of the Lord is on me, because he has anointed me to preach good news to the poor. He has sent me to pro-

---

L. Grant McClung served as a missionary educator at the European Bible Seminary and in leadership training among the Asian community in Los Angeles. As coordinator of education for the Church of God World Missions Department, he oversees the work of some seventy Bible institutes, colleges, and seminaries around the world. He also serves as associate professor of missions and church growth at the Church of God School of Theology in Cleveland, Tennessee.

claim freedom for the prisoners and recovery of sight for the blind, to release the oppressed, to proclaim the year of the Lord's favor (4:14-19).

I greet you as colleagues, sisters and brothers in the name of this Lord and Savior, Jesus Christ, whom we serve together in one body and one Spirit (Eph 4:3). It is this Jesus whom Pentecostals and Charismatics love to preach and whom we all honor as Lord of the universe, Lord of nature and nations, Lord of the church, and Lord of God's harvest.

The communions I represent (seen on one hand as identical, that is, Pentecostal/Charismatic, or on the other as distinct, Pentecostal *and* Charismatic) have been mistakenly labeled over the years as a "Spirit movement" or a "tongues movement" at the expense of a firm, biblical Christology in the tradition of historical theology. Nothing could be further from the truth. It is our confession that the presence of the Holy Spirit will only give more and more honor to the unique and indispensable revelation of God in the powerfully present person of the Lord Jesus Christ. Arthur F. Glasser relates this witness of the Holy Spirit to the lordship of Christ in Pentecostal/Charismatic spirituality:

> Many evangelicals have been challenged by the immediacy and reality of God that Pentecostals reflect along with their freedom and unabashed willingness to confess openly their allegiance to Christ. The achievements of their churches are equally impressive, reflecting their settled conviction that the full experience of the Holy Spirit will not only move the Church closer to Jesus at its center, but at the same time, press the Church to move out into the world in mission (1985b).

Pentecostal and Charismatic theology maintains the necessity of the baptism in the Holy Spirit as indispensable for Christian mission (Lk 24:49; Acts 1:8); that Jesus, the exalted mediator between God and humankind, is the Baptizer in the Holy Spirit (Mt 3:11; Mk 1:8; Lk 3:16; Jn 1:33); and that Jesus Christ continues *today* to do all that he began in his earthly mission (Acts 1:1). It confesses the trinitarian proclamation of Peter, "Being therefore exalted at the right hand of God, and having received from the Father the promise of the Holy Spirit, [Jesus] has poured out this which you see and hear" (Acts 2:33).

My concern is shared by other Christian traditions: that the missing ingredient in mission and in much of today's missiological education is *passion*—a passion for God and God's glory, and a passion for the lost. We will find technical terms for this dimension in our training—the so-called "affective domain." We will even schedule space for a chapel or convocation here and a Bible reading or meditation there as a nod toward "spiritual formation" and then go back to business as usual—statistics and structures, curriculum and consultations, minutes and methodologies, news and networking. We may as well be chief executive officers of multinational corporations or lecturers on mechanical engineering! These misplaced priorities tend to leave us dry and wanting, as was the case with one of William Booth's Salvation Army officers, who wrote to his general with complaints about his own ineffectiveness. Booth's two-word prescription by return telegram was, "Try tears."

We complain about the rise of modernity and of our technocratic cultures being captivated by secularism, making them resistant to the gospel, without realizing our *own* captivity to the same. As helpful as they may be, and given by God as wider gifts to all humanity, we move toward subtle dependency upon the "arm of the flesh" with too much dependence upon the social sciences in church extension, or upon the latest educational procedures and techniques in leadership training, or upon Western business-style management-by-objective in our missiological strategizing. One marks the encroachment, for example, of a management/marketing paradigm in recent North American church growth emphases such as "marketing the church."

My question is, Where is Jesus in all of this cultural accommodation? As Lord of His church, he said, "If *I* be lifted up, I will draw everyone unto me" (Jn 12:32) and "*I* will build my church, and the gates of hell shall not prevail against it" (Mt 16:18). In missiological education for the twenty-first century we must enter into the passion of our suffering King, described by the prophet Isaiah: "He will see the result of the suffering of his soul and be satisfied; by his knowledge my righteous servant will justify many, and he will bear their iniquities" (Is 53:11). Some Pentecostals and Charismatics may be too quick to point to the Day of Pentecost, but the heart of missiology begins in Gethsemane and proceeds to Golgotha before getting to the upper room.

This "burden of the Lord" in missiology cannot be reduced to a simple slogan, motto, or catchword such as "The Great Commission in this generation," "A church for every people by the year 2000," or "Reaching into the 10/40 window"—however grand and true these are. The passion for God and God's mission is expressed in the deep pathos of Paul, "I have great sorrow and unceasing anguish in my heart. For I could wish that I myself were cursed and cut off from Christ for the sake of my brothers, those of my own race, the people of Israel" (Rom 9:2-3). It is the plaintive and desperate cry of Jeremiah, "Oh, that my head were a spring of water and my eyes a fountain of tears!" (Jer 9:1). These were the servants, said one Jewish writer of the Old Testament prophets, who could hear the "silent sigh of God." This is the passion carried over a hurting world by the "Christ of the Emmaus Road," who has walked along so powerfully in the life and missionary ministry of the newest dean of the School of World Mission of Fuller Theological Seminary (Woodberry 1989).

Missiological education for the twenty-first century needs the preeminence of Jesus and the presence of the Holy Spirit. Our training must follow the pedagogy and paradigm of the Spirit in a Spirit-directed, Spirit-driven missiology that openly confesses with Moses:

> If your presence does not go with us, do not send us up from here. How will anyone know that you are pleased with me and with your people unless you go with us? What else will distinguish me and your people from all the other people on the face of the earth? (Ex 33:15-17).

David Barrett's description of our tradition, now numbering more than 400 million and growing by 19 million a year and 54,000 a day, is that we come in an "amazing variety" of 38 major categories, 11,000 Pentecostal denominations, and 3,000 independent Charismatic denominations spread across 8,000 ethnolinguistic cultures and 7,000 languages. A cross section of worldwide Pentecostalism reveals a composite "international Pentecostal/Charismatic who is more urban than rural, more female than male, more Third World (66 percent) than Western world, more impoverished (87 percent) than affluent, more family oriented than individualistic, and, on the average younger than eighteen" (Barrett 1988; see also McClung 1991b).

To ask, for example, for Pentecostal/Charismatic perspectives may take us across the landscape of Barrett's five umbrella categories, first used in his *World Christian Encyclopedia* (1982):

   a. Classical Pentecostals (with North American/European roots)
   b. Neo-Pentecostalism (main-line Protestant)
   c. Catholic Charismatics
   d. Independent Charismatic Churches
   e. Indigenous non-white Pentecostals/Charismatics in the Southern World (especially Africa).

Obviously, with this backdrop, it is difficult to bring a monolithic, homogeneous view, but the following seven perspectives would be generally representative of Pentecostal/Charismatic missiology.[1]

MISSION IS EXPERIENTIAL AND RELATIONAL

This has long been the millstone my tradition has had to carry, that we are too emotional, placing experience over objective, revealed truth. A few Latin American Pentecostal leaders openly critiqued their own movement during the recent Latin American Congress on Evangelism (CLADE III) in Quito, Ecuador. They felt, says reporter John Maust (1992), that Latin Pentecostals (representing an estimated 75 percent of the forty million Latin evangelicals) have overemphasized subjective experience as over against God's objective truth as revealed in the Scriptures.

As a generic assessment, this may be questionable. If this *is* true of the rank and file in the pulpits and pews of Latin American Pentecostal churches, however, it is because believers have seen first-century Christians experiencing the power of God on the pages of the book they have so diligently sought to obey and emulate as God's objective expectations of the normal Christian life.

It seems to me that there will be no relevant and pungent missiological education in the twenty-first century unless it is fired with the passion and presence of God so characteristic of the *first* century and so desperately needed in the present, final days of the *twentieth* century.

MISSION IS EXPRESSLY BIBLICAL AND THEOLOGICAL

Pentecostals and Charismatics are "people of the Book." Eugene Nida called Latin American Pentecostals, "The Church of the Dirty Bibles." There, he observed, the Bible is used frequently in worship services, being read along by the poor with their soiled fingers as a reading guide.

For us, biblical authority will be central to missiological education for the twenty-first century, and rightfully so. Due to the rising deterrence from non-Christian religions and lifestyles and the alarming drift toward theological "slippage" on the part of some in the Christian community, we will need the ballast and the balance of biblical exegesis and theological scholarship conducted under the rubric of missiology. Exegesis and evangelization need not, and cannot be mutually exclusive.

In this light it is encouraging, as one case in point, that national and regional meetings of the Evangelical Theological Society and the Evangelical Missiological Society in the United States are held in the same venue with integrated plenary sessions. This "piggy back" arrangement, besides making school administrators and accounting departments happy, makes a fundamental theological statement of unity.

With increasing interaction between those within and outside of Christian faith, discussions of revelation, authority, hermeneutics, and eschatology are inevitable. I believe *the primary missiological issues of the nineties and beyond will not be methodological, but theological.* In the case of the lostness of humanity and questions of eternity, for example, our high-tech methods of demographic research have now allowed us to find the lost (even pinpointing the numbers and locations of people groups), but some are not sure that those we have found are lost!

MISSION IS EXTREMELY URGENT

Eschatological urgency is at the heart of understanding the missionary fervor of Pentecostals, producing in our early days what historian Vinson Synan (1992) calls "missionaries of the one-way ticket."

I'm reminded daily of this urgent missiology by the fact that my office sits next to our county rescue squad and ambulance station. Repeatedly, sirens and flashing lights atop rushing rescue vehicles remind me of yet another emergency in our community.

Regardless of one's views on eschatology, it must be allowed that our *world* community is currently filled with urgent emergencies: "ethnic cleansing" in the Balkans; famine moving south from Ethiopia and Somalia; continued unrest and political violence in virtually every corner of the globe. We began the first year in this last decade of the twentieth century with encouraging signs of hope: the end of totalitarianism in Eastern Europe, advances in human rights in South Africa, encouraging political developments in Central America. Christians in the capitalistic West breathed a triumphant sigh of relief that the Cold War was over and communism weakened.

Euphoria tends to hide reality, however. One must be reminded that democratization is not evangelization, that crying needs remain across Eastern Europe and the Commonwealth of Independent States; that third-world debt, ecological disasters, the squalor of deplorable urban environments, and the despair of the poor—also in the United States—continue to be powder kegs ready to explode, social time bombs that will form the context of missiological education for the twenty-first century.

MISSION IS FOCUSED YET DIVERSIFIED

Pentecostal/Charismatic missiology is obviously focused on, but not limited to the prioritization of evangelization and church planting. What will come to light as more inside interpreters from these traditions articulate a self-definition of their mission (a process that began to mature in the 1980s) is that the "broader mission" of the church has been part and parcel of this branch of the family as an automatic outgrowth of our prioritization of "Great Commission" missions. Pentecostal pastor Juan Sepulveda of Chile states:

Pentecostalism—in spite of its popular origin—did not develop a social ethic which would encourage the participation of believers in social, labor union or political organizations, which promote social change. This does not mean that Pentecostalism failed to have any social impact. Rather, to the contrary, the Pentecostal communities meant a powerful offering of life-meaning for wide sectors excluded from our societies.

"What is overlooked," says William Menzies (1988), "is that Pentecostals have quietly gone about social renewal in unobtrusive ways, working with the poor of this world in unheralded corners."

When social activist Ronald Sider gathered representatives from the Evangelical and Pentecostal/Charismatic communities for a dialogue on social action, there was an interesting blend of "words, works, and wonders" seen in the Pentecostal/Charismatic churches (Sider 1988). The non-Pentecostal world cannot afford to typecast all Pentecostals and Charismatics (especially internationally) into the affluent Hollywood media images we saw during the heyday of American TV charisma in the 1980s.[2] Pentecostals and Charismatics are more politically and socially involved than most casual observers suppose, but evangelization and church multiplication will continue as our main priority.[3]

MISSION IS AGGRESSIVELY OPPOSED

Missiological education for the twenty-first century will not go unchallenged either within or outside of the Christian community. Sending churches from any region or country will have to swim against the tides of nationalism and isolationism that foster nonsupportive attitudes in parishes, denominational headquarters, and, unfortunately, in many training institutions.

There is an aggressive "to the gates of hell" mentality in true Pentecostal/Charismatic life style. Contrast this with an equally determined missionary fervor and growing intolerance from cults and non-Christian religions. These contrasts make for one result: religious persecution (Woehr 1992; McFadden 1992; McCurry 1992). Sociologist Peter Berger has observed in his Foreword to *Tongues of Fire*, David Martin's study of the growth of Protestantism in Latin America, that there are two global movements of enormous vitality on the religious scene today: conservative Islam and conservative Protestantism (Martin 1990, vii). Both are expressly committed to missionary expansion. This makes for a potentially volatile mix.

Pentecostals and Charismatics believe, however, that the primary source of deterrence is spiritual. They would echo the sentiments of Neuza Itioka, who writes, "Certainly one of the most important issues worldwide missions must face in the 1990s is how to confront the destructive supernatural evil forces that oppose the missionary enterprise" (Itioka 1990, 8). For this reason, expect the proliferation of "power literature" and publications on spiritual warfare to continue. It is currently one of the most frequent topics in Pentecostal/Charismatic publications.[4]

MISSION IS INTERDEPENDENT

With the dramatic growth of the Pentecostal/Charismatic churches we will need to avoid the twin perils of triumphalism and elitism, says Pentecostal insider Russell Spittler, who relates the insights of church historian Martin Marty. Marty, says Spittler, "once observed that Pentecostals used to argue God's approval upon them because they numbered so few. But more recently he said the proof has shifted to the fact that there are so many" (Spittler 1990, 120). David Shibley has urged the cooperation of Charismatics and Evangelicals, saying that neither can complete the task of world evangelization without the other (1989, 26-27). I would broaden that to say that the Pentecostal/Charismatic tradition and all the other major traditions—Eastern Orthodox, Roman Catholic, Protestant, and Evangelical—need one another, and that Pentecostals and Charismatics need each other. Not until five years ago at the July 1987 North American Congress on the Holy Spirit and World Evangelization (in New Orleans, Louisiana) did main-line Pentecostals and Charismatics meet together around the task of world evangelization. Subsequent congresses were held in Indianapolis, Indiana (August 1990), and internationally in Brighton, England (July 1991). In addition, Pentecostals and Charismatics have been more recently engaged in the Lausanne and the AD 2000 and Beyond movements and have participated in common projects with the Commission on World Mission and Evangelism of the World Council of Churches (see Hollenweger 1986; Hayford 1990).

Beyond the already established years of involvement in missiological training programs from the main-line Pentecostal groups, missiological training programs could also benefit by reaching out to three rapidly growing Pentecostal/Charismatic type ministries: local congregations (many of them mega- and meta-churches), missions agencies, and media ministries.

Local Congregations

In the United States alone, there have been scholarly estimates of more than 100,000 new independent Charismatic congregations formed during the decade of the 1980s, representing the fastest-growing segment of American Christianity this past decade. Edward K. Pousson produced the landmark study on the missions involvement of these congregations, *Spreading the Flame: Charismatic Churches and Missions Today* (1992). Pousson's study found that more and more Charismatic churches are hiring mission directors and sending out missionaries. This is a trend that missiological educators cannot ignore. The growth of these churches has also resulted in the growth of Charismatic missions agencies, many of them now linked together in a network called AIMS—The Association of International Missions Services.

Missions Agencies

Whereas the number of indigenous Pentecostal/Charismatic missions agencies in the non-Western world grew to some 40 percent of the total of non-Western agencies by 1988, researcher Larry D. Pate is concerned that many more need to be created to keep pace with the general growth of Pentecostal/Charismatic churches, expected to represent 85-90 percent of the Christians in the two-thirds world by the year 2000 (Pate 1991). As these agencies grow, they will look for help in training. Thus the need for interdependence.

Media Ministries

A third type of "growth ministry" among Pentecostals and Charismatics is outreach through the media, both print and electronic. Tracing the growth of "mega-media" ministries and their potential for missiological education is a doctoral dissertation waiting to be written. Since the early days of this century—when no fewer than thirty-four Pentecostal periodicals came into existence between 1900 and 1908 (McClung 1986, 78)—Pentecostals have seized the popular media as an instrument of evangelism and discipleship training. Imagine the potential of the major Pentecostal/Charismatic television and publishing networks in providing basic missiological education to their viewers and readers through a variety of innovative "distance learning" type instructional formats. The time is ripe for older established missiological training programs to explore creative training cooperatives.

MISSION IS UNPREDICTABLE

The understatement of the year for the international roller-coaster ride of the thirty-six months (beginning in Eastern Europe in the fall of 1989) could have been provided by Habakkuk 1:5: "Look at the nations and watch—and be utterly amazed. For I am going to do something in your days that you would not believe, even if you were told."

The dawning of the last decade of the twentieth century has brought a new wave of evangelical futurists, eager to update the rest of us on trends at the touch of a computer keyboard. There are some things in the information age, however, that the Lord of mission sovereignly intends on keeping to himself, including the "times and dates the Father has set by his own authority" (Acts 1:7).

Should we, in God's mercy, be granted the remainder of this decade and see a new century before that day when time shall be no more, the glory of the Christian mission and harvest (Mt 9:38) will be God's alone. All branches of the Christian family will be awed by the initiative (Acts 13:1-4) and the unpredictability of God in mission (Acts 8:26ff.; 9:10ff.; 10:9ff.).

Charismata cannot be contained. For that matter, signs and wonders cannot be reduced to a mere methodology or curriculum elective. "All these are the work of one and the same Spirit," Paul instructed, "and he gives them to each one, just as he determines" (1 Cor 12:11).

Along these lines, I suppose the quote that has imbedded itself in my heart and mind the last three years since Lausanne II in Manila involves the words of Eva Burrows on the next to the last day of the congress. Judging from the number of times her statement has appeared in a variety of publications, it obviously had international impact. She noted how, in reflection before the Lord over her many years of ministry, a clear word from the Lord came to her: "I have seen your ministry. Now, let me show you mine."

Notes

1. In addition to Pomerville (1985) recent expositions on an emerging Pentecostal/Charismatic missiology include L. Grant McClung, Jr., *Azusa Street and Beyond: Pentecostal Missions and Church Growth in the Twentieth Century* (1986); Gary B. McGee, *This Gospel Shall Be Preached: A History and Theology of Assemblies of God Foreign Missions to 1959*, Vol. 1 and 2 (1986, 1989); David Shibley, *A Force in the Earth: The Charismatic Renewal and World Evangelism* (1989); Byron D. Klaus, Murray W. Dempster, and Douglas Peterson, *Called and Empowered: Pentecostal Perspectives on Global Mission* (1991). Extensive bibliographical references are included in the following articles by McClung: "Mission in the 1990s," (1990); "The Pentecostal/Charismatic Contribution to World Evangelization," (1991c); "Forecasting the Future of Pentecostal/Charismatic Church Growth," (1991a).

2. See Quentin J. Schultze, "The Great Transmission," (1990); and articles on "Evangelism," "Bakker, James Oren (Jim) and Tammy Faye (La Valley)," and "Swaggart, Jimmy Lee" in Burgess and McGee (1988).

3. See the following for just a sampling of reports and case studies on Pentecostal/ Charismatic social involvement: Margaret M. Poloma, "Pentecostals and Politics in North and Central America," (1986); Paul Brink, "Las Acacias Evangelical Pentecostal Church, Caracas, Venezuela," (1990); Brian Bird, "Reclaiming the Urban War Zones," (1990); Ron Williams, ed., *Foursquare World Advance* (1990); Irving Hexham and Karla Poewe-Hexham, "Charismatics and Apartheid," (1990); Thomas Fritch, "It Started at the Dumpster," (1990) (dealing with an Assembly of God local church ministry to the homeless).

4. Kevin Springer, ed., *Power Encounters among Christians in the Western World* (1988); John White, *When the Spirit Comes in Power: Signs and Wonders Among God's People* (1988); Don Williams, *Signs, Wonders, and the Kingdom of God: A Biblical Guide for the Reluctant Skeptic* (1989); Charles H. Kraft, *Christianity with Power: Your Worldview and Your Experience of the Supernatural* (1989); John Dawson, *Taking Our Cities for God* (1989); Opal L. Reddin, ed., *Power Encounter: A Pentecostal Perspective* (1989); Steven Lawson, "Defeating Territorial Spirits," (1990); John Dawson, "Winning the Battle for Your Neighborhood," in *Charisma and Christian Life* (1990); C. Peter Wagner and F. Douglas Pennoyer, eds., *Wrestling with Dark Angels* (1990) (the spectacular title may obscure the contents of this compilation of papers and responses presented during the Academic Symposium on Power Evangelism at Fuller Seminary School of World Mission on December 13-15, 1988; forty scholars representing some twenty institutions of higher learning attended).

6

Theological Issues for Missiological Education

An Ecumenical-Protestant Perspective

Jerald D. Gort

In considering the question of this chapter, I was reminded of the extent to which human thinking is influenced and shaped by personal biographical and situational factors. It is in full awareness of these very real circumscriptions that the argumentation outlined in this chapter is offered and ought to be viewed.

In my interpretation of it, the topic calls for identifying and delineating selected theological issues which, from an ecumenical-Protestant perspective, now require, and for the foreseeable future will continue to require, priority attention in missiological reflection and education. To do this, I have had to face the necessity of making a difficult choice between a more or less simple listing of a broad range of issues or a more concentrated treatment of a few selected problem areas. I have opted for the latter, choosing to deal at some length with five constellations of challenge that seem particularly urgent; the first three of these will be dealt with at some length and the latter two more briefly.

METHODOLOGICAL APPROACH

Most, if not all, missiology takes its departure from one or another broadly termed definition of mission. Initial conceptual constructs of this kind are important because they provide us with a working understanding of the essential nature and main contours of the missionary task. Their usefulness for further reflection, however, is strictly limited. For example, one might

Jerald D. Gort is associate professor of missiology on the faculty of theology at the Free University, Amsterdam, The Netherlands, and an editor of the series *Currents of Encounter.*

define Christian mission as the mediatory participation of the community of believers in the liberating coming of God in Christ to people in need (cf. Gort 1980, 156), or as "the church's participation in the work of the Spirit to renew the face of the earth" (Bosch 1987, 14). But what do the concepts and notions employed in such definitions mean in concrete terms? What, precisely, is the message of mission? In what does human need consist? What, specifically, does the missionary task involve? In other words, what constitutes human lostness, liberation, and missionary mediation? Missiology is called to provide systematic answers to these three central questions. But how does it go about doing this? How does it gain insight into these matters?

These latter questions point to the vital perennial need for a suitable epistemological model, a responsible hermeneutics for mission. Formulation of theory always requires a methodological medium. Articulation of appropriate and effective principles of mission interpretation is both fundamental *to* and an indispensable part *of* the task of missiological reflection and education. Arguing from the fundamental nature of mission, I should like to contend that the most obvious and trustworthy methodological approach to the specific understanding of mission is neither that of rationalistic deduction (which takes no genuine account of empirical reality) nor that of positivistic induction (which recognizes no reality beyond the world of time and space) but rather that of contextualization, which, in my view, must involve the *correlation of text and context—of theory and practice.*

From the biblical witness and the history of the Christian church we learn that mission is incarnational in its basic structure. There is only one salvation, wrought by God in Christ: "I believe in one God . . . and in one Lord Jesus Christ . . . who, for us . . . and our salvation, came down from heaven" (Nicene Creed). This great and profoundly moving affirmation, *Jesus Christus pro nobis*, stands at the very heart of the biblical witness and of the faith, doctrinal teaching, and proclamation of the Christian church. However, it is only within actual human social and cultural settings, which often differ significantly from one another, that this one salvation provided by the one God assumes specific content. Indeed, this is true of Holy Scripture itself: in it documents of human life and experience, a whole "series of social worlds" (Schreiter 1982, 430), are interwoven with revelations *of* and witnesses *to* God. What implications does this bear for reflection on mission?

Adequate missiological reflection will be reflection on the normative biblical witness *to* and the historical continuation *of* the dynamic mediated relation between heaven and earth, whereby the multiplicity of human need is met by the plenitude of divine mercy. Legitimate reflection on mission, thus, will consist of "a reading of the Bible that goes hand in hand with a reading of human history," as was said at the Commission on World Mission and Evangelism meeting at Melbourne in 1980. That is, it will take full account of the correlativity of text and context as that came to expression in the missionary praxis of the past and does so now in that of the present.

It is not possible to learn everything there is to know about mission from biblical texts or the teaching of the church alone. The textual witness cannot be satisfactorily comprehended apart from contextual circumstances. The text, in other words, cannot be read properly without the aid of the context used as "interpretive dictionary." The context helps us to understand the nuances and richness of God's liberating Word. In correlation with the text, the context discloses the myriad shapes of human want, the manifold dimensions of God's salvation, and the precise forms of missionary mediation required in a given situation. In sum, careful exegetical reading of the context contributes significantly to the hermeneutical understanding of the text.

On the other hand, no socio-cultural context can be sufficiently fathomed without the help of the text. In the Christian view, earthly reality and the true meaning and purpose of human existence can be brought into clear focus only if viewed through the "reading glasses" of the biblical message and its historic interpretation. When "we study the Bible from within a missionary context . . . the Bible . . . opens our horizons and unlocks 'envisioning possibilities' to us" (Bosch 1987, 10). Scripture reveals the depth-dimensions of human need, the deepest intentions of the gospel of God's Kingdom, and the foundational dynamics of the mediation and realization of salvation in this present life on earth and the life to come in the hereafter. In short, careful exegetical reading of the text contributes significantly to the hermeneutical understanding of the context.

Contextual missiology also involves a correlation between mission theory and practice, which is first of all creative. Contemporary hermeneutical discussion "has taught us that . . . the application (*Anwendung*) of a text is integral to the whole experience of understanding it" (Bosch 1987, 9). It is only in or on the basis of the actual missionary practice of bringing the gospel into rapport with culture that it will be possible to formulate suitable missionary theory. Conversely, proper mission praxis requires solid theoretical grounding. But this interplay between missionary reflection and action also has a critical dimension. In this connection one might well refer to Walter Freytag's dictum: *Mission ist mehr als Mission* ("Mission is more than mission") (Freytag 1961, 109), which means, among other things, that the theological concept of mission and empirical missionary practice transcend one another (cf. Spindler 1992, 103). Each acts as a corrective to the other; theory is tested on the touchstone of praxis and praxis on that of theory.

Application of this model of contextual correlation will, as an ongoing dynamic process, confront missiology with new challenges on a regular basis and lead it to renewed reflection on unresolved older issues, including the following areas of concern.

COMPREHENSIVE MISSION

We are living in a world in which, despite the spread of Christianity and the presence of the Christian church nearly everywhere, there are still many millions of people who have never heard of the salvation and liberation offered by God in Jesus Christ. In this "the Church cannot acquiesce" (Bosch 1987, 12). These so-called "unreached" people—huge numbers of whom today are found in North America and certainly in Western Europe—must remain a central concern of Christian mission of whatever stripe: not only evangelical but also ecumenical, Catholic, and Orthodox. Those who have not yet come into contact with Christ need to be invited to put their faith in him and to join his church, a local manifestation of the koinonia of believers, the sign and agent of human reconciliation with God, of restored partnership with the God of the Kingdom (cf. Vandervelde 1993, 136). The call to accept the gospel always has been and will remain an absolutely essential aim and focus of the Christian missionary task. And on that account the challenge of the oral communication of the message of God's salvation must always occupy a central place in missiological reflection and education.

But there is more to be said in this connection. We also live in a world that is increasingly falling under the influence of modern Western culture, a culture in which people's lives are divided into two separate spheres: a public world of "facts," science, and politics, and a private world of "values," beliefs, and religion (cf. Newbigin 1986, 21ff.). As a result of this profound cultural fragmentation, people both in the West and more and more in other parts of the world find themselves in a universe characterized by a lack of a sense of the holy, a sense of the sanctity of nature and even of human life (cf. Griffiths 1985, 15).

There can be little doubt that, certainly since the collapse of Communism, we live in a world shot through, at the level of the "haves," with the idolatry, the destructive acids of consumerism, acquisitiveness, and selfishness (cf. Amaladoss 1990, 274); a world, in other words, in which the "laws" of the market economy—ever greater profits, ever higher levels of production—ultimately count for more than the lives of human beings. As Ana Langerak has rightly pointed out, the world in which we must carry out our mission crucifies untold millions "of its population by calling them irrelevant and removing them from its political, social and economic map"; it crucifies the hope of these helpless victims "by irresponsibly dismissing options and alternatives for change" (Langerak 1992, 448). Everywhere in the world today hunger, homelessness, structural unemployment, racism, human and environmental exploitation are *on the increase*. America today contains within itself an entire underdeveloped country, and the same is true of Western Europe taken as a whole.

Of course, it is part of the missionary calling of the Christian church to engage to as great a degree as possible in the diaconal alleviation of human need. But it is also the duty of Christians in mission, as I see it, actively to oppose all forms of abuse of power and to work for the transformation of unjust social and economic relationships. As William Nottingham rightly argues: "The good news of God's eternal love in Jesus Christ cannot fail to challenge the conditions in which the poor are forced to live" (Nottingham 1992, 436). And this emphasis becomes even more urgent if he is right in asserting that "the temptation [in the nineties] will be to turn 'mission' into denominational expansion and individualistic personal piety" (ibid.). In a world "of economic dependency and exploitation," Christian churches and mission agencies "are called to be advocates for the poor" (Report 1992, 470), lobbyists at the centers of power on behalf of the oppressed and marginalized. And it is the particular responsibility of the North Atlantic churches and missionary organizations that are "beneficiaries of the present economic system to fight for a new political and economic world order" (ibid.). This does not represent advocacy of triumphalistic activism or arrogant Christian attitudes. As Mouw and Griffioen have rightly argued, Christians must at all times assume a stance of public civility and eschew all ostentation. Their attitude must be one of patient tolerance based in expectation of the Kingdom, founded in the eschatological trust that *God in Christ* will overcome and triumph. Since this interim ethic of public civility is thus not rooted in indifference, it leaves full room for and even requires Christians to make full use of all available opportunities for political cooperation and action with a view to the realization of Kingdom goals in human society, the erection of signs of God's Kingdom in the public arena (see Mouw and Griffioen 1993, 173-77).

What would be involved in a genuinely missionary encounter between the gospel and the present world disorder? It is incumbent upon missiology and missiological education to take up the challenge of this question with a view to helping churches and mission agencies to embrace or overcome any remaining hesitations regarding the necessity for a holistic, Kingdom-oriented understanding of human need, divine salvation, and missionary mediation. To this end missiology will have to give much more serious attention than it has in the past to the absolutely vital task of biblically informed social analysis. In cooperation with Christian economists, political scientists, and historians, missiologists must seek to discover and spell out the causes and structural dynamics of, and the possible solutions to, hunger, poverty, racial injustice, etc. I would like to call attention in this connection to the impressive WCC brochure *Economy as a Matter of Faith: An Ecumenical Statement on Economic Life*.

RELIGIOUS PLURALISM

Some Christian observers contend that church and mission stand at the frontiers of a new phase in their history: namely, that of encounter and interaction with the other religions. I strongly agree with this assessment.

Of course, the church has always lived in a religiously plural world. After the first period of its existence, however, from the time of Emperor Constantine, this issue ceased for many centuries to figure significantly in Christian theological reflection. Later, in reaction to the Enlightenment, the church was forced to expend nearly all of its theological energy on the encounter—or more often, confrontation—with modern philosophy, natural science, and critical historiography.

In recent decades Christians have become more conscious of the other religions. There are many causal factors involved in this new awareness, three of the most important of which are the following: first, the availability of vastly improved knowledge and information about other religious traditions; second, the continued existence and unmistakable vitality of the other religions, despite two thousand years of missionary activity; and third, the fact that nearly every human society and even community in today's world is multireligious to a greater or lesser degree. Furthermore, recent years have witnessed increasing "ecclesiastical sanction for disparate theological views" and religious beliefs, a "new latitude for pluralism" (Coalter 1995, xix). There is "an increasing awareness that [all of] this brings with it serious theological issues for the Christian Church" (Race 1983, 1).

Many Christians throughout the world in East and West, North and South, experience these religions, according to Karl Rahner, as "a question posed," "an offered possibility," "something that calls the Christian claim to absoluteness into question." Many are asking what the proper Christian stance is with respect to other faith systems. Should the Christian attitude toward other religions be one of disapproval, rejection, and confrontation or respect, recognition, and reconciliation? Should Christianity isolate itself from these religions or enter into certain forms of cooperation with them?

Experiences and questions such as these have given rise to an important new discipline within missiology called *theologia religionum* or theology of religions (TR), which explores and seeks to provide answers to three main questions. First, do people beyond Christianity and the Christian gospel have a share in salvation, and if so, in what does that salvation consist? Second, if people of other faiths share in salvation, can their religions be viewed as "ways to salvation"? Third, if other religions represent salvific ways, in what sense may the Christian gospel be said to be of a definitive character and to have decisive meaning and universal validity?

These are questions with potentially far-reaching implications. The possibilities for interpretation of the relation between Christianity and other religions are not unlimited, however. In my considered opinion TR must meet at least three conditions of validity.

First, any legitimate TR must recognize that God, the Father of Jesus Christ, has never left himself without witness anywhere and that his salvific intentions and actions embrace the whole of history, the whole world, and all people.

No longer can we state categorically . . . that there is light only in the church and darkness outside. No longer dare we say that God is at work only in the church. We have to recognize light and God's presence also in other faiths (Bosch 1987, 11).

Second, if TR is to retain validity, it needs to affirm the decisive significance of the *acta et dicta et passa tota Jesu Christi in carne* ("the totality of the deeds, words, and suffering of Jesus Christ in the flesh") within God's plan of salvation for the world. This does not mean that we should refrain from all further reflection on the person and work of Christ. What it does mean is that no model of the doctrine of Christ is acceptable if it undermines the clear biblical claim of ultimacy for Christ, as does, for example, Paul Knitter's concept of "theocentric Christology" (see Knitter 1985, 171ff.).

Third, adequate TR is required to acknowledge fully the missionary nature of the Christian congregation. It is by no stretch of the imagination sufficient to maintain, as does Knitter, that the

central purpose of mission is being realized as long as, through mutual witnessing, all are converted to a deeper grasp and following of God's truth . . . [and] that the goal of missionary work is being achieved when announcing the gospel to all peoples makes the Christian a better Christian and the Buddhist a better Buddhist (Knitter 1985, 222).

I agree fully with David Bosch that the Christian faith "would turn against itself, its origin, nature and history, if it ceases to challenge people of all persuasions to put their trust in Christ and join a community of his disciples" (Bosch 1987, 12).

The questions raised by TR are by no means easy ones. This discipline was not designed for the fainthearted. As early as 1958 the well-known English missiologist, the late Max Warren, warned that the confrontation between the Christian faith and agnostic modern science would turn out to be child's play in comparison with the coming challenge of encounter between Christianity and the other religions of the world (cf. Race 1983, 3). But it is precisely on these grounds that this challenge will have to be given a place very high on the list of priorities for present and future missiological research and education. There is no doubt in my mind that this issue will come to occupy our attention in increasing measure for decades to come.

MUTUALITY AND SPIRITUALITY: A BRIEF SKETCH

I am very conscious of the fact that there are other important issues that could have been advanced at length in this chapter. It is tempting to expound on them, but that, as indicated above, is not possible. I will have to limit myself to a brief treatment of two additional matters that appear to me to be of fundamental significance for mission and hence also for missiology.

The first of these concerns the theological insight that the church's mission and the church's unity are essentially and reciprocally related to each other. This points to, among other things, the vital importance of international ecumenical cooperation for mission. There is a pressing need to find ways through reflection and education to promote convergence and cooperation especially between evangelicals and ecumenicals, for "from the perspective of wholistic mission, there is no place for the polarization between an ecumenical outlook and an evangelical one" (Padilla 1992, 381). We must also continue the search for genuine mutuality between the churches and mission agencies of the North and the South. Present relationships of dependency and inequality need to be transformed, not because partnership and mutuality are ends in themselves, but rather because they are means to a vital goal: "Striving for the unity of the church has a missionary intention" (Report 1992, 469). No Christian church anywhere in the world can properly read the Bible and adequately carry out the task of mission in isolation. Every church and mission agency everywhere must be enriched by all the others. On that account, it is imperative to find ways to operationalize the concept of "mission in six continents."

Some gains have been made in this regard (see Van Beek 1992), but there are also many obstacles standing in the way of ecumenical cooperation today. In his magisterial book *Transforming Mission: Paradigm Shifts in Theology of Mission* David Bosch speaks of the dawning of a new ecumenical paradigm. On the evidence of present circumstances, however, one might be somewhat doubtful as to whether a paradigmatic change of this nature is really in the offing. Many churches, mission agencies, and Christians seem to be withdrawing into their own private "corners." Moreover, contextualization and mutuality are being threatened, in my opinion, by the post-modernist project with its rejection of meta-narrative and its celebration of "local experience and pluralism" (Meyers 1992, 397) as opposed to global experiences and ecumenical theologies.

Finally, another concern of great importance, in my view, is that of the relation between mission and spiritual vitality. This can be examined in terms of the present serious crisis of faith in the churches of Western Europe. "It is a remarkable fact that at a time when the Christian Church as a whole is growing . . . in Europe [it] is in decline—timid, defensive, apologetic" (Newbigin 1992b, 1). It is often said that it is due to this faith-crisis that the Western European churches have lost interest in ecumenical cooperation and have almost ceased their involvement in evangelism and cross-cultural mission. On this construction of things, renewal of mission and ecumenical fervor depends on spiritual renewal of the churches. The question is whether this is a valid assessment of the matter. My judgment is that it is the privatization of faith and the abandonment of commitment to mission, evangelism, and ecumenism that are the causes of this crisis of faith, which in reality is a crisis of *life*. For privatization of religion leads to religious etiolation. In failing to "exhale" properly these churches are unable to "inhale" fully. The antidote to this spiritual torpidity, therefore, is renewal *through* mission. In the words of Walter Arnold, a German missionary leader, "God will give us new joy and will fill us with his Spirit where we meet in love for the common task of evangelism" (cited in Hauser 1989, 24). This thinking is also echoed in the recent papal document *Redemptoris Missio*, which "has as its goal an interior renewal of faith and Christian life. For missionary activity renews the church, revitalizes faith and Christian identity, and offers new enthusiasm and new incentive" (John Paul II 1990, no. 50).

It is only to a living, breathing, working church that the salvific words *sursum corda* ("lift up your hearts") are addressed; they are meant to comfort the struggling church in the midst of the adversity it meets in its pursuit of mission and unity. For this reason it will always be necessary through missiological reflection and education "to demonstrate, to the church and to the world . . . that the Christian faith is a missionary faith or it is no faith at all" (Bosch 1987, 9).

In conclusion, I should like to emphasize the supreme importance of having a firm foundation for our missiological reflection and education. In Darrell Guder's words, the well-known German New Testament scholar Martin Hengel recently

> pointed out that the dominant approach of New Testament scholarship in this century has replaced [the] view [that Jesus was consciously and intentionally messianic in his ministry] with the idea that a very creative and constructive early church created a messianic Jesus out of a remarkable human being who was a great prophet or wisdom teacher or moral example or a combination of these, but no more (Guder 1995, 171).

In order adequately to meet the very real and very acute challenges with which we are confronted, we will need to take our stance on the solid ground of biblical Kingdom and trinitarian theology. If we are not to be found floundering about, searching in vain for answers to issues and challenges that prove incapable of resolution, we will have to affirm, with Lesslie Newbigin, that "the Christian hermeneutic key is Jesus Christ and His death and resurrection" (Newbigin 1992a, 3). In other words, we must always take great care to remember that, no matter how difficult, complicated, confusing, and even imponderable the task may seem at times, in the final analysis the object of our reflection is the "balm in Gilead to heal the sin-sick soul, to make the wounded whole."

7

A Roman Catholic Perspective on Missiological Education

Mary Motte

A concerted ecumenical effort to understand mission in a changing world is the result of several years of endeavor. David Bosch describes this emerging ecumenical mission paradigm in *Transforming Mission*, and illustrates the broad expanse of common ground attained (Bosch 1991, 368-510). Roman Catholics began to participate in this process as a result of the Second Vatican Council. A whole new series of questions arose as Catholics shifted the position from which they looked at the world. This required a different understanding of mission.

As I attempt to delineate the principal elements of Roman Catholic mission perspectives, I am aware that, contrary to a commonly perceived image of Catholics, there is a diversity of views among us. Hence, there is room for further discussion from within the Catholic community about the issues I will address in this chapter. With that caveat, I will focus on three aspects in relation to missiological education: tradition, new developments, and emerging questions.

At the beginning I wish to note that missiological education among Roman Catholics takes place generally within the formation programs of missionary orders rather than in a school or university. Due to this, formation largely influences the kind of missiological education given. In the first place, missionary spirituality has a significant role. Being a missionary within

Mary Motte, FMM, is a Sister of the Franciscan Missionaries of Mary and Director of the Mission Resource Center, North Providence, Rhode Island, engaged in ecumenical missiological research, consultation, and education. She is a member of the board of the Overseas Ministries Study Center and formerly Roman Catholic consultant to the Commission on World Mission and Evangelism of the World Council of Churches.

these orders or communities requires a lifestyle undergirded by a way of relating to God through Jesus Christ, and of relating to all human beings and creation within that relationship by the grace of the Holy Spirit. Profound transformations in theological insight about how one relates to God produce changes in missiological understanding. A changing spirituality leads to a changing missiology. Such an integrated approach is positive, but there is likewise a negative aspect requiring a corrective, which I will address later. I should add a note here that the lay mission movement is beginning to introduce some changes into missionary formation, but there is still much that is similar.

TRADITION

The Catholic community weaves a sacramental view of nature and ecclesial awareness throughout the long fiber of its history. This strongly influenced the foundation and development of missionary orders and consequently the formation of missionaries and their understandings of mission.

Sacramental View of Nature

Francis of Assisi perhaps best exemplifies this view within Catholic tradition. For him, all creation—human persons, animals, sun, moon, stars, day and night—conveyed something about the mystery and magnificent goodness of God. In his "Canticle of Brother Sun" Francis praises God through the gift of creatures; for example, "Praised be You, my Lord, with all your creatures, especially Sir Brother Sun, who is the day and through whom you give us great light." This view recognizes that God is beyond our finite understanding and can break through all creation. As Gerard M. Hopkins, a Jesuit poet, says so well, "the world is charged with the grandeur of God." And the dying priest in Bernanos's *The Diary of a Country Priest* exclaims, "Grace is everywhere."

Awareness of God's sustaining love and creative power leads to a missionary spirituality that is basically contemplative. By this I mean a spirituality that regards everything from the view that God's love is a creating love, embracing all persons and all creation. This is God's plan for creation; namely, that all be saved (cf. Ti 2:11). A contemplative stance before the world and creation requires commitment to seek out those signs of God's presence, especially among peoples where the Good News is not known, as well as among those who no longer hear or understand its message.[1]

Ecclesial Awareness

The church is central to the self-understanding of missionary orders. While there are canonical procedures that foster this relationship, one cannot fail to recognize examples of outstanding figures who exemplify a genuine love for the church. This love is grounded in a vision of the church as mystery, holding the Holy Trinity and the community of believers in a mutual, dynamic relation. Conditions of time and place do not place limits on this community. The concept of church extends beyond but includes all particular expressions of life and authority in the church. It is a community living a relation to God, who, though hidden at times by sin, always calls the community to repentance and renewal. It is the pilgrim community on the way, in communion with all those from all times and places who constitute the People of God (*Lumen Gentium*, ch. 2). The church is a sacred mystery encircling the missionary. As *Evangelii Nuntiandi* notes:

> The Church is the depository of the Good News to be proclaimed. . . .
> Having been sent and evangelized, the Church herself sends out evangelizers. . . . She gives them the mandate which she herself has received and she sends them out to preach. To preach not their own selves or their personal ideas, but a Gospel of which neither she nor they are the absolute masters and owners, to dispose of it as they wish, but a Gospel of which they are the ministers, in order to pass it on with complete fidelity (Paul VI 1975, no. 15).

There are not many examples of isolated missionaries, unattached from a community. Rather, the opposite is true. Missionary orders have grown up around outstanding persons who wanted to communicate the gospel message in a particular way or time, but always in relation to the church. This has been true even when the central administration of the church has made cooperation difficult. Consequently, fidelity to the church is a concept cherished in missionary orders and shapes the formation and education. However, this is not a blind affection or loyalty. It is a vocation lived in a tension between truth and charity.

NEW DEVELOPMENTS

Assessing the impact of Vatican II is a continuing process. In relation to mission and missiological education, a number of key factors are useful in deciphering the impact to date. Since the Council, it is important to include present experience in theological reflection in order to discern the signs of the times, or how God is speaking to us in this age. There is a deeper appreciation for human activity in relation to salvation and communicating the gospel.[2] Social analysis owes its development largely to these new orientations and is now generally part of missionary education. Most important, social analysis is an essential missiological tool, helping to reshape missionary understanding. It uncovers injustice and societal structures of sin. It is largely responsible for the way missionaries moved from a condescending way of relating to the poor and marginalized to a position of solidarity.

Today the option for the poor significantly affects choices for missionary insertion of most missionary communities (cf. Motte 1991). This option is also an important missiological concept for formation and education of missionaries.

Discerning the signs of the times, social analysis, a preferential option for the poor, and solidarity with the poor are elements of an overall missiological process at work over the past several years. Within the larger process, inculturation, liberation, dialogue, and the role of the local church emerged as new dimensions defining mission. Eventually, the missiological process refining its analysis identifies its parameters more accurately (see Jenkinson and O'Sullivan 1991; Lang and Motte 1982, Sedos papers).

The post-conciliar process is correcting what I cited earlier as two aspects of tradition, a sacramental view of nature and ecclesial awareness. *Dei Verbum*, the Council's *Dogmatic Constitution on Divine Revelation*, insisted upon the need for solid scriptural foundation for all those engaged in the proclamation of the gospel (nos. 21-25). Serious study of Scripture is part of formation and continuing education programs; this was not customary for Catholics prior to the Council. Basic Christian communities owe their development and impetus to their intentional study of the Word of God. Scripture study leads to keener insight into the reign of God and the church's relation to it as sign and sacrament of that reality larger than itself. *Evangelii Nuntiandi* further describes how this emphasis on Scripture, interacting with ecclesial awareness, results in a constantly renewed missionary dynamism—an important corrective in Catholic tradition:

> For the Christian community is never closed in upon itself. The intimate life of this community—the life of listening to the Word and the Apostle's teaching, charity lived in a fraternal way, the sharing of bread—this intimate life only acquires its full meaning when it becomes a witness, when it evokes admiration and conversion, and when it becomes the preaching and the proclamation of the Good News (Paul VI 1975, no. 15).

Scripture provides a corrective also to a sacramental view of nature, enlarging its missiological perspective. God's presence in all creation poses new questions today about salvation in a world and universe where human greed appropriates resources for a few. The gospel emphasis on the reign of God suggests an even deeper sacramental awareness of how all matter is important in some way to the plan of God.

The internal change process affecting these various movements includes a number of features. Understanding justice as constitutive to evangelization or proclaiming the gospel, recognizing that Catholics share one faith with all Christians, admitting that the laity have an important role to play in the life of the church, human dignity, freedom of conscience, and grasping new insights into the relation between local and universal church are constant references in any effort to discern what missiological questions are the questions for our time. Missionary formation reflects these elements. Dialogue and respect for the other are paths toward new ways of relating; lay people increasingly share in missionary work as missionaries in their own right. Justice and peace are key to interpreting reality. Most missionary orders accept the theory of working together with other Christians, and a number are committed to evolving praxis.[3] Human freedom and dignity require listening, respect and a search to understand the other as God's creature. This approach is critical to formation for mission. It is not a question of providing a clear recipe for action, but rather of enabling a missionary to enter into a dialogical process with adequate missiological resources that will permit further discernment about how to proclaim the reign of God in a given place and time. It continues to explore the relation between human freedom and the mystery of Christ.

The impact of Vatican II is taking some time to unfold. The reasons are multiple. Many Catholics do not understand the Council's implications. Missionary orders, having dealt rather intently with the Council documents, incorporated many changes. However, now they often speak a language the average Catholic does not understand. There is also a serious problem of retrenchment from directions taken by the Council. Some exhibit an unwillingness to stay with the process of change and transformation, preferring to seek what is "tried and true." Some are concerned about how freedom of conscience relates to belief in Christ, and ultimately to salvation. This in turn raises questions about the validity of dialogue as a way of communicating faith (see *Dialogue and Proclamation*, intro b, c). Some efforts at direct evangelization seem to ignore the premise of freedom of conscience. Laity is rapidly assuming a new role in the church's mission. But this is happening in a church where there is strong resistance to reconceptualizing the ministry of the church.

NEW QUESTIONS

At the beginning of this chapter I remarked that spirituality has been the overarching framework for missionary formation and missiological education within the Catholic missionary orders. While this approach fosters personal integration and is holistic, in practice it leads to a certain downplaying of more formal missiological education. This results in an incapacity on the part of many missionaries to grasp the more subtle interplay between gospel and culture. Consequently, they fail to understand adequately their role in the world today (cf. Knight 1992, 201). Some missionaries have a confused sense of vocation due to the Council's retrieval of the essential missionary nature of the church. The further failure to emphasize missiological education along with spiritual formation for mission now results in a lack of identity. More important, there appears to be a certain incapacity to identify the missiological questions in today's context. One needs to be able to articulate the missiological question within the complexity of questions posed globally. That question asks, What furthers or prevents God's reign? For example, within larger questions about the role of women in church and society today we need to ask missiologically, What is feminine in the gospel images of God's reign? Then we must go on, asking ourselves what we do to foster or prevent those images from enlivening our understanding of community gathered in God's name.

Michael Amaladoss suggests that recovering the meaning of prophecy as the task for mission will lead to clearer missiological focus (Amaladoss 1992). I believe this stress on prophecy as proper to mission is something new emerging from the missiological experience accumulated since the Vatican Council. As Amaladoss notes, mission has focused on different orientations such as inculturation, liberation, development, and interreligious dialogue at different moments. Yet the central meaning of mission is *a call to conversion*; it is a challenge to *transform culture* (ibid, 270-72). A true renewal in the understanding of mission, something sought avidly since the time of the Council, needs a sharpened missiological focus. Such a scientific focus would enable a sharper perception of the relation between God's reign and present experience. Those responsible for missionary formation, both the formation of new missionaries and the continuing formation of those who have already become missionaries, must find ways of promoting more solid, formal missiological education.

Roman Catholic perspectives on missiological education will of necessity incorporate a sacramental view of nature and ecclesial awareness. They will also include a transformed way of looking at the world/church relationship brought about by Vatican II. Traditionally, missionary thinking developed within the missionary orders, and spirituality provides the basis for this reflection. While this is an integrating approach, and is commendable, Roman Catholics need to provide a more formal and solid missiological education for their missionaries. Except for some notable examples, such as the Society of the Divine Word (SVD), missiological focus in the formation process is gravely lacking or greatly diminished.[4] If we do not make this effort collectively, then the missionary vocation could be lost. Stephen Bevans points out that "mission is not really about transplanting the church from one culture to another, but about searching for the seeds of that church that are already hidden in another culture's soil" (Bevans 1991, 56).

The missiological task of prophecy perceives what is hidden, and issues a call, directing people's attention to the reign of God. Bevans goes on to say, "Mission is the prophetic preaching by word and deed alike that God, who is present in every culture, is also the God who calls every culture to perfection in the light of the incarnate Divine Word; often that prophetic task is carried out by being a grateful guest and a respectful stranger" (ibid.).

The concept of mission expanded with the new insights of Vatican II, and consequent efforts of missionaries to find their place in that broader field of endeavor have been difficult. Amaladoss suggests that prophecy conveys the essential meaning of mission, "Mission is a call to conversion, a challenge to change, an invitation to realize the Reign of God, an exhortation to enter into the creative dynamism of divine action in the world, making all things new" (Amaladoss 1992, 270, my translation).

In a recent study published by the U.S. Catholic Mission Association, missionaries placed a high priority on their personal experience of God as basis for proclamation (Motte 1991). While this offers evidence of integration in formation and certainly provides a solid basis on which to build, this deepening awareness needs further strengthening through formal missiological education. The insight into reality in relation to God's plan and compassion has made missionaries see into the sufferings of peoples. New processes in mission have helped missionaries to grow in their experience of the healing power of the gospel, to the extent that at least some are recognizing their lack of knowledge of what is beneath the surface (see Knight 1992, 260-61).

The capacity to recognize the signs of God's reign requires a profound relationship to God and a keen insight into the realities of the present context. This can never be a static attainment. It requires a continual penetration into the mystery of God and a constant inquiry into the scientific meaning of historical events. Roman Catholic formation stresses the former; it needs to incorporate more of the latter to realize the prophetic role of mission in the world today.

Notes

1. Cf. John Paul II (1990), *Redemptoris Missio*, art. 37, where he speaks of the parameters of the church's mission *ad gentes*, including "new worlds and social phenomena" and "cultural sectors: the modern equivalents of Areopagus."

2. See *Gaudium et Spes*, no. 34, where it says, "Christians ought to be convinced that the achievements of the human race are a sign of God's greatness and the fulfilment of his mysterious design."

3. In 1987 the Division of Overseas Ministries of the National Council of Churches and the U.S. Catholic Mission Association held a joint mission consultation to consider the question of divided churches and common witness in mission. The resultant commitment to pursue further collaboration led to plans for another consultation held in 1994.

4. The SVD set up a center for missiological education and research in its Asia-Pacific Zone almost ten years ago. It is concerned precisely with the relation between formation and missiological education.

8

Orthodox Missiological Education for the Twenty-First Century

Michael James Oleksa

The task of training Orthodox Christian missionaries for the next century worldwide is a topic too great and too grand to discuss adequately in a chapter, for the Orthodox Church embraces tens of millions of believers, dozens of languages and cultures on every continent. This chapter will therefore initially present some historic and theological principles of Orthodox missiology globally, and in the second part focus on Orthodox Christian mission in America, specifically in Alaska.

HISTORY OF ORTHODOX CHRISTIAN MISSION

The Eastern Orthodox Church traces its origins historically and geographically to Pentecost, when with the coming of the Holy Spirit the ancient Christian community began the evangelization of the world. Already on the first day of missionary outreach two basic principles were eternally established: (1) each nation must hear the wondrous works of God, that is, the gospel—and not some other message—(2) in its own language.

The message the missionary is to deliver is the salvific story of Jesus Christ, Emmanuel, crucified, dead, risen and ascended in glory. Each person and each culture and nation will receive this message differently, uniquely, and respond accordingly. This difference or uniqueness in hearing and receiving is inevitable. The gospel becomes incarnate in each hu-

Michael Oleksa, rector of St. Nicholas Church, Juneau, Alaska, teaches cross-cultural communication at the University of Alaska, South East, and is Outreach director of Seaalaska Heritage Foundation. He is author of several publications, including *Alaska Missionary Spirituality* (Paulist Press) and *Orthodox Alaska: A Theology of Mission* (St. Vladimir's Seminary Press).

man personality and in each cultural setting in a unique and irreplaceable way, and this variety is not only to be anticipated and respected but treasured. The same gospel, the same Christ, manifests itself in multiplicity. The story must be "translated" into the language and the cultural categories, the world view, of the hearers with meticulous attention to the accuracy and adequacy of their language. Finding "words adequate to God" in Greek required eight centuries of debates, discussions, and decisions, the history of the ancient councils of the undivided Christian church of the first millennium A.D. The first missionaries must approach any new situation with humility, learn its language, study its customs, ideas, and ideals, and present the Christian message within this framework.

The Greeks had a particular advantage in that the Christian Scriptures were already available in their language. Other nations have had to rely on translations of the Greek texts into theirs, and this has been the special initial task of Orthodox missionaries, who have often had to create an alphabet for peoples who lacked any literary tradition. St. Cyril invented a writing system for Slavonic before traveling to Moravia, in Central Europe, at the invitation of Prince Rastislav in the ninth century. St. Stephen of Perm had to create a Zyrian alphabet at Perm in Siberia. The Tatars received the written gospel from St. Hourg and St. Barsanuphius at Kazan. St. Innocent of Irkutsk continued this tradition near Lake Baikal in the seventeenth century, as St. Innocent Veniaminov and St. Nicholas Kasatkin did in Alaska and Japan respectively in the nineteenth century. The initial goal of every successful Orthodox mission is to incarnate the gospel in local language and culture, realizing that this task will require centuries to complete. The model for this enculturation of the Christian message historically has been the experience of the eastern Mediterranean, essentially that of Byzantium.

This does not mean, however, that in order to become authentically Christian each person or nation must be culturally or linguistically Hellenized, for the very struggle between the gospel and its original cultural context was precisely between Greek culture and philosophy and the Hebraic God of Abraham, Isaac, and Jacob. Ultimately, it was Hellenic culture that was Christianized, not the gospel which was Hellenized, at least in the East. The missionaries, therefore, must be thoroughly familiar with the process by which the living God triumphed over or rather transformed this first culture as a paradigm for the process they are initiating. The experience of the first thousand years and the correct decisions, the consensus, of the undivided ancient church—what the Orthodox call Tradition (upper case T)—is not only informative but normative for Orthodox theology, worship, spirituality, and mission. It is faithfulness to this heritage rather than any cultural or administrative unity that constitutes the unity of the Orthodox communion.

Preparation for missionary outreach must necessarily focus on the Holy Scriptures, church history, and patristics, and the indigenous language and culture of the particular tribe or nation, so that the people too may hear the wondrous works of God in their own language, conducting the worship and celebrating the sacraments of the ancient undivided church in their own musical tradition, architectural heritage, and artistic expression. The ultimate goal would be the eventual creation of an autonomous or autocephalous (self-governing) church within the worldwide community of Orthodox churches.

THEOLOGICAL CONSIDERATIONS

The theology of the Eastern church tends to emphasize certain aspects of the Christian faith that Western theology has tended to neglect, and this also has an important bearing on missiology. The Greek fathers understood the creation of human beings in God's "image and likeness" in a variety of ways, never arriving at a precise definition of what constituted these. The consensus, however, distinguished between the two terms, *image* being the unique status of human persons as existing and eternally existing, as free, creative, autonomous creatures—characteristics humanity still possesses— and *likeness* being those divine attributes humans have distorted or lost through sin—kindness, gentleness, generosity, patience, joy, peace, love. This likeness-to-God was not Adam's static condition, but a goal he was to attain. Sin has redirected humanity in a harmful and self-destructive direction, but it has only distorted, not destroyed, the image of God in humanity. This distinction between image and likeness allows Eastern Christianity to be more open, more tolerant and accepting of creative expressions and spiritual impulses that may be culturally different but not necessarily alien or antithetical to the gospel. Orthodoxy rejects cultural or linguistic uniformity as incompatible with respect for human beings created in God's image, as free, unique, autonomous creatures.

Likeness to God, however, is not only a goal Adam did not attain but no people can now reach by their own efforts. God has revealed himself in these latter days as Father, Son, and Holy Spirit, three divine (uncreated, eternal, omniscient, almighty, transcendent) persons so united in love that they are also undivided. No individual person can be "like God," for God is a community of persons. Orthodox doctrine affirms personal but not individual salvation, for to be saved is to attain to the condition of God-likeness, to become, by grace, by God's energy and power as well as by human consent and determination and effort, like God in "goodness and wisdom," as the holy fathers say.

This process of divinization (*theosis*), which the catechumens are invited to begin at baptism, constitutes an eternal quest for and growth toward restoring the likeness of God in each Christian. Salvation, defined as becoming God-like, is a never-ending transformation "from glory to glory" undertaken as a member of the body of Christ, in communion with God and in unity with one's neighbor. It is a communal process which no one can undertake or accomplish alone. To be saved is to be in the right relationship with God, neighbor, and the entire created universe. No one is ever, from this perspective, permanently or irreversibly "saved," not even the missionary.

All humankind is either actively pursuing this goal, fulfilling this task, or not. The non-Christian or pre-Christian or even anti-Christian person may be already on this quest or completely unreceptive, unresponsive, or hostile to it, consciously or not. The missionary's task is to clarify and articulate this message, knowing, as Alexei Khromiakov wrote, where the church is, but never knowing where it is not. One might say the Christian is one who knows where Christ is, but can never be certain where he is not. It is his identity which will constitute the essence of the good news the missionary will bring to another person, place, culture, or nation. Jesus is the good news. Jesus is salvation. It is he who restores the proper balance, the harmonious relationship between God and humanity, between Creator and creation, and between humankind and the entire cosmos. This vision of God, the world, and the human place in it is celebrated and affirmed in public worship, the liturgical life of the Christian community. It is in the context of the liturgy that the individual believer becomes embued with these biblical, doctrinal, theological, and spiritual principles, and is restored to communion with God, neighbor, and the created universe in Christ. He is the origin, the means, and goal of Christian life.

ORTHODOX MISSION IN ALASKA

In September 1794 the first Orthodox Christian missionaries arrived in the New World to announce the good news of salvation as described above. They discovered at Kodiak, Alaska, that before they could begin to challenge their target population to orient their lives toward the living God, they had to defend and protect them from the abuses and exploitation to which they were subjected by officials of the Russian-American Company, the trading monopoly which dominated colonial life from 1784 to 1867. It is impossible to initiate the process of growth toward God-likeness in a community oppressed by violence, injustice, and immorality. If Alexander Baranov, the governor, and his regime were representative of Christian behavior, mass conversions would be extremely unlikely, so the mission had to denounce his inhumane treatment of indigenous peoples immediately upon arrival, not only to their ecclesiastical superiors at home but to company officials and Baranov's victims on site. This led to strained and eventually hostile relations between the missionaries and the governor, but faithfulness to Christ demanded that they assume this position. To act in a Christ-like way in any given circumstance is basic to the Christian life, and the missionary is called not only to talk about, to teach and preach the gospel, but also to live and to exemplify it.

Risking their lives to visit and tend to their flocks, the missionaries familiarized themselves with the beliefs and religious practices of the Kodiak

Aleuts and began presenting Christianity as the fulfillment of their age-long spiritual strivings. They were tolerant and respectful of traditions that were foreign to them, seeking a way to accommodate these within the broadest possible Christian setting. While they were critical of polygamy, they were more concerned with promoting harmony among peoples rather than introducing new sources for strife among them. Most impressive was their positive evaluation of Alaskan spirituality, which affirmed the sacredness of life and life-sustaining forces.

Western Alaskans spoke of this life force as the Inua, Yua, or Sua, depending on the language, each term closely related to their word for human being—Inuk, Yuk, or Suk. Their traditional art depicted various animals with a human figure or face "inserted" somewhere inside, an iconic depiction of the life that enlivened not only all humans but all creatures. Tribal ceremonies annually "recycled" the inua/yua/sua of the animals whose lives had been voluntarily offered to the hunters so that the human beings could live. The walrus, whale, seal, sea lion, and otter, as well as the salmon, were considered intelligent, sensitive, and therefore willing victims of the hunters, and their cooperation was considered necessary for the success of any hunt. If people wasted meat or spoke disrespectfully of the animal, the entire species would withhold itself, and the people would suffer deprivation or even starvation. Hunting and eating were therefore rituals by which the people and the animal respected each other, and all the implements of the hunt, together with cooking and dining utensils, reflected aspects of this interdependence.

THE MISSION FROM ALASKA

This reverential awe of the mystery of life is celebrated and affirmed in Orthodox worship and sacramental theology. Mission extends beyond the human community to the natural world God so loved. St. John the Evangelist could have chosen to use the word *oikoumene* and written, "For God so loved the inhabited earth that he sent his son . . . " but the text reads instead "For God so loved the cosmos"—the entire creation, the whole universe—that he sent his son. The whole creation suffers the effect of human sin. The modern ecological crisis only demonstrates that individually and collectively humans are getting better at disrupting and destroying the natural environment, using more efficient technologies to desecrate and destroy it. Christians are often accused of complacency regarding the pollution and exploitation of the world's natural resources, since Genesis confers dominion of the earth on Adam. But this status as ruler of the world predates sin. Humans were indeed intended to be God's image and likeness and therefore his presence in the world, but in their fallen, sinful condition they only appropriate the world and each other for their own self-centered and self-destructive purposes. Sin and the mortality it has introduced into earthly existence set each person and creature against every other. Darwinian survival of the strong over the weak has become the new norm. But this is unnatural, against nature, against God's *oikonomia*, his saving plan. The Holy Scriptures are the historical record by which he has acted to restore and transfigure the cosmos he still loves.

Confronted with this reverence for life, Orthodox missions everywhere have affirmed rather than denounced it. In the agricultural societies of the Middle East and southern Europe the Great Blessing of Water at Epiphany each year resonates with the pre-Christian spiritual intuition that water is life-sustaining and essential to life. God has used water throughout the history of salvation. In the old covenant, he began the creation of the world with water, separating the waters of the universe into seas, oceans, and rivers. Paradise is bounded by rivers, as is the Promised Land. Sin is drowned by the flood in the days of Noah. The infant Moses is taken from the waters of the Nile. Water gushes from the rock in the wilderness when Moses strikes it with his staff. The children of Israel are saved from bondage by passing through the Red Sea. Elijah uses water in his contest with the priests of Baal on the mountain top, and crosses over the Jordan before ascending in his fiery chariot. And Christ begins his public ministry by coming to the river to be baptized, to begin anew the re-creation of the world, the Spirit of God again appearing on the face of the waters. All of this is recounted in the church each January. The sacred history is "applied" to this place, to these waters in the midst of the congregation, the water in this way "projected" into the kingdom "which is to come" in order to be for the believers an eschatological sign, a tangible, visible, drinkable symbol of the cosmos as it will all be on the last day.

In fact, for those who are acquiring the "mind of Christ" the whole creation is already filled with his presence. The Aleuts and Eskimos were right, but they never could have guessed the personal identity of the Inua/Yua; it is all Christ. By conforming ourselves to the paradigm he is, each person becomes fully the human being God intended from all eternity. By behaving in a humble, reverential, and respectful way to all creatures and to all creation, each believer affirms the vision of the created universe the New Testament conveys in Colossians 1. This is not "paganism" but a Christian understanding of the eternal significance of the cosmos as a sacramental sign, the means by which God reveals and communicates himself to humankind.

In addition, therefore, to the traditional disciplines of scriptural, liturgical, patristic, and historical studies, Orthodox missiological education in the next decades must concentrate deliberately on this cosmic dimension in the Orthodox exegesis of the Bible, celebration of worship, the patristic theological legacy, and the history of missions. Besides having a mission to Alaska and similar places, the church must recognize that it is in dialogue with these cultures, and that they have something to offer the church. Alaska has a mission to the Christian community in the United States and the world beyond. This mission is to remind the church of its own history and theology, the ecological significance of which may have been dismissed in some earlier age as merely poetic or marginal, and to focus the church's attention on the cosmic dimensions of Christian doctrine, Scripture, and liturgy. Eastern Christianity is not pantheistic. It does not believe that God and the creation are contiguous, for God is transcendent, pre-existing, having no necessity to create the world. He exists beyond, outside, and without the cosmos. But within the world he is present in every person and every thing. There is no place where he is not, for he is before all things and in him all things hold together and in him all things subsist. Having created the universe because of his pre-existing love for it and all that is in it, God sustains it at each moment by his energy, his grace, his agape. Creation is not a long-ago act, the first in an infinite sequence of historical events, but an ongoing process. God creates the world at each moment.

Christians are therefore not pantheists but *pan-en-theists*, and it is the function of liturgy to manifest this experience and apprehension of reality, to move it from mental concept to concrete realization, from doctrinal proposition to a cosmic event. This is what is fulfilled in the sacramental and liturgical life of the church, but it is poorly appreciated or understood, even by Orthodox theologians, hierarchy, clergy, and pastors, especially in the secular West. The peasants of eastern and southern Europe and the hunters and gatherers of Africa, Asia, and Alaska probably understand it better. A dialogue needs to be reestablished between them "for the salvation of the world."

The Christian, as my beloved teacher of blessed memory, Father Alexander Schmemann wrote, is a person who, wherever he or she looks, sees Christ and rejoices in him. This is the vision, the experience of the world which the missionary of the next century must convey to and celebrate before all people everywhere, not only in remote tribal communities of the developing world but in the cities and suburbs of the developed world, where this witness is, perhaps, more desperately needed. Orthodox theologians must look afresh at their rich heritage from this perspective and bring forth as crucial to the *oikoumene*, and, indeed, the cosmos, the biblical, liturgical, and patristic heritage of the ancient Orthodox Catholic faith. Appropriating that heritage, the church can be more truly herself, the body of Christ, existing for those outside her, for their transfiguration, redemption, and eternal salvation,

In most of the millennium now ending, the Orthodox churches have been suppressed by hostile rulers—the Islamic Arabs and Turks in the Middle East, Greece, and the Balkans, the Tatars, the secularized Western-oriented aristocracy, and later the Bolsheviks in Russia. These silenced the free voice of the Orthodox churches beginning in the seventh century. Only now, with their collapse in this century, do most Orthodox Christians enjoy freedom to explore their spiritual legacy and begin their mission to the world unfettered by political oppression or interference. This too seems providential, not only for Eastern Orthodoxy but for the planet. The missiological task is enormous, but certainly no greater than that which the church faced two millennia ago at Pentecost. May the same "Heavenly King, the Comforter, the Spirit of Truth, who is everywhere present and fills all things, Treasury of Blessings and Life-Giver," as the Orthodox prayer to the Holy Spirit begins, guide, inspire, and sanctify this evangelical mission as the third Christian millennium begins. *Maranatha.*

REGIONAL CONTEXTS

Sandals from Other Lands

9

The Training of Missiologists
for an African Context

Tite Tiénou

The formulation of suggestions or especially the development of a program for the training of missiologists for an African context depends on the answers one gives to the following questions: Are the missiologists to be trained Africans or non-Africans? What is Africa, particularly in relationship to Christian mission in the continent in the twenty-first century?

The preceding questions are, of course, interrelated, for the personal identity of the missiologist determines, to a large extent, the characteristics he or she ascribes to Africa. This, in turn, raises questions such as: What should be the ancillary disciplines of missiology for an African context? Should we expect Africans to be consumers of mission or producers of mission and full participants in it?

With the foregoing in mind, I will explore issues related to the training of missiologists for an African context by endeavoring to answer the following two questions: What is Africa? What missiology is necessary for twenty-first century Africa?

WHAT IS AFRICA?

What is Africa to me? So asked Countee Cullen in his poem "Heritage." One need not be an African American, one or three centuries removed from the African continent, to seek an answer to the question, What is Africa? The peculiar and strange way in which the continent is perceived in the

A citizen of Burkina Faso, **Tite Tiénou** was professor of theology and missiology at Alliance Theological Seminary, Nyack, New York. He is now president and dean of the Evangelical Seminary of the Christian Alliance in Abidjan, Côte d'Ivoire.

world today and its marginalization by the West result from answers given
to the question raised here. What Africa is to most non-Africans is what
they are told about the continent or what they read about it. This is usually
limited to the superficial, the sensational, and the exotic. It is no secret that
the Western press, for instance, focuses its interest in Africa on "the coups,
the starving refugees, the monumentally mismanaged governments, the ugly
dictatorships" (White 1992, 52). For example, *Time* "honored" the continent by devoting much of the September 7, 1992, issue to "The Agony of
Africa." One sentence seems to sum it all up: "Nowhere is there a continent
more miserable" (Morrow 1992, 40). Misery and despair, we are led to
believe, are the chief characteristics of Africa. Is it any wonder that the
continent's inhabitants are perceived as helpless children or junior members of the human race and in constant need of benevolent care?

In the last one hundred years or more, Africans have seen a plethora of
adventurers and philanthropists, religious or otherwise, come and go. Some
have risen to the status of hero in the West because of their African experiences. Yet all their efforts seem to have availed little for the continent. Africans are still poor and languishing. Indeed, Africans have been aware of
their own vulnerability for some time (see N'Diaye 1979). One wonders: Is
Africa only good for promoting outsiders to hero status?

Christian mission agencies have for a long time recruited workers for
Africa on the basis of the continent being "the land of deepest, darkest,
heathen night."[1] The belief that Africa is the target par excellence of mission could be the religious expression of the phenomenon mentioned above.
How could it be otherwise when so many people easily associate material
deprivation, technological simplicity, color of skin, and spiritual need? Since
Africans are the poorest of the poor, since Africa is inhabited by dark-skinned
backward people, it must follow that Africans are most in need of
missionizing. This kind of missiology has been with us for a long time, is
still too much with us, and is not about to disappear. Witness one of the
current missiological slogans: The poor are the unreached and the unreached
are the poor. Such a slogan is supported by research (or what is presented as
research) summarized in this statement: "There is a remarkable overlap
between the fifty poorest countries of the world and the least evangelized
countries of the world" (Bush 1990, 7). And, as we all know, since Africa
has the highest number of the world's poorest countries, would Africa not
logically be a place where the unreached are found? When both trainers
and trainees in missiology are convinced of this, an inevitable link between
mission and charity develops. Missiological training and training for charitable work become synonymous. I contend that this has been an important
aspect of missiological training for Africa and it comes out of definitions of
Africa.

Why, you say, do I go out on a limb to make you uncomfortable? I do so
because missiological education, like any education, begins with language
learning. As Lesslie Newbigin reminds us, "We have to learn a language in

which to express what we think we have learned, and the language is itself the form of our knowing" (1991, 32). The language of missiology, in spite of adjustments here and there, has remained substantially the same since William Carey. We remember that, for Carey, the inhabitants of "the greatest part of Africa, the island of Madagascar, and many places besides" were "in general poor, barbarous, naked, pagan, as destitute of civilization, as . . . of true religion" (1891, 63). Since Carey's book was first published in 1792, we have been using the same language in missiological descriptions and training for two hundred years. The time has come, it has more than come, to change this language, the first tool of missiological training. This is particularly crucial for the training of missiologists for an African context.

The language of our missiology has prevented us from taking seriously the significant Christianization of Africa that resulted from more than one hundred years of missionary and other Christian witness. We know, thanks to the work of Barrett and others, that Africa is Christianity's most fertile soil. Yet we find it difficult to train missiologists for the African context in any other way than viewing the continent primarily as an object of mission. We do not take the time to reflect on the contradiction inherent in viewing the African continent simultaneously as a place with vital Christianity and as the continent most in need of missionizing. That may be the reason why significant African participation in global mission is usually greeted with skepticism or condescension: how can the recipients of charity provide charity to those who do not need it?

The linkage of mission and charity has turned our attention away from the essential focus of Christian mission, namely, the passionate call to all peoples to turn to the true and living God, the Father of the Lord Jesus Christ—regardless of whether they are poor, rich, ignorant, learned, dark-skinned, or light-skinned. What is urgently needed in Africa is missiological training that will liberate African Christians from perceiving themselves solely as recipients of mission. For it is increasingly difficult to hold these two convictions simultaneously: Africa should be a primary target of mission; African Christianity has remarkable vitality. For this raises the inevitable question: why do we not expect this vitality to result in major African involvement in mission? Surely Christian mission will continue in Africa as in other continents. Missiological training for Africa must nonetheless prepare African Christians to be responsible and full participants in global mission.

What then is Africa? For missiologists in the twenty-first century the answer will have to be that it is a continent just like any other continent of this planet. Missiologists will have to heed the words of Chinua Achebe and "see Africa as a continent of people—just people, not some strange beings that demand a special kind of treatment. [Because] if you accept Africans as people, then you listen to them" (1989, 335). In my judgment, listening before speaking is the first act of sound missiology; it must therefore be incorporated into missiological training. Listening enhances the possibility of reflection. Missiological training which includes serious reflection will prevent the practice of mission from being mere activism. Christian mission in Africa in the twenty-first century will need to be more than Christian activism if it is to contribute to making qualitative and permanent impact on African Christianity.

WHAT IS MISSIOLOGY
FOR TWENTY-FIRST CENTURY AFRICA?

Missiological education for Africa in the twenty-first century will depend on what kind of missiology one envisions for the continent in the coming century. In general, missiology will have to be done in a perspective of taking Africa and Africans seriously. Taking Africans seriously means that missiologists consciously will have to rid themselves and other Christians of the sequels of the theology of curse which has informed much of the evangelization of Africa in the past (Mbembe 1988, 41-42). Those who are charged with training missiologists for the Africa of the twenty-first century will have the grave responsibility of preparing them to deal with the multiple challenges of Christian life and ministry in the continent. Some of the challenges missiology will face in Africa in the twenty-first century are intellectual probity, theological grounding and responsibility, spiritual fervor and credibility, rethinking the ancillary disciplines of missiology, and making Christianity count in the moral, political, and economic rehabilitation of the continent.

Missiologists trained for twenty-first century Africa will need to develop and sustain intellectual probity. According to Achille Mbembe, the mediocrity of the intellectual formation of African clergy is undeniable (1988, 175-76). A similar observation can be made about African missiologists in general. This is so despite the increase of advanced credentials in missiology granted to Africans and other missiologists working in the continent. The fact is that credentials alone do not create intellectual probity. They may, in fact, produce the opposite result. Intellectual probity is manifested through characteristics such as competence, courage, creativity, and patient discipline. These characteristics can be acquired by all missiologists regardless of the level of training.

The lack of intellectual probity causes African Christianity in general, and its missiology in particular, to suffer from what Mbembe calls ready-made thought (1988, 50). Missiological training institutions do, of course, share part of the responsibility for that. All of them, whether they are within Africa or outside the continent, should be careful not to just satisfy people's need and desire for degrees and other credentials. In this respect the ability to do critical reflection, analysis, and synthesis is more crucial for African missiologists than the mastery of the various missiological theories and strategies currently proposed. Without intellectual probity African and other missiologists will continue to be unable to deal seriously with the specific issues of Christian mission in Africa.

A major component of the training of missiologists for an African context should be devoted to theological study, reflection, and grounding. By this I do not mean that we need to devote more time and attention to biblical and theological justification of mission. Rather, we need to train missiologists to be competent in theology and biblical teaching. I am advocating the view that missiologists in Africa must be full theologians. If missiologists were competent theologians, missiology would cease to be relegated to the practical side of the theological curriculum. This viewpoint is shared by my friend and colleague missiologist from Mali, Yiranou Traoré. In a recent letter he made this unsolicited suggestion: "In your courses in missiology, you must insist on the fact that the missionary needs to take biblical teaching seriously."

Theological grounding and responsibility in the training of missiologists for Africa mean that missiological training institutions should not dismiss hastily the so-called classical theological curriculum. Specifically, familiarity with the biblical languages, acquaintance with the history of Christian thought including systematic theology, and ability in hermeneutics will be of utmost importance.

Missiologists trained for an African context need to have spiritual fervor and credibility. It is true, of course, that spiritual fervor and credibility cannot be taught or created on demand; they must be demonstrated by example. That is why institutions of missiological training must be more than factories producing people equipped with techniques and a body of knowledge. They must be communities where spiritual fervor is valued. But the spiritual fervor must be credible. In other words, spirituality which fails to relate to the world as it is today cannot be credible. Let missiologists, in this regard, learn lessons from the renewed vitality of African "traditional" religions. As in other continents, "old" religions are resurgent because, in the eyes of the people, they seem to relate better to ordinary life and spirituality. Raymond Deniel reports these words uttered by a Catholic layman in Abidjan: "Our [Catholic] religion is made of advice for us to follow so that we can be well in heaven tomorrow" (1975, 190). We fail to prepare people to communicate "the whole counsel of God" as long as our missiological training teaches them to promote a Christianity good only "for heaven tomorrow."

Some may view the opinions expressed here as a particularly harsh and negative evaluation of African Christianity. After all, there is ample statistical evidence that all sectors of Christianity are experiencing numerical growth in Africa. But the numerical increase of a religion cannot, in and of itself, constitute proof of its spiritual vitality and relatedness to people's ordinary life. The religious scene of contemporary Africa resembles the selling and buying of insurance. Multiple religious affiliations, like buying several insurance policies for various purposes, are common. Consequently, people may choose to identify themselves with a form of Christianity for reasons other than those envisioned by the communicator of the Christian message. Missiologists trained for Africa must therefore be equipped to communicate and deepen the Christian faith in the total religious context of the continent. Such a preparation may help them articulate ways of developing Christian spiritual fervor and credibility in keeping with the concerns of the general public.

In the twenty-first century missiology will need to promote vigorously the study and living of Christianity in Africa in the total religious and sociopolitical context of the continent. This raises the question of the ancillary disciplines necessary for such a missiology. Anthropology has been the obvious ancillary discipline to missiology for a long time. The dialogue between missiology and anthropology has had positive as well as negative results. On the positive side, for instance, anthropology has helped missiologists develop techniques for the cross-cultural communication of the gospel. On the negative side, an "anthropology-based missiology . . . tends to reduce everything to 'the West and the rest'" (Bediako 1992, 6).

Since "the West and the rest" missiology cannot adequately prepare non-Western missiologists, the ancillary disciplines of missiology must be expanded especially for Africa. The curriculum for training missiologists for an African context must be expanded to include, among other disciplines, African history, sociology, urban studies, political thought, African philosophy, Islamics, and African literature. African as well as non-African missiologists will benefit greatly from such a multidiscipline-based missiology.[2] In addition, such a missiology is the only responsible way to address the numerous publics of contemporary post-colonial Africa as opposed to a missiology which is only helpful in dealing with so-called traditional Africa.

Missiologists trained for the African context must be able to articulate ways of making Christianity count in the moral, political, and economic rehabilitation of the continent. In order to do so, they will need to reflect seriously on suffering in the African experience, and they will also need to rediscover dignity in poverty.

Africa, more than any other continent on earth, is in need of healing in all its dimensions. Her sons and daughters have endured untold suffering and humiliation. One wonders, with Kwame Bediako, "Why has there been so little reflection in African Christian thought so far, on the African collective experience of suffering?" (1992, 3). Could it be that a certain kind of triumphalist missiology has successfully marginalized the theology of the cross and suffering? Yet suffering has been part of the experience of God's people throughout the centuries. Indeed, pagan "people are not only persuaded by the triumphs of Christianity, but also by its trials" (A. Anderson 1990, 73). If serious reflection on suffering were part of training missiologists for the African context, African Christians would be able to show how the continent's problems can be dealt with realistically. For they would be able to demonstrate how God—Father, Son, and Holy Spirit—sustains them through life's tragedies even in the absence of visible and immediate success.

Since the suffering of the continent is related to its poverty when compared to other continents, missiologists trained for the African context will need to do more than pity Africa or be ashamed of being "poor black men." Equipped with solid biblical and theological evidence, they will have to show how poverty is no shame for the poor. They will courageously unmask the hypocrisy of those who seem to pity the people while simultaneously deriding them and doing little to change the situation. They will warn all Christians of how easy it is to seek to missionize through gold power rather than God's power.

Africa has three characteristics that can be the basis for new directions in missiological theory and practice in the twenty-first century. First, the continent is enjoying unprecedented Christian growth. Second, the Christians share with other Africans the experience of suffering. Third, Africans lack the obvious means of power, particularly that of money. The convergence of these three factors provides missiologists in Africa with the greatest challenge and opportunity: the power of the gospel does not depend on the earthen vessels which carry it. The training of African missiologists for the African context will therefore be a laboratory for elaborating a missiology from the wretched of the earth.

The training of non-African missiologists for the African context will differ slightly from the above. The ideas expressed above apply to them. But since they are outsiders to the continent, their training needs to prepare them to recognize the fact that in cross-cultural Christian service, as in any Christian service, the first priority is respect for, appreciation of, and love for people. The cross-cultural dimension of their work should not cause them to think that cultural sensitivity and learning about different customs take precedence here. After all, culture is not independent of people. One does not become a neighbor to people by studying their customs; rather, closeness comes with sharing and mutual respect. As Gérard Toffin reminds us, one does not draw near people by understanding their customs; they remain distant and closed before and after the study (1990, 210). Consequently, missiological training for Africa that succeeds only in explaining customs and cultures will remain inadequate. One thing is certain: missiologists cannot continue to be trained for Africa as they have been up to now. I have tried to sketch here major aspects of what may be involved in training missiologists for Africa in the twenty-first century.

Notes

1. For instance R. S. Roseberry of the Christian and Missionary Alliance states that A. B. Simpson's poem "Meet Me in the Dark Soudan" "became the rally song of the pioneers" of Alliance mission efforts in West Africa (*The Niger Vision.* Har-

risburg, PA: Christian Publications, Inc., 1934, p. 6). Note especially these two lines from Simpson's poem: "Land of deepest, darkest, heathen night, Thou shalt yet be called the Land of Light."

2. In this regard, Basil Davidson's recent book, *The Black Man's Burden* (New York: Times Books, 1992) should be required reading for all missiologists interested in Africa.

10

The Training of Missiologists
for a Latin American Context

Samuel Escobar

Latin America is a unique missiological laboratory where the missionary and the missiologist can find at the same time the most traditional situations as well as the most daring experiments. That gives a unique relevance
to the subject I have been assigned, and I want to address it in a very specific way. My subject is not the training of *missionaries* but the training of
missiologists, and I think that there is a clear difference between these two
types of training. You can train a "missionary" by teaching the person to
memorize a particular version of the gospel, giving him or her some communication techniques, adding some cross-cultural awareness that may include your own ethnocentric interpretation of the other cultures, and whatever specialized techniques the particular task of the missionary may demand.
But what is a "missiologist," and how do you train one?

I propose that the key difference between a missionary and a missiologist
is that while the missionary accomplishes the task that his or her call demands, the missiologist *also* reflects about that task in a *critical* and *systematic* way. Such reflection is necessary in order to adapt, correct, and
improve missionary methodologies. Such reflection benefits from the use
of classical theological disciplines such as biblical studies, historical theology, history of the church, as well as the social sciences. Such reflection
should be the source of the missiological content, which is then arranged in
the form of a curriculum for the training of missionaries and missiologists.

Samuel Escobar, born in Peru, was a missionary among university students for
twenty-six years in several Latin American countries and Canada. He specialized
in evangelism and leadership training. Presently he is the Thornley B. Wood
Professor of Missiology at Eastern Baptist Theological Seminary in Philadelphia,
Pennsylvania.

Missiology is an interdisciplinary kind of study, and missiologists agree that in theological education there is the constant difficulty of an adequate integration of different disciplines. That is not a problem limited to theological education but is a serious problem of higher education in general. Close contact with missionary activity plays an integrative role in the academic formation of missionaries and missiologists. Spirituality in its diverse forms also plays an integrative role in missiological education, because the best moments of missionary history and practice are always related to moments of renewed spiritual vitality. In this way we come full circle to our initial statement. The best missiologist will be a missionary whose commitment to mission and spiritual vitality are the integrative part of his or her own reflection about missionary practice. The missiological reflection is no mere academic exercise; it is part of missionary obedience.

THE LATIN AMERICAN CONTEXT

Let us look at some notes of the Latin American situation that are specially significant from a missiological perspective today.

Catholicism on the Defensive

Before this decade ends, half of the Roman Catholics of the world will be living in Latin America. For missiologists, this means that if there is to be Catholic missionary activity next century, Latin American Catholics will have a special role to play within it. However, less than 2 percent of the Catholic missionary force in the world comes from Latin America. Moreover, Catholic missiologists observe that the rate of conversions from Catholicism to different forms of Protestantism in Latin America has been such that today comparatively more Catholics have become Protestants than in all of Europe during the sixteenth century Reformation (Damen 1987, 63). During CELAM IV, the most recent Assembly of Latin American bishops in Santo Domingo (October 12-28, 1992), Pope John Paul II used the expression "rapacious wolves" to refer to evangelical churches (Steinfels 1992). Language and attitude betray the same defensiveness of CELAM I in Rio de Janeiro, 1955, almost forty years ago.

Popular Protestantism Grows

In 1916, when Protestant missionary forces working in Latin America held their first continental conference in Panama, they counted 126,000 Protestants. Though no precise information exists today, a conservative estimate puts the figure of Latin American Protestants beyond the forty million mark in 1992. Even Catholic journalists believe that Latin America may have an evangelical majority by the early twenty-first century, because "actually in terms of church participation, 'practicing' evangelicals may already outnumber 'observant' Catholics" (McCoy 1989, 2). The churches that grow faster are the popular churches of the Pentecostal type, the most contextual in liturgy and evangelistic methodology. These are also the ones that have almost no foreign connections or influence.

Emergence of Marginalized Sectors

Migration patterns and massive urban accumulation have brought to the fore segments of the population that had been almost invisible in the past. This new visibility of those who were absent before has been described by theologian Gustavo Gutiérrez as "the emergence of the poor," who are coming to be new actors in the historical processes. This movement is well exemplified by the significant church growth that has taken place among native communities in Guatemala, Mexico, Peru, Bolivia, and Ecuador. The fact that they have now the complete Bible in their own language allows us to expect significant theological challenges in the future. More than forty-five thousand copies of the complete Bible in Quechua have been sold in Peru in the first three years of its existence, in spite of the suffering imposed by Maoist terrorists on the one hand and military repression on the other.

Missionary Enigma

In view of the fact that five centuries of the Iberian evangelization of Latin America were commemorated in 1992, it is puzzling to realize that from the missionary force going out of North America, both Catholic and Protestant, the largest contingent of missionaries is still being sent to Latin America, more than to any other region of the world. Most of them do not go to work among pagan populations but among nominal Christians. The context of Protestant growth is actually a superficially Christianized population with no pastoral attention, because the Roman church is too weak to even keep its faithful within the fold. Honest reflection about this fact is filled with missionary lessons.

The Worsening of the Social Conditions

The decade of the eighties has been described as "the lost decade" because of the visible deterioration of the social conditions all over Latin America. A recent evangelical document describes dramatically the area in this final decade, "The Latin American world is left with a sad legacy of unaltered structures of land ownership, stagnation of rural communities, invasion of aboriginal territories, deterioration of the quality of life in the large cities, unemployment, hunger, violence, child and old age abandonment, illiteracy, housing shortage, deterioration of public services, particularly in the areas of education and health, slow judicial processes, overcrowded prisons, generalized corruption and inflation" (Powell, et al. 1992,

9). All this has affected significantly the patterns of church life and theological education.

Christian Activism

As a spiritual counterpart to the growth of poverty and marginalization, but also prompted by it, the life and testimony of Christian communities has intensified. Through Latin America the name of Jesus is being proclaimed loud and clear in crowded streets of megalopolises as well as in remote villages. There are simple peasants as well as sophisticated intellectuals ready to risk their lives for what they consider the demands of their faith in Jesus Christ as their Lord. Faithfulness to the faith becomes a question of life and death rather than an academic debate about fundamentals. Some churches are declining in numbers and influence, but other churches are flourishing.

Missionary Activism

Enthusiasm for mission at a global level has begun to flourish among evangelicals, and several missionary organizations have appeared in the last two decades. For instance, there are now missionaries from Brazil, Costa Rica, Peru, and Colombia working in other Latin American countries as well as in Europe, Africa, and the Middle East. Moreover, among the hundreds of thousands of Latin Americans that go into voluntary or forced exile in other parts of the world, there is a small but significant number of evangelicals who cultivate their faith in the midst of transition and are enthusiastically engaged in spreading it "as they go." The significant growth of Protestantism among Hispanics in North America is made dynamic by the active engagement of lay people, which the Roman Catholic Church finds very difficult to foster.

Growing Awareness of Holistic Mission

One of the most significant Protestant gatherings of our century took place in Quito, Ecuador. It was CLADE III, the Third Latin American Congress on Evangelism (August 24-September 4, 1992). The success of this event, which attracted more than a thousand delegates from all of Latin America, demonstrated the existence of hundreds of projects of holistic mission born and developed by Latin Americans themselves, and a new generation of mission theologians that are also missionary activists (Escobar 1993). It is evident that with missionary enthusiasm there is also creativity and a reflective concern to do mission in Jesus' way and not simply to repeat classic Anglo-Saxon patterns. Holistic mission takes place here through the amazing resilience of the poor and the creativity of those committed to service for their neighbor.

In a continent with these characteristics, the training of missionaries and missiologists has to be designed anew. We cannot limit ourselves to the curriculum and methods of the predominant missiological schools in North America or Europe, especially when it is evident that they are going through a crisis of adjustment to new conditions in the world. Our training program in Latin America has to be designed on the basis of biblical convictions, experience of life, historical awareness, and pastoral concern. My outline in what follows is basically a reflection on current practice, not a theoretical proposal.

WHERE TRAINING BEGINS

The preparation of persons for mission is provided by life experience long before college, university, or mission school offers them information through a curriculum. The zeal, the vision, and the basic qualities of character that are the "raw material" of which missionaries are made, are fostered at home, in churches, and in para-churches. In times of social and moral crisis and transition, such as the ones Latin America is going through, it is important to keep this fact in mind. When you have a growing number of candidates for missionary work that come from dysfunctional families, drug addiction, or involvement with spiritism, there is a need to revise the presuppositions which were the bases for previous forms of missionary training. Neuza Itioka, who trains missionaries for *Avante* in Brazil, has stressed this point (1991), and I have also written about my own experience (Escobar 1992).

We should not forget that before a person teaches, evangelizes, translates Scripture, fosters self-supporting development, reflects missiologically, or does whatever missionaries are supposed to do, that person *is*, that person has a *way of being*. His or her presence communicates something to others, especially to those on the receiving end of mission. At CLADE III we heard a Brazilian missionary in Angola refer to the long process of learning that humility was the first mark that should characterize a missionary. And that virtue cannot be taught in a Humility 101 course of the missions curriculum!

Observing training situations in Latin America and reflecting about discipleship processes in churches and para-churches, I have come to the conclusion that forming people for mission is an activity that should take place within the frame of a "person to person" relationship, which is as fundamental as the environment for the educational process. No amount of academic excellence or doctrinal orthodoxy can substitute for this personalized dimension of the training for mission. This is difficult in North America, where theological institutions depend so much on the need to market education and the constraints imposed by accrediting agencies. At least in Latin America there is still room for a more careful process of selection of students, which allows a better job at the entrance level, and careful monitoring along the way.

EDUCATIONAL ATMOSPHERE

The nurturing and formation of persons is an aim based on the biblical model of the practice of Jesus and the apostles, and also in the historical models of the charismatic personalities that started some of the missionary orders. Within the student movements in which I have worked, the healing of persons through life together and interaction has been a key element in the preparation of missionaries (Escobar 1987, 540-44). Unidad Cristiana Universitaria in Colombia has been a seedbed of missionaries to other parts of Latin America and Europe, and it has developed a personalized curriculum for their training. The questions posed by the discipling of future missionaries at this personal level took missiologists like René Padilla (1985) or Neuza Itioka (1990) to a rediscovery of a biblical anthropology in contrast with the current evangelical reductionism.

Another important element here is the dialogical style that the educational process must adopt. Paulo Freire's pedagogical credo has some points of missiological significance, even if his ideological presuppositions may be questioned. Freire makes a clear distinction between education and "domestication." Instead of the magisterial monologue, learning happens better through dialogue that is based upon the conviction that no one ignores everything and no one knows everything. The openness to hear and discuss the experience of everyone contributes to a liberating educational atmosphere. The process may be facilitated and enriched by including in the student body people with missionary background and experience, on the basis of equality and mutuality. When teachers are encouraged to abandon the magisterial pose, they are better able to help students *reflect about their own experience*. Transmission of information and the fostering of new abilities become more meaningful and acceptable within the context of that active reflection.

Interaction with a variety of practitioners of mission also has a formative effect. Foreign or Latin American missionaries who visit training centers share their experience and interact with students. That kind of presence has to be more than simply the promotional kind of deputation with which we are familiar. Its formative value is related to the degree to which authenticity and the personal touch are kept by all means. A more formal version of this principle has been to encourage students to research the history of their own denomination and to focus on the life and work of specific missionaries, with sympathy but also with rigorous realism. This is what my colleagues Stewart McIntosh and Tito Paredes have done in the Orlando E. Costas School of Missiology in Lima, and I have done at Eastern Baptist Theological Seminary.

A Brazilian missionary who leads the *Magreb* project in North Africa has described the serious difficulties Latin Americans have accepting the poverty and deprivation of some of the Muslim communities in which they work (Acosta 1991). He sees no answer but incarnation. Mission can never be achieved from a distance, from the safety of a detached bureaucratic style. The clue to move from one culture to another with the gospel is the kenotic experience of incarnation, according to the Christological model of mission outlined in Philippians 2: 5-11. It is costly and painful, but it is the only one that produces lasting results. If the sowing of the seed of the gospel demands that kind of incarnational style in the missionary, it gives birth to a form of Christian life that is also incarnate in a given culture. These are perspectives about mission that do not come from either books or computers but from incarnation in grassroots situations, by the power of the Holy Spirit. This kind of experience is the starting point to which insights from social sciences and cultural history can be added in order to provide a basic awareness of cultures.

THEOLOGY AND MISSION

Within recent theological developments in Latin America, theology actually has been missiology. It has been pointed out that Liberation theologies, for instance, are really explorations into the meaning of mission for the church today. Among evangelicals the beginning of an indigenous theology was linked to a Congress of Evangelism (CLADE I, Bogota, 1969), which was the cradle of the Latin American Theological Fraternity. The only way we could explore the depths of our faith in order to appropriate it within our context was by relating that exploration to evangelization. An important reason for this was that our questions about the faith came from our practice as evangelists and pastors and not from questionnaires provided by translated textbooks. Another reason was that for the average Latin American evangelical, evangelization is still at the heart of the mission of the church; it is the church's reason for being.

I have studied this point in relation to Christology, for instance, which for us is more than an exploration into the creedal formulas of the fourth century. Rather, it must be an exploration into the biblical material in search for a model for the contemporary missionary, that is, a missiological Christology (Escobar 1991). Evangelical theologians in Latin America do not theologize for the academic gallery or for the fundamentalist watchdogs. The theological agenda must always be close to the point where the missionary agenda is. This is an exciting task but not without its difficulties and struggles.

I think that in relation to mission the theological task moves constantly between two poles: the *ideological* and the *critical*. Some conceive the task of theology as that of providing an "ideology" for the missionary enterprise as it exists. The function of ideology is to explain (provide rationality) and justify (sanction or legitimize) a social fact. Some conceive the task of mission theology precisely along those lines: the creation of a missionary theory which will undergird one particular expression of the missionary enterprise. Missiology becomes simply methodology. Others conceive the task of a theology of mission as a critical task in which the missionary enterprise is put under the light of the social sciences in such a way that all shortcomings become evident, to the point that eventually the missionary task in itself is abandoned. This is one of the ways through which missiology becomes a purely academic activity, taking the form of a detached, permanently negative commentary. I believe that by keeping close to missionary activity, missiology avoids the trap of academic sterility. But I also believe that by being faithful to God's Word, missiology avoids the trap of merely providing a convenient ideology for the missionary establishment.

During the recent CLADE III, both Federico Bertuzzi (1992) from COMIBAM and Carlos Mraida (1992), a pastor and professor of missiology in Buenos Aires, spoke to the need for a drastic revision of the curriculum of theological institutions patterned after the Anglo-Saxon system. They think that this system is actually geared to the training of monocultural ministers. Mraida believes that the whole curriculum has to be affected by the rediscovery of the missionary nature of the church, of the missionary obligation of every believer, and of the participation of Latin America in mission at a global level. This is much more than simply adding a missiology course to the curriculum. It means a reformulation of the disciplines by placing the mission of the church at the center of their object of study. Missiologists in Europe and North America know that this is not an easy task in theological institutions, and that we have a long way to go.

ECUMENISM AND COOPERATION

This is probably the area in which Latin Americans have the greatest difficulty. In North America evangelical missiologists have been able to cooperate with conciliar Protestants and Roman Catholics in the American Society of Missiology; in Latin America, missions are the bone of contention that separates these three groups. The report of the Evangelical-Roman Catholic Dialogue on Mission (Stott-Meeking 1986), which explored an amazing amount of common ground, has been ignored by both Catholics and Protestants. Even inter-Protestant dialogue is not practiced, partly because missionary promotion is based so much on the rules of market competition. Let me mention two developments within Roman Catholicism that Protestant missiology in Latin America cannot ignore.

The nineteenth Assembly of the Latin American bishops in 1983 was the occasion that Pope John Paul II used to propose a "new evangelization" for Latin America. The concept developed and was clarified later on (CELAM 1990), detaching it from any idea of "re-evangelization" as if the first evangelization in the sixteenth century had failed. The "new evangelization" had to be "new in its fervor, its methods, and its expression," but it presupposes that the first one was successful in spite of its shortcomings. As the bishops said at Puebla, "Despite the defects and the sins that are always present, the faith of the church has set its seal on the soul of Latin America.

It has left its marks on Latin America's essential historical identity, becoming the continent's cultural matrix out of which new peoples have arisen" (Puebla Document 1979/80, 445). Using categories of Vatican II and the document *Evangelii Nuntiandi* of Pope Paul VI, the concept of "evangelization of cultures" has been developed as an effort to understand groups of people within the unique circumstances in which they live. Missionary-missiologist Roger Aubry presents the Catholic missionary task of the future in Latin America focused around a threefold challenge: the "ancient cultures" (indigenous and Afro-American peoples), "changing cultures" (masses of migrants to the great cities), and "new cultures" (peoples affected by the impact of modernization) (CELAM 1990, 76-80). Here is a concept that Protestant missiologists cannot afford to ignore.

What kind of missionaries are necessary today according to Roman Catholic missiologists? The most courageous answers to this question have come from North American Catholics who have evaluated their own experience of mission during the critical days of the 1960s. At that time "a new mission approach began to emerge, radically new. . . . The missionaries who remained began to learn instead of to teach, to serve instead of to lead" (Costello 1979, 5). A veteran of twenty years of missionary work in Nicaragua describes it this way: "Unless a person wants to 'put on the mind of Christ,' he'd do better not to enter Latin American work. . . . Christ came as one of the oppressed with a message of life for the oppressors. We, the church today, tend to come as the oppressors to the oppressed telling them we have a message of life—and they say, 'Oh, yeah? Show us!'" (Costello 1979, 41). Another American missionary who serves in Peru has used his Christological perspective of Matthew 25:31-46 to describe the experience of "the recognition of the face of Christ in the faces of the Latin American woman, *campesino*, or laborer," an experience that "grows out of the concrete day-to-day experience of those who have pitched their tents among the poor . . . not those who occasionally visit the world of the poor as they would a county agricultural extension worker, but to those who dwell among the poor" (Judd 1987, 7). This missiology that comes from a new missionary practice cannot be ignored by Protestants in their search for new models of mission relevant to our times.

The training of missiologists in Latin America demands the opening of the mind and the heart of Latin American evangelicals to the missiological reality of Catholicism in their continent. There are in other parts of the world some signs of practical ecumenism that may be announcing new trends for the future. I am not thinking necessarily about the well-known, organized patterns of ecumenical activity and discourse, but of the grassroots level at which both training for mission and the practice of mission takes place. I have found it a fascinating sign of our times that a conservative evangelical missionary like Viv Grigg, the author of *Companion to the Poor* (1990), doing evangelistic work in the slums of Manila, may find value, inspiration, and guidance in the model of a great ecumenical leader like the

Japanese Toyohiko Kagawa and in the pioneering incarnational style of
Francis of Assisi.

Missiological training in Latin America demands a new understanding
of our history. The more I know contemporary mission history, the more I
respect the missionary work of Spain and Portugal in the sixteenth century.
Stewart McIntosh in Peru has been teaching how Jesuit Jose de Acosta in
the sixteenth century was responding creatively and biblically to some of
the contemporary dilemmas of transcultural mission (McIntosh 1989). Protestant historians of the church and mission in Latin America have done
good work in terms of showing continuities and discontinuities within a
continuum in the missionary methods and styles of Catholics and Protestants (González 1970, Prien 1985). Along this line, a good work of
missiological scholarship published recently by the Latin American Theological Fraternity is a book written by Pablo Deiros (1992), a historian and
a pastor of a large Baptist church in Buenos Aires. However, neither the
irenic spirit of these historians nor the content of their works has reached
the pastoral and missiological level of the daily life and practice of evangelical missionaries. Let us hope that this scholarship will contribute to a
more mature missiological understanding in the future.

A MISSIOLOGICAL PARADIGM SHIFT

We have pointed out that one of the effects of accelerated urbanization
in Latin America has been to bring to light the emergence of new segments
of the population and that popular forms of Protestantism have flourished
among them. Social scientists who used academic Marxism to evaluate this
growth considered it negative, because it would not mobilize social forces
into a Marxist-style revolution. That is also the way in which liberation
theologians approached the Pentecostal phenomenon. However, David
Martin, a well-known sociologist of religion, has come to the conclusion
that the most helpful paradigm that can be used to study and interpret this
Latin American phenomenon is the Wesleyan movement of the eighteenth
and nineteenth centuries (David Martin 1990). Here we can see a redemptive evangelistic spiritual experience and the social dynamism it provokes.

If we approach this reality with the standards of a missiology that takes
seriously New Testament teaching and church history, we realize that we
are faced by a phenomenon of tremendous missiological significance. The
expansive power of this popular Protestantism comes from its ability to
mobilize lay people and to adopt truly contextual forms of worship, congregational life, and pastoral practices. For the masses in transition, these
churches are the only available way to find social acceptance, achieve human dignity, and survive the impact of dehumanizing forces at work in the
big cities.

Pentecostal communities emphasize the ministry of the Holy Spirit and
the spiritual conflict involved in mission. Pentecostal missiologists are work-

ing at a renewed understanding of the New Testament teaching on this point. Thus Argentinean Norberto Saracco finds in his reading of the gospels that they emphasize the atmosphere of conflict that surrounded the ministry of Jesus and constituted the context in which the Kingdom of God and the power of the gospel are to be understood. He goes on to say, "Unfortunately contemporary evangelicals, especially in Latin America, have been influenced by a dispensationalist theology that has given them a gospel without kingdom, and by a Western worldview that has deprived them of a holistic understanding of human beings and the world" (1992, 4).

In their own way Latin American missiologists are asking for a post-Enlightenment missiology that will take seriously spiritual realities. Neuza Itioka, a Brazilian who spent several years of missionary life in her country and carried on missiological research at the doctoral level, finds a close connection between spiritual oppression and the social conditions of poverty and exploitation. In this she comes to conclusions similar to those of other missionaries in the Third World, such as Daniel Fountain, a medical doctor in Zaire (Fountain 1989), and Viv Grigg, a church planter in the slums of Manila (Grigg 1990).

For Itioka, "The rational intellectual approach we have used for so long brings only new information, a new way of thinking. What we need to reach people who coexist daily with the supernatural is the powerful presence of the risen Christ. He is the missionary and evangelist par excellence. Without his intimate involvement we have no mission and there will not be transformation in the lives of people" (Itioka 1990, 9).

The training of Latin American missiologists has started to emerge from its dependence upon imported models. It must leave behind the shackles of curriculums, methods, and textbooks from North America and Europe, dominated by intellectualism, a Western imperial view of the world, an authoritarian pedagogy, and sectarian denominationalism. As the Holy Spirit moves the church of Latin America into new frontiers of mission, God's Word will show again its inexhaustible renewing power for the new generations of missionaries that will carry on the Great Commandment and the Great Commission into the twenty-first century.

11

The Training of Missiologists for Asian Contexts

Ken R. Gnanakan

The challenge of mission in Asia is staggering, with a multitude of forces—political, cultural, religious, and economic—increasing their impact on all that the church has to do. Pertinent questions need to be asked, and fresh answers must be sought. In this situation, the training of missiologists is urgent, but top priority needs to be given to evaluating what is being done in order to develop more effective people and programs for the future.

THE CHALLENGE OF RELIGIONS

A brief reminder about some aspects of history will be useful, with both successes and failures underlining some valuable lessons. With the pluralistic challenge looming large, it is good to start with those from religious encounters. The Jerusalem Conference of the International Missionary Council in 1928 gave much time for discussion of the attitude of the church to other religions, acknowledging the reality of the pressure exerted by them on the mission field. This was timely.

However, long before this the West had been reminded quite forcefully of the claims of the world's ancient religions. The 1893 World Parliament of Religions in Chicago had heard the powerful oratory of a dynamic Indian, Swami Vivekananda, reminding the delegates of the continuing influence of Hinduism. His stay in the United States after the conference for

Ken R. Gnanakan is a well-known Christian evangelist, missiologist, theologian, educator, and author. He is founder of the ACTS Institute, Bangalore, and General Director of ACTS Ministries, an affiliate of International Needs. He is the General Secretary of Asia Theological Association.

over a year was memorable. Jawaharlal Nehru records, "Wherever he went, he created a minor sensation not only by his presence but by what he said and how he said it. Having seen this Hindu Sanyasin once it was difficult to forget him or his message. In America he was called the 'cyclonic Hindu'" (Nehru 1990, 337).

Vivekananda was not impressed with the kind of Christianity he had seen, and as a result his commitment to Hindu philosophy became all the more firm. The American press, carried away by his charisma, criticized the churches for sending missionaries to the East when there was so much for Westerners to learn from the Asians. It went on to state that there was nothing unique that Christianity had to offer to the East. Following the Jerusalem Conference William Hocking had summed up a similar conclusion (Hocking 1932).

While most Asians themselves would deny such claims, it must be noted that by and large there have been questions about the role of "foreigners" peddling "foreign religion" in various countries. The term *missionary* itself had become synonymous with the Westerner, and as a result the missionary enterprise also smacked of a foreign intrusion. In Asia, with the resurgence of traditional religions, the threat of communalism, and politically motivated nationalism, the priority is to spell out our mission and to train people within the context of each situation. In fact, there is an urgent need to spell out Christianity itself within each of its contexts.

Rapidly intensifying religious fundamentalism as well as the continuing fanatical nationalism need to be reckoned with even more seriously. Political independence has played a major role in reviving traditional values, customs, and beliefs which had been stifled and suppressed under colonial culture. It is imperative that Christians also get involved in this struggle, as long as there is no conflict with personal commitment to Jesus Christ. This struggle must ultimately be seen as a struggle for our own identity within the nation as a whole rather than being viewed as agents of Western Christianity. Current realities must be taken seriously and the challenge accepted by both the church and theological/missiological education.

COLONIALISM AND EDUCATION

We have heard it said over and over again that the history of colonization and Christianization have been synonymous. Several aspects of colonial rule have come under attack, but relevant to this chapter is a brief reference to education. The powers that ruled most of the world between 1500 and 1900 were instrumental in introducing education wherever they were established. In India, Western education was welcomed by the national reformers. Western patterns were preferred to traditional methods. Some of the earliest missionary institutions were established by missionaries, mainly William Carey and Alexander Duff. Their approach was heavily Western, assuming that Indians needed to be "civilized," as Duff believed. Education was a powerful tool, easily exploited. The British claimed they wanted to train Indians for their civil and professional services. However, there are those who conclude that Western education was yet another form of cultural imperialism, which aimed to dominate the Third World. One Western scholar writes, "The primary purpose of schooling was *control*, not change. Britain did not want India to become an independent capitalist country. British manufacturers wanted the Indian trade—but not competition" (Cornoy 1974, 81).[1]

Such theses could well be one-sided, but nevertheless need to be looked into carefully before theological and missiological education follow a similar path. There easily could be a colonial mentality in institutions that believe their influence must be exerted worldwide. Already there is the phenomenon of some influential institutions extending their influence in Asia with little reference to the existing seminaries or to national or continental bodies. This kind of insensitivity can cause more harm than good to the mission of God in Asia, or anywhere else.

The questions that need to be asked, therefore, concern relevant patterns for training to produce effective men and women of God who will be concerned for God's mission in their own countries. Any assistance from outside will need to strengthen these indigenous efforts. No universal patterns or formula will be effective, no matter how much statistics testify to their success.

TRAINING MISSIOLOGISTS FOR ASIA

A quick look at opportunities for training missiologists in Asia will reveal that there is no dearth of institutions all over the continent. These are being conducted at varying levels and cater to a wide variety of needs. For instance, in India there is the South Asia Institute of Advanced Christian Studies in Bangalore, which offers post-graduate programs in missiology, some jointly with the Union Biblical Seminary in Pune. The Asian Center for Theological Studies and Mission and the Asian Missiological Graduate School in Taiwan similarly cater for higher degrees. These are at a seminary level.

However, there are many others that offer short-term courses, some largely patterned on Western models. Some train raw hands in three- to six-month courses to be sent out to flounder through the mission field. Efforts made by the World Evangelical Fellowship Missions Commission to evaluate mission training programs should concentrate on assisting such centers as top priority.

However, there are effective courses being conducted directly by churches and denominations or mission organizations themselves. In Indonesia, some very successful church-planting programs are linked directly with training institutions. In India, the Indian Evangelical Mission's Outreach Training Centre and the Friends Missionary Prayer Band training programs are noteworthy. The Alliance Biblical Seminary in the Philippines and the Kyoritsu Christian Institute in Japan offer missiological training at a master's level to students directly involved in mission.

A scanty survey such as this is hardly sufficient to give an idea of the enormous amount of activity related to training of missiologists in Asia. But it amply justifies the fact that no more institutions need to be set up to confound the confusion that already exists. A related question arises: Do Western institutions have any role to play in training Asians for mission? My argument so far could easily suggest that they do not! But, that is not true. Here are a few suggestions.

Offer Expertise as Partners

The West has any number of specialists qualified both in academics and experience. Such experts need to be sent to Asia and Africa. There are programs where faculty can participate in even three-week assignments to teach intensive modules. Library resources are a desperate need. The West could loan some of its abundant resources, could it not? A carefully worked out international library lending service would add immensely to the strengthening of existing programs.

Offer Programs in Partnership

There are some institutions that definitely have programs offering training in Asia. Where there is such demand, programs or even degrees could be offered in partnership with credible institutions. For instance, would it not be possible for Fuller or others to offer degrees to students with as little a residential requirement in the United States as possible? The casualties indicated by the number who stay behind in far more attractive missions is reason enough for steps to be taken for such ventures. Moreover, costs of residing in the West are becoming more and more prohibitive. There are credible institutions in Asia through which such partnerships could be worked out. ATA's Asia Graduate School of Theology, backed by the major evangelical institutions in Asia, could become a viable avenue for such a partnership.

Accept Mature Students for Post-graduate Studies

One of the ways in which the casualty rate referred to above could be curbed is accepting students only for specialized studies at the post-graduate level. This would ensure the admission of more mature candidates already committed to responsibilities to which they will want to return. Added to this, if residential requirements were trimmed to the minimum, we would be involved more responsibly in training Asians in the United States.

TRAINING FOR THE FUTURE

In conclusion, I would like to spell out some of my concerns for missiological training in the Asian context. The comments above have underlined some of these concerns as priorities both for institutions in Asia and for Western institutions committed to training Asians. However, I am primarily concerned for our own indigenous efforts and their effectiveness at a time when the prospects are promising but mistakes could be disastrous. Here are some needs.

Training within Each National Context

There is hardly any doubt that in our approach to training missiologists we need to be extremely sensitive to context. The political climate will compel us to address our training to issues that are larger than merely people in a social context. There is an intricately linked nexus of social, economic, and political realities that play a powerful part in the attitudes and the behavior of people all over the world. All these factors have already been adequately addressed, and I do not need to belabor the point.

They point, however, to an issue needing strong emphasis. Missionaries need to be trained within their particular settings. It is here that a true sensitivity to one's context can be developed. Students can definitely come out to the West for specialized training in skills that could only be imparted here. But this should be encouraged only after sufficient foundational training has been acquired in their own contexts.

Less Theory, More Praxis

The whole approach to "missiology" has become a very specialized pursuit with highly theoretical studies in sociology, anthropology, etc. These tend to make the student a good theoretician concerned for statistics rather than a practitioner with a heart for people. It is when these tools become the end rather than the means that missionary training itself degenerates into an ineffective academic pursuit of degrees devoid of the fruit intended to be produced.

Faithful to the Bible

The best way to keep mission training practical is to stress the centrality of the Word of God in the life and training of the missionary. The theoretical approaches referred to above could easily result in the Bible taking second place.

ATA's Seoul Declaration emphasized, "Being faithful to the Word of God necessarily implies being relevant to the context" (Ro 1987, 4). This should be understood in the sense that there ought to be an overriding concern for us to *demonstrate* the relevance of the Bible by *making* it relevant to our training.

The "Whole Mission"

Surprisingly, many institutions in Asia still carry on with the view that mission training must be restricted to training for evangelism and church growth. Undoubtedly, this is the carryover of the limited idea of mission that we evangelicals earlier entertained. Our understanding of God's mission has progressed into a much more holistic involvement, and with this our training must also evolve into all that will make the missionary an effective part of any community.

This holism must be reflected not merely in the curriculum but also in training. Our training has been restricted to imparting knowledge to the mind when education must be seen as so much more. Innovative approaches to training along with a concern for the total development of the missionary will be more effective than clever strategies that merely show skill in the manipulation of figures and the creation of exaggerated reports.

Holism refers to an interrelatedness. Missionary training must enrich the student in seeing the interrelatedness of all of life. When training has been holistic, the missionary's whole approach to the ministry will be truly holistic. The missionary then will become part of the community and culture in such a way that what he or she says will not only display a sensitivity for the context but will also be accepted by the hearers as part of that context.

Mission Training Must Become Part of Seminary Training

My primary concern is for a bridging of the gap between what we may refer to as seminary training and what we see as missionary training. In fact, unless and until mission training is seen as part of overall seminary training, the division between missions and theology will itself continue to grow to damaging proportions.

With the growing specialized approach to missionary training and the increasing threat of missionary training institutes producing "missionaries" through short-term crash courses, we face new problems. Why is it that a pastor or a Bible teacher needs to go through several years of study but "missionaries" are churned out in a matter of months? Is it that the mission field is any less demanding than the church or Bible school?

My plea is for missionary training to be fitted right within the setting of the seminary and for pastors, teachers, evangelists, missionaries, and any others to receive the same kind of foundational training. The specialized elements could then be imparted over and above this foundation. In passing, I am similarly concerned that seminaries don't appear to be concerned for equipping students committed to the teaching ministry to be real teachers with adequate teaching methodologies and pedagogical as well as "people" skills that will prepare them for this ministry. A successful student does not necessarily become a successful teacher!

Not Just Cross-cultural, Also Intra-cultural

Most mission training institutions in Asia continue to stress mission as a cross-cultural enterprise. This is mainly due to the limited stress on mission being a cross-cultural involvement, as it was in the previous missionary era. While Western institutions will undoubtedly continue to emphasize cross-cultural mission, the intra-cultural dimension to mission needs to be emphasized in order to make mission all that the Bible makes it out to be.

The success of the Western missionary movement, apart from the outworking of the power of God, could well be attributed to the needed stress on crossing cultures to take the message far and wide. But what we need today is a greater awareness of the localness of mission in the sense of every church and every country being part of the mission of God. This in itself could well have remedial effects on the whole explosive situation in some countries where the very existence of the church is being threatened.

When mission is seen as an intra-cultural concern, the church arises to its task in a much more responsible way. The church is not just "sending" missionaries; it is itself inescapably planted within God's world and mission. There are enough casualties among men and women who have "crossed" cultures before they have been effective in their own, and this calls for an evaluation of our understanding of the outworking of our mission within our contexts.

A biblical understanding of mission spelled out anywhere today must seek to rediscover from within the pages of the Bible the universality of mission in such a way that the localness of its manifestation is not ignored. It is only then that the inescapable responsibility laid on every committed Christian to be involved in God's mission will be recognized.

Stress Total Formation

With all the modern analytical approaches to the mission field, the impression is given that proper patterns and carefully worked out strategies will automatically ensure results. Some worldwide movements and their claims are frightening. While I am convinced that God will continue to use all forms of attempts to accomplish his purposes, the most successful channels will always be men and women in tune with God.

Shoki Coe, at the outset of an address given to Tainan Theological College, stated,

> I have a specific text from the Apostle Paul in mind which sums up
> for me as a life-long theological educator not only the question about

theological education but also its answers. Here is the text, in Galatians, chapter 4, verse 19: St. Paul says "My dear little children, with whom I am again in travail until Christ be formed in you" (Coe 1988, 546).

Coe speaks in terms of "theological formation," "ministerial formation" and "life formation." And by ministerial formation he is not speaking merely of skills and techniques for service. Beyond skills and beyond techniques we must be in travail until the ministry of Christ is formed in each one, the ministry of which he himself spoke when he said, "I came not to be ministered unto but to minister" and "I am in your midst as one who serves—*ho diakonon.*" We should be so caught up in that ministry that each one of us can say, "It is no longer I who work but Christ who is working in me" (Coe 1988, 547).

We Asians clamor after degrees, most times as an end in themselves. But degrees will not produce effective missiologists, just as our plans and strategies will not ensure effective mission. Missiological training must keep its emphases right, and it must start with concern for the formation of the total person of the men and women committed to God's mission all over the world.

Note

1. Cornoy refers to some influential Indian writings such as Ramakrishna Mukherjee, *The Rise and Fall of the East India Company* (1958); R. C. Dutt, *The Economic History of India* (1950); Syed Narullah and J. P. Naik, *A History of Education in India* (1951); and M. N. Srinivas, *Social Change in Modern India* (1963).

12

The Training of Missiologists for Western Culture

Wilbert R. Shenk

In 1990 and 1991 I conducted a reconnaissance of mission in several Western countries to determine 1) if there were programs whose object was the training of missionaries to the peoples of modern Western culture; and, if so, 2) what comprised the curriculum. I never advanced beyond the first question.[1]

Frequently my interlocutor would assure me that within that institution a course or unit in evangelism was offered. But when I would press the question whether they trained people for missionary service in the West in a manner analogous to that prescribed for cross-cultural ministry, the answer was consistently in the negative. It seemed evident that if such training was not being offered, a supporting missiology had not been a priority concern.[2] From the evidence at hand, mission training programs and missiology continue to be defined by the "foreign missions" paradigm of the past two centuries.

I would be the first to speak in defense of the modern mission movement. But poised as we are on the edge of the twenty-first century, not the nineteenth, that paradigm is untenable for two reasons. First, neither biblical nor theological justifications can be adduced for the dichotomy which

Missionary in Indonesia from 1955 to 1959, **Wilbert R. Shenk** was director and associate professor of the Mission Training Center, Associated Mennonite Biblical Seminaries, Elkhart, Indiana, from 1990 to 1995. He served as consultant to the Gospel and Our Culture Programme, Birmingham, United Kingdom, from 1990 to 1992. He was vice president of Overseas Ministries, Mennonite Board of Missions, from 1965 to 1990 and has been editor of *Mission Focus* since 1972. In 1995 he became professor of mission history and contemporary culture at the School of World Mission, Fuller Theological Seminary.

stands behind this historical pattern.[3] Second, the church in the West has long been marginalized and on the defensive in relation to the culture of modernity because it is confused about mission to its own culture.

The Protestant Reformation in the sixteenth century breached the wall of sacramentalism-sacerdotalism and reclaimed for the church the liberating reality of justification by faith (Shaull 1991, ch. 1). Through the modern mission movement the church rediscovered its responsibility to the regions beyond. I submit that nothing less than a reformation on that scale will deliver the church in the West from captivity to its mission-less identity relative to its own culture.

My argument may be summarized as follows: The church's recovery of mission is deeply indebted to the modern mission movement of the past two centuries, but that movement was understood to be directed beyond the culture of the sending church. Mission to modern culture will have to reckon with the history of Christendom in the West, for the ancient cathedral spires continue to cast long shadows. The training of missiologists and missionaries for this culture must be in full view of that history but based on a renewed understanding of the apostolic character of the church as embedded in the Great Commission.

MISSION CONSCIOUSNESS: WELLSPRING OF MISSION

The church always lives out of the consciousness of its fundamental identity. The self-consciousness inculcated by Christendom was non-missionary (cf. Neill 1968, 71-77). We may posit that there is a direct link between this historical fact and the present lassitude of the church in Western culture. What is required is a fundamental reorientation of the church in modern culture to mission to its culture. This means ecclesiology must be at the top of our agenda.

Some theologians began to take ecclesiology seriously in the twentieth century, but it was at most a partial recovery (Berkhof 1979, 344; Van Engen 1991, 35-45). The idea that mission is constitutive of the identity of the church has been acknowledged by some theologians (Brunner 1931, 108). Less clear is what impact this has had on the theological curriculum and particularly on the concept of pastoral formation. If we measure the effects of theological education by what happens in the congregation, then we would have to say that little has changed by way of self-understanding. For the majority of congregations ecclesial consciousness is shaped by the agenda of self-maintenance as a community of worship and pastoral services, a perspective pandered to and reinforced by the emphasis on "marketing the church."

The Great Commission

In our reading during the past two hundred years of the Great Commission—the charter of the mission movement—we have been captive to the hoary Christendom tradition. The result has been an emphasis on territory, that is, the territory of heathendom versus the territory of Christendom, on going as the imperative rather than making disciples, mission defined as what happens "out there." Apart from being faulty exegesis, this reading reinforced the traditional view that mission had no place within Christendom.[4] The church in the West must be set free of this deformed understanding of the Great Commission, a notion shaped by the powerful Christendom reality and reinforced by the way it was interpreted during the colonial era.[5] Indeed, the Great Commission judges this deformation and points the church to missionary faithfulness. The training of missiologists of Western culture ought to be one of the key points where this fundamental reorientation takes place.

Reading the Great Commission in its biblical context has the potential to radicalize the church's vision of itself in relation to the world, the environment in which the church exists.[6] The Great Commission is a powerful ecclesiological statement, for it is addressed to the disciple community, not autonomous individuals. It conjoins ecclesiality and apostolicity. The Great Commission thus sets the permanent agenda of the church: making men and women disciples of the reign of God wherever the church is until the end of time. Discipling men and women involves enabling them to embrace the fullness of God's reign in their lives. The training of missiologists of Western culture ought to be based on a biblical understanding rather than historical precedents and theological distortions. The task of the missiologist is to help the disciple community to live out the Great Commission.

We need to rethink the function of the Great Commission biblically and theologically. The modern mission movement did indeed reclaim and restore this portion of Scripture to the church's awareness, but this was done without a fundamental rethinking of the nature of the church as it had been redefined from the fourth century within the matrix of the *corpus Christianum*.[7] Instead, the Great Commission was understood primarily in terms of motivating individual Christians to go or to support missions (in the same way appeal has been made countless times to a text like Isaiah 6:14). This inspirational and motivational dimension has indeed been indispensable to the modern mission movement, but it does not begin to exhaust the meaning and function of the text in the canon (Michel 1983, 35; Bosch 1991, 56f.; Legrand 1986, 302ff.).

The Great Commission structures or institutionalizes the church's relation to the world. To put the matter in sociological terms, institutions mediate the relations between an individual or group and the world. These include such matters as conventions which regulate social relationships and extend to all realms where interaction is occurring (Bellah 1991, 287-93). The Great Commission institutionalizes mission as the raison d'être, the controlling norm, of the church. To be a disciple of Jesus Christ and a member of his body is to live a missionary existence in the world. There is no doubt that this was how the earliest Christians understood their calling.

Training for mission in the region of "Jerusalem, Judea, and Samaria" that comprises our Western culture will require that we approach this frontier in missionary rather than pastoral terms.[8] We must come to grips with a culture that is in crisis and transition. At the same time we should become more self-aware of the assumptions which have controlled mission studies and missionary action up to the present. We cannot appropriate wholesale the cross-cultural model(s) of mission as the basis for the training of missiologists and missionaries to Western culture, even though there is important overlap.

The Model of Mission

Luke's account of the Acts of the Apostles describes the working out of this missionary existence from the beginning. At his ascension Jesus gives the still disconsolate and disoriented disciples their defining purpose (1:8); forty days later at Pentecost the church is constituted on the basis of that mission (2:41-47); and the remainder of Acts records the unfolding of that mission.[9] In two descriptive passages Luke provides what we may regard as the normative twofold model by which the church works out its missionary existence in the world.[10]

Acts 11:19-26 depicts what may be called the organic mode. Under the impact of fierce persecution in the environs of Jerusalem (11:19), the disciple community scattered, with a contingent going to Antioch, at that time the third largest city in the Roman world. Far from being intimidated by the persecution they had endured, the disciples continued their evangelizing activity—the very thing that got them into trouble in Jerusalem—and were indiscriminate as to whether they witnessed to Jews or Gentiles. The result was that "the hand of the Lord was with them, and a great number that believed turned to the Lord" (11:21). Luke presents no honor roll of outstanding evangelists. Reading this account in the context of the varied encounters the young community was having, it is evident that the disciple communities challenged the regnant plausibility structure of their culture on the basis of the claims of the reign of God (cf. Acts 17:6f.). Witness to God's reign, present and coming, was at the heart of the disciple community's life. The church grew organically. This mode has been the main vehicle of the expansion of the church historically and is an authentic outworking of the Great Commission.

Acts 13:1-3 describes a contrasting but complementary mode. The Holy Spirit leads the church at Antioch to an innovation. Certain individuals are set apart for an itinerant ministry that will enable the faith to spread to key cities and regions throughout the Roman world. This creates the precedent for the sending mode and, by extension, cross-cultural mission, which has played a critical role in the expansion of the church precisely because it guards against the parochialism—the entropic syndrome—which is the slow death of the faith. The Great Commission continually holds this dimension before the church.

Luke's account of the development of the early church may be seen as proceeding from the thesis statement in Acts 1:8. The model for mission is the missionary church actualizing its true existence through the two modes (11:19-26 and 13:1-3). From Acts we understand that the Holy Spirit leads the church in working out its obedience to the Great Commission. There is no place here for dichotomous thinking—home versus foreign missions. The Antioch church is the base from which both expressions of missionary obedience emanate. The authenticity and vitality of the church in its local environment are validated by the fact that the Holy Spirit calls out of it select individuals, with confirming action by the church, as witnesses to the gospel among Jews and Gentiles farther away and where cultural and linguistic barriers may be greater. But those individuals also feel themselves accountable to the church through which they receive their commission.

Reign of God as Criterion

The phrase *Kingdom of God* occurs only eight times in Acts (1:3, 6; 8:12; 14:22; 19:8; 20:25; 28:23, 31). This does not mean it is of little importance. Luke reports that Jesus was occupied with expounding to his disciples the meaning of the reign of God (1:3). And the last thing we hear of Paul is that he is prisoner in Rome where he "welcomed all who came to him, preaching the kingdom of God and teaching about the Lord Jesus Christ" (28:31). The emerging Messianic movement is based on the reign of God as criterion. The Great Commission calls the church to keep the Kingdom as central focus. The model of mission identified by Luke guides the church in witnessing to, and living out, the reality of God's reign in the world. Whenever the church lives out of that dynamic, there will be a strong mission consciousness. Conversely, when awareness of the Kingdom of God is weak, there will be a correspondingly feeble sense of mission or reliance on missionary approaches motivated by sources other than the reign of God.

MISSION CONSCIOUSNESS: THE WORLD

I have emphasized the importance of the church renewed in mission consciousness in response to the reign of God. Discussion of mission and the role of training would be incomplete without a consideration of the world which is the object of this extraordinary undertaking. This means the world of Western culture. More particularly, it requires that we become self-critically aware of the "kingdom of the Western world" which is counterposed to the reign of God. All cultures are human constructs. None, including the culture of Christendom, approximates the Kingdom of God. Consequently, wherever "this gospel of the Kingdom" is proclaimed, deep tensions with the world appear.

We who are indigenous to this culture too easily accept the dubious assumption that we know it in its depths. But many Western Christians have considerable difficulty distinguishing between God and Caesar in their loyalties. That we must subject the fundamental presuppositions on which our culture rests to rigorous missiological scrutiny and criticism is a foreign notion. They accept that the individual needs to be saved from personal sin, but this concerns personal status before God rather than social relations and the wider culture.

To train missiologists concerned with Western culture will require adopting a countercultural stance in the sense that we must overcome the undertow of resistance, especially by other Christians, to raising these fundamental questions concerning our culture. Any profile of modern culture would need to include such basic themes as the view of the human being, the importance of technique, and the role of power and violence.

The Modern Self

The crowning achievement of the Enlightenment was the emergence of "the autonomous self." Traditional society had no place for such autonomy. The individual's place was assured by virtue of conformity to the role or station defined by society. The Enlightenment proclaimed freedom for the individual from such arbitrary constraints (Colin Brown 1968, 90-106). It was argued that the human being can achieve fullest potential only if set free. The corollary conviction was the potential to solve all problems through human reason. The ideals of freedom and rationality soon entered political discourse and were enshrined in both the United States Declaration of Independence (1776) with its "self-evident truths" and the French Statement of Human and Civil Rights (1789). "Life, liberty, and the pursuit of happiness" became hallmarks of modern culture.

Since the eighteenth century the West has idealized and pursued the autonomous individual. Positively, this has encouraged people the world over to resist and reject political tyranny and inhumane conditions. A new appreciation of the dignity of the human being and consequent "human rights" are fruits of this movement. But certain other facts are inescapable. Two hundred years after Immanuel Kant defined the Enlightenment as the "coming of age" of humankind through the throwing off of external constraints and vast socio-political changes that have greatly enlarged individual freedoms, we are a culture driven by the quest for self-esteem, a totally elusive goal.

The temptation to "be as God" in modern culture has taken the form of making the self the goal. Ironically, Enlightenment has fostered alienation (Gunton 1985). Modern culture's love affair with "expressive individualism" is "corrosive of both true love for the self as well as love of others. Conceiving of persons as unrelated and finally unrelatable social 'atoms' allows one to recognize self-seeking and self-expression, but not self love" (Pope 1991, 397). This has produced far-reaching consequences for inhabitants of modern culture.[11] We can do no more than note several issues. First, it may well be asked whether we now have a sound understanding of personhood at all. Second, our long preoccupation with the "self" has resulted in the atrophying of our sense of what makes for a viable society (Bellah 1985, 1991). And, third, we urgently need to reconsider the meaning of Christian conversion in light of the impact of modern culture on Christian thought and practice.[12]

Technique

Modernity is the culture of scientific technology, a point made with great force forty years ago by Jacques Ellul. This means not only that we have developed more and more machines to do our work, but it also points to the fact that technique has come to pervade our lives. The ways we communicate and relate to others are shaped by technique. The impact of the modern system on the human being has been the subject of sustained study by social scientists. A central conclusion is that technological culture results in anomie and alienation. The rise of the counterculture movement of the 1960s was, in part, a reaction to this feature of modern culture.

Modern technology is displayed at its most brilliant, perhaps, in modern appliances of warfare. The United States government force-fed the military-industrial complex over the past fifty years with huge infusions of capital to enable continual technological innovation in order to build the most sophisticated weapons. It is worth noting that the way a nation wages war reflects profoundly its culture. The technological sophistication of the Western military machine is a projection of modern culture. It is salutary to recall, therefore, the failure of the United States military campaign in Southeast Asia, in which technological warfare was defeated by a poor peasant army which was fighting for its political, not simply its military, life (Baritz 1985).

There are important questions begging to be considered in terms of Christian witness in modern culture. On the one hand, we must reflect on the extent to which the church has understood the nature of modern culture and its impact on the human—individually and collectively. On the other hand, the church can ill afford to rely uncritically on technique in its witness. If technique leads to alienation, and the church bases its witness on technique, what reason do we have to believe that "witness" will not result in alienation rather than reconciliation with God and fellow humans? To ask the question is not to presume to have an answer. But if we wish to engage modern culture with the gospel, it is a question we cannot evade.

Power and Violence

Power is central to human existence. Life can be lived only because of power—the means—to set goals and work them out. More than we recognize, we are preoccupied with power. The consciousness of power in modern culture has been heightened by the confidence that we possess the means, through scientific technology, actually to bend the forces of nature to our purposes, control our environment, conquer disease, and be masters of our destiny. These achievements have been real but remain relative and ambiguous at best. More sobering still is the extent to which modern culture is a culture of violence, power turned destructive.

In his Nobel Lecture on Literature, Aleksandr Solzhenitsyn characterized modern culture thus: "Violence, continually less restrained by the confines of a legality established over the course of many generations, strides brazenly and victoriously through the whole world . . . [which] is being flooded with the crude conviction that force can do everything and righteousness and innocence nothing" (1972, 25). This should not surprise us when we examine the myth of violence, which can be traced to primal creation myths but continues to give legitimacy to so much in modern culture, from children's cartoons to foreign policy (Wink 1992).[13]

In spite of the pretenses and illusions of mastery of life forces which are purveyed in our society, modern culture is incapable of delivering itself from the forces of death. Only the message of the reign of God, in which power is defined by the cross, holds out hope to modern culture. It is through metanoia, a turning toward God's new heaven and new earth, that we have the promise of salvation.

THE TASK OF MISSION TRAINING IN MODERN CULTURE

In such brief compass I can only present a rough sketch of work that needs to be done if we are to develop a responsive missiological approach to modern culture. The task is threefold. First, we must have a clear conceptual framework. This may not be quickly accomplished. One of the reactions I get is that of puzzlement: "What is it you think you are doing that we are not already doing through our well-honed evangelism training program?" This implies the interrogator is not thinking in self-critical terms regarding modern culture. At that point one can appeal to the cross-cultural example and indicate some of the learnings that might apply in modern culture. Second, we must seek to reorient the whole of theological education so that theology is informed by mission and mission is strengthened by theology (Kirk 1990). The proper anchor of all theology is the *missio Dei*, and that needs to be worked out in modern culture. Third, training programs are needed that equip people for mission to modern or postmodern culture. Specialized training will be required to meet needs that the usual theological training program cannot offer. Above all, we need to take the long view and lay a solid foundation for what promises to be as demanding a mission frontier as the church has yet faced (Newbigin 1983).

Notes

1. A few mission departments now designate as "domestic missiology" what formerly was evangelism and church planting.

2. Training for evangelism and church development is not at issue; this is essential to the theological curriculum. However, evangelism has generally been conceived to be an activity conducted within the cultural assumptions that govern the life of the church in a particular society or as an extension from the West to other parts of the world. (It is beyond our purpose here to pursue this theme. See such standard works as Autrey [1959], Sweazey [1953], Templeton [1957], and Scharpff [1964]. Orr [1973, 1974, 1975] continually emphasized the linkages between revival movements as they spread round the world.) By contrast, mission takes as its point of departure the Kingdom of God with an agenda for challenging the reigning plausibility structure. The sine qua non of mission is formation of communities of the reign of God which live by its plausibility structure. To be sure, certain evangelists—one thinks especially of E. Stanley Jones—have made the Kingdom their central theme, and some missionaries have never gone beyond replicating the socio-religious culture from which they originated. But I hold the basic typology to be valid. Orlando Costas was a vigorous exponent of evangelism based on the reign of God (1989), a conviction intensified by his multicultural background and experience as an evangelist-theologian. Abraham (1989) devotes a chapter to "Evangelism and Modernity." One of the most innovative attempts to rethink evangelization of modern culture by drawing on experience and insights from the non-Western world is Alfred C. Krass (1982).

3. See Robert Wilder's (1936) history of the Student Volunteer Movement where he quotes *in extenso* reflections of Nettie Dunn Clark, who wrote: "One reason for the great impression created by the Movement was that it made a clear, definite appeal for one cause only, and . . . a great mistake would be made if [it] were now to be made to cover both foreign and home missions, or the enlistment of young people for anything other than definite missionary work" (48). This is a purely pragmatic and tactical argument, but one which has long held sway. Samuel Zwemer (1943) based his interpretation of the Great Commission firmly on this dichotomy.

4. The genius of Christian faith is that it is not tied to a particular geography— holy city, holy land, holy language. Whence comes then the recurrent quest for total conquest of a particular country or people for Christ? Another such campaign to capture America for Christ is being reported in the news media as I am writing. Both Old and New Testaments are based on the conviction that the faith is preserved and transmitted through God's faithful remnant, a theme sadly ignored in contemporary theology. Crusades and conquests comport well with Christendom but not with the biblical tradition.

5. It is not our purpose here to evaluate the modern mission movement. Recent studies that examine the reflex action of the modern mission movement on the Western church include Walls (1988) and Shenk (1984, 1992).

6. Mortimer Arias (1992) demonstrates the importance of the Great Commission for full realization of the mission of the church. I wish to press the point

further: this can be achieved only by reconceptualizing the nature of the church in terms of the Great Commission.

7. A viewpoint that was important in the missiology of Gustav Warneck, from whose pioneering work (forged during the High Imperial period) much of modern missiology descends.

8. Sacerdotalism is irreconcilable with the prophetic office. While one must maintain the distinction between the apostolic and prophetic vocations, neither fits easily with the role of the priest, whose role is to modulate conflict between church and society.

9. Modern commentators help to perpetuate a "Christendom" reading of the Acts account by the way they divide up the material and insert editorial heads and commentary that draw on modern practice and assumptions. Taking a random selection of commentaries, one notes that the majority introduce the term *mission* only at 9:32, with the start of the Gentile mission, or at 13:1-3 (Barclay 1953, Bruce 1954, Marshall 1980); in contrast, Munck 1967 entitles 1:6-14, "The Mission to the World and the Ascension."

10. This does not mean all cultures are of the same moral caliber. Cultures may be deeply influenced by values that move them closer to the Kingdom of God ideal. But at their best, such cultures remain marred by human fallibility.

11. Space limits disallow pursuing this important point. Rollo May (1969) has argued that the rise of psychiatric science is a direct response to modern culture but criticizes psychotherapy for being itself a part of the problem. See further, Rieff 1966, Menninger 1973.

12. One might start with an examination of the classical evangelical expression of conversion: "I have decided to accept Jesus as my personal Savior." Revivalist culture arose concurrently with the Enlightenment and in its preoccupation with the self bears its imprint. This reduces conversion to an instrumental understanding of religion, hardly to be reconciled with the call of Jesus to discipleship.

13. One area of modern culture where the role of violence is rising steadily is sports. On the one hand, sports dominate our culture to an extent frequently not acknowledged. On the other, it is becoming clear that exploitation and violence are essential to the sports system. The relation of sport and religion deserves close scrutiny as reported by Frank Deford, the sports journalist (1976) and more recently Shirl J. Hoffman (1992).

MISSIOLOGICAL CONTEXTS

A Variety of Books and Circles

13

The Role of the Behavioral Sciences
in Missiological Education

Darrell Whiteman

A few months ago while living in Hong Kong on sabbatical I had an opportunity to meet with some Chinese Christians over lunch. As we sat down to the table, spread with white linen and delicious food, a Chinese man who had just returned to Hong Kong from the United States picked up his chop sticks, turned to me, and asked what I was doing in Hong Kong. I explained that I was an anthropologist and missiologist doing research on various issues of gospel and culture relevant to East Asia. With derision in his voice he sneered, "Oh, there are no issues here. We just need to give people the gospel and make sure they are grounded in solid theology and correct doctrine. We don't need all that culture stuff." He then asked me if we had any famous professors at my seminary. Concluding that we had none, he ended the conversation.

That incident in Hong Kong frequently came to mind as I prepared this chapter. In microcosm it captures a popular attitude among far too many people involved in cross-cultural ministry today. Naively assuming the gospel can be communicated and understood in a hermetically sealed environment, free of cultural contamination, they proceed with good intentions and abundant enthusiasm to win the world for Christ. They believe that as long as they get the content of the gospel down, they don't need to worry about understanding the context in which it is communicated.

Darrell Whiteman teaches missiological anthropology in the E. Stanley Jones School of World Mission and Evangelism at Asbury Theological Seminary, Wilmore, Kentucky. He has had research and mission experience in Central Africa and in Melanesia, where he served on the staff of the ecumenical Melanesian Institute researching issues of Christianity and culture. He is the editor of *Missiology*.

Despite such naiveté on the part of some missionaries, there is nevertheless a growing awareness of just how important it is to understand the social and cultural antecedents in every missiological encounter. But lest one quickly conclude that this awareness is a modern, present-day phenomenon, it should be noted that there have always been missionaries, from the beginning to the present, who have been culturally sensitive and aware of the important issues surrounding the interaction between the gospel and culture.

Today in missiological education we acknowledge the value of insights from the behavioral sciences in the conversation between text and context, between gospel and culture, between the universal and the particular. I believe my interrogator in Hong Kong was wrong; there are many critical issues surrounding the gospel and culture in Asia as well as elsewhere. And until they are dealt with, non-Christians will continue, for example, to perceive Christianity as a foreign, Western enterprise. The relevance of the transforming power of Christ in their own life will escape them, and they will dismiss Christianity as something alien to them or of little consequence for their society.

My task in this chapter is to discuss the role of the behavioral sciences in missiological education. Such a wide-ranging topic cannot be encompassed adequately within these few pages, so I must necessarily be selective and brief. I will begin by quickly noting who needs missiological education and for what ministry contexts is it necessary today and in the twenty-first century. I will then note three conceptual areas where the behavioral sciences can contribute to missiological education. Following that, I will discuss why some missionaries have resisted some of these insights, note the various disciplines that are contributing, and finally discuss the limitations of the behavioral sciences in missiology.

MISSIOLOGICAL EDUCATION FOR WHOM?

The most obvious group of people who need missiological training are Western missionaries, whose numbers have greatly increased in the postcolonial era. Despite the cry of "missionary, go home" a generation ago, the numbers keep growing even though the roles Western missionaries fill are changing. For example, at the turn of the century John R. Mott published *The Evangelization of the World in This Generation* (1900) and concluded there were fifteen thousand missionaries from Europe, Great Britain, and North America. The 1989 edition of the *Mission Handbook* noted there were 75,167 career and short-term Protestant missionaries from North America. The numbers are increasing, and these people need missiological education even though for many their theology tells them they don't need it and their pocketbook indicates they can't afford it.

Another category of missionaries that is growing in even greater numbers is the mushrooming phenomenon of what is often called third-world missionaries (see Pate 1989). These are people engaged in ministry across cultural boundaries both within their own nation and beyond its borders. Providing adequate missiological training and education for these people is even more problematic, but not less necessary.

A third group in need of missiological education is perhaps not so obvious. I am referring to North American pastors ministering to other North Americans who are embedded in a secularized and materialistic culture shot through with values and assumptions that are often antithetical to the Kingdom of God. As Lesslie Newbigin (1986, 1989) and others (Hunter 1992; *Missiology* 1991) have helped us see, it will require a cross-cultural missionary encounter to evangelize people in this setting.

A fourth not so obvious group of people for whom missiological understanding is necessary includes non-Western workers ministering among their own people within their own culture, such as Chinese pastors with Chinese congregations, or Melanesian pastors working with their own Melanesian people. Lacking a missiological perspective that enables them to contextualize their ministry, they often struggle in a cross-cultural encounter because they have been trained in a Western mode. The form of the gospel that was introduced in the past and handed down to the present is one that does not readily relate to the needs of people within their own culture. How often I have heard international students admit that it was not until they studied missiology in the United States that they gained an appreciation for how the gospel could relate to the needs of people within their own culture.

These four categories of people in need of missiological education present us with quite a challenge; unfortunately, I believe most missiological education is reaching only a fraction of these people, and as Eugene Nida said to me recently, "There are more Christian missionaries today than at any period of history, yet they are more poorly prepared than ever before."

If these are the men and women in need of missiological education, then what are the different contexts for which they must be prepared, today and in the twenty-first century?

MISSIOLOGICAL EDUCATION FOR WHAT CONTEXTS?

As we consider the role of the behavioral sciences in missiological education, we become aware of a number of different contexts for which people need training. Anthropology as one of the contributing behavioral sciences will be most helpful in some contexts, but other behavioral sciences, such as sociology and political science, may contribute more salient insights for different contexts of cross-cultural ministry.

The first one worth noting, because of its growing importance, is the urban context. As we enter the twenty-first century the world will be more urban than rural, and it is projected that by the year 2025 two-thirds of the world's population will live in cities. The dominant context for ministry will be an urban one, and the size and complexity of these cities of tomorrow are almost beyond belief and comprehension today. Cross-cultural witnesses will need to understand the structure and dynamics of cities and the impact they have on the people living within them if their ministry is going to be effective.

A second context for which people will need missiological education is an impoverished context. Poverty, hunger, and oppression characterize so many places today, and all the available evidence indicates that this desperate scenario will only multiply in the twenty-first century. The gap between the rich and poor will widen, and the poor will increase in number. Recognizing this pattern in Brazil, one of our students said to me on a recent visit to his country, "Unless our Methodist church becomes a church of the poor, it will die." He was recognizing that unless his middle-class Brazilian church and his denomination begin an incarnational ministry among the poor, their future as a church will be bleak. There are many insights from the behavioral sciences that can help us understand how to minister to people in situations of poverty and oppression.

Pluralism characterizes many contexts of ministry today. Despite what appears to be the growing influence of Western commercial culture around the globe, the social and cultural worlds in which people live are becoming more diverse and pluralistic, not less so. Social and cultural fragmentation is happening everywhere from Eastern Europe to Ethiopia to Canada. Cross-cultural witnesses must face this reality, recognizing that in the marketplace of religious ideas Christianity will face stiff competition. This reality underscores the need for an incarnate gospel to be communicated and lived out in creative and innovative ways if people without Christ are ever really to hear and understand the gospel and if they are to see it demonstrated in transformed human lives and renewed structures of society that reflect Kingdom values.

A fourth context is the closed context. And of course one must ask immediately, "closed to whom?" When we use the term *closed*, it normally refers to countries that are closed to formal outside Christian influence, especially to Western missionaries. Therefore, to minister in these places will require creative imagination and the development of informal ways that use low-profile methods. It is important that the search for effective ways of ministry in closed contexts be informed by missiological education.

I have suggested four categories of people in mission and four primary contexts in which they minister. We now want to explore how the behavioral sciences can help in preparing them missiologically.

CONTRIBUTIONS TO MISSIOLOGY
FROM THE BEHAVIORAL SCIENCES

I want to limit my discussion to three areas in which I believe insights from the behavioral sciences can make a contribution to missiology:

1. They can help us understand ourselves and the social and cultural antecedents that shape who we are, influence our denominational and/ or institutional loyalty, and affect our theological reflection.
2. They can enable us to understand the social, cultural, economic, and political contexts in which we are engaged in cross-cultural ministry.
3. They can contribute to our ability to distinguish between the gospel and culture, between the universal and the particular.

Understanding Ourselves

For missionaries, the greatest value of studying anthropology, for example, is not in what we learn about exotic cultures that are different from our own, but rather, in what we discover about ourselves. It is critically important for cross-cultural witnesses to distinguish our universal human nature, which we share in common with all humanity, from that part of our being that is shaped and molded by culture. Human beings everywhere reflect the fact that we are created in God's image, but we also show plenty of evidence that we are sinful. As our humanness is shaped and molded by culture, it influences how we understand God, how we define what is moral and good, and how we deal with evil. Although Christians from every culture are required to confess "Jesus is Lord" and to give him their allegiance, the myriad social and cultural contexts in which they live will influence the diverse ways in which Christians function as a body, relate to one another, and interact with non-Christians in their society.

When we do not understand, for example, how much our culture influences our theology, we are easily seduced into believing that we are communicating a gospel free of cultural bias, when, in fact, we may be blind to our own cultural and denominational ethnocentrism. We will confuse what is cultural with what we *think* is biblical. Many American Christians have this problem when they fail to distinguish the American dream from the Kingdom of God, believing, at least unconsciously, that they are one and the same. But of course they are not. In fact, one could argue that in many ways they are antithetical. Americans, however, are not the only ones with a corner on ethnocentrism. For example, as more and more Korean Christians go as missionaries to other cultures, they are discovering the challenge of separating the gospel they wish to proclaim from their peculiar Korean understanding and practice of Christian faith. They are discovering the difficulties of cross-cultural living and experiencing the damaging effects of culture shock. Many are returning to Korea discouraged and bewildered, wondering what went wrong with their ministry.

Understanding ourselves as persons both created in God's image and shaped by our culture is a necessary prerequisite to effective cross-cultural ministry. The behavioral sciences can contribute enormous insights to this aspect of our missiological formation and training.

Understanding the Context of Our Ministry

Another important area of missiological education that can be informed by insights from the behavioral sciences is the need to understand the context in which we are ministering cross-culturally. Many people in ministry recognize the necessity of exegeting the text but are woefully unaware of the need to exegete the context as well. In seminaries and Bible schools students are taught exegetical tools to discover the deeper meanings in Scripture. But where are they taught the skill of how to listen to the culture in which they propose to minister? The consequence is that we get ministers and missionaries who are full of biblical and theological content but are clueless about how to communicate that content in ways that make sense to people in contexts different from their own.

A few months before Bishop Stephen Neill died in 1984, Gerald Anderson interviewed him on the topic "How My Mind Has Changed about Mission." Anderson said, "If you had it to do all over again, what would you do differently?" Without a moment's hesitation, Neill said, "I would listen a lot better." Cultural anthropology, semiotics, and communication theory can teach us to listen more effectively.

In the past we have drawn on insights from cultural anthropology and linguistics to overcome cultural barriers in communicating the gospel to non-Christians. Today, however, we are realizing more than ever that we need to listen to a culture, not simply so we can get our ideas across to someone else more easily, but so we can better understand where God's prevenient grace has been at work among a people.

Understanding the Difference between Gospel and Culture

Once we understand the power of culture on ourselves, and once we begin to learn how to understand the context in which we are ministering, then we are ready for the third and perhaps most difficult area of missiological reflection and training; namely, distinguishing the difference between the gospel and culture, between the universal and the particular, between one, eternal, and apostolic faith and the multifarious ways people come to understand and practice Christian faith. It is important, for example, to be able to at least analytically distinguish *Christian* meanings from the forms used to express those meanings. This is sometimes hard to do in practice, but without this kind of sensitivity to the difference between form and meaning we will not know the difference between syncretism and indigenous expressions of Christianity.

The gospel is, of course, good news, but it is also offensive news for sinful people in need of God's redeeming love. How often in cross-cultural ministry have we offended people for the wrong reason? We have offended them culturally, so they turn off or turn away and never hear the offense of the gospel. Like the Judaizers in Acts 15, we feel compelled to erect cultural barriers for potential converts to overcome before we are willing to extend to them the right hand of Christian fellowship.

The issues of gospel and culture are critical, and until they are satisfactorily dealt with, non-Christians outside the West will continue to perceive Christianity as a foreign, Western religion. For example, in China before 1949 a common phrase went like this: "One more Christian, one less Chinese." In 1949 there were only 1.5 million Chinese Christians, equally divided between Protestants and Catholics. There were also about ten thousand missionaries. In the intervening forty years between 1949 and 1989, the church in China grew by leaps and bounds to fifty million or more. I suspect that, among other factors, this growth can be traced to the fact that the Chinese discovered they could be Christian and Chinese. Christians across the face of the earth are yearning to discover how to be Chinese, Japanese, Melanesian, Aymara, etc.—and also Christian. Insights from the behavioral sciences can help us in that quest by equipping Christians to use aspects of their culture to understand the gospel, organize themselves as a fellowship group, and express their worship and praise to God in ways that are culturally appropriate for their time and place.

RESISTANCE TO THE BEHAVIORAL SCIENCES IN MISSION

I believe that understanding in the above three areas will enable cross-cultural witnesses to be more faithful to the gospel, to be less imperialistic and ethnocentric in the way they share the gospel across cultures, and to understand more profoundly that the gospel can become incarnate in every cultural context.

If the behavioral sciences can contribute as much to missiology as I have argued, it is therefore unfortunate that a tendency has emerged among some missionaries and mission leaders to argue that the behavioral and social sciences have had too dominant a role and have even been guilty of hijacking the mission agenda. For example, Lois McKinney in her 1992 presidential address to the American Society of Missiology noted that when future historians evaluate missions in the late twentieth century, they will likely conclude that "we allowed the theological base for missions to erode and replaced it with a shallow reliance on the social sciences" (McKinney 1992, 18).

I empathize with this concern, but I think it is misplaced. I agree wholeheartedly, however, with the argument that ideological agendas reinforced by the cultural compulsives of the moment can easily misguide our understanding and practice of mission. There is abundant evidence that this is taking place today. However, I do not believe this has occurred because the behavioral sciences have gained the upper hand in missiology. My observations and interviews with missionaries and national pastors has led me to conclude *not* that they have had too much exposure to behavioral science insights, but, rather, they have not had enough, or what they have had has often been inadequate. I don't believe that an over-reliance on insights from the behavioral sciences has caused missionaries to water down their understanding and practice of the gospel. To the contrary, it is their lack of this kind of understanding that has caused them often to confuse the eternal gospel with their own culturally bound interpretation of the gospel.

Of course, there is always the bent to remove the stinging offense of the gospel, to move, for example, from a Christocentric missiology to a theocentric one that will be less offensive, some believe, to brothers and sisters influenced by other religious traditions. To blame the impact of the behavioral sciences for this theological erosion I believe is misplaced and misdirected.

In recent research in East Asia I interviewed and observed well over a hundred American missionaries and national pastors. I discovered that many of them were confusing Western culture and tradition with the gospel, and, of course, this was creating a major stumbling block for non-Christians coming to faith. The American dream and the Kingdom of God appeared to be synonymous in the minds of many. Over and over again I saw the tenacious grip of ethnocentrism and witnessed the enervating drag of missionary lifestyles that were inappropriate for the context. These unconscious behavior patterns erected formidable barriers for non-Christians coming to faith. Ethnocentrism and inappropriate lifestyles weaken our ministry, but frequently we do not realize it. They create unnecessary cultural offenses which prevent non-Christians from experiencing the offense of the gospel. We must learn to discern the difference and to avoid unnecessary cultural offenses, thus enabling the gospel to have a sharper and more penetrating focus, to become more prophetic and less parochial, to be more scintillating and less syncretistic.

I believe the lack of behavioral insights in the preparation of missionaries from any culture sets them up to be even more victimized by the ravages of culture shock. The high attrition rate—50 percent of missionaries quitting after one term—is due in no small measure to the culture shock that hits them broadside; they do not know what is happening to them.

BEHAVIORAL SCIENCE DISCIPLINES AND MISSIOLOGY

Cultural anthropology has been the dominant behavioral science discipline that has contributed to missiological education, reflection, and research. The field of missionary anthropology has emerged as a hybrid between cultural anthropology and applied anthropology with insights, concepts, and theories applied to the mission task. I prefer the term *missiological anthropology* over *missionary anthropology*, because I believe it is more appropriate for the post-colonial age of mission. This shift is also reflected in the subtitle of Luzbetak's 1988 masterpiece, *The Church and Cultures: New Perspectives on Missiological Anthropology*.

Missionaries have made significant ethnological and ethnographic contributions as far back as Las Casas (1474-1566) and Sahagun (1499-1590) in Mexico in the sixteenth century, and Lafitau (1681-1746) in Canada and Ziegenbalg (1682-1719) in India in the seventeenth century. Yet the intentional application of anthropology for missionary training and missiological reflection began in this century, going back at least as far as Fr. Wilhelm Schmidt in the Roman Catholic tradition and to Edwin Smith (1924) and Henri Philippe Junod (1935), who both argued that anthropological study was essential for missionary education.

Then there is Eugene Nida's classic *Custom and Cultures* (1954), which will soon be back in print in a revised edition. Louis Luzbetak's *The Church and Cultures* (1963) was applied anthropology in the context of mission at its best. Although Alan Tippett never wrote a major text on missiological anthropology, he nevertheless demonstrated the value of an anthropological perspective in missiology in his dozen books and scores of articles and therefore can be rightly considered the dean of modern missiological anthropology (see Whiteman 1992). Marvin Mayers's *Christianity Confronts Culture* (1974) was helpful in that it discussed the dynamics of cross-cultural communication of the gospel in light of anthropology, social psychology, sociology, and educational theory, and was illustrated with many memorable and helpful case studies. Then in 1979 Charles Kraft broke open the field with his book *Christianity in Culture*, which I regard as the most important landmark in the discussion of Christianity and culture to appear in the past twenty-five years. Kraft combined cultural anthropology with communication theory to demonstrate over and over again the value of behavioral science insights for missiology.

Kraft was in the stream of others like Eugene Nida, William Reyburn, Bill Smalley, Charles Taber, and Jacob Loewen, that creative and insightful group of Bible translators who, through their publications in *Practical Anthropology*, developed some important missiological insights by relating anthropological linguistics to Bible translation.

The focus of much of this anthropological writing and research in missiology has been on language and culture learning, understanding other world views, and discovering the cultural factors that shape indigenous churches and theology. Anthropological insights have been used mostly to illuminate our understanding of the complexities in communicating the gospel across cultures. Much of the writing and research in missiological anthropology has been from the perspective of third-world tribal groups in rural villages. This heavy "jungle perspective," done by "bush anthropologists," as some would characterize missionary anthropology, is sometimes viewed with suspicion or even antipathy by those who are ministering in modern, urban contexts such as one finds in many parts of Asia or Eastern Europe today.

Other areas within anthropology, such as social organization, structuralism, symbolic anthropology, political and urban anthropology, are fields that can bring significant insights to the missiological tasks in the modern world. For example, insights from the field of social organization and social structure can help us better understand the natural social groupings in a society and how the fellowship of believers should select its leaders and organize itself so that Christians can relate more naturally and winsomely to non-Christians in their culture. The concept of social networks as applied to urban environments will help us know how the church in the rural area will differ from the church in the city. Psychological anthropology and studies in cognition can help us better understand what happens or does not happen in conversion across cultures. The field of cross-cultural pastoral counseling is a growing one that will continue to draw insights from anthropology and contribute to missiological education.

There are many areas of anthropology that have never yet been applied to missiology. For example, Victor Turner's model of structure, *communitas*, and liminality promises to help us learn more about the process of crossing cultural boundaries and forming strong bonds of friendship and identification with local people, a burden that most missionaries struggle with. Sherwood Lingenfelter (1992) has recently applied Mary Douglas's powerful model of gird and group to understanding how Christianity can transform culture. There is no doubt that missiological anthropology will continue to be a vital field and contribute to missiology. Helpful books like Paul Hiebert's *Anthropological Insights for Missionaries* (1985a) will continue to encourage and assist missionaries in their task. But it is interesting to note that despite the developments in this field, we still do not have a missiological anthropology textbook that explores the wide field of anthropological theory from a missiological perspective.

Anthropologists used to hold out the promise that if we could first comprehend the microcosm of the village, we could then better understand the complex macrocosm of the nation-state and the interconnectedness of global economics, geo-political strategies, and international levels of social organization. But to do so we will need to move beyond the field of anthropology, which can still tend to be myopic and get bogged down or obsessed with detailed data such as kinship charts while ignoring the impact of global conflicts that create millions of refugees who are permanently severed from their relatives.

I believe the time is long overdue to draw on a wider range of behavioral sciences for missiological education. As helpful as cultural anthropology has been, it nevertheless has its blind spots. For example, the discipline has been slow to face up to how much it was influenced in its formative years by its ties to colonialism. Anthropology has had a built-in conservative bias against culture change, and missionaries have often been the brunt of anthropologists' jokes and derision. They have frequently claimed that in their zeal to save people's souls, missionaries have often destroyed their cultures. This functionalist view, which sees change as primarily disruptive, has sometimes made it difficult to recognize that cultures everywhere are in need of transformation and redemption.

Drawing on insights from a wide range of behavioral sciences will encourage us to avoid the spurious distinction between evangelism on one hand and issues of social responsibility on the other. We will better understand the connection between global economics and the personal, social ethics informed by Kingdom values. Bridging the gulf between the global and personal is important. We need the macro-level understanding of society for such things as church-planting strategies in urban settings, understanding structural evil and inequalities, the impact of global economics, and the consequences of political instability and change in nation-states, but we also must use the micro-level concepts and perspectives to understand how individuals are influenced by the gospel as a result of their encounter with Christ.

I want to conclude by drawing attention to a cross-cultural encounter in the New Testament that I believe is paradigmatic and instructive for cross-cultural ministry and missiology today. I am referring to Peter's experience with Cornelius as recorded in Acts 10. The important principle that emerges out of this event is that God has no favorites and that God is willing to come into the lives and cultures of all people. It is interesting to note, however, that before Peter was able to lead Cornelius and his family to faith in Christ, he had first to undergo a cultural conversion that was as significant as his spiritual conversion. In other words, in the same way that God led Peter to confess to Jesus, "You are the Christ," he also brought him by way of a vision to confess, "I now realize that it is true that God treats everyone on the same basis. Whoever fears him and does what is right is acceptable to him, no matter what race he belongs to" (Acts 10:34).

Peter needed to be converted cross-culturally in order for the Lord to use him in effective cross-cultural outreach to the Gentile world. Today we are like Peter; we need to have the blinders of our own culture removed so that we understand one another better. Missiological training informed by insights from the behavioral sciences can help us make that important cross-cultural conversion so that we can be God's people in the world, sharing God's love and grace across all social, cultural, and economic barriers.

14

World Urbanization and Missiological Education

Roger S. Greenway

From this point on in history, educating people for mission will require careful attention to worldwide urbanization and its many implications. Roughly half the world's population now lives in cities, and these cities are multiracial, multiethnic, multilingual, and multireligious. They are the change-makers and power centers of the globe. It is no exaggeration to say that as cities go, so goes the entire world politically, economically, socially, and religiously (Barrett 1986, 17).

Cities are challenging places. They are filled with social, religious, and cultural differences. Opposing world views, value systems, and lifestyles stand toe to toe in urban centers. From these same places emanate most of the negative and disintegrating forces that wage havoc on the natural environment and on human life in general. Cities are like battlefields where issues of many kinds are raised and fought over daily.

When we speak of cities and the nature of the urban environment, we largely describe what in contemporary parlance is called *globalization*. Globalization is predominantly, though not exclusively, an urban phenomenon. In describing the theological challenge of globalization, especially the dimension he calls "deprovincialization," Max L. Stackhouse observes that in today's urban world, deprovincialization occurs less often through immersion in classical texts than through immediate exposure to everyday occurrences.

Islam is on TV, Hinduism is in the religious section at the bookshop, Confucians are members of the PTA. The daughter of a church mem-

Roger S. Greenway is professor of World Missiology at Calvin Seminary, in Grand Rapids, Michigan. He served as a missionary in Sri Lanka and Mexico. He has published numerous books and articles on Christian mission, with a special focus on cities.

ber marries a Buddhist, a relative converts to Judaism, a lay leader in the church becomes fascinated with the Samurai sense of duty to a corporate unit—which threatens both his sense of the superiority of the Protestant ethic and his job—while his wife signs up for yoga class and his son becomes a Marxist (1989).

If this is the city, the conclusion is inescapable that fierce spiritual battles rage here and the chief struggle is for the allegiance of human hearts and lives. Therefore, the sharpest, best-trained minds Christian churches produce should be focused on the city and the urban masses. Here lies Christianity's chief challenge. In view of this, missiological education in the decades ahead must expect heavy demands as answers are required to complex urban questions not raised before. Somewhere down the future's unmarked streets there will emerge an urban form of Christianity that may be more like that of the early church than of the century now behind us.

ACCEPTING URBAN REALITIES

Generally speaking, Protestant schools and churches have not found it easy to accept the realities of urban life or to shape their ministries and training to meet those realities. Yesterday's world, molded largely by village values and small-town viewpoints, is still the world many institutions cling to, though it is a world that will not return. Mission training schools need to recognize that there will be serious consequences if they delay urbanizing the education they offer.

It may be helpful to those who harbor misgivings about cities, and hence are reluctant to consider urbanizing the curriculum, to reflect on the fact that urbanization as a present fact of life for most of the human family is a reality under the providential control of God. In Acts 17:26-27 the apostle Paul observes that God's rule in the affairs of human beings includes their location:

From one man he made every nation of men, that they should inhabit the whole earth; and he determined the times set for them *and the exact places where they should live.* God did this so men would seek him and perhaps reach out for him and find him (NIV).

Viewed in the light of these verses, city growth is not something to be perceived as entirely the work of the devil, but as part of God's providential plan in history. God's redemptive purpose behind urban growth is that "men would seek him and reach out for him." By means of these enormous gatherings of people, God provides the church with one of history's greatest opportunities for evangelization. Pressed together in metropolises, the races, tribes, and diverse people groups are geographically more accessible than ever before. In some cases the processes of change that new urbanites pass through make them more receptive to the gospel.

If this is the case, then world urbanization should be viewed in an eschatological as well as a missionary framework. God in our time is moving climactically through a variety of social, political, and economic factors to bring earth's peoples into closer contact with one another, into greater interaction and interdependence, and into earshot of the gospel. By this movement God carries forward his redemptive purpose in history. A sign of our time is the city. Through worldwide migration to the city God may be setting the stage for Christian mission's greatest and perhaps final hour.

This adds a note of urgency to the task of urbanizing missiological education. To ignore the plight of the urban masses or refuse to grapple with the trials and complexities of city life is worse than merely a strategic error. It is unconscionable disobedience to God, whose providence directs the movements of people and creates special moments of missionary opportunity. The world of the twenty-first century will be urban, and so will Christian mission.

URBANIZING THE MISSIOLOGICAL CURRICULUM

Missiological education takes place through a variety of institutions and programs, both formal and informal. Bible colleges have traditionally prepared a large share of North American missionaries, and most mission agencies require that candidates take a number of mission courses on a college or seminary level as part of their pre-field training. Likewise, almost all seminary curriculums include one or more mission courses that all students seeking a degree are required to take.

In the past the focus of most of these courses was on mission work among tribal and village people. This was an appropriate focus up until the latter part of the twentieth century. But now that a majority of the world's unreached and unevangelized people lives in cities, it is reasonable to expect that colleges and seminaries will be redesigning their basic mission courses so as to address an urbanizing world in an accurate and balanced way. This will involve changes in the content of the courses and the textbooks that are used. Likewise, it can be expected that schools offering mission majors and advanced degrees in missiology will seek ways to expand their curriculums by introducing new courses designed to educate students for urban ministry.

For schools engaged in urbanizing their curriculum, the following areas of study should be built into the program:

1. A biblical theology of cities and of urban ministry.
2. Urban anthropology, sociology and demographics.
3. Contextualization of the gospel in the urban environment.
4. History of urban mission and ministry.
5. Nature of urban poverty and of community development.

6. Urban political structures, social systems, and justice issues.
7. Research techniques for urban evangelism and church growth.
8. Effective methods and models of urban ministry.
9. Physical and mental health in urban environments.
10. Accessing urban resources, particularly through networking.
11. Advocacy systems and empowerment in the city.
12. Leadership development in diverse urban contexts.
13. Communication methods in the city.
14. Non-Christian religions, cults and alternative world views.
15. Principles of education and methodologies appropriate to various cultures and social contexts.
16. Urban spirituality and spiritual warfare in the city.

Each of these areas of study contributes something vital to the equipping of people whose special task it is to communicate the gospel to urban dwellers, build churches, combat injustice, relieve suffering, and by every possible means extend Christ's Kingdom in the cities of the world. No school can offer everything an urban worker may need. Yet it is hard to imagine anyone engaged in urban work for very long who does not recognize the importance of acquiring knowledge and skill in all or most of these sixteen areas (Rooy 1992).[1]

In view of the breadth of subjects needing to be covered, an ideal arrangement is for Christian colleges, seminaries, and specialized mission training schools to link their resources. By working together, a more complete and balanced curriculum can be developed. The personal involvement of faculty and students in hands-on ministry is a matter of high priority (Greenway 1985).

GOING BEYOND CURRICULUM REVISION—
NEW URBAN MODELS

A degree of fear exists among urban ministry specialists that, well intentioned as they may be, traditional seminaries and Christian colleges are so ill equipped to understand the urban world or to train ministers and missionaries adequately for that world, that no amount of curriculum revision can accomplish what is needed. To compound the problem further, the Western school model is widely exported to other parts of the world. In places such as Asia and Latin America, where city growth is especially rapid, old Western models of mission education prove to be inadequate (Bosch 1991, 490).

The simple fact is that in cities throughout the world new and different forms of church and mission are emerging. With each new form fresh demands appear for more appropriate ways of training leaders. But it is almost impossible to imagine that traditional educational institutions can make the changes, and make them quickly enough, to equip the wide range of leaders needed by emerging urban ministries. Traditional schools understandably are contextualized to meet the dominant needs of their own realities. But in varying degrees this makes them ineffective in meeting the needs of other groups.

Urbanization, which by its very nature involves a variety of peoples, races, and cultures, with constant changes of many kinds, calls for bold new thrusts in leadership and missionary training. Awareness is growing in a number of places that merely tinkering with existing models will not be enough. Already some of the bolder institutions are helping establish new types of schools in the city and creating new training processes where the needs of minority leaders and ethnic groups can better be met. This is just the beginning of what will probably be one of the educational frontiers of the twenty-first century.

Mexico City

More than twenty years ago in Mexico City I wrestled with the inappropriateness of much of the education given by the Presbyterian seminary where I was teaching. I pleaded with the school's administration to alter the pattern of sending seminarians every weekend to minister in distant villages and instead to expose them to evangelism and church development in Mexico City. I pointed out that from the very towns and rural communities where our students spent their internships droves of people were moving to the city, leaving empty houses and dwindling churches behind. But rural-oriented leaders were in control of the church and seminary, and they were not minded to change the school's direction.

My response at that time was to link up with a Mexican pastor, a former priest who understood city people very well, and to start a new school dedicated to educating urban evangelists. The school was located on one of the city's main arteries (Avenida Tlalpan). Its purpose was to break the rural orientation of leadership training and raise up a new breed of pastors and evangelists who understood the city and were urban-oriented in their education for ministry. Besides other things, students learned how to plant and nurture city churches, especially churches located in the new and growing segments of the population. Dozens of young churches resulted. But after a few years an administration took over that failed to sustain the vision, and the school was eventually handed back to the traditional seminary from which it had come (see Greenway 1973, 213-23).

Philadelphia

In Philadelphia I have worked with the Center for Urban Theological Studies (CUTS), which I consider one of the best North American models of contextualized urban education. The curriculum is designed to enhance the educational levels of inner-city Christian leaders.

Everything is designed to fit inner-city people, from the location of the buildings to the schedule of classes. At CUTS, students can follow a non-degree program or earn a college diploma from Geneva College and degrees in theology from Westminster Seminary. Classes meet in the evening from six o'clock to ten, and on Saturdays. Every enrollee must already be engaged in a significant church ministry.

It is exciting to teach at CUTS. The students are mostly African American and Hispanic. For students from traditional schools in the suburbs who choose to add an urban component to their education by taking some classes at CUTS, it is invariably an eye-opening experience. CUTS does not call itself a mission agency, nor does it openly pursue new church development. Yet a mission atmosphere prevails in the school and every year one or more new churches are started by CUTS students. This results from the fact that when God's people are empowered through appropriate and effective education, the Spirit is sure to light the fires that cause new ministries to emerge (Greenway and Monsma 1989, 89, 254).

What are the best ways to equip Christian leaders to serve in urban ministry? That is the key question, and finding the answers requires combined efforts by professional educators, theologians, and missiologists. Models of effective urban leadership training need to be found and analyzed with a sensitivity to their theological content, cultural relevance, and educational value (Elliston and Kauffman 1993). In pursuit of the answers, the wise words of Johannes Verkuyl should be remembered, for they were never more true than in the city:

> Theological education is an ongoing process. If it is carried on properly, it is not done in immovable cathedrals, but in portable tents which can be transported by the pilgrim people of God. Theological educators must not become too firmly attached to one place or way of doing things, but must be ever ready to change and adapt as the situation may require (Verkuyl 1978, 307).

URBANIZING THE ENTIRE CURRICULUM BY INFUSION

The enormous demands of mission in an urban world, with its critical needs and endless issues, are too great to be left in the hands of a minority of faculty members, namely, the missiologists. This leads me to a suggestion, perhaps unrealistic, that the entire curriculum of ministry training institutions, beginning with core courses, be urbanized in such a way that urban concerns are infused throughout the curriculum. This means that urban issues will be addressed from the standpoint of many disciplines: biblical, historical, theological, and pastoral, and by all members of the faculty. In addition, urban field-work positions will be expanded, with supervised internships in city churches and urban-mission programs. Men and women coming from non-urban backgrounds will be strongly encouraged to live in interracial communities and involve themselves as much as they can in urban life (Dayton and Nelson 1974, 116).

The goal of the infusion approach is the urbanization of the entire educational process in such a way that the themes, questions, and inter-cultural issues that stand out in urban mission and global ministry will be approached from a variety of standpoints. Each of the educational disciplines will contribute from its own perspective, and the missiological task will not be restricted to a handful of mission specialists. It seems to me that this approach, if it can be implemented, offers the most to persons being educated for mission in an urban world.

The integration approach is fully in keeping with the viewpoint that "just as the church ceases to be church if it is not missionary, theology ceases to be theology if it loses its missionary character" (Bosch 1991, 494). The business of theology is the mission of God and his church. Hence, we are just as much in need of a missiological agenda for theology as for a theological agenda for mission (ibid.; Soltau 1988, 6-10). Urbanization offers something special to that agenda, and schools would be wise to address it with vigor.[2]

If for some reason schools choose to pay scant attention to urban realities they will not meet the needs of the twenty-first century. The call of the hour is for cities, seminaries and schools specializing in training missionaries to be brought together for total engagement, lest the world's most strategic positions be lost to the church and the gospel. As the late Donald McGavran reminded us often: "We must speak to today, not to yesterday" (McGavran 1988, 99).

Notes

1. Rooy describes a tranformational role for theological education in the city and outlines four major areas that theological education should address to advance Christ's Kingdom in the city.

2. David Bosch pointed out that aberrations result when non-missionary churches get involved in the missionary enterprise: "The church imparts its own ghetto mentality to the people it 'reaches.' It engages, not in mission, but in propaganda, reproducing carbon copies of itself." The same can be said of seminaries and other training schools that define as their "mission" the propagation of a particular narrow viewpoint, frequently in opposition to another church or school, which they make the central criterion of truth. It is unlikely that such institutions will show much interest in the broad challenges of an urban agenda (Bosch 1984, xxx).

15

The Training of Missiologists
to Develop Local Bible Translators

Philip C. Stine

In a recent management exercise I had to write down various things in the course of my life which had given me a sense of accomplishment and pleasure. One of the things I listed was success I had in several translation projects in West Africa in shifting the work from missionary to native-speaker African Christian translators. I recalled in particular one project that I would like to describe briefly.

When I first had contact with this New Testament project in 1975, I found that two or three missionaries were doing most of the drafting, and then checking it with African reviewers to find out if it was grammatically and lexically correct. The missionaries were fluent in the language and had been responsible for developing other materials such as grammars and lexicons. They had all attended one or two SIL courses, as well as a UBS translation workshop. They all had good biblical studies and worked directly from the Greek. They had made every attempt to produce a translation in common language which followed principles of what was then called dynamic equivalence, and consequently their work wasn't bad. I didn't find very many exegetical problems at all, but what I did sense was that it wasn't natural. There were too many expressions which sounded to me like circumlocutions, too many things that one did not normally find in that language family, for example, passive constructions or the frequent use of direct speech.

Over the next few months I began to introduce issues of discourse to the translators, and they decided that a native speaker must completely redo the

---

Philip C. Stine is director for Translation, Production and Distribution Services for the United Bible Societies. Prior to that he served as a translation consultant in West Africa and also as the global coordinator for the translation program of the United Bible Societies.

work. I well remember a conversation I had two years later on the day of the launching of that New Testament. I was speaking with some of the older pastors who had been reviewers, and I asked them what they thought of the work. One of the men said to me, "You know, with that first translation, we would say 'You can say that.' But now with this translation, this is the way we would say it."

When I began thinking about this chapter, my first thought was of that project. What would I have liked those missionaries to learn before they undertook translation? If their children were to attend Fuller, what would I like Dan Shaw to teach them? Given the title of this chapter, you will see that Fuller must already be thinking along lines similar to ours in the United Bible Societies, for the topic is not training missionaries to become Bible translators, but rather to train missiologists to develop local Bible translators. What, then, are some of the areas that must be covered in training missiologists to develop local Bible translators?

THE ROLE OF THE NATIVE SPEAKERS

This is by no means self-evident. Among the most important requirements for Bible translators are that they have an understanding of the biblical texts, some theological or exegetical training, and skill in using commentaries and lexicons. In most areas of mission work in the last two hundred years it has been the missionary who has had those skills.[1] Consequently, it was they who spent time learning the language and then, with native speakers as helpers, drafted the translation. But usually the expatriate missionaries did not realize that the native speakers bring certain kinds of knowledge and linguistic skill to the translation which the missionaries, as non-native speakers, could neither easily acquire nor fully comprehend. The translations the expatriates produced were therefore usually lacking in several key ways, and readers understood the message either with difficulty or not at all. Let me describe here briefly two of these areas: discourse structure and metaphor. They are, I believe, essential elements in the curriculum we are considering.

Discourse Structure

In the mid-1970s a church in what is now Burkina Faso contacted me, asking if I could help them with a New Testament as soon as possible. Up to that time they had been using the Bambara Bible, and one of the initiation rites for new believers was to learn how to read and understand it. But now the church was growing rapidly and the pastors were not able to train everyone in the Bambara Bible. They therefore realized that they had to have Scriptures in their own language.

They told me this might not be too difficult, since fifteen or twenty years earlier a missionary had prepared a translation of the New Testament. It had never been published; basically it had been rejected by the people. The leaders now wanted to find out if it could be corrected and used. The manuscripts had been lying around in a box for many years. Everything was there except a couple of the shorter epistles—I think the epistles of John—which had been eaten by termites.

I spent some time looking at the discourse patterns in that language, and when I then looked at the old manuscript of the New Testament, it became very clear why it had been rejected. No one had been able to understand it! Here are some of the reasons.

First, sequence of tense. The way we keep track of the time line in a narrative varies a great deal from language to language. In most Indo-European languages we narrate a story with a sequence of past tense forms, but in most African languages to do this would not only be unnatural, but would in fact distort what was happening. Unfortunately, this translation had followed the Greek tenses.

Second, the translation had a problem with passive voice. The passive is a form which languages use in different ways. Many African languages have no passive at all. When the Bible translator is faced with divine passives used to avoid the name of God, there is a real problem. Take, for example, in Mark 2, where Jesus says to the paralytic, "Your sins are forgiven," and the African translator has to supply an agent. Should Jesus say, "I forgive your sins" or "God forgives your sins"? The problem is theological, and the translator in this language had created a passive even though the language itself does not have one.

Third, many African languages do not commonly use direct speech. If the preacher reads on Sunday morning, "Jesus said, 'I am the way, the truth and the life,'" the audience can only understand that it is the preacher who is the way, the truth, and the life. But the literal phrase has become so precious to us that this translator, as many others have done, decided to use direct speech even though it was not understood.

This translation of the New Testament had been tested sentence by sentence and had seemed perfectly grammatical and acceptable. But when one read an entire paragraph, it was almost gibberish.

Metaphor

Figurative language in general is highly culture-sensitive, and every translator has to learn how certain figures of speech from the Bible will be understood. Anyone who has learned another language can offer examples of misunderstanding, often hilarious. One example I have often used in teaching is "heap coals on the head." More frequently than not even pastors would explain this as a form of torturing one's enemies. "Children of the bride chamber" was another one. Interpretations offered ranged from the children conceived on the wedding night to the children born before the wedding.

But I really am interested in something more profound. Recent work in cognitive linguistics has demonstrated the degree to which metaphor becomes a principal means of organizing and processing information in a language. A number of recent scholars (see, for example, Sweetser 1990 or Lakoff 1987) have shown that there is an enormous range of metaphors across a large number of languages which are motivated by correlations between external experience and the internal emotional and cognitive states. These connections are unidirectional; the bodily experience is the source of vocabulary for the psychological state. Thus we use the physical concept of hearing to mean comprehend or obey, and seeing becomes connected with knowledge. But as cultures experience their bodies differently, they have different starting points for the metaphors they use to organize and process information.

The point I am making is that we have had until recently very little understanding of the different ways by which we categorize entities in different cultures, or why. But what the non-native speaker may spend years struggling to understand fully, the native speaker will do naturally and instantaneously. My conclusion is, therefore, that few non-native speakers will ever be able to deal with such issues effectively in translation. Hence the need for native-speaker translators, and the goal of missiological education becomes to sensitize the missiologists to train the native speakers, not to do the work themselves.

TRAINING THE MISSIOLOGIST

Somehow we have to help the missiologists not only become sensitive themselves to the issues I've described, but also show them how to help the native speakers become aware of these issues. Lecturing on theory isn't the way to teach this. I think I can tell if someone really understands a concept when he or she can describe (adequately) something about his or her own language to speakers of another language. Inevitably that isn't done with much theoretical talk; it will always be with practical examples. So one thing we can do to prepare our missiologists for training translators is to supply them with example after example. The second part of this training is to make them use these and their own examples to teach speakers of a second language.

Incidentally, one thing that the School of World Mission might consider is developing a database of metaphors and idioms in languages from around the world. This would be a great resource for cross-cultural training.

THE ROLE OF THE MISSIOLOGIST

A third major topic on the curriculum relates to the role the missiologist should play in translation work.

Training

As already discussed, the missiologist will frequently be the one to train the translators and reviewers. That training covers several areas. The first area is in theory and practice. In the United Bible Societies and the Wycliffe Bible Translators/Summer Institute of Linguistics the principal emphasis in recent years has been what is now called functional equivalence translation, whereby the goal is to produce a translation which is the closest natural equivalent of the original texts.

A missiologist can only teach others if he or she has had some experience using the theory, and so I would suggest any curriculum be highly practical in nature. The prospective missiologist should not only practice translating in his or her own language, but also practice helping someone in another language, thereby developing a better feel for translation issues. Traditionally, translation teaching started off with basic things such as who we are translating for, how to analyze certain grammatical problems, how to do a componential analysis of lexical items, and how to transfer these units of meaning across to the second language. Now it seems more important to begin with discourse so as to sensitize the native speakers from the very beginning to the overall text, and only after they have developed an understanding of discourse issues bring them down to the lexical and grammatical categories. Helping the missiologist understand why this should be the starting point would be a crucial goal of the training.

It is also important to learn how to teach. I am not referring here to any great training in educational theory. A pattern I have followed in workshops is to lecture in the morning and have the translators practice in the afternoon. My experience over the years was that the translators all went home with much of what they learned in the afternoons, and very little from the mornings. So give the translators material to work on, and use those materials to draw out the principles of translation. Let's teach the missiologist to avoid a lot of lecturing.

Of course, teaching and learning styles are not the same in all cultures. What I learned in the African context may not work everywhere. Therefore we should set up several models of teaching. Using different models as examples, we could at least sensitize the missiologists to the fact that they will find different learning and teaching styles in different cultures, and they will have to learn how to adapt the material to those styles.

The missiologist must also know whom to teach. Every church, every individual, has an idea of what it thinks a translation should be like. If the translation produced does not come close to that, it will be rejected. More than one excellent translation sits on Bible Society warehouse shelves because not enough people in the church learned what the aim of the project was or what to expect from a good translation. Therefore, several different groups will need training: expatriate missionaries, native-speaker translators, reviewers, and others. Church leaders and people of influence must also be given training. Here the training will have somewhat different goals, including the purpose and goals of the project and the translation principles being followed.

More important, training should be given on how to use the new translation. There are many languages where the church uses a Bible in another language or a very old translation in its own language. The result is sermons that explain this "foreign translation" to the people. These pastors may not have experience in preaching on a biblical text which the people in the church can understand clearly. So it is not out of place, in fact it is extremely important, for a great deal of effort to go into training Sunday School teachers, catechists, and pastors in how to prepare their sermons and Bible studies in a new way. Such training can also help the church leaders understand the issues behind key theological terms in the translation such as "prophet," "Holy Spirit," "Kingdom of Heaven," "Son of Man," "righteousness." Church leaders will better appreciate the new translation, they may be more willing to accept it, and they will be able to teach the Scriptures more effectively to their people.

Another important area is related to exegesis. An important feature in the curriculum should be an introduction to translator's handbooks and helps from the United Bible Societies, exegetical guides and other helps from the Summer Institute of Linguistics, commentaries that are particularly useful to translators (most aren't), and Bible dictionaries and lexicons which are most useful to translators. The United Bible Societies and the Summer Institute of Linguistics have prepared annotated lists of the various helps that are available, because many of the materials used by theologians or pastors are not what the translator needs. Our training must include an introduction to these materials and the ways to use them. Missiologists will need to advise translators about these materials.

Management

A major area of neglect, and the reason that most translation projects take too long, are too expensive, are inefficient, or are not done well, has to do with the management of the project. Most people who undertake translation recognize the need for training in theory and practice and for certain biblical skills, but few recognize the importance of knowing how to help translators organize a project properly. Recently, the United Bible Societies conducted research regarding about 120 New Testaments and Bibles published in recent years. Among other things we discovered the following:

1. The best translations had been produced by two or three, no more, translators with at least some secondary education, working full time;
2. There had often been in place an incentive bonus scheme;

3. The churches had been financially involved in the project to some degree, providing either a portion of salaries or facilities as a minimum;
4. Often a plan had been worked out with the churches in advance of the project as to how long it would take and what it would cost. As a result, all parties involved—the churches, the translators, the reviewers, and the Bible Societies—were held accountable for their areas of responsibility;
5. There was provision for a secretary or keyboarder;
6. There was one person who served as the coordinator of the project.

One of the most successful projects I ever saw involved a language in South America where the missionary coordinator happened to be a psychologist. Before the actual work of translation began, he had the team come together for a week to go through a number of team building exercises so that questions about decision-making were resolved long before the work was begun. As a result, potentially explosive disagreements between the translators were handled easily and to the satisfaction of all. I have since been wondering if maybe we shouldn't hire him to help us in a lot of other projects. My point is that basic management training is crucial for even a small translation project, and the missiologist should be given training in how to help a team organize and run a program.

Of course, the hard part about this advice is that management techniques will vary considerably in different cultures. So the training in basic management must be carried out in conjunction with training in cross-cultural sensitivity. One cannot impose a system on a team if it is not going to be accepted in that culture. So although the missiologist should receive training in managing a project, ideally what he or she needs to learn is how to work with a church in the target culture and how to organize and manage the work in a way that works in that culture.

As an example, consider the organization of review committees. What we like to do in the Western world is send draft materials to the reviewers and ask them to send back written comments. The reviewers rarely meet, but when they do, it is simply to discuss places where the translators find themselves in disagreement with the reviewers or where there are crucial issues that should be brought up. But the committee would rarely go through a passage verse by verse, as a committee.

In many traditional societies in Africa and Asia this matter of individual contribution is culturally inappropriate. Instead, decisions are reached by consensus, within a group, and there is a strong need for the reviewers to sit together and go through the materials verse by verse. When this actually takes place, the reviewing can take five or six times as long as translating. So other patterns must be sought. For example, one pattern that worked successfully in some contexts in West Africa was to assign different churches or towns different books of the Bible to review. There would be a committee in that town of four or five or ten people who would sit together and go through a book verse by verse. But they only had one or two books assigned to them, and everyone knew that town was responsible for reviewing those books. While they were working on Amos, another town worked on Hosea, so that the project was not unduly delayed and the cultural needs were met.

Computer Literacy

One final topic that must be in the curriculum is the use of computers. At some stage most translations today get keyboarded. It is our experience that the earlier that takes place, the better. Not only is word processing faster than retyping a manuscript several times, but there are a number of programs that help us with the checking process and quality control of the translation. Production is enormously sped up and made cheaper by the preparation on the computer of camera-ready copy or by use of computer typesetting.

So all translators should be computer literate. This skill should not be the sole property of the expatriate, but must become an integral part of every translation program. All the translators should have some familiarity with the process, and the missiologist must be prepared to train people to use computers. If for no other reason, this training means the work is not held up when the missionary goes on furlough.

This leads to one final point. If the missiologist does his or her job properly in training local native speakers to serve as translators, then leaving the field temporarily or permanently will not hurt the translation program. The translators will use the tools they have acquired and keep on drafting; the secretary will key in and print out drafts; the reviewers will feed in their comments in an appropriate manner; the coordinator will see that the project keeps moving; and the church will prepare to use the translation in evangelism and worship.

Note

1. Given the limits of time, I will not discuss one point which I consider completely self-evident; namely, that the first step in training Bible translators is to extend biblical studies to a level which is not easily available in most parts of the world now. Our greatest lack is translators who have good Greek and Hebrew and the kind of biblical study which will help them in translation work. If we want them to be truly independent and not to have to rely on the expatriate, then we must do everything possible to increase the amount and level of biblical studies offered in seminaries and Bible schools in developing countries of the world.

16

Training Missiologists for Jewish Contexts

Stuart Dauermann

Stimulated by David Bosch's masterful *Transforming Mission: Paradigm Shifts in Theology of Mission*, my effort in this chapter proceeds from a concern for an ongoing revitalization of mission among my people, undergirded by my hearty agreement with Bosch's contention that new and rediscovered paradigms often engender new perspectives, new questions, and new answers that can bring new vitality to the entire mission enterprise.

Bosch reminds us that one way in which such revitalization often occurs is through the revival of almost forgotten paradigms (1991, 186).[1] But are there forgotten or neglected paradigms in Scripture which reflect especially upon the interrelatedness of Jew and Gentile in the *missio dei*? Are these paradigms of sufficient weight that no missiologist can afford to neglect them? I submit that the answer to both questions is a resounding yes.

THE EPHESIANS PARADIGM

In considering the nature of the people of God, the Western church has traditionally leaned heavily upon the model presented in the Epistle to the Ephesians, which stipulates that throughout the ages God has called forth a people for his own name from among Jew and Gentile, thus forming "one new person"—the church.

This "one new person" carries quite a bit of theological freight, filled with heavy missiological implications. First, this Ephesians paradigm is an us/them model: Once we were one of them, but now we are separated out from among them and part of the one new man, the new community which

---

Stuart Dauermann is rabbi of Ahavat Zion Messianic Synagogue in Beverly Hills, California, and director of the Messianic Teaching Our Rituals and Heritage (TORAH) Institute. Dauermann served as a missionary and music director with Jews for Jesus from 1973 to 1989.

God is building. Once we were them, now we are us; once we were there, now we are here. In brief, this model is grounded in a before and after presupposition.

The Ephesians paradigm is certainly a valid one. However, we can only rightly understand it if we recognize that Paul is here addressing the issue of how Gentile believers ought to view themselves with respect to the God of Israel and people of Israel. The model affirms the interrelatedness of Jew and Gentile, as well as their unity and equality in the body of Christ. We need to bear in mind that this model was never intended to explain the interrelationship of Jewish believers in Jesus and the wider Jewish community. In fact, using it in this manner damages and hinders effective intracultural mission among the Jews for reasons that will become more apparent as we contrast this paradigm with another Pauline model.

THE ROMANS PARADIGM

In Romans 11, Paul indicates that for as long as there has been a Jewish people, there have only been two kinds of Jews: the remnant and the rest. True, the limitations of human perception make it impossible to discern unerringly the boundary between these two categories. We are always in danger of mistaking wheat for tares and vice versa. Yet, despite the difficulty in iron-clad identification, the fact remains that all Jews fall into one of these two categories, the remnant and the rest. According to this model, we Jews after the flesh who have embraced God's grace in Christ are part of that remnant within the Jewish people.

Such a paradigm produces an entirely different understanding of mission by Jews to Jews than does the Ephesians model. More important, it creates and nurtures an entirely different feeling and posture in the intracultural context. Under this paradigm, the evangelization of Jewish people by Jewish people is an "us/us" affair. Indeed, even when I as a Jew who believes in Jesus get together with other Jews hostile to my faith, it is still "us" getting together with "us."

I am suggesting that, due to the influence of the Ephesians paradigm and other factors, mission to the Jews is too often conceptualized and conducted as an "us/them" affair. While this attitude is almost universal in Gentile mission to the Jews, it is also generally apparent in intracultural mission by Jews to Jews. Such a flawed approach is predicated on a theologically erroneous and overstated discontinuity between the Jewish community as a whole and those Jews who have embraced Christ.

Sadly, the pronouncements and theologies of the Western church have often institutionalized, sanctioned, and sacralized this woeful fracturing of the Jewish community. Historical reflection reveals that this presupposition of discontinuity has served to discolor and distort the entire Jewish mission enterprise, resulting in an unnecessarily adversarial posture, gap-oriented strategies, undue defensiveness, and a siege mentality. Surely, mission among the Jews will be profoundly transformed as we explore the implications of an "us/us" paradigm involving the remnant "us" pursuing mission grounded in a deeply felt, warmly lived, and jealously guarded commonality with our brethren after the flesh.[2]

THE RELAY RACE PARADIGM

Having discussed the interrelationship of the remnant and the rest within Israel, Paul goes on to discuss the relationship of the Jews as a people and the Gentiles seen as an aggregate entity. This teaching may be expressed in terms of the relay race paradigm.

In this model, the saving purposes of God may be compared to a relay race in which Jew and Gentile are partners on the same team. The baton being passed from runner to runner is God's salvific purpose for humankind. From Abram's time until some time in the book of Acts the "baton" was in the hands of the Jewish people. Then the baton was passed to the Gentiles, who took their place in the spotlight, "running" their lap in accordance with God's purposes. Meanwhile, being an active part of the same team, the Jewish team members should be vigilantly following and cheering the progress of their Gentile partners. Finally, Paul mentions that a time is coming when the "baton" will again be passed to the Jews, and then the race will be concluded as both Jew and Gentile rejoice together.[3]

What is the value of this paradigm? Much in every way! First, it reminds us that the church among the Gentiles is not the sum total of what God is doing in the world—God's continuing purpose embraces the Jews as well. We Jews and Gentiles are on the same team. Second, when the baton is passed from one team member to another in a relay race, it is not always easy to tell who is controlling the baton—the boundary between one runner's possession of the baton and the transfer of control to the next runner is indistinct. Similarly, a clear demarcation between the era of Gentile preeminence and that of Jewish preeminence in the *missio dei* is not possible. The baton may have already been passed to the Jewish people; the baton may still be entirely in the hands of the Gentiles; the two runners may be running together, each with a hand on the baton, with the transfer having not yet been completed. We cannot know for sure exactly at what stage we are in this process.

What we *can* know is that neither the Jewish nor the Gentile partner can afford to take his or her eyes off the other. Just as in sports, when one's teammate is rounding the corner, preparing to pass the baton, one must start running, ever keeping an eye upon the other team member so that the baton may be passed at the right time in the right way, without being dropped or disrupting the running of the race. So under this paradigm Jewish and Gentile participants in God's salvific purpose must be diligent students of each other's progress; there must be no passivity, no self-congratulation, what Paul calls being "wise in your own conceits." There must be no disassociation from one another as if we weren't on the same team. The race is still going on, and Jew and Gentile must remain alert and active partners, laboring together toward that culmination when Jew and Gentile will celebrate together at God's finish line. Truly, as Bosch reminds us, the destinies of Jew and Gentile are irrevocably coordinate (1992, 164).

The relay race paradigm has transformational implications for the entire missiological agenda, not only in the area of attitude but also in that of action. If it is only when the fullness of the Gentiles has come that God will again turn his spotlight upon the Jews, then even if solely on the basis of self-interest, we Jews who have embraced Christ must vigorously support and energetically promote mission advance among the Gentiles. The culmination of God's purposes for *us* awaits the culmination of God's purposes among *them*.

Similarly, since it is only when all Israel is saved that God's saving purpose will reach its culmination, Gentile partners in faith all ought to be zealots about Jewish mission. They ought to bend every effort to aggressively pursue and actively assist mission among the Jews, remembering that their full acceptance will mean nothing less than life from the dead (Rom 11:15).[4]

The conclusion of the matter is this: Despite our small numbers (currently about 12.8 million), it is impossible to overstate the crucial importance of the salvation of the Jews in God's great scheme of things. On the basis of Paul's clear teaching in Romans, as conveyed in these paradigms, no missiological agenda can rightly be called comprehensive until it gives due weight to the interrelatedness of the destinies of Jew and Gentile and to the mutuality and reciprocity of our responsibility to serve the mission cause with all the strength that God supplies.[5]

THE PARADIGM OF THE ANTIOCH-JERUSALEM CONTINUUM

From the macro-context of God's broad salvific plan, we turn to the micro-context of mission to the Jews in particular. Does Scripture provide any models or paradigms to help us more effectively pursue the missiological task in this context? Again, the answer is yes.

Despite their far-reaching distribution and diversity, it seems clear that there was no New Testament church without at least some Jewish representation. In accordance with the particular details of its locale and founding, each of these churches differed from the others in demographic constitution and cultural norms. For example, Timothy, who lived as an uncircumcised Jew in Lystra (Acts 16:1), could scarcely have done so freely in the Jerusalem congregation, which James characterized as being composed of "many thousands of Jews . . . and all of them . . . zealous for the law" (Acts 21:20).

The point of all this is that today, as then, there is a wide spectrum of cultural preferences and habits represented within the general population and within the Jewish community itself. We may see this graphically portrayed if we posit a continuum with Antioch at one end and Jerusalem at the other. On such a continuum Antioch would represent the most demographically and culturally "Gentile" of contexts, and Jerusalem the most demographically and culturally "Jewish" of contexts. This being the case, it is obvious that mission and congregational life among Jews in Antioch would differ substantially from that among Jews in Jerusalem.

Now, as in the first century, Jewish people may be found distributed across the continuum from Antioch to Jerusalem. Accordingly, mission effort among them must reflect their cultural, geographic, generational, and demographic diversity. We who do mission among the Jews and who train others to do so must commit ourselves to the discipline of seeing Jewish people as they truly are in their various changing contexts. We must see them as they are, not as they were or as we imagine them to be, and we must gauge our approaches and programs accordingly.

We must continually pursue the quantitative aspects of mission research, being diligent students of the vast wealth of demographic and sociological data already extant about the Jewish people. And where no satisfactory research has been done, we must mobilize to do it. This will also mean that we must get out there and meet Jewish people, getting close enough to take their demographic pulse.

The Antioch-Jerusalem continuum reminds us that some Jews will always feel more comfortable in an Episcopal, Baptist, Presbyterian, Charismatic, or other church than in a Messianic Synagogue. Therefore, we must prepare such churches to reach and enfold them, as Jews for Jesus and other mission organizations have sought to do. This also means that approaches which address the needs of Jewish punk rockers will have little if any resemblance to what touches their parents, and young Jewish punk rockers will be more likely to line up homogeneously with punk rockers of other ethnic groups than they will with their conservative and respectable Jewish peers.

Concerned missiologists and church and mission leaders will need to continue devoting themselves to preparing the church—in all its diversity—to reach and receive the Jewish people in all of *their* diversity. We will even need to develop modalities that look and feel entirely secular.

And at the other end—the Jerusalem end—of the spectrum, we in the Messianic movement will need to develop a rich variety of Messianic Jewish congregational and communal expressions, corresponding in ambiance and emphasis to mainstream Judaism's Orthodox, Conservative, Reform, and Reconstructionist Synagogues, and to the more communal, less institutional Havurah modalities, which bear a striking resemblance to first-century house churches. I am currently devoted to developing this "Jerusalem" end of the spectrum, because I believe passionately in the urgency of developing truly indigenous models of corporate life, together with all the instructional, spiritual, and communal supports this entails. With Larry Brandt and Mark Stover, graduates of Fuller Seminary and Westminster Theological Seminary respectively, I have recently established a nonformal educational and training institute to enrich and inform Messianic communal life and witness. Such congregation-based lay training institutes seem to be the wave of the present and perhaps of the future in strengthening and multiplying congregations.

As this age draws nearer its close, I believe Jewish people will increasingly be searching for vital and credibly Jewish spiritual options. We in the Messianic Jewish community will need to be there at the Jerusalem end of the spectrum to meet those whose spiritual quest drives them there.

When Jewish people consider faith in Christ, it is common for them to succumb to social pressure to validate their new spiritual journey through "meeting with the rabbi." We must strengthen the Jerusalem end of the continuum, because we need to develop leaders and laity sufficiently intimate with the shape and content of Jewish theological discourse to equip them to articulate the Messianic Jewish position against the background of Jewish arguments which often seek to discount our faith as "illegitimate," "ignorant," and "non-Jewish." This calls for "building up Jerusalem." And the time is *now*.

THE PARADIGM OF COMPASSIONAL MISSION: JOB AND HIS FRIENDS

In today's theological climate the very propriety of mission to the Jews is itself under attack, and recent decades have witnessed a wholesale abandonment of the Jewish mission enterprise. Although my current mandate affords neither space nor opportunity to speak comprehensively to this issue, I cannot close without discussing a paradigm which addresses this crucial issue from an unexpected direction.

There is a certain common denominator of the Jewish psyche, a component of the Jewish world view which prevails in every Jewish context. More than an idea, it is actually a question and accusation, which, like an organ pedal point, resonates continually at the root of the Jewish soul. Although each Jewish person and community improvises differently over this ringing fundamental, the pedal tone remains the same. It is actually a question. In fact, I regard it as *the* Jewish question. The question is: Why? More precisely, the question concerns the problem of suffering and, from the Jewish point of view, God's apparent failure to intervene, despite his covenant relationship with his people.[6]

It is true, of course, that this question is not solely the province of Jews. But for the Jewish people, especially for older Jewish people, by virtue of our historical experience and theological orientation, *this* question is *the* question: "Why?"

You might say that all of us who didn't die in Europe are survivors or the children of survivors. Many Jews view themselves to be bound together in a holy obligation not to let the question die, not to leave the question unasked, not to let God and reality off the hook. Somewhere in his gut, when confronted with the memory or experience of suffering, the average Jew cries out viscerally, "My God! My God! Why hast thou forsaken us?"

Although some may view this posture to be arrogant and theologically flawed, nevertheless this is where many of my people are "stuck" with reference to God. And especially in the case of Holocaust survivors and their families, it seems presumptuous in the extreme for us to deny them the right to their pain-filled anger. If we are going to meet them where they are, we must meet them here.[7]

Against this background, perhaps the best metaphor for understanding the mission task as it applies to the Jewish people is that of Job and his friends. I suggest we all henceforth see Job as a symbol of the Jewish survivor who contends with God in his bereavement and pain, bellowing "Why?"

Under this model, the trainer of missiologists may then best be likened to the coach whose responsibility it is to orient, to educate, to sensitize, and to prepare a new generation of Job's friends for ministry to him and his bitter wife. The trainees will need help in understanding who Job is, what his experience has been, and his current state of mind. They will need to listen and to hear Job and his wife in the many ways in which they speak.

We must accept the fact that most Jewish people are not yet existentially at the end of the Book of Job. They have not yet come to the point of revelation and of deep contrition over the foolishness of trying to argue with God. Perhaps we'd like them to be there; perhaps some *demand* that they be there. The fact is, they are *not* there.[8] Ministering to such people requires that we ponder the profound mysteries of theodicy. We will need to learn what it means to stand in the uncomfortable place of knowing that for some people pain is so deep that our best answers don't seem to matter. And yes, some will be so angry that they will spit in our faces instead of heeding our words. Perhaps, most of all, we will need to learn to cry.[9]

What I am commending here is "compassional mission." We must get close enough to Jewish people for them to share with us their tears, their grief, their anger, and eventually their questions. If we really care, if we really feel their pain, then we simply *must* share with them Jesus Christ and him crucified, for only in the Crucified One do we find an adequate response to the twentieth-century Jewish controversy with God.

THE PARADIGM OF THE CRUCIFIED ONE

Without the Crucified One, most Jews perceive themselves to be left with a God who has been both silent and unresponsive in the face of howling terror, unremitting pain, and a covenant commitment apparently dishonored. Without the God-man on the cross we leave such people with a God who not only has failed to respond to their cries of "Why," but has also seemingly avoided the pain, preferring to remain uninvolved. Without Jesus

Christ and him crucified, such people feel themselves to be confronted with a deity who is simply the ultimate bystander.

Only the cross of Christ can adequately demonstrate to the post-Holocaust Jew that God is neither apathetic (in the formal sense of being "without feeling") nor distant from the mysteries and agonies of suffering. Looking at the cross through Messianic Jewish eyes, I recognize that the Messiah functioned as a prophet of the entire Jewish historical experience when, echoing the psalmist, he asked his father, "My God! My God! Why?" Yeshua (Jesus) is the ultimate, and in the deepest sense, the only *truly* innocent Suffering Servant, who alone, by virtue of his purity, is totally justified in asking the big Jewish question concerning undeserved suffering. He, as it were, takes up this Jewish question, and, amplifying it through his own holiness, wails louder than all of humanity could, "Why does the innocent one suffer? Why have you forsaken me?"

At the cross we see Christ as the human prophet, the ultimate Jewish questioner, although asking his question within the context of undiminished trust. We also see in him the evidence that God himself has not remained aloof—that in Christ he too has experienced the terror of helplessness and pain in the midst of an anguished "Why?" In Christ we see both the Jewish question and the divine answer that God has himself entered into the mystery of suffering and that through Christ and his resurrection he has emerged from the morass with redemption in his hand.

For this reason, even though the Jewish context requires skillful contextualization, we *must not* forsake a high Christology.[10] We dare not reduce the Incarnate One to the status of being simply the finest and best of Jewish rabbis. We Jews don't need another suffering and tormented rabbi—Hitler gave us thousands. Give my people nothing less than Emmanuel.

If the Jewish people are to find the answers they seek, they will need to know that indeed, God was in Christ. Contrary to those who proclaim the ethical impossibility of mission to the Jews after Auschwitz (see Bosch 1992, 163), I am suggesting that it is precisely *because* of Auschwitz that we must redouble our efforts to proclaim to my people the good news of Jesus the Messiah. Salvation is found in no one else (Acts 4:12).[11]

Notes

1. Bosch illustrates this phenomenon through reference to the "rediscovery" of Paul's Letter to the Romans by Augustine in the fourth century, Martin Luther in the sixteenth, and Karl Barth in the twentieth (1992, 186).

2. Although especially applicable to the Jewish experience, one might extend this remnant model to viewing the church universal as being comprised of the sum total of all remnants among all the people groups of the world. This approach, unlike the Ephesians paradigm, does not presuppose a discontinuity between the redeemed and not-yet redeemed or unredeemed in a given people group. Instead, it supports a sense of commonality which, I would suggest, is much more conducive to effective intracultural communication and mission.

3. I would contend that Zechariah 8:20-23 speaks to the same effect. In his 1747 sermon "A Humble Attempt to Promote Explicit Agreement in Prayer," Jonathan Edwards linked the fortunes of the church and Israel on the basis of the same text, stating that "Blessings on Jews mean incomparably greater blessings on the church" (Edwards 1854, 430).

4. Of course, the identity of the "all Israel" of Romans 11:26 has been a much-debated *crux interpretum*. As for those whose theological constructs oblige them to equate the "all Israel [which] will be saved" with the church, comprised of all the elect, both Jews and Gentiles, Cranfield's response seems determinative, at least for me: "[This position] must surely be rejected, for it is not feasible to understand *Israel* in v. 26 in a different sense from that which it has in v. 25, especially in view of the sustained contrast between Israel and the Gentiles throughout vv. 11-32. That *pas Israel* does not include Gentiles is virtually certain" (1979, 576-77).

5. Commenting upon Romans 11 and its implications for the church's obligation to the Jews with characteristic clarity, Cranfield states, "Where the church fails to fulfill this duty, where it fails seriously and wholeheartedly to will, and earnestly pray for, the unbelieving Jews' salvation, its identity as the true church of Jesus Christ is called in question" (1980, 73).

Declaring the imperative that the church pursue mission to the Jews, the Lausanne Consultation on Jewish Evangelism (LCJE) meeting in 1983 at Newmarket, England, stated: "Mission to the Jewish people is the foundation stone upon which the Christian mission to all the peoples of the world is built. . . . If this foundation stone is dislodged, then the universal mission of the Church is in danger of theological collapse" (Lausanne Consultation on Jewish Evangelism 1986). The LCJE continues to generate theologically mature position papers and articles delineating and defending the church's evangelistic responsibility to the Jews. For a tersely stated, well-considered survey of Christian responsibility vis-à-vis the Jewish people, see also the "Willowbank Declaration on the Christian Gospel and the Jewish People," developed at a consultation conducted April 26-29, 1989, sponsored by the World Evangelical Fellowship.

6. This theme of ongoing controversy with God, seen against the background of covenant relationship, has a history coterminous with that of the Jewish people themselves. For an excellent and comprehensive survey of the data, see Anson Laytner, *Arguing With God: A Jewish Tradition* (1990).

7. The flood of literature on the Holocaust is enormous and shows no sign of abating. It is impossible to overstate the centrality and impact of this experience upon all aspects of Jewish life and thought. Those interested in understanding and communicating with Jewish people must become informed about the Holocaust and sensitized to its dominance in Jewish life. For its comprehensiveness, intelligence, and clarity, I highly recommend the recent volume by Jonathan Sacks, Chief Rabbi of the United Kingdom and the Commonwealth, entitled *Crisis and Covenant: Jewish Thought after the Holocaust* (1992). It is a tour de force which will serve well to orient and update people concerned with the communal, theological, and personal impact of the Holocaust. From a Jewish-Christian point of view, though dated, Jakob Jocz's *The Jewish People and Jesus Christ after Auschwitz* (1981) is still required reading.

8. Psychologist Aaron Hass is the child of Holocaust survivors. His book *In the Shadow of the Holocaust: The Second Generation* (1990) poignantly and perceptively portrays the continuing pain, suffering, and dysfunction Holocaust survivors

and their descendants experience and the attitudes which are transmitted intergenerationally. In his eighth chapter, "Can I believe in God?" he writes:

> At the very best, most survivors struggle with God, and, in the process, express their anger. "I go to synagogue to accuse God. I used to go to ask forgiveness of my sins. Now I demand He ask forgiveness for His." "I go to synagogue to remind Him I owe Him nothing. He owes me." The second generation also wrestles with God. As their confidence in his ability or willingness to protect his children is shaken, their vulnerability is felt more acutely. ... The most disturbing question, of course, would involve God's complicity in the Holocaust. Why did he do this to us? (1990, 1147)

9. I find it interesting that in John's gospel it was not until Jesus wept at the tomb of Lazarus that the Jewish neighbors commented, "See how he loved him!" (Jn 11:36). For us as well, our love for the Jewish people and our bond with them will be best demonstrated and established as we are able to weep with those who weep.

10. In regard to Christology in the Jewish context, among the other excellent works available, I heartily recommend the highly provocative and seminal work of Norwegian scholar Oskar Skarsaune. See, for example, his *Incarnation: Myth or Fact?* (1991). It is his contention that the orthodox creeds, contextualized documents that they were, nevertheless were written to defend an authentically Jewish Christology which the apostles articulated using categories and terminology from Jewish Wisdom literature. No one seeking to find a credible bridge between the Jewish community and an Orthodox Christology can afford to ignore his work.

11. Although I am well aware of the theological controversies surrounding this text, I remain unconvinced by those who attempt to blunt its edge in regard to Jewish evangelization, as Krister Stendahl does in his article "In No Other Name (Acts 4:5-12)" (Stendahl 1976), where he dismisses the plain sense of the text as being attributable to the apostle's excessive spiritual ardor and devotion. This interpretation strikes me as being more indicative of the "table manners" prevailing in religious dialogue circles than the demands of the text. I myself have never been able to escape the force inherent in Peter's confronting the Sanhedrin, the religious "superstars" of the Jewish community in his generation, with the supreme authority and sole sufficiency of Jesus Christ as Lord and Savior. Is it not clear that the context demands that Peter intended that the "we" who must be saved through the name of Jesus Christ alone must certainly be the Jewish people? Where's the problem? If there is a problem with this text and its consequences for Jewish evangelization, it seems obvious to me that the "problem" resides not in the text itself but in its unfashionable implications.

17

Missiological Education for Lay People

Ralph D. Winter

I would like to propose the following ideas:

1. That *missiological education for the lay person* is the best hope of rescuing our generation from a "Great Commission-less" Christianity, a form of Christianity which is a deadly and widespread heresy within the Western churches and as such is a fatal disease striking at the very root of the global Christian mission.

2. That *missiological education for the lay person*, therefore, even outranks the strategic importance of training professional missionaries.

3. That *missiological education for the lay person* can best be achieved by off-campus education, and that—believe it or not—the off-campus education of "lay people" is also the only way that the best selections can be made for the ordinary pastors/evangelists without whom the Christian movement cannot continue.

4. The idea, finally, that the massively growing trend in university circles toward *off-campus education* is also the only way the average post-secondary educational institution will survive in the increasingly "on the run" world in which we live.

After serving ten years as a missionary among Mayan Indians in western Guatemala, **Ralph D. Winter** spent the next ten years as a professor of missions at the School of World Mission at Fuller Theological Seminary. He is the founder and general director of the U.S. Center for World Mission, Pasadena, California, a cooperative center focused on people groups with no culturally relevant church. Winter has also been instrumental in the formation of the movement called Theological Education by Extension, the William Carey Library Publishing House, the American Society of Missiology, and the Institute of International Studies. In 1990 he became president of the William Carey International University.

INTRODUCTION

My concern for the strategy of educating the laity clearly derives in part from Donald McGavran, with whom I worked for ten years, and who was subsequently a member of my board for most of his years beyond that. While he certainly believed in professional training for certain people, he always kept in mind "the five kinds of leaders" essential to any vital church movement. Note that most of these five kinds of leaders were lay people. Indeed, his major reason for inviting me to help out in the early years of the School of World Mission at Fuller was because of my involvement with the Theological Education by Extension movement, a growing phenomenon that brought high quality theological studies precisely to lay people in their local context.

However, over a much longer period of time I was exposed to the influence of another man, who was also a founder of the Fuller School of World Mission. He was the one who decided that there ought to be a School of World Mission. His concerns set in motion the search for a founding dean for the projected school. I still recall the lengthy search process and the serious energy invested in it long before McGavran was chosen. Who was this other founder? He was himself a lay person named Charles E. Fuller, who, like Dwight Moody, did not get his theological training in what we consider "the proper way." Earlier, of course, Charles Fuller was the founder of Fuller Seminary itself, a temporary compromise of his original intentions. Thus, once a standard seminary was well established, the School of World Mission became his attempt to make a mid-course correction. A course correction to what?

Charles E. Fuller was a lay person who had been able to get a bit of Bible and mission education in a school of a type that no longer exists, the Bible Institute of Los Angeles. Note that if he had not gained biblical education *as a lay person* there never would have been a Fuller School of World Mission, much less a Fuller Seminary, or a global Old Fashioned Revival Hour.

Like Moody, Fuller's passion was for the lay person. We know him as the one who launched the first religious radio program in this country, a program with a radio audience which at its height was larger than any other at that time. But few people realize that he took hold of radio for the special purpose of reaching people in the out-of-the-way places in this country— just as his father, Henry Fuller, before him personally supported forty missionaries in out-of-the-way places around the world. Charles E. Fuller, drawing on family wealth, at one time supported a couple dozen full-time evangelists who were sent specifically to the "scattered populations" of this country—the mines, the lumber camps, the rural towns. Yes, his passion was for the forgotten, the overlooked, the little person, the lay person. Radio was merely his method of reaching them. Thus, both McGavran and Fuller would have been especially interested in the topic assigned to me.

Nevertheless, for me this is a curious topic. I don't think I have ever thought about the training of lay people (as a subject) until this topic was handed to me. For example, I have always thought that the network of classes across this country and around the world with which I am involved has been simply a case of trying to educate people who might subsequently become missionaries, mission pastors, mission mobilizers, and so forth. Most missionaries are and always have been lay people.

Indeed, the education and honor accorded to lay women missionaries was the primary force producing the elite women's colleges and later the early feminist movement in this country. The serious education of lay women explains why, in the vast majority of the multitudinous house churches of China, the theological "anchor man" is actually a Bible-trained *woman*. This curious and enormous reality on the field in China shows, I believe, how much more effective was the *non-seminary training* of lay women, even if conducted by only the women missionaries, than was the much more cumbersome *seminary training* of men in China—the totally different technique with which certain specialized male missionaries struggled, and which accomplished relatively little by comparison.

However, the principal reason for being asked to deal with the topic "Missiological Education for Lay People" is likely due to the fact that for more than two decades following the Urbana Student Missionary Conference of 1973 I have been involved—as a sideline—in an off-campus study program for thousands of lay people. I cannot here recount that story in great detail, but a brief synopsis may be expected of me.

Case One: The "Perspectives" Network

In the United States alone, more than twenty thousand people have taken our 150-hour, 3-semester-unit course "Perspectives on the World Christian Movement," which is essentially an introduction to missiology. Students who wish can get transcripts from cooperating seminaries and colleges, and then often transfer that credit into a state university or other college as a humanities elective. This possibility of transfer of credit to a secular school is one reason we don't call the course "Introduction to Missiology." That is, the wording "Perspectives on the World Christian Movement" is more likely to allow secular schools to accept transfer credit for such a course.

Already this year we have accepted the plans for fifty-eight locations in the United States where the course will be taught this coming spring. It will be taught in a number of other places again later in the year in some of the same as well as additional places. For example, it will be taught six times in the Spanish language in Los Angeles. In other countries we are not in charge, so we are less aware of the statistics. However, in New Zealand we hear that they project thirty locations for the course next year. Overseas it is likely that the combined enrollment for courses in Spanish and Portuguese as well as in English would loom at least as large as the enrollment in this country.

Having awakened a sleeping giant we are now virtually forced into offering further studies. In order to do that we are in the process of asking the
help of a consortium of about a dozen seminaries and graduate schools
which have shown a willingness to offer some of the constituent elements
of an additional curriculum ten times as large as the Perspectives course—
namely, a 32-semester-unit program in mission studies. We are guessing
that, in general, about one out of twenty of those who take the introductory
Perspectives course will want to go on with these additional units toward a
degree—*if we can deliver the goods to these lay people in an off-campus
location.* Let's look more closely at the nature of what is involved in off-
campus education.

It is not new for us to draw on the help of other schools. Even now, in
order to operate in fifty-eight places at the same time, we have had to
build up over the years a pool of over five hundred lecturers who typically
take on a single weeknight three-hour class—one of a series of fifteen
lessons spread over fifteen weeks. We need fifteen different professors
for each fifteen-week course. Note that fifteen weeks times fifty-eight
places is 870 evening lecturers just for the spring session. Since we only
draw on 500 different professors, and it is very rare for anyone to teach
more than one of the fifteen lessons in a given location, it is obvious that
some of the many friendly people who teach for us must teach in more
than one place. One reason we find it so easy to attract help of this kind is
the unusually high interest on the part of the lay people in these off-campus classes.

Three professors in one of the accredited Christian colleges that gives
transcripts to people in these classes cornered me recently when I happened
to visit their campus. They told me over and over again how elated they
were to be teaching off-campus in this program. Why? Because of the as-
tonishingly high motivation and interest of the students in these off-campus
locations. One said, "Never in twelve years here at this college have I had a
group of students like that."

The incredibly high spirit in these off-campus classes explains why we
do not need to pay professors astronomical honoraria, although what we do
pay is substantial. The tuition paid by students covers air travel, honoraria,
other class overhead, credit transcription costs, and so forth. Even so, the
program has been entirely self-funding from the beginning. No one has
gotten rich, but cooperating schools have benefited from the millions of
dollars that have been generated in this operation. While over a hundred
residential schools also employ the same text materials, what I have described is purely the off-campus version of the program, which we ourselves directly supervise.

However, enough of these details. I am sure many of my readers are
familiar with the nine-hundred-page *Perspectives Reader* and the accom-
panying three-hundred-page *Study Guide*, both of which have undergone
major revisions over the years.

Let me move on to an earlier experience with lay people which might also be expected of me under this topic—the activity which provided the basis for McGavran's invitation to me to join the faculty of the School of World Mission in 1966.

Case Two: Theological Education by Extension

I remember an incident which happened shortly after I first arrived on the field in the highlands of Guatemala. My wife and I had been assigned to work with a tribal group numbering a third of a million, one of thirty-three language groups in the Mayan family. While there were many congregations of believers in this group already, no one from this tribe had ever gone to the Presbyterian Seminary for training, and it was not very likely that the seminary (located far away in the capital city) would be able to contribute anything very soon to the well-being of the far-flung network of mountain Indian churches.

A good friend of mine, Jim Emery, had arrived five years earlier and had worked extensively down on the coast with Spanish-speaking churches. It was apparent to him that there was a similar problem with the coastal congregations; very few of their actual, local leaders would ever make it to the seminary in the capital city or, therefore, ever be properly ordained as ministers.

He and I were talking about the problem of theological education one day, and he observed that most of the congregations lacking "properly trained" pastors nevertheless had at least one person within the congregation who did a creditable job of leading the group. *The curious fact was that the absence of ordained pastors in these many tiny rural and mountain churches was more an ecclesiastical inconvenience than a serious deficiency in local congregational dynamics.*

But why were there not more *ordained* pastors? Well, in our Presbyterian system "proper training" (defined by an approximation to U.S. standards) was considered essential for ordination. But of course if anyone down on the Pacific coast of Guatemala ever got "proper training," the cultural shift involved would leave him feeling very much out of place within either the coastal Spanish culture or the highland Indian culture. Therefore, we decided that if the people could not come to the seminary, we ought to try to figure out how the seminary could go to the people.

Seven years later we were running a nationwide extension program that enabled any rural adult studying part time anywhere in the country to gain a government diploma for the first six grades of general education. We wrote the textbooks, drawing on the collaboration of the various missions in different parts of the country. We gained government recognition for this process, and within a short time over a thousand rural adults gained the highly esteemed sixth grade diploma—quite an achievement since very few of the rural schools went beyond the third grade. A sixth-grade diploma was something like the Ph.D. (except that it was much more rare in that rural world than the Ph.D. is in ours). Meanwhile, the government was astonished at the high grades many of these rural adults achieved. (They were equally astonished by our willingness to flunk those of our own students who did not make it.) At first they assumed the whole thing was a phony process. They found it hard to believe that people can learn outside of school!

This sixth-grade level then provided the basis for enrollment in the lowest of four levels of training offered by an extension seminary program we had simultaneously devised—which was our real goal. No, the real goal was not a seminary program accessible to rural people. Our real goal was to give rural church leaders the silly academic credentials without which they could not be duly ordained and function as fully ordained leaders. I'm not saying what these rural leaders learned was silly. I'm saying that the missionary-imported delivery system was silly. We were teaching the same things that were taught in the seminary, and what our students learned in our off-campus extension pattern was valuable. What we did could have been done (and was done) earlier when an apprenticeship pattern (dominant in the United States and on our mission fields until at least as late as 1900) made it unnecessary to go to the capital for a period of years for such studies. But by the close of the Second World War (1945) standards were now "higher," and it was unheard of not to have to go off to the seminary in the capital once this new "seminary education" had been established as the way to go, even though, historically speaking, it was a relatively recent invention. With our new extension system, however, the paper barrier was broken, and the two hundred rural churches could look forward to having real pastors again. But there was a problem we had not anticipated.

After four years of the new off-campus program, 140 rural leaders were enrolled. Now came the opposition. At the annual meeting of this particular church movement, a meeting which took place in the capital city, a strong challenge was voiced against this new program. By now our Extension Seminary had enrolled seven times as many students as any previous total in the residential seminary. Pastors in the capital city were feeling uneasy at the sheer numbers but even more threatened by the impressive leaders who had found their way into this new program.

The telling accusation was made on the floor of Synod, "Those 140 students you have enrolled are mere lay people; you are letting lay people into the ministry." In other words, the whole operation was merely for *lay people*—meaning *lay people* should not be ordained on the basis of off-campus training. True, the 140 students in this extension program *were* lay people, with jobs and families located out in the Spanish and Indian worlds of rural Guatemala.

At this point in the meeting Jim Emery stood up. He was at that time probably the only person who could stand up in a synod meeting and be listened to with respect by both missionaries and Guatemalans. What he said I'll never forget: "When I went to seminary I was a lay person." Then, directing his comments to the city pastors who had gone through the capital-city seminary, "When you went to seminary you were lay persons, were you not? So what is the problem? Why is it so strange that our students are lay people?"

When the vote was taken, the simple fact was that most of those 140 students were present. They tended to be, for the most part, ordained elders who had a vote in Synod, and they out-voted the city pastors. The whole thing was a kind of palace revolt, but the experiment survived and continued. One city pastor later told me, "You missionaries are trying to dethrone the pastors with all these lay persons." He was right. He himself later left the ministry and ran a Christian bookstore—a job for which he was much better qualified. However, since very few of the two hundred congregations had "properly trained" pastors, not very many existing pastors lost their jobs.

However, a whole new kind of leadership soon flooded the church. *We had dramatically forestalled the professionalization of the movement.* By means of this extension trick, so to speak, our church movement had now gained almost the growth and nurture capability of the Pentecostal churches, which were, in that era at least, still untrammeled by a seminary tradition.

Our idea, basically, was merely that of setting up an educational delivery system which did not implicitly exclude the more mature leaders of the church congregations. It became an approach that was employed in other parts of Guatemala and Central America, and later in South America. An entire extension seminary association was formed in Brazil. I recall being invited in 1977 to its tenth annual meeting where association members were eager to display all of the marvelous progress they had made with study materials especially designed for off-campus students for the ministry.

In 1968, a joint committee of the EFMA/IFMA sent people around the world introducing the concept of training lay people where they are. At one point it was estimated that over 100,000 people in over five hundred programs around the world, mostly in humble congregations (but also doctors and attorneys in capital cities), were taking studies that would allow them, or at least could allow them to be ordained.

But I recall even more vividly when I was invited a second time to Brazil for the *twentieth* anniversary of the same extension seminary association that had been organized on my first visit in 1967. This time, unknown to me during the first two days of the conference, I was lecturing to a group which had changed its name. The Brazil extension association had decided *to be respectable*, and had dropped the word *extension* out of its title! By now, a good number of the seminary leaders present were not even acquainted with the concept of off-campus training. A massive reversion had taken place! "Respectable" seminary residential training had regained its culturally approved position of power. With the exception of some evening schools in the big cities, former extension schools, trying once again to live up to the U.S. pattern, were back to training young people who were footloose and free with no families or daytime jobs and were thus able to attend a residential school. In many cases they were young folks who needed the literal care and feeding of a subsidized institution. Those young people were not bad people; they simply are not as good a bet for church leadership as the older, functional leaders in the congregations, who are not very likely to be able to go away somewhere for years in order to be qualified for ordination.

I am afraid this same sort of reversion has taken place in most of the world. The global influence of the U.S. pattern is just too strong. The desire of leaders who are not significantly gifted for a tangible basis of leadership authority, a professional status, is too powerful—and deadly.

It was an interesting experiment. The initial activities in Guatemala were in 1961. The Latin American and global movement gained significant strength by about 1968. But by 1987 the whole idea of extension education had come and mainly gone, and in its place the more respectable (yet untried and untrue) seminary pattern from America had regained even greater strength in more and more places across the world. As a result, the irresistible pressure of an established American tradition continued to be carried like a disease germ out across the world. What else can we expect from missionaries who had not themselves been trained in an off-campus model? As Jerald Gort says in an earlier chapter, it is surprising how much theological education is influenced by personal, biographical, social, and geographical factors.

Well, maybe we don't need to worry. In Latin America, at least, the Pentecostal pattern has picked up the slack. That movement has thus far not erected artificial barriers to lay people with leadership gifts who are found in the real world of the local church. However, in the United States the older Pentecostal denominations are, in fact, slowing down as they insist upon "professional training" for their leaders. And, as the classical Pentecostal movement slows down in America, for example, the growing edge becomes the Costa Mesa Calvary Chapel movement, the Vineyard movement, and the thousands of independent Christian Centers, or the "house churches" in England. The well-known Pentecostal characteristics may blind us to the simple fact that around the world *their leadership selection pattern is not hobbled by the requirements of certain kinds of largely inaccessible institutional training.*

So, who cares if the so-called main-line churches commit slow suicide by allowing Rube Goldberg complexities in their ministerial delivery system? Who cares? Well, at least the newer, untrammeled movements need to care simply because they seem likely to be headed in the same direction, like sheep being led to the slaughter.

The key word in this discussion is *access*. Ken Mulholland uses it in his chapter. It is one of the main secrets of the Pentecostals, although it is not uniquely Pentecostal. The Moody Bible Institute in its early period gave *access* in evening classes to all kinds of real leaders who could not go to daytime classes. This was the secret of the surprising and massive new power injected into the evangelical tradition through the mushrooming Bible Institute Movement. But like Samson, who knew not from whence his strength had come, the Bible Institute Movement had no sooner come into existence for the benefit of *giving access to lay people*, including leaders who could not go to daytime classes, than it turned away from that secret strength—perhaps in order to support its professors but more likely because of a desire to ape the other daytime schools and thereby gain "legitimacy" and "respectability."

Charles Fuller was one of those lay people whose great gifts became evident only after some years as a lay person, and who then gained enough from the Bible Institute of Los Angeles to get him going in personal studies that hoisted him to the level of national and worldwide influence. He then intuitively tried to contribute further to the movement that had given him *access*, but eventually was persuaded to create a conventional seminary that seemed, as usual, designed to deny mature, gifted *lay people* access.

By now the reader may be asking, "You have been talking about theological education for lay people, but what does all this have to do with missiology and the specifically missiological education of lay people?" These two case studies provide the context for our reflection on the three terms in our title: *missiology, lay people*, and *education*.

MISSIOLOGY?

Let us go from the general to the specific. All I have said thus far has been an extended illustration of the concept of mobilizing gifted lay people into leadership versus the defensive survival of institutional school patterns promoting a professional ministry. What does this have to do with missiology?

Three Kinds of Missiology

The introductory course mentioned in our first case study, "Perspectives on the World Christian Movement," talks about the whole world. It employs the word *mission* here and there. Does that make it *missiology*? Let's look more closely at what *missiology* can mean nowadays.

My discussion of missiological education for lay people falls to the ground if what we are teaching in these lay programs is not missiology of some kind. But words do gain expanded meanings. We have come a long way from the classical missionary activity of the Apostle Paul, in which believers from one nation or people reached out to begin work within a different nation or people. Paul himself distinguished his major ministry from the ministry of Peter in Galatians 2:7 when he said, "I had been entrusted with the Gospel to the Gentiles, just as Peter had been to the Jews." I may add that Paul did not simply plant Gentile churches and then stay around. His constant passion was to go "to the regions beyond . . . where Jesus Christ is not named."

That Pauline type of mission activity has been going on for many centuries. However, three quite different concepts of missiology have by now emerged, causing considerable confusion to the church. A candid look at the budgets of the main-line denominations reveals that millions of dollars that once were committed to one kind of mission are now routinely committed in other directions, and the growing pew-level awareness of this transformation in the definition of *mission* has virtually paralyzed the national offices of such denominations due to a resulting fall-off in giving.

Intracultural missiology. I realize that no one owns the word *mission* or the word *missiology.* Note that the *purposeful* element in the meaning of the word *mission* allows us to describe any purposeful activity as mission. When pastors *purposefully* expand their congregational membership into the same cultural stratum, that kind of activity can logically be called mission (and thus missiological, if we pursue that subject academically). There is, thus, the *missiology of church growth*, whether that growth is growth in internal quality, in expanding congregations, or in planting new churches within the same people group. This is what Gnanakan in his chapter calls "intracultural missiology." That is one kind of missiology talked about today.

Interchurch missiology. There is then, logically, the more exotic cross-cultural kind of missiology, in which the study is of the purposeful (for example, *mission*) activity of believers in one part of the world who are working among other believers at a distance, across significant cultural barriers, perhaps in other countries. This is preeminently the missiology of the global Christian fellowship. Call it *interchurch missiology.* It involves ethno-theology, the staggeringly fascinating wonderland in which we compare notes with other believers in other cultures. In this arena it is easy to suppose that we can and should beat our pioneer mission swords into the plowshares of the concerns of the church wherever in the world it has become domestic. Or we may channel our remaining pioneer mission courage into doing battle with the domestic problems that may plague the new churches which our mission labors have planted. We may ponder the need to fight alongside these wonderful overseas believers in their battles with their own social and political problems. We can join them in their own intracultural missiology. *Interchurch* missiology is thus cross-cultural *intracultural* missiology. It is as fascinating as it is helpful for two church movements in two different parts of the world to compare notes on their own intracultural challenges.

Why haven't missionaries and mission agencies kept moving on further to other peoples? You might have thought that Western mission forces by now would have often become aware of having "worked themselves out of a job." But Parkinson's law comes into effect: "Work expands to fit the time available" (or the number of workers available). Where Western agencies completed the pioneer stage, they often saw no reason to go elsewhere. Why not stay where they had planted churches and revise the Great Commission to read, "Go ye into all the world and meddle in the national churches"?

Indeed, after the Second World War a whole new variety of mission agencies jumped into being. Eleven million service personnel returned from the far corners of the earth with a new awareness of other peoples. Within five years 150 new agencies appeared in the United States. These new "service missions" did not go out to plant the church, nor go to new places particularly; they went out across the world where the church was already planted to be of service to the new churches, carrying to them our back-home Sunday School materials, church programs, airplanes, radio stations, evangelistic techniques—and, yes, seminaries. In view of the immensely gratifying existence of the churches in the former mission fields, some organizations are proposing that missionaries are not needed at all, but that the money we spend to send our own people ought to go rather to pay the much lower stipends of national evangelists who can do a better job for less money. This perspective would not be entirely unreasonable *if there were no remaining untouched fields.*

Classical or frontier missiology. Beyond interchurch missiology, however, there should continue to exist the Pauline kind of missiology; namely, believers reaching out from their own culture to begin work in *new groups in which Christ is not yet named,* or at least within those peoples where there is not yet "a viable, indigenous, evangelizing church movement." This kind of pioneer work is now being attempted by some of the Western missions as well as by some of the agencies in the vast new category of the two-thirds-world missions.

Thus we have at least three kinds of missiology to talk about: (1) the missiology of the church in relation to its own society (*intracultural* missiology), (2) the missiology of interchurch relationships on the global level (*interchurch* missiology), and (3) the missiology of continuing pioneer efforts within unreached people groups (*classical* or *frontier* missiology).

My own primary concern in the last fifteen years has been with classical or frontier missiology. Probably less than 10 percent of missiological literature today focuses on this missiology. Clearly both interchurch and classical missiology are cross-cultural studies of great value to the world church. It is unfortunate if their respective functions are confused with each other, because they are both needed.

"Re-missiologizing" the Bible

Clarifying the differences between these three kinds of missiology, however, still leaves unanswered the questions, Why take interchurch or classical missiology to *lay people*? Why not give lay people standard theology? There are at least two reasons.

One reason has to do with the survival of our own authenticity as true followers of Christ in our own culture. Missionaries go not only to give but to receive. But missionaries generally carry a cultural mix of Christianity to their overseas posts. The indigenous church movements that result must eventually free themselves from the lingering elements—or at least the undesirable elements—of the foreign (missionary) culture by means of what is usually called the process of contextualization.

In this process (in which national and expatriate should take part) the missionary may learn some important things he can take back to his own people. Eventually the new leaders in the overseas churches will be able to take the lead in contextualization, comparing notes with the missionary's own theological tradition. The result can be a precious refinement of the missionary's theological thinking and even his understanding of the Bible. This is the first reason why classical missiology is inevitably of high interest and value to lay people in our own culture. Hopefully, it will assist them in refining their understanding of the treasure we have in the earthen vessels of our own culture—essentially in the *decontextualization* of our own Christianity. Every church movement in the world deserves this kind of cross-cultural critique of its own cultural mix of Christianity.

Briefly, it is very easy for the Bible to become within any one nation the means simply of that nation's own salvation. Much of conventional theology contributes to ethnocentric soteriology. The Westminster Confession (and every other theological statement clear back to the Nicene Creed) falls desperately short of allowing the central thrust of biblical revelation to shine through. I refer here simply to the impartial concern of God for all nations.

Thus, lay people who don't go as missionaries—those who support missions—surely deserve to receive insight from missiology so they can see the Bible with the eyes of a different culture. This process can rescue them from what Samuel Escobar calls "culture Christianity" and can also allow them a much better grasp of the Bible and a deeper understanding of the central meaning of the subject matter of theology.

"Re-missiologizing" Theology Itself

We are already talking about the second reason for sharing missiological insights with lay people. In a much more specific sense, missiology (intracultural but especially interchurch or classical) can help to restore central meaning to theology, and thus to balance out a hundred specific and very crucial areas in the theological diet lay people inevitably receive within the cultural cocoons of their own mainly monocultural world at the hands of monocultural pastors, monocultural Bible scholars, and monocultural theologians.

THE LAY PERSON?

The phrase *lay people* is the most shocking element in the topic assigned to me. Its use often implies that lay people who go full-time to residence schools for seminary knowledge are no longer lay people the moment they decide to go to seminary—an assumption we have already questioned. On the other hand, if I do not yield to that assumption, it would appear that I should talk about what goes on in seminaries, not merely what goes on off campus. I feel I was handed a topic that was probably meant to avoid the role of the traditional seminary, which trains people for ordained ministry, not just to be better lay people. That perspective implies that once a person sets out to be a professional minister, he or she should no longer be considered a lay person. To underscore this, some church traditions apply the special term *ordinand* to a lay person at that point where he or she decides to seek professional training for ministry.

But I ask you, is there on the one hand a significant difference between the kind of lay people our nationwide off-campus program has been teaching and, on the other hand, the kind of lay people who attend seminary? Is there a significant difference, for example, between a hundred M.Div. students enrolled in the Conservative Baptist Seminary of the East (who may be in Boston, New York City, Philadelphia, or anywhere between) and a different hundred who pull up stakes, "give up a secular career," and move to a residential seminary program? Less than half of those who attend residential seminaries are there due to a special decision to give up a secular calling.

However, it is probably not good enough simply to maintain the point of view that most seminary students are still in fact lay people. The key fact is that they are getting a professional education that will allow them to become something other than lay people—that is, professionals. In fact, seminaries solicit funding from donors on the basis that they are providing ministers to the church. Even granting that some of the students will become ordained (which in some schools is less than 30 percent), this still does not provide a rationale for the seminary to command a monopoly on the training of ministers. Historically, a handful of seminaries functioned for a full century as a rather rare option for ministerial training. Only recently with the massive assistance of the "GI Bill," have seminaries become part of a normative path into the ministry.

It would thus be understandable if seminaries were unenthusiastic about moving off campus and educating just anyone. What if what is taught off campus were to allow just anyone into the ministry without requiring the full, formal on-campus ministerial education that is now conventional? Wouldn't that undermine the financial base of the entire seminary movement? Wouldn't you expect dire warnings against "watering down" the quality of ministerial training—even if the real fear were the financial viability of the residential schools? Recently a seminary leader remarked in my hearing that if it were not for the incredible influx of relatively affluent Korean students, at least six evangelical seminaries in the United States would be bankrupt.

This kind of dependence should alarm us about the inherent financial fragility of the seminaries, since it must not become a marginal concern to the church that the seminaries continue to exist, especially in their crucial role as the guardians of the Christian historical and intellectual heritage.

In seminaries, scholars guard and treasure the biblical manuscripts, the historical records, and theological truth, constantly updating our understanding of the present-day meaning of our faith. The problem is that in order to carry out that crucial role, seminaries have all along depended on what I have come to regard as a pragmatic, secondary function, namely, the training of young people for ministry. The seminary-church linkage involved in the passing on of that heritage to future ministers is quite natural. This kind of linkage between theological centers and the training of new ministers is financially beneficial to the survival of the seminaries. But we need to ask, "Is it harmful to the quality of church leadership?"

Many people feel that this linkage is prejudicial to the welfare of the church movement, because it settles on an institutional experience *that is not available to the average lay person*. This fact is a nearly fatal complication in what should be a normal selection process in which lay people may rise to church leadership.

That is, insisting on the institutional experience of the traditional seminary for all ordained leaders extensively skews the selection process. Gone are the possibilities of lay people becoming "farmer-preachers," as in the Baptist tradition, a movement that grew very large and very fast before it adopted the seminary experience as essential for ordination. Gone is the lay preacher of the Methodist tradition, a mighty movement that also experienced fast growth as long as it employed an extension form of theological education—a method which for a hundred crucial years of Methodist growth did not put any artificial limitations on the church leadership selection process. Gone are the apprenticed pastors who provided the backbone of a strong Presbyterian tradition long before seminaries dominated that tradition. By now in history we have accumulated extensive worldwide experience—*missiological* experience—confirming the damaging interference in church growth resulting from a mandatory residential seminary experience for all pastors.

In the global context to which we are introduced by missiology, we see a vast laboratory of very different experiences from our present situation at home. It is safe to say that virtually the only church movements in the history of the world that are growing, or once grew mightily, are those that enable lay people to become leaders in the church *without the disruptive extraction of a residential seminary program leading to a professionalized ministry*. Those movements that adopt a pattern requiring all future ministers to take the seminary detour find that their growing days are over. From the village churches to the super-churches, the real leadership resources of a healthy church movement do not consist of professionally trained people.

In a word, then, as with mayors, governors, congressmen, and presidents in the civil sphere, the vital, living, growing church movements around the world draw their leaders directly from the laity. They would not think of drawing upon untested young men and women out of the graduating classes of seminaries—even if that kind of institutional process were prolific enough to keep up with the rate of growth of an expanding church. In Latin America, specifically, the "night Bible schools" throughout the hemisphere—which give access to the whole of the laity—have fueled a movement that has surpassed the other groups employing seminaries for pastoral training as if those movements were standing still.

Is it not somewhat the same in the United States today? What proportion of the twenty-five thousand most recent new churches have started out with standard, seminary-trained pastors? Would it be higher than 5 percent? The Calvary Chapels, the Vineyards, the Christian Centers of our time generally display surprisingly capable leadership. It is becoming clear that congregational leadership is something other than what is acquired in school or through a course on leadership. Do we have to choose between (1) untrained but gifted leadership and (2) less gifted but academically qualified people?

I don't believe the key point here is whether lay people are being given the Bible or not, or seminary training or not, since in fact most seminary students really are *lay people*. The key point is *which* lay people are able to get the necessary training to be effective pastors and Christian leaders. Our seminaries are not teaching the wrong things. They may be teaching the wrong people. The awesome reality is that the *right* people, for the most part, are unable to gain access to the traditional institutional structure of the seminaries.

The kind of leaders the Bible defines for the church is not easily discernible at the time people in their early twenties register in a seminary. Granted, the gradually increasing age of the average seminary student has brought a lot more mature people into seminary, as has the increasing tendency for seminary students to be married (a change from 2 percent in 1945 to maybe 65 percent today). Yet not all the older students who find their way into seminary are especially gifted.

As a result, no matter how high the quality of education seminaries offer such people, that *quality* may not be able to transform them into the right kind of *gifted* people. It is thus not a matter of what seminaries do to their students—how much field work is required, or whether the seminary professors have had, or continue to have, pastoral experience—but it is a matter of whether or not the particular lay people who find their way into seminary classes in a daytime residential program are those within the church who possess the strongest pastoral gifts. It seems to me that unless seminaries make what they teach *accessible* to the full spectrum of believers, the greatest leadership potential of the church cannot be harvested—nor can the seminaries survive (without counting on Korean students!).

This leads us to the final term in our topic: *education*.

EDUCATION?

Education is thus not merely a matter of the right curriculum but the right students. It is more crucially a matter of *whom we are training than what we are teaching*. It is not merely a matter of the quality of the classroom or the library but the quality of the selection of those who benefit from the education that is being offered.

Many years ago David Hubbard and I happened to be speakers at the same meeting (about off-campus theological education) held at the Denver Seminary. He was introduced by a man who gushed effusively about the many illustrious pulpits held by Fuller graduates. Dave began by courteously declining the praise offered for these well-known examples of outstanding leadership, going on to note that if he did not decline these honors he might with equal logic be blamed for those many Fuller students who had not turned out so well.

He was not merely gracious; I feel he showed great insight. There is only so much a seminary can do for a student. No amount of field training can guarantee to create the kind of gifts possessed by those who have already distinguished themselves in lay leadership. At any given time the vast majority of the saints who have the gifts of ministry are to be found in the churches and will never darken the door of a seminary.

The healthiest church movements across the world are not limited for their leadership selection to those relatively few who do somehow make it through seminary. No, they draw their leadership right out of their congregations. This is true especially in the super-churches where the crucial cell groups are all led by lay people. For the growing movements of the world today, it is better for the seminaries to figure out how to add high quality training to those who have manifested *giftedness* than to hope that an indiscriminate slice of a relatively small handful of young people given professional training will someday manifest the necessary *giftedness* on which the church desperately depends.

I am convinced that (1) the seminaries must survive in order to perform crucial functions other than the direct training of the ministry, and that (2) they can readily survive only if they are willing to bend sufficiently to make their riches accessible to lay people, and that meanwhile (3) this shift happens also to be a matter of life and death for the churches, which cannot forever digest professional pastors—professional administrators, perhaps, professional organists and choir directors, perhaps, even professional orators, but not professional pastors.

Missiological education also must extend to lay people. Most missionaries—whether intracultural, interchurch, or frontier—like most pastors must be recruitable from the entire spectrum of the laity. It is a matter of life or death for the Christian world mission that we allow lay people access to missiological education whether they become part-time or full-time workers, whether they become home-front mobilizers, cross-cultural interchurch workers, or front-line pioneers, and whether or not they are able to go off for years to school for professional training.

FUTURE

Toward New Books, Circles, and Sandals

18

The View
from a Refurbished Chair

J. Dudley Woodberry

The year 1992 was a milestone year for an installation: the 200th anniversary of William Carey's booklet *An Inquiry into the Obligations of Christians to Use Means for the Conversion of the Heathens*, which launched modern Protestant missions from a church that is now a mosque, and launched some paternalism too; the 500th anniversary of Columbus's voyage, which brought Christianity and exploitation to the new world; also the 500th anniversary of Christendom's recapture of Granada, the last Muslim stronghold in Spain, which led to mass conversions and massacres; and the 250th anniversary of Handel's inspiring *Messiah* and Voltaire's satirical *Mahomet the Prophet.*

The title "The View from a Refurbished Chair" notes my two tasks: describing the Chair of Islamic Studies and describing the view of a dean in that chair. We shall look first at the chair and then at the view. But due to limits of space, we can only look at the contours of the chair, without the intricate designs, and the main features of the view, without the details of the horizon. Illustrations will be drawn from a Chair of Islamic Studies at al-Azhar University Mosque in Cairo, because it has influenced academic

---

This chapter was initially the address given by J. Dudley Woodberry on the occasion of his installation as dean of the School of World Mission and occupant of the Chair of Islamic Studies through the stewardship of Mary Belle Varker, M.D., November 2, 1992. In this collection of essays, it serves as a transition between the section on missiological contexts and the one on future contexts, because it deals both with the teaching of Islamic studies and points to possible future directions for the School of World Mission. The latter are developed more fully in the conclusion, "Till the Final Book Is Opened in the Final Circle."

chairs around the world. And al-Azhar, like Fuller Seminary's School of World Mission, trains missionaries to serve all over the world.

THE CHAIR

What kind of chair is the Chair of Islamic Studies at Fuller? Since I prepared this part of the presentation in an airplane with my seatbelt on, I am tempted to think of it as an airline seat. Or since all of us work on the shoulders of others, it might be a sedan chair. It certainly is not a museum chair, roped off to keep it from being used.

The Making of the Chair

When we look for the origin of the teaching chair, we turn first to the model of our Lord, who on the Mount of Beatitudes used a rock, as we saw in the New Testament reading (Mt 5:1-2, 13-16). Before he exchanged the rocks of Palestine for a throne, he taught his disciples two lessons that were to become a part of endowed teaching chairs: make disciples and teach "all that I have commanded you" (Mt 28:29), and "freely have you received, freely give" (Mt 10:8).

From Monasteries to Mosques

In the post-apostolic period Christians chipped those rocks into the pillars for monasteries and churches (like the Church of the Apostles in Constantinople), which became recipients of endowments and centers of teaching. When the Christianized lands of the Middle East were overrun by the advancing Muslims, teaching mosques in turn became the recipients of endowments and centers of teaching.

Al-Azhar Mosque, founded in Cairo in 972, became prominent among these—especially after the Mongol invasions robbed rival centers like the Nizamiyah Madrasa in Baghdad of their former glory. What developed became a model for subsequent universities in Europe, Britain, and ultimately the United States. Students traveled from great distances to study with a noted scholar. They sat in a circle in front of him while he sat next to a pillar of the mosque, which became identified with him and his subject.

Through the years his position was elevated from sitting on the floor with the students, to sitting on a skin, then a cushion, and then a chair. Religious endowments began to be given to pay the salary of the occupant of the chair—the origin of "endowed chairs." Other practices developed, like students kissing the hand of the professor when they came or left—an element of academic etiquette I have been singularly unsuccessful in instilling in my students today.

From Mosques to European Universities

Many things suggest that the academic chairs of Islamic centers like al-Azhar served as models for the subsequent academic chairs of Europe and Britain. First, there was sufficient contact between Islamic and European civilizations. In addition to contact through traveling scholars, the two cultures lived side by side in Spain and Sicily. Also, a flourishing trade continued between the two, right on through the Crusades as dozens of Arabic words in English attest—words from *alcohol* to *sofa*.

Second, other aspects of Arab scholarship were clearly borrowed by the nascent European universities—most notably the textbooks. Nestorian Christians had passed Greek learning on to the Abbasid Muslims, who kept it alive and developed it with the help of Jewish and Christian subjects while schools were decaying in Christendom. By the thirteenth century Aristotle had come to Europe in Arab dress. The adaptations and paraphrases of his writings by Ibn Sina (called Avicenna in the West) were translated into Latin in Toledo and read in Paris, Louvain, and Montpellier, making a great impact on the resultant philosophy and theology in Europe.

Third, there are many similar forms of instruction that appeared in Europe after they were found in older Muslim centers of learning. Al-Azhar Mosque became a center of theological instruction in 989, and its major rival, the Nizamiya Madrasa in Baghdad, was founded between 1065 and 1067. Major parallel forms of education did not appear in Europe for a century and did not flower in European universities until the thirteenth and fourteenth centuries. Some of the earliest examples of these forms in Europe are at Bologna, where there was the greatest contact between the two civilizations. Similarities in the form of instruction included the following: Students traveled from professor to professor who, in places like Bologna and Paris, personally signed a certificate that the student had studied the material and was qualified to teach it—all this originally without the authorization of a guild or university senate. The lecturer's seat was reported to have been elevated above the students in Bologna in 1235. By 1289 Bologna had permanent chairs endowed with salaries. Endowed hostels provided living quarters and rooms for students and in Paris were divided into four "nations," according to the geographical region from which the students came. These "colleges" were developed still further at Oxford and Cambridge. Permanent charitable trusts, however, are not found in English law until the thirteenth century. The practice was adopted by the early Muslim community from Byzantine monasteries and churches and was apparently introduced into England by the Franciscans, an order that had contact with Muslims during the Crusades.

Of particular interest for this survey were chairs of Oriental languages that were attached to the universities at Rome, Bologna, Paris, Oxford, and Salamanca by Pope Boniface VIII and the Council of Vienna in 1311. The establishment of these chairs for the teaching of Hebrew, Chaldee, Arabic, and Greek was a result of the efforts of Raymond Lull, a Franciscan missionary to Muslims, and was primarily to promote the conversion of Muslims and Jews in the Orient rather than increase the understanding of the Scriptures (Mykelbust 1955, 32; Peers 1969, 350-52). Lull's efforts were doubtless influenced by Ramon de Penyafort, who persuaded the Monicans of Spain to propose such study in 1250 (for accounts before 1311, see Peers 1969, 35-36).

Academic chairs were started in North America with the establishment in 1721 of the Hollis Chair of Divinity at Harvard, which, of course, was patterned after Cambridge. The present Chair of Islamic Studies now bears no such name, because the donor, Mary Belle Varker, would not let her name be affixed to it—in keeping with years of donating her medical skill to the poor of Philadelphia without remuneration and, even in her final hour, donating her body for medical training rather than a commemorating grave.

The Legs of the Chair

Having looked at the making of the chair, we now turn to its refurbishment at Fuller Theological Seminary. Unlike the three-legged and triangular-based chair that Harvard presidents are squeezed into—perhaps to keep installations short—the Chair of Islamic Studies here stands on four legs.

The first points to the east and has been crafted primarily by orthodox and orthoprax Muslim artisans. The second points west and has been shaped by scholars from Paris and Leiden. The third points to the shrine across the street and has been made by the folk practitioners from Marakesh to Kuala Lumpur. The final one points toward Jerusalem and was carved by the Master Craftsman as he commanded his disciples to make other disciples and teach them.

Leg 1: Muslim Sources

The first leg, made by Muslim artisans, includes both the scholarship and everyday lives of those who practice formal Islam. Our approach at Fuller Seminary must start with what phenomenologists of religion call empathy—trying to enter into the religious experience of Muslims. This means

- taking off our shoes because we are in a sanctuary,
- performing mental ablutions to cleanse away preconceived ideas,
- and sitting at the feet of Muslims to learn from both scholars and common people.

My students and I have sat in a circle with an imam in a mosque in Cairo during Ramadan, the Muslim month of fasting. After asking him about the role of fasting in Islam, we asked his eleven-year-old son, proudly abstaining for the first time, what it meant to him. Muslim scholarship is a rich source. Learning has been revered and the spoken and written word carefully preserved and transmitted, even when Europe was in darkness. But this leg can support only part of the chair. Dogma has often limited research. Thus refusal to acknowledge any human element in the reception of the Quran or error in its codification and transmission has hindered textual studies. The canonization of Traditions of Muhammad that at times are conflicting has complicated the reconstruction of his biography. The focus backward on memory and transmission rather than creative research has hampered new ideas. Conservatives, against the protests of reformers, closed the door to individual interpretation of law and theology at the end of the Classical Period. Yet some Islamic thought is still adapting and growing to meet the challenges of today's world. Christian witnesses should be willing to deal with Islam as Muslims define it and with the ideals it espouses.

Leg 2: Non-Muslim Sources

The second leg was painstakingly carved by Western Orientalists and other non-Muslim scholars. They have added tremendously to the knowledge of Islam by editing manuscripts, compiling concordances and encyclopedias, and gathering and interpreting masses of material. Yet each group of scholars has tended to use its own tools rather than borrow tools from other disciplines. Orientalists, who have done most of the in-depth work, have used historical and linguistic tools—emphasizing the textual rather than the behavioral. As a result, they often have not had empathy for those they study and their religious experience.

Interest in area studies has grown dramatically in recent years. To meet the need, many professors have been hired because they are native speakers of required languages. Often, however, they have not had the critical training or discipline to teach religious studies.

Missionaries and theologians, in turn, have tended to analyze Islam by the theological categories of the Christian experience with which they are familiar. The result has been that Islam has been asked questions that are not her own and has been forced into categories that are not inherent to her.

Perhaps the greatest weakness in non-Muslim studies of Islam has been the lack of a meaningful relationship between Islamicists and historians of religion. Islamicists have studied the necessary languages and have sifted the historical sources but have made little use of the behavioral sciences. Historians of religion have focused on Islam as it is experienced and lived by its devotees but often do not have much philological and historical training.

What is needed in Islamic studies is interdisciplinary cooperation that utilizes the historico-philological methods of the Orientalist, the participant-observer skills of the anthropologist, and the balance of empathy plus objective description of the phenomenologist of religion. Christian witnesses need all the tools that are available to help them deal with the history and present experience of Muslims.

Leg 3: Popular Beliefs and Practices

The third leg of the chair is shaped by folk practitioners and includes the study of popular beliefs and practices. Students study formal Islam at al-Azhar, but across the street is a shrine where devotees go, not for knowledge but for power. They rub their hands against the tomb to derive blessing from it.

Although the cult of saints has been decried by reformers for centuries, there is some magic even in formal Islam. The black meteorite stone in the corner of the Kaaba in Mecca is touched or kissed by pilgrims to derive blessing, and the Zam Zam water there is used with similar intent. Magical practices are scattered throughout the Traditions of Muhammad, second only to the Quran in authority.

The problem is that most Islamicists are trained in formal Islam but know almost nothing about folk religion, while anthropologists are trained in folk religion but know almost nothing about formal Islam. A large percentage of Muslims, however, blend both formal and folk beliefs and practices, and we must learn both if we are to understand them and meet them where they are.

The perceived needs of folk Muslims are not identical to those of orthodox Muslims. They will probably feel the need of a savior from fear more than a savior from sin. Christian witnesses must be able to show the relevance of the gospel to these needs.

Leg 4: Mission

The fourth leg, shaped by the Master Craftsman, is our mission to Muslims. This is what makes a chair of Islamic studies in a school of world mission different from chairs with the same name in other schools. This leg is connected to and needs the other three, but the chair is unstable without it. The other three give understanding, but understanding without commitment to any need is irresponsibility.

Our mission to Muslims is a response to our Lord's command, "Go and make disciples," an answer to the Islamic call to prayer, "Come to salvation," and an echo of the worshiper's, "I bear witness"—a witness of word and deed.

As our eyes drift up to the pinnacle of the mosque, we see a crescent moon—the symbol of Islam. The crescent portrays for us the light Islam reflects and the darkness it contains, the light that recognizes Jesus as prophet and the darkness that does not see him as priest and king.

The light, of similarities with and affirmations of biblical faith, calls for bridges and contextualization. The darkness, of differences and denials of biblical faith, calls for interpretation and, especially when combined with occult elements, power encounter. Our mission calls for all the tools of the other missiological disciplines to contribute toward the goal of the establishment and multiplying of communities from Islam who have found Christ to be more than a prophet.

THE VIEW

Next we turn to the view of a dean of the School of World Mission sitting in that chair.

The Prayer Niche

The view straight in front of the chair is the prayer niche, because all teaching chairs face that direction. As prayer precedes teaching in the mosque, it must also in a school of world mission. Our Old Testament reading (Is 6:1-8) reminds us that our mission starts with a vision of God and God's call to us. Prayer is far more important than any methods; the school must be a worshipping community.

The present Muslim direction of prayer faces Mecca, but the occupant of our chair will want to turn mentally toward Jerusalem, the original direction of prayer even for Muslims. The places, of course, are not of prime importance, but the tale of these two cities describes the differences in our mission. The crowning prophet of each preached "Repent for the Kingdom of God is at hand," but

> One saw it as an earthly kingdom,
> the other as not of this world.
> One chose to rule rather than suffer,
> the other to suffer before ruling.
> One sought to center the kingdom on law,
> the other on transformed hearts.
> One felt the kingdom could be extended by the sword,
> the other only by weapons that are not carnal.
> One denied the cross,
> the other accepted it, that all might have life.

The Pillars and Arches

In the mosque each pillar was identified by the subject that was taught there, and the pillars were connected by arches. As such, they picture the interconnection between the disciplines that make up missiology, for missiology is the interaction of various disciplines toward the goal of fulfilling the Great Commission. There are three clusters of pillars in the wing of the sanctuary devoted to missiology. These clusters center around the Word, the World, and the Church.

The Word cluster is by the lectern (called literally a "chapter chair" after the quranic material read from it). The central pillar in this cluster is for the theology of mission. The Bible must remain central. The World cluster is near the door and includes pillars for the behavioral sciences and world religions. The Church cluster, as in some ancient mosques, includes pillars from earlier churches. These include church growth and the history of its expansion. Missiological education strengthens the arches between these clusters and a student's or a professor's specialty so that they create unity and strength.

The Sheikhs

The sheikhs, or deans at the School of World Mission, have sat at different pillars but have all related their disciplines to the other clusters. Donald McGavran sat by the church growth pillar but related his writing and teaching to Great Commission theology and the principles he learned in the world of India. Alan Tippett was the first professor he hired to put the pillar of anthropology at the center of the World cluster. Arthur Glasser, the second dean, was chosen to strengthen the theology of mission pillar at the center of the Word cluster. Then Paul Pierson, the third dean, was added to the Church cluster to give it historical depth and breadth. With the centers of each cluster firmly in place, the new dean's pillar of Islam is in the World cluster.

The challenge is to determine which new pillars should be named and to strengthen the arches between pillars in the missiological wing and any related pillars in other wings. Teaching mosques like al-Azhar commonly developed a cruciform plan of four wings off a central courtyard for the four Sunni Schools of Law. These would be comparable to our three schools at Fuller plus a university. Thus the arches need to be strengthened between missiological pillars like the history of the expansion of the church and church history in the theology wing, between missionary family concerns and the marriage and family program in the psychology wing, and between missionary anthropology and anthropology in the university wing. We need to interrelate all so that, like arabesque designs, they create harmony, add strength, and result in beauty.

The Book, the Study Circle, and the Sandals

The Book, either in the hand or head of the sheikh, represents the *theory* of a subject. The Study Circle of the professor and students represents the *reflection* that takes place, and the Sandals by the door represent the *practice* in the streets of life. Our missiological education has always made the three interact. Since the beginning the school has been named the School of World Mission and the Institute of Church Growth, indicating the need to relate theory and reflection to practice. To date, no professor has been given a pillar unless he or she combines academic training with years of experience. Other specializations besides church growth have been added, but the book, the study circle, and the sandals must always remain together.

Through the Door

The view through the door shows many things, and the challenge is to determine which require a pillar in an academic institution. First, we see the *colleges of different nationalities* across the street, which remind us of the need

- to listen to the voices from other lands,
- to hire more international professors to teach by pillars, sometimes in rotation so as not to increase the "brain drain" overseas,
- and to establish creative partnerships, particularly in two-thirds-world centers.

Second, we observe *women*—some liberated professionals walking confidently and some with modest head coverings. They challenge us to meet them where they are and to place more of them by teaching pillars.

Third, we see the congestion of the *city* with the urban poor and new skyscrapers. These represent a challenge to add more urban pillars that deal with urban anthropology and sociology, the church, ministry and development, and contextualized theology, and to strengthen the arches between these pillars and complementary ones in the other schools in the connected wings.

Fourth, we see the *crosses* on various churches, from the ancient to recent storefront types. These call for creative partnerships with the multiple branches of the church, where they help us with relevance and we help them with tools for ministry.

Fifth, we observe in the distance *stars of David* in the old Geniza district and on the Israeli Embassy. These challenge us to increase our training for the encounter with world religions and our attention to peace and justice issues along with our central call to evangelism.

Sixth, we see *locked gates outside many embassies*. They remind us of the increasing need to train people to serve in creative access countries as tentmakers.

Seventh, we observe the *booksellers* in the bazaar immediately outside. They have added cassettes challenging us to be accessible by upgrading continually our multimedia delivery systems, with videos, computers, electronic mail, and consultants on-site to provide personal instruction, information, interaction, and reflection so that our circle of students can extend from these pillars to those on many shores.

Cupola

As our eyes drift up the pillars to the cupola above al-Azhar, we are reminded of a higher chair by the quranic words inscribed there: "God . . . His throne extendeth over the heavens and earth." And the Apostle John, who got his certificate at the rock on the Mount of Beatitudes, describes the view from that final chair—a circle of students from every tribe and nation.

19

Missiological Education through Decentralized Partnerships

Viggo Søgaard

At this late stage in this book, most likely everything that could be said about missiological education for the twenty-first century has already been said. The reader has possibly wearied of the topic: your "RAM" is over-loaded and there is no more storage space on the "hard disk." All I may be able to add is a "virus" that will wipe out enough material to make space for what I am going to present, and to try to turn all you have learned into a concentrated form that will only be restored and made usable through a new type of "applications program": the one I am going to suggest!

THE COMMITMENT TO RELEVANT MISSIOLOGICAL EDUCATION

Fuller School of World Mission Commitment

Let us read from the catalogue:

Fuller Theological Seminary:
is dedicated to the preparation of men and women for the manifold
    ministries of Christ and his Church;
seeks to serve the Body of Christ in its worldwide ministry;

A native of Denmark, **Viggo Søgaard** and his family spent thirteen years as missionaries in Thailand. He is now associate professor of communication at Fuller School of World Mission, and spends much of his time as a consultant to Christian groups around the world. He is presently media consultant for the United Bible Societies with responsibilities for developing principles and practices for communicating scriptures to people who do not read. He is also the director of the Asian Institute of Christian Communication.

(is committed) to flexibility in curriculum design, to allow room for innovation and growth to recognize individual needs and specialized ministries;

(is dedicated) to the growth of the church in every culture of the world confronted with rapid change and unrest;

(and) because of the rapidly growing non-Western Christian missionary movement, Christian mission is now the most international, interracial, and intercultural movement in history. The goal of the School of World Mission is to be a resource to this growing movement.

Thus the aim of the School of World Mission is to help prepare leadership for the task of world mission in today's emerging world (p. 98).

The Lausanne Covenant

The Lausanne Covenant to which we subscribe says,

A reevaluation of our missionary responsibility and role should be continuous. Thus a growing partnership of churches will develop and the universal character of Christ's church will be more clearly exhibited. We also thank God for agencies which labour in . . . theological education. . . . They too should engage in constant self-examination to evaluate their effectiveness as part of the church's mission (article 8).

We also acknowledge that some of our missions have been too slow to equip and encourage national leaders to assume their rightful responsibilities. Yet we are committed to indigenous principles, and long that every church will have national leaders who manifest a Christian style of leadership in terms not of domination but of service. We recognize that there is a great need to improve theological education, especially for church leaders. In every nation and culture there should be an effective training programme for pastors and laymen. . . . Such training programmes should not rely on any stereotyped methodology but should be developed by creative local initiatives according to biblical standards (article 11).

Receptor-oriented Communication

Receptor orientation, or true love in communication (according to Charles Kraft), means that our primary concern is what is best for the other person, irrespective of the cost to ourselves.

So, as we respond to the need for missiological education, it is comforting to know the principles and commitment on which we stand. The challenge to us is to put these good words into action in the twenty-first century. The need is overwhelming.

THE NEED FOR MISSIOLOGICAL EDUCATION (WHO? WHY?)

In this chapter I will focus on three groups that have caused me to work on this topic. This does not exclude other groups with big needs, but let me start here.

Ongoing Training of Missionaries and Church Leaders

In a way this is starting at home, where we at SWM are already working. We have been able to develop relevant and effective advanced training programs, but we are only scratching the surface. In today's world an education is not finished when you complete seminary. You need to go on learning, in-service, through seminars, by way of advanced training, etc. The number of people in this category who need training counts into tens of thousands.

New Emerging Missions

In 1990 there were over twenty thousand missionaries from non-Western countries.

By the year 2000 their number will probably be higher than those from the West. Only a tiny fraction of them receives relevant missiological training. Of those who call themselves Christians, 60 percent now live outside Europe and North America. Thirty-five hundred churches are planted each week in Africa. Opposition and persecution seem on the increase. Church leaders and missionaries from such countries need training—tens of thousands of them—and only a handful of them can come to Pasadena.

Pastors

Here I will just mention pastors in European churches. The continent has been called a Christian continent, but today we have a situation with extremely low biblical literacy. New Age and other religious movements with a Hindu base claim up to one-third of the population, and the many immigrants bring in other religions. Pastors in European churches need missiological training. The need is enormous, and the response needs to permeate all our pastoral training institutions: seminaries as well as universities.

For most of the people I have mentioned above, Fuller's School of World Mission is priced out of reach. The challenge is to make the School of World Mission a global campus. I believe it can be done, but it will take courage, resolve, dedication, and a lot of work. My suggestion is to initiate *decentralized partnerships*, a system that could increase our ministry ten, twenty, or maybe even a hundred times. I realize objections and problems may seem almost unsurmountable. But let us turn the problems into chal-

lenges and opportunities. The quotations from the Fuller catalogue challenge us to be creative, so let me be bold. The challenges relate to:
— academic requirements (which we ourselves have established)
— coordination and planning (which we ourselves can control)
— finance (which can be found)
— library needs (which can be solved)
— faculty (which is available)
— credits (which can be worked out)
— facilities (which are in existence)
— development of trust and relationships (which is the practice of what we preach).

PRESENT OUTREACH

Presently, Fuller's SWM is teaching a wide variety of courses on the Pasadena campus. Students come from all over the world to study with world-class faculty. There are core courses and concentrations, special interest courses and excellent opportunities for study, research, and personal development. Some 300-400 students come to campus each year.

The advantages of on-campus study are many: All faculty members are present on campus; library resources are readily available; degrees are offered; and being away from home makes study easier. On the other hand, the disadvantages are also many: Few students can attend due to lack of finances; leaders cannot get away from responsibilities for such a length of time; teaching is done outside of the student's context and culture; children get American education or face family separation for a year or more.

A few extension centers have been established, but again only very few can attend these. The centers are controlled by the Pasadena requirements, including finances. The students are the losers in such a situation. In Papua, New Guinea, extension courses have been conducted. Students there pay half-price, but only a minority has been able to use the credits toward completing a degree at SWM. Ninety-five percent of the students have been missionaries, so local leaders are not trained. Course size is only sixteen on the average. In Nigeria the students have been primarily nationals, but few of them can get to Fuller to complete their programs. Finances have had to be different, and even the books are paid for by a Nigerian businessman who has been to Fuller.

A third approach is individual ministry by faculty members. We all teach courses all over the world, but Fuller gets no help from that (apart from public relations), and the students get no seminary credits. Even though a significant ministry is carried out, it is not a "win" situation for either Fuller or the students, and it is a hassle for the individual professor. A slightly improved format is that conducted by the Asian Institute of Christian Communication, where we have been able to establish more regular faculty-student contact, and credit has been approved. Illustration 1 shows the current course offerings.

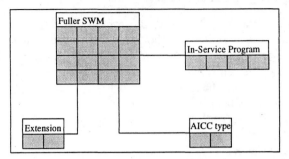

ILLUSTRATION 1: FULLER SCHOOL OF WORLD MISSION PRESENT COURSE OFFERINGS
Most courses are offered on the Pasadena campus (many more than indicated on this illustration). Several courses are available through self-study programs, called Individualized Distance Learning (IDL). Individual course modules are offered as intensive courses at various sites around the world. Eight-unit courses are offered in cooperation with the Asian Institute of Christian Communication (AICC).

A Northern Europe Illustration

If we look at the situation in northern Europe, we can define an area where English instruction is possible at the graduate level. We will find that there are many institutions that have similar interests to those of Fuller, yet due to lack of faculty and students they are not able to offer degrees in missiology. Each teacher is required to teach a wide variety of subjects.

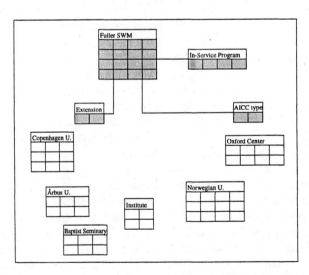

ILLUSTRATION 2: EXISTING INSTITUTIONS THAT OVERLAP FULLER SWM
The types of institutions available in northern Europe cover a wide spectrum. There are the state universities with faculties of theology. In both Århus in Denmark and in Oslo there are free faculties. Several seminaries and colleges teach courses in theology and mission. As the English language can be used for graduate-level education in Scandinavia, it is possible to include a number of institutions based in the United Kingdom.

By way of illustration, let me mention a few of these situations and place SWM in the picture with them. Eventually, several other institutions will be involved, and there may also be other American institutions involved.

If we look more closely at these institutions and their courses, we will find that each of them has courses that could be part of a missiology curriculum, and each one may in fact have courses that even Fuller would like to add to its curriculum. There are also faculty resources that are unique and of world class. The picture can therefore be expanded as shown in Illustration 3.

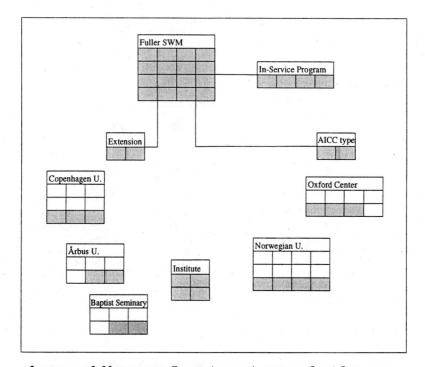

ILLUSTRATION 3: MISSIOLOGICAL COURSES ALREADY AVAILABLE AT LOCAL INSTITUTIONS

Many of the existing institutions have courses in missiology, but suffer from a lack of faculty and variety of courses. Few, if any, could provide enough courses for a degree in missiology. On the other hand, many local institutions have outstanding faculty members who could teach their specialties in a wider coalition, and several existing courses could be integrated in a degree program.

Taking a little closer look, we might discover that the number of courses could easily be expanded without any extra resources. Fuller faculty who are already spending weeks of ministry in different countries could align their courses with these institutions. Faculty at such institutions might also add new courses. There are also local resource persons who would be more than willing to teach a course. Without much extra work the number of missiological courses offered in northern Europe could be vastly increased and made very rich.

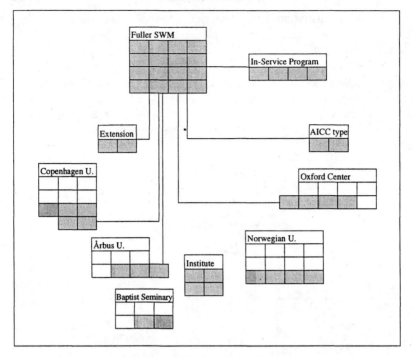

ILLUSTRATION 4: POSSIBLE COURSE OFFERINGS

By utilizing existing courses and faculty members, and by appointing adjunct faculty, a very wide selection of course offerings is possible in Scandinavia and northern Europe. Several faculty members with top qualifications can be recruited for teaching special courses. Present faculty members can be asked to develop new courses at their institutions. In addition, special institutes can be developed where intensive courses can be offered. So, together with the offerings from Fuller School of World Mission, it is possible to provide the necessary courses, libraries, and facilities for degrees in missiology.

Decentralized Partnerships

Let us leave the illustration for a moment and try to define the words in our topic:

What Is a Partnership?

A partnership is more than we presently know as networks of cooperation. It is a higher degree of mutual commitment. The word partnership makes us think of issues such as:

Shareholders: shared responsibility, shared vision;

Mutual dependency: quality performance, interdependency, cooperation, trust;

Mutual interest in success: commitment to each other, common cause, interest in mutual success ("win-win" situations);

Quality: consistency, quality control, standards.

What Is Decentralized?

A *network:* several units involved, diverse resources and background;

Off base: located at different centers, diversity in location;

Shared authority: equality in decision-making, commitment to democratic tradition, autonomy of partnership;

Resource networking: respect for divers resources, each making resources available for common cause, joint resources development;

Diversity: cultural, social, applications, priorities;

Local answers: close to need, relevant solutions, relations to local authorities and institutions, international parameters.

For Fuller SWM, this means a world mission training program on a world campus.

Motivation for Partnerships

The biblical records challenge us to partnership and relationships. Unfortunately, Western individualism has caused much division in the life and ministry of the church. A partnership dedicated to missiological education will in itself be a testimony to the fellowship that exists among the servants of the Lord.

The needs of the world for missiological education require coalitions and partnerships. In the business world we see the formation of strategic alliances all the time, and it is now assumed that such alliances are an integral part of any successful strategy. I could mention the European Airbus Consortium. In missiological training we need to bring our resources together to meet the challenges and needs of today. Competition is a luxury that we should not allow to continue to shape our service.

The whole issue of effectiveness is at stake. Each school can only do so much and span so wide. A decentralized partnership will pool resources, include new and exciting resources, and expand drastically. The overall quality can only increase, and the participating institutions can only gain from such partnerships.

We could also mention a number of practical problems that can be solved by a decentralized partnership. Fuller is located in southern California, far removed from most of the world. Only a few can make it to study at Pasadena. If we accept the world-campus challenge, the practicalities of providing advanced missiological education for the twenty-first century suddenly become much more realistic. We should not even ask if we need to form partnerships. The question is how do we do it?

A Northern European Partnership

Now let me continue with my illustration for northern Europe.

Partnership of Institutions

We need to develop real partnerships with institutional commitments and not just one-way controlled extension centers. It could also be a traveling institute, shifting base from one institution to another. The partner institutions will be represented on the board of the partnership.

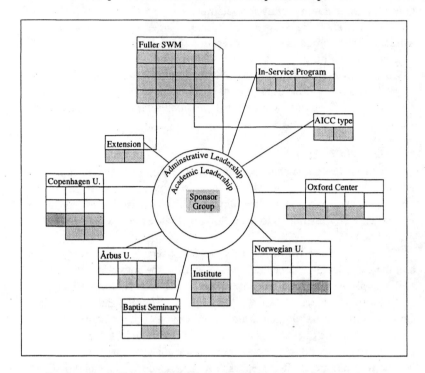

ILLUSTRATION 5: PARTNERSHIP OR COALITION LEADERSHIP AND ADMINISTRATION
A partnership as illustrated in this chapter will need good coordination and leadership. A sponsoring group of agencies will need to form a committee or board. Appointed academic leadership will coordinate and provide quality control as well as provide necessary administration.

There are several precedents to such a net, such as the Graduate Theological Union at Berkeley, where it is the GTU that issues the degrees, coordinates, and provides for library and other resources. In India, the Christian University at Serampore (started at the inspiration of the Danish government in the 1800s) has a similar function as it validates exams from some thirty-five colleges and provides quality control of faculty, students, and courses.

Administration
The partnership will need its own administration, possibly a self-governing body under the authority of the partner board/agencies. An academic council could be responsible for approval of some courses and faculty, but this responsibility will need to rest primarily with the partner institutions.

Facilities and Study Centers

The partnership will use the facilities of the member institutions, making full use of resources already available in the countries we serve, but special regional events/courses may take place at other facilities.

Library

The partner institutions will already have libraries, and these can be expanded. New developments with CD-ROM also make it possible to store hundreds of books on a single CD at a reasonable cost (currently, three hundred or more books at approximately two hundred dollars). It should be possible to produce CDs on major areas of interest, and such material can be made available at study centers, in organizations, or for personal use.

Faculty

The partnership will draw on faculty members from partner educational institutions. Fuller SWM professors can be a major source, but faculty from other institutions and regional experts also can be recruited for special courses. This will significantly expand the pool from which resources can be drawn.

Courses

There can be agreement regarding a common core of courses, but one of the advantages of a partnership is that the partner institutions can develop different courses, building on their strength and experience, making the whole program flexible and rich. A student can then study at various centers under the guidance of a wide variety of faculty members. This will advance receptor-oriented training one step further.

20

Specialization/Integration
in Mission Education

Charles Van Engen

The thesis of this chapter is that missiological education at Fuller's Institute of Church Growth/School of World Mission (ICG/SWM) involves a delicate balance between specialization and integration in a three-arena approach to missiology.

The purpose, shape, styles, and delivery systems of missiological education cannot be determined in a vacuum. Rather, to be a faithful servant of the church, missiological education for the twenty-first century must derive from the changing nature of mission itself. Our definition of mission then influences our perspectives of the nature and purpose of missiology, which in turn shape missiological education. And, due to the multidisciplinary nature of missiology, the heart of the discussion is found in the tension between specialization for a task and integration for understanding.

Specifically in relation to Fuller's ICG/SWM, this means a difficult search for a balance between specialization and integration, between being an *institute* for fostering the growth of churches and being a *school* that develops new missiological theory and fosters reflection concerning the world mission of the churches. In what follows I will discuss the tension between specialization and integration in missiological education from five perspectives: (a) the location of missiology in theology education, (b) the definition of missiology, (c) the ICG/SWM as a case in point, (d) a three-arena approach to missiology, and (e) a pyramidal model for finding a dialectical synthesis between specialization and integration in our understanding of mission and missiology. Finally, I will list what appear to be the minimal components of a missiological education that bridges the specialization/ integration dialectic.

SPECIALIZATION/INTEGRATION
AND THE LOCATION OF MISSION EDUCATION

The shape of missiological education depends on the place it is given in the larger curriculum of formation for ministry and mission in church and world. The place of missiology (and thus missiological education) in the larger theological curriculum has been a subject of much discussion for the past hundred years and is an issue not yet resolved, as Johannes Verkuyl pointed out. Verkuyl offered an excellent overview of this, mentioning Friedrich Schleiermacher, Abraham Kuyper, J. H. Bavinck, Karl Graul, Gustav Warneck, Walter Freytag, J. C. Hoekendijk, Charles Forman, Creighton Lacy, and William Richey Hogg (see Verkuyl 1978, 6ff.).[1]

Olav G. Myklebust and James Scherer, among others, concentrated on the question of the relation of missiology as a discipline to the rest of traditional theological education, asking whether missiology should remain independent from theological education, or should somehow be incorporated as part of it.[2] James Scherer summarized this issue in 1987:

As Myklebust's studies have shown, early continental missiology was set up largely on the "independent model," designed to give status and recognition to the autonomy and worth of the then unproved discipline alongside the more venerable and recognized fields of theological instruction (Myklebust 1955).[3] Recent continental missiology, by contrast, has taken a decidedly more integrative and interdisciplinary approach. Missiology in the United Kingdom, to the extent that it was done, showed a preference for complete integration into the field of church historical studies (Myklebust 1959), the assumption being that ecclesiology properly understood would generate missiological reflection. Here the discipline was never really established at the university level, and only in training colleges such as those at Selly Oak is missiology taken seriously. Missiological reflection in the U.K. was mainly done in mission executive offices by able administrators such as Max Warren and John V. Taylor. . . . In our view, missiology needs freedom from a too tight embrace by ecclesiastical structures so as to be unimpeded in fulfilling its primary task of permeating the entire *world* with the knowledge of God's saving acts (Scherer 1987a, 520).

The upshot of this was that during the last several decades, missiological education followed four general models in its struggle to find a place in the sun.

Universities

In the first place, much missiological education became resident in university faculties (the Netherlands, Germany, and Scandinavia), as a "science of missions" or as "mission studies." Whatever it was called, in the university setting missiological education emphasized the integrational perspective rather than task-oriented specialization for mission action. Specialization happened only as a secondary matter, primarily through the particular directions that individuals chose for their doctoral studies. These, however, were located more generally in an integrational approach to missiological reflection.

Seminaries

A second model placed missiology within theological seminaries that trained professional clergy for church ministries in the United States and Canada. This pattern is being followed in many places in Africa, Asia, and Latin America, as well. But here too, missiology struggles to know in which department or division it belongs, and how it may fit within the larger curriculum of standard theological education.[4]

Recently in North America a new type of relation of missiology with traditional theological education developed around the interest in "globalization," sparked by the Association of Theological Schools (ATS) (see, e.g., Thomas 1989).[5] Even so, missiological education remained subsumed under the larger agendas of general theological education. And although many persons who graduated from these programs went into full-time cross-cultural ministries, their preparation was by and large oriented to the agendas and forms of traditional theological education, not toward specialization for cross-cultural mission action. Thus these programs usually provided a minimum of familiarity with missiology from an integrational point of view, with little formation for mission in terms of specific task-oriented specialization.

Bible Schools

A third model found in Europe and North America involved the Bible school movement that offered grass-roots, practical biblical training for Christian ministry and mission. During the last hundred years, Bible colleges, Bible institutes, and Bible schools arose all over the world, specifically oriented toward equipping people for the tasks of ministry and mission. In this volume, Ken Mulholland speaks about this phenomenon—a development that radically changed the face of ministry formation, of mission education, and of mission praxis.

The Bible school movement was strongly oriented to the practice of ministry and mission. So it is no surprise to find that in the movement's approach to missiological education there arose a host of specializations in mission, supporting the many tasks of missions. Although biblical studies were considered foundational, and these provided a degree of integration in mission education, yet the final purpose was praxeological and activist. Reflection was considered important, yet right action was essential.

All three of these models can be found today in Africa, Asia, Latin America, and elsewhere. And all three models were represented by speakers at the conference from which this book resulted. It is beyond my scope here to delineate the resulting differences they represent in terms of their understanding of mission, their perspective of missiology, and the pros and cons of their respective modes of missiological education.

Schools of World Mission

Of more recent vintage, a fourth model provides the contextual setting of this book, and the subject of this chapter. During the last half century or so we have seen the birth of schools of world mission or centers for mission studies. Although these have depended on, and interacted with, the three models we saw above, they created something new that differed from all of them. Rather than opting for either specialization or integration, this fourth model is a dialectical one that is oriented in both directions. Structurally semi-independent from the regular channels of theological education, these schools of mission pursue research, reflection, historical recording, or data-gathering *about* mission and, simultaneously, they seek to advance the training of professional missionaries for *doing* mission more effectively. These schools of world mission have tended to gather a group of highly specialized scholars, who contribute their individual expertise both to further the missiological insights of their students and to train those who practice mission.

But the "school of mission" paradigm contains a built-in dialectical tension between specialization and integration—a tension that has gone mostly unexamined and unresolved. As an activist school with specific agendas, Fuller's ICG/SWM belongs to this fourth type. The particular venue of this book provides us with an excellent case in point to explore one of the most timely, complex, and essential questions facing missiology and therefore missiological education. This has to do with the relation of specialization to integration in missiology. Before we go on to examine the ICG/SWM, however, we need to examine the way we define mission and missiology, because the way one defines mission (and thus missiology) influences the emphasis one adopts in terms of the specialization/integration continuum, which in turn affects the way one carries out missiological education. This continuum can be appreciated better by examining three sample definitions of mission and/or missiology.

SPECIALIZATION/INTEGRATION
AND THE DEFINITION OF MISSION OR MISSIOLOGY

There is an intimate relationship between the issue of specialization versus integration, and the way mission is defined. In this section I will first explain how I see the continuum between specialization and integration as this influences missiology. Then I will give three examples of definitions of mission (or missiology) that differ markedly in their relation to the continuum. That will prepare us for the next section, where we will examine how the inherent tensions in the continuum affect the ICG/SWM.

As I see it, missiology struggles to live between two radically different ends of a continuum that looks like the following:

SPECIALIZATION	INTEGRATION
Action	Reflection
Mission defined by action/goals	Mission defined by concepts
Results	New insights
Task-oriented	Understanding-oriented
Present/future-oriented	Past/present-oriented
"Strategies/Methods"	"Mission studies"
"*Institute of . . .*"	"*School of World Mission*"

At one end are those missiologists who are interested in asking about the assumptions behind concepts of mission. They are committed to discovering new insights about mission and missiology. They are dedicated to profound reflection about mission and to listening to those who have been involved in, and reflected upon, the mission enterprise. Research at this end of the continuum involves predominantly the recent or distant past: who did what, why they did it, and how they articulated the vision that shaped their mission. The search at this end is for understanding and deeper wisdom. Mission is defined in terms of a consistent, coherent, appropriate, and clear relation to various concepts, perspectives, and assumptions as to what mission ought to be.

At the other end of the continuum one finds the activist missiologists. For the sake of clarity, I will describe them over against the other end of the continuum. Viewed thus, the activists appear concerned about the doing of mission. They are committed to discovering new methods and strategies for mission and missiology. They are dedicated to more effective evangelization, and want to mobilize the churches for mission. Research at this end of the continuum involves predominantly an examination of the results of mission action. Did the methods bring about the desired missional goals? This missiology is predominantly future oriented, interested in past and present primarily as they point to new, more effective action. The search at this end is for increased transformation, brought about by effective missional action. How one defines mission is of concern not so much in terms of the idea of mission but in relation to the actions and resulting effects of mission.

Now, of course, this is a continuum. Missiologists at the "integration-reflection" end would want me to clarify that they are interested in action; those at the "specialization-for-action" end would want me to state that they are interested in "right" action, based on appropriate reflection. And yet, the approach to mission and missiology differs markedly in terms of the two extremes of the continuum.

The tension between integration and specialization in missiology is closely related to the way one defines mission or missiology.[6] David Bosch and James Scherer have written about the difficulty of such definition. In 1987, Scherer stated:

> The quest for an agreed definition of *missiology* remains elusive, and neither the ASM (American Society of Missiology), nor the teaching fraternity represented by the APM, has been able to come up with one. The reasons, I would suggest, are partly attributable to *internal* differences in aims and viewpoints between those who teach the discipline, and partly to *external* factors such as unresolved relationships between missiology and the goals of theological education in general, as well as profound changes in theological trends and attitudes in the past 25 years which have had their impact on thinking about both mission and missiology. Indeed, the most serious for *missiology* . . . is current indecision, or at least divergence of opinion, about what *mission* fundamentally is.[7]

Earlier, David Bosch sounded a similar note:

> In many circles, there is a great deal of uncertainty about what mission really is. . . . The picture is one of change and complexity, tension and urgency, and no small measure of the confusion exists over the very nature of mission itself. Our task is to enter the contemporary debate and seek answers that are consonant with the will of God and relevant to the situation in which we find ourselves (Bosch 1980, 8-9; see also in Scherer 1987b, 519).

Here let me highlight three definitions that, although they do not contradict one another, differ markedly in their perspectives. I have chosen these three, because, in spite of their differences, all three definitions have affected, and will continue to influence, the nature of Fuller's ICG/SWM and may help us better understand the tensions in which the ICG/SWM exercises its missiological education. The samples I have chosen are not extreme. It would be inaccurate to place any one of these definitions at one extreme or the other of the continuum. However, by laying them side by side, we may gain a clearer sense as to how they tend to emphasize one end or the other.

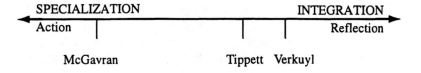

Johannes Verkuyl

Standing on the "mission studies" end of the continuum, Johannes Verkuyl's definition demonstrates a "from above" perspective that tends to be more reflective, although it is still oriented toward missional participation. [8]

> Missiology is the study of the salvation activities of the Father, Son, and Holy Spirit throughout the world geared toward bringing the Kingdom of God into existence. Missiology's task in every age is to investigate scientifically and critically the presuppositions made of structures, methods, patterns of cooperation, and leadership which the churches bring to their mandate. In addition, missiology must examine every other type of human activity which combats the various evils to see if it fits the criteria and goals of God's kingdom which has both already come and is yet coming. . . . Missiology may never become a substitute for action and participation. . . . If study does not lead to participation, whether at home or abroad, missiology has lost her humble calling (Verkuyl 1978, 5-6).

Alan Tippett

Verkuyl's approach to missiology and mission might be characterized as reflection that leads to action. In contrast, Alan Tippett's definition has the marks of a researcher who is interested in researching and reflectively analyzing the actions and events of missionary practice, especially as they are influenced by (and influence) the cultures in which they occur. Tippett says:

> Missiology is defined as the academic discipline or science which researches, records and applies data relating to the biblical origin, the history (including the use of documentary materials), the anthropological principles and techniques and the theological base of the Christian mission. The theory, methodology and data bank are particularly directed towards:
>
> 1. the processes by which the Christian message is communicated;
> 2. the encounters brought about by its proclamation to non-Christians;
> 3. the planting of the church and organization of congregations, the incorporation of converts into those congregations, and the growth and relevance of their structures and fellowship, internally to maturity, externally in outreach as the Body of Christ in local situations and beyond, in a variety of culture patterns (Tippett 1987, xiii).

Tippett's definition lies slightly further toward the activist end of the continuum than Verkuyl's. But Tippett does not go as far in the activist direction as Donald McGavran. Notice in the following that, although Verkuyl and Tippett offered definitions of *missiology*, McGavran's is a definition of *mission*.[9] Nowhere have I been able to find Donald McGavran defining *missiology* as such.[10]

Donald McGavran

Donald McGavran's definition of mission (his basis for what we could assume to be his view of missiology) is similar to, but differs in important ways from, both of the above. Although McGavran begins his thinking "from above," with regard to God's desires and plans, the heart of his perspective is "from below," in the sense of being most thoroughly concerned with the results of the action of the missiology in question.

> To many, mission is widely defined as, "God's total program for humans," and we have considered the alternatives arising from that definition. Mission may now be defined much more narrowly. Since God as revealed in the Bible has assigned the highest priority to bringing men and women into living relationship to Jesus Christ, we may define mission narrowly as *an enterprise devoted to proclaiming the good news of Jesus Christ, and to persuading men and women to become his disciples and responsible members of his church* (McGavran 1990, 23-24, emphasis his).

Donald McGavran's definition of mission is thoroughly activist. His concern is with effective missional strategy and action that yields specific results. The reason to research and reflect is for the sake of mobilization and action.

The interplay of the three definitions offered above provides a good springboard for considering the dialectical tension between specialization and integration that affects the missiology of Fuller's ICG/SWM.

SPECIALIZATION/INTEGRATION IN DYNAMIC TENSION IN THE ICG/SWM

In 1965, when Donald McGavran moved from Eugene, Oregon, to Pasadena, California, he founded an institute devoted to fostering the growth of churches. In a soul-searching article entitled "Church Growth at Fuller," Arthur Glasser reminded his hearers[11] that McGavran's book *The Bridges of God* was published in 1955, and was said by some to be, "the most read missionary book in 1956." Still, Glasser says, "In my judgment the church growth movement actually began in January, 1961, when McGavran founded what he called the *Institute of Church Growth* (ICG) in an unused corner of the library of a small Christian college in remote Eugene, Oregon" (Glasser 1987, 403).[12]

Specialization

McGavran's founding of a specialized Institute of Church Growth placed him at the "specialization-activist" end of our continuum. It was quite clear in those early years that research, writing, speaking, and thinking were to be devoted to mobilizing people for church growth. Church growth defined the integrating center and determined the outer limits of the Institute's missiology. Those who cared about the same missional activity could come and join McGavran in researching church growth. Mission, mission education, and missiology were all seen through the lens of church growth principles that were to foster the numerically verifiable growth of churches. McGavran's publications from the mid-1960s to the early 1970s were clear, focused, and insistent on this point. Here there is no tension, no dialectic. Integration is only relevant as it incorporates various cognate disciplines that foster the main agenda: church growth. Such a specific focus is necessary if one is to gain a hearing by the larger mission community, not be ignored, and start a movement. And McGavran had all the right stuff to do just that.[13]

Yet this is not the whole picture. To see McGavran and his associates in the ICG exclusively as church growth enthusiasts is an inaccurate caricature. McGavran's founding of a specialized Institute of Church Growth did not thereby exempt him from the integrative nature of missiology.[14]

Integration

To see McGavran as an integrational missiologist, we must look to the antecedents from which he drew his missiology. We have space here for only a few related examples. We could go all the way back to Gisbertus Voetius, the Dutch missiologist. Voetius (1589-1676) spoke of the threefold goal of mission as being the conversion of the heathen, the planting of the church, and the glorification and manifestation of divine grace (see Bavinck 1977, 155). I'm not sure that Donald McGavran drew directly from Voetius. But in a real sense McGavran's missiology was a restatement of Voetius, 375 years later, and represented the best of a historic and biblical understanding of mission. Yet even Voetius, in the combination of those three goals, was involved in a tension between specialization of *means* and integration of *goals*.

Donald McGavran's well-known dependence on the Great Commission of Matthew 28 places him as an heir of William Carey.[15] And even though Carey went to India to work toward the conversion of those who did not know Jesus Christ, in fact, Carey became more of an integrative missiologist than a specialist: a farmer, a merchant, a linguist and translator, a trainer of leaders, and so forth.

The German missiologist Gustav Warneck (1834-1919), considered by many to be the father of Protestant missiology, was very influential in the European scene. Although he may have exerted little direct influence on

Donald McGavran, echoes of Warneck's concern for the integration of missiology can be heard in McGavran's writings. This is especially so as these are then mediated through the administrative missiology of Henry Venn and Rufus Anderson. Their strong emphasis on what later would be known as the "indigenous churches"[16] shows the influence on McGavran of Venn and Anderson's "three-selves" concept, strengthening the ecclesial emphases of McGavran's approach. But this too involved McGavran and his friends in a tension between the integration of all that it meant for their churches to be "indigenous" and specialization of methodologies to produce the desired results.

Then came the Student Volunteer Movement and John R. Mott, along with Roland Allen, both of whom deeply influenced McGavran.[17] We could go on to mention Hendrick Kraemer and John Mackay, along with J. H. Bavinck, Arthur Brown, and many others whose influence on McGavran can be traced in his writings. In each case McGavran the integrative missiologist stands in tension with McGavran the "father of church growth" (cf. Stafford 1986).

When McGavran started the Institute of Church Growth, he immediately brought in Alan Tippett, an anthropologist by trade—but also a reflective missiologist, as we saw earlier in his definition of missiology. Then the ICG began to add faculty: Peter Wagner, Ralph Winter, Charles Kraft, Arthur Glasser, J. Edwin Orr, and so forth. The "School of World Mission" side, multidisciplinary, more reflective, and more integrational, was developing. It appears that McGavran was able to keep the two sides (action/specialist and reflection/integrationist) functioning in a mutually supportive manner. Even so, McGavran's dominance in the ICG/SWM meant that the bottom line was that mission was to foster the numerical growth of churches. In the final analysis, McGavran was an activist.

By 1973 the two sides of the school could be seen delicately balanced in the volume that Alan Tippett edited in honor of Donald McGavran, *God, Man and Church Growth* (1973). This volume, with all the ICG/SWM faculty contributing, was an interesting representation of the two sides of the continuum, showing how carefully folks struggled to preserve a dynamic tension between the two perspectives of missiology. Yet clearly, church growth activism was central.

Another example of this tension was the Lausanne Covenant. The strong influence of the ICG/SWM on the Congress on Evangelism in Lausanne in 1974 is well known, and the activist, results-oriented emphasis on church growth is clearly at the center of the Covenant. What some may miss, however, is the tension evident in the documents of the conference between specialization-for-a-task and integration-for-understanding. I believe this tension is a direct result of the impact that the faculty of the ICG/SWM had on Lausanne and the subsequent movement.

When Arthur Glasser read a paper called "Church Growth at Fuller" at the 1986 meeting of the American Society of Missiology, he spoke of the relationship of the Institute of Church Growth to the School of World Mission. It was only a couple of years later that David Bosch was invited to make an oral presentation to the ICG/SWM faculty and highlighted similar issues (cf. Bosch 1988). In both cases, the foundational issue had to do with the balance of the ICG church growth activist side and the SWM integrational side of the school's missiology. A comparison of these two papers is very interesting. Art Glasser was concerned that the church growth focus not get lost, a matter of deep concern to me as well. I also share David Bosch's concern that church growth activism (which he supported) not skew the perceptions and valuations by which the school's missiology was being integrated.

Creative Tension

Clearly this is an important continuum, and the ICG/SWM must hold together both ends. So the matter of balance is crucial, and here we come back to considering the venue and occasion of this conference. During the late 1970s and 1980s, as other faculty and programs were added, the ICG/SWM continued to multiply its arenas of investigation and specialization. Eventually, church growth as a subject of inquiry began to appear as one part of a larger missiological whole. As of 1993, the ICG/SWM counted at least eighteen different specializations, known as "concentrations," structured in a number of masters' and doctoral programs.[18] This might be seen as bringing about a reduction in the activist church growth side of the continuum, resulting in a lowering of the creative and dynamic tension between the two sides of the continuum. This would be unfortunate.

The creative tension between "institute of" and "school of world mission" may be one of the most powerful forces that propels this school forward. The tension itself may give rise to the creativity for which this school has been known. If the school were to lose the tension, if it were to go in either direction, it might lose its creative, innovative edge. Curricular considerations, the mode of integration, and the deepest values do in fact differ between the two perspectives. The "institute of" has as its most basic issue the *doing* of mission and measures its success in terms of tangible results in the growth of churches. The "school of world mission" perspective, on the other hand, has as its bottom line the doing of *appropriate* mission and measures its success by its insight, understanding, and biblical/theological fidelity, with less emphasis on church growth.

Is there a way to affirm the whole of the continuum—to continue to be the ICG/SWM, both institute and school? Is there a way whereby the ICG/SWM can serve mission agencies who want professional training for their personnel within their own individual agendas and missional tasks (especially in relation to church growth)—and at the same time serve the world church, which needs teachers of reflective missiological integration, related to the larger missiological academy, and participating in global missiological theorizing?

SPECIALIZATION/INTEGRATION
IN A THREE-ARENA APPROACH TO MISSION EDUCATION

One way to begin to address the inherent tensions between specialization and integration is to look at three of missiology's major arenas of investigation and consider what they include and how they interface with each other. In so doing, we can affirm all three definitions of missiology given above without losing their individual emphases. Together, the three-arena integration can show us how both the specialist-activist and the reflective-integrationist viewpoints of ICG/SWM may come together in a creative synthesis.

At the ICG/SWM, we have been finding it helpful to work with missiology as an integrated sum of three major areas, clearly not original with us: text, context, and community (or Bible, world, and church).[19] Here we seek to define missiology as a multi- and interdisciplinary discipline that might be represented by a series of interlocking circles. As shown in Figure 1, missiology deals with three arenas individually and simultaneously: biblical and theological presuppositions and values (A) are focused in the context of specific missional activities that happen in particular times and places (B) and are applied to the enterprise of the ministry and mission of the church (C).

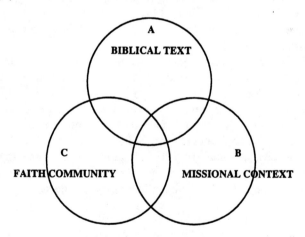

FIGURE 1: TEXT, CONTEXT, AND COMMUNITY

Text (Word)

First, missiology is *biblical* and *theological* (circle A in Figure 1), because fundamentally it involves reflection about God. It seeks to understand God's mission, intentions and purposes, use of human instruments in God's mission, and working through God's people in the world. This demands a careful yet creative interaction with Scripture, bringing both old and new questions to the text—an endeavor David Bosch called "critical hermeneutics" (Bosch 1991, 22-24).[20] Reflection on the text moves missiology to deal with all the traditional theological themes of systematic theology—but it does so in a way that differs from how systematic theologians have worked down through the centuries. The difference arises from the multidisciplinary, missiological orientation of its theologizing, and the range of questions (contextual, ecclesial, and praxeological) that are brought to Scripture.

In addition, because of its commitment to remain faithful to God's intentions, perspectives, and purposes, missiology shows a most fundamental concern over the relation of the Bible to mission, attempting to allow Scripture not only to provide the foundational motivations for mission, but also to question, shape, guide, and evaluate the missionary enterprise.[21]

Context (World)

Second, missiology is *contextual* (circle B in Figure 1). Missiology is an applied science. At times, due to this applicational nature, it looks like what some would call pastoral or practical theology. Thus missiological reflection focuses specifically on a set of particular issues—those having to do with the mission of the church in its context. Missiology draws its incarnational nature from the ministry of Jesus, and always happens in a specific time and place. Thus circle B involves the missiological use of all the social science disciplines that help us understand the context in which God's mission takes place.

Missiology borrows from cognate disciplines like history, sociology, anthropology, art, economics, urbanology, linguistics, psychology, the study of the relation of Christian churches to other religions, and the study of the relation of church and state, among others, to understand the specific context in which it does its reflection. Such contextual analysis moves us, then, toward specific reflection about the context in terms of a hermeneutic of the reality in which we are ministering. This, in turn, calls us to hear the cries, see the faces, understand the stories, and respond to the living needs and hopes of the persons who are an integral part of that context.

Community (Church)

Third, missiology is *ecclesial*—it is specially oriented toward and for the church in its mission (circle C in Figure 1). The most basic reflection in this arena is found in the many books, journals, and other publications dealing with the theory of missiology itself.[22] But the "community" arena represents much more than this. It also includes the historical pilgrimage of the way the church in its mission has interfaced with that context down through history. The attitudes, actions, and events of the church's mission that have occurred and continue to take place prior to our particular reflection will color in profound and surprising ways the present and the future of our missional endeavors.

Thus we will find some scholars dealing with the history of theology of mission[23] who, although they are not particularly interested in the theological issues as such (they don't engage very much in questions of history of dogma), are concerned about the effects of that mission theology upon mission activity in that context. They will often examine the various pronouncements made by church and mission gatherings (Roman Catholic, Orthodox, Ecumenical, Evangelical, Pentecostal, and Charismatic) and ask questions, sometimes polemically, about the results of these for missional action.[24] The documents resulting from these discussions become part of the discipline of theology of mission.

Neither missiology nor theology of mission can be restricted to reflection only. As Johannes Verkuyl wrote:

> Missiology may never become a substitute for action and participation. God calls for participants and volunteers in his mission. In part, missiology's goal is to become a "service station" along the way. If study does not lead to participation, whether at home or abroad, missiology has lost her humble calling. . . . Any good missiology is also a *missiologia viatorum*—"pilgrim missiology" (Verkuyl 1978, 6,18).

Thus a full-fledged missiology must eventually emanate in biblically informed and contextually appropriate missional action. If it does not emanate in informed action, we are merely a "resounding gong or clanging cymbal" (1 Cor 13:1). The intimate connection of reflection with action is absolutely essential for missiology. At the same time, if our missiological action does not itself transform our reflection, we have held great ideas, but they may be irrelevant or useless, sometimes destructive or counter-productive—and even our commitments to "acts of faithfulness"[25] may come to naught because they derive from uninformed reflection.

SPECIALIZATION/INTEGRATION
IN A THREE-DIMENSIONAL PYRAMID

The foregoing discussion has led the ICG/SWM to experiment with taking the three-arena perspective one step further to perceive a unified whole that is at once integrational and activist. We have found that a pyramid seems to represent most clearly the way we can bring together the three arenas of missiology, tie them to specific specializations, and integrate them all within the purpose of church growth.

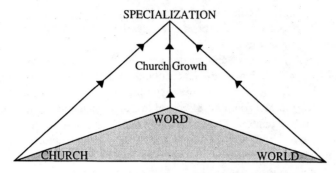

FIGURE 2: THREE ARENAS OF MISSIOLOGY

In Figure 2 the pyramidal, three-dimensional relationship brings three things together: the three-arena base of integrational missiology, the particular specialization of the mission practitioner, and the central core purpose of church growth. In this way, specializations in mission are grounded on a broader base of integrational missiology, directed toward the growth of churches, yet affirmed in their specific tasks in mission. By the same token, the three-arena base of mission needs to be expressed in concrete action (usually through specifically specialized tasks) for the sake of church growth. Finally, the church growth agenda of Donald McGavran that forms the raison d'être of the ICG/SWM becomes the central core that integrates the entire pyramid, draws the edges together toward the center, and offers the core motivations and goals of the ICG/SWM's missiology. The dynamic interrelation of these four aspects can be more clearly understood if we look at the pyramid as being at once praxeological, integrative, paradigm-forming, and limited.

Praxeological

First, as reflected in the pyramid, missiology is *praxeological.* One of the most helpful ways to interface reflection and action is by way of the process known as praxis. Although there have been a number of different meanings ascribed to this idea,[26] it appears that Orlando Costas's formulation is one of the most constructive:

> Missiology is fundamentally a praxeological phenomenon. It is a critical reflection that takes place in the praxis of mission. . . . [It occurs] in the concrete missionary situation, as part of the church's missionary obedience to and participation in God's mission, and is itself actualized in that situation. . . . Its object is always the world, . . . men and women in their multiple life situations. . . . In reference to this witnessing action saturated and led by the sovereign, redemptive action of the Holy Spirit . . . the concept of missionary praxis is used.

Missiology arises as part of a witnessing engagement to the gospel in the multiple situations of life (Costas 1976, 8).

The concept of praxis helps us understand that not only the reflection but profoundly the action as well is part of a "missiology on the way" that seeks to discover how the church may participate in God's mission in God's world. Just as in Scripture word and deed are coupled together in the narrative of God's revelation to humans, so missional action is seen as itself being theological, and it serves to inform the reflection, which in turn interprets, evaluates, critiques, and projects new understanding in transformed action. Thus the interweaving of reflection and action in a constantly spiraling pilgrimage offers a transformation of all aspects of our missiological engagement with our various contexts.

Integrative

Second, missiology is *integrative*. What is increasingly forcing itself on our attention is the way in which the three circles *in their difference* must be brought together *in their integration* for transformational missiology to work. Bible, church, and world (or text, community, and context) cannot be affirmed integratively and simultaneously unless we become very clear about how we define the integrating theme that holds the whole together. The various corners of the pyramid are drawn together by means of an integrating theme.[27] Because of the complexity of the inter- and multidisciplinary task of missiology, missiologists have found it helpful to focus on a specific integrating idea that would serve as the hub around which one may approach a rereading of Scripture. This integrating theme is selected on the basis of being contextually appropriate and significant, biblically relevant and fruitful, and missionally active and transformational. Clearly a host of different integrative themes is possible, yet all must be held together in terms of their proximity to Jesus Christ, the head of the body, the church (see Van Engen 1987; 1991, 59-71; 1981, 237-39; Berkhof 1979, 409). I would suggest that for the ICG/SWM, in faithfulness to its founder and to its raison d'être, this integrating theme is church growth. Even so, my personal suspicion is that the meaning and content of "church growth" will change as it is influenced by differing praxeological issues arising from different contexts in relation to different specializations.

Clearly we are trying to avoid bringing our own agendas to the Scriptures and superimposing them on Scripture. This was the mistake made by liberation theologians, from which they have not recovered. Rather, what is being sought is a way to bring a new set of questions to the text, questions that might help us see in the Scriptures what we had missed before.[28] As we pointed out above, this new approach to Scripture is what David Bosch called "critical hermeneutics" (Bosch 1991, 20-24).

As we reread Scripture we are faced with new insights, values, and priorities that call us to reexamine the motivations, means, agents, and goals of our missiology. This, in turn will call for rethinking each one of the traditional theological loci. Thus we will find ourselves involved in a contextual rereading of Scripture to discover anew what it means to know God in context. Robert McAfee Brown called this type of reflection *Theology in a New Key* (1978) and *Unexpected News* (1984).

In Latin America, for example, this missiological and praxeological process has especially focused on issues of Christology and ecclesiology.[29] In today's missiological enterprise, it appears that we need to allow our rereading to offer us new insights into the scope and content of our missiology, derived from a profound rethinking of all the traditional theological loci (see Conn 1993a, 102-3).

In 1987 the Association of Professors of Mission discussed at length what missiology is, and how it does its reflection. In the subsection dealing with theology of mission, it was said that,

> The mission theologian does biblical and systematic theology differently from the biblical scholar or dogmatician in that the mission theologian is in search of the "habitus," the way of perceiving, the intellectual understanding coupled with spiritual insight and wisdom, which leads to seeing the signs of the presence and movement of God in history, and through his church in such a way as to be affected spiritually and motivationally and thus be committed to personal participation in that movement. . . .
>
> Such a search for the "why" of mission forces the mission theologian to seek to articulate the vital integrative center of mission today. . . . Each formulation of the "center" has radical implications for each of the cognate disciplines of the social sciences, the study of religions, and church history in the way they are corrected and shaped theologically. Each formulation supports or calls into question different aspects of all the other disciplines. . . . The center, therefore, serves as both theological content and theological process as a disciplined reflection on God's mission in human contexts. The role of the theologian of mission is therefore to articulate and "guard" the center, while at the same time to spell out integratively the implications of the center for all the other cognate disciplines (Van Engen 1987).

When we look at the central core of the pyramid, we see the "integrating idea" or "habitus" (cf. Van Engen 1987, 524-25) of missiology as an interdisciplinary discipline. David Bosch has used the term "elements" in a similar vein to describe the component parts of an "emerging ecumenical missionary paradigm" (Bosch 1991, 368ff.). I believe one way to view these thirteen different "elements" is to see them as thirteen interrelated but differing "integrating ideas," each seeking in its own unique way to apply the three general arenas to a particular context in time and space. We could, then, see each one of them as if they were differing elliptical orbits, tracing each in its own way a unique path around the Center, Jesus Christ. But all of them are also in some way related to each other. As Bosch says:

> The elements discussed below should by no means be seen as so many distinct and isolated components of a new model; they are all intimately interrelated. This means that in discussing a specific element each other element is always somewhere in the background. The emphasis throughout should therefore be on the wholeness and indivisibility of the paradigm, rather than on its separate ingredients. As we focus our torchlight on one element at a time, all the other elements will also be present and visible just outside the center of the beam of light (Bosch 1991, 369).

Might this not offer a way whereby the ICG/SWM in its many specializations could be held together, integrated, as each concentration draws its own elliptical orbit around word, world, and church (or text, context, and community)?

Possibly one of the sources of our confusion in defining missiology, and thus missiological education—and a reason why such definition is so elusive—is that missiologists have too easily spoken past each other, against each other, and opposite each other in terms of the "integrating ideas" that hold their particular missiologies together. In actual fact, whether our missional goals be numerical church growth or Bible translation, socioeconomic liberation or interreligious dialogue, cross-cultural proclamation, evangelism or international relief and development—each missiological agenda can be seen to represent a different orbit around the Center of the three circles. The question, then, becomes one of the proximity or distance of that orbit from Jesus Christ.[30]

Paradigm-Forming

Third, missiology involves *paradigm-formation*. The central integrating idea that draws together the corners of the pyramid is that which serves to *focus* our missiology. However, we must also be concerned with the *limits* of our missiology, so that we may prevent our missiological education from getting so broad that it becomes meaningless. The integrating idea asks, What is our bottom-line agenda? But we must still work to avoid the pitfall Stephen Neill highlighted so well when he said, "If everything is mission, nothing is mission."[31] This involves something that philosophy of science has called "paradigm-construction" or "paradigm-shift."[32]

We know that paradigm-shift is normally understood (especially in philosophy of science) as a corporate phenomenon that occurs over a rather long period of time and involves the reflective community interacting with reference to a particular issue. However, David Bosch has initiated many of us into seeing paradigm-formation as a powerful way of helping us reconceptualize our mission with reference to specific communities, in specific contexts.

In these terms, a paradigm becomes "a conceptual tool used to perceive reality and order that perception in an understandable, explainable, and somewhat predictable pattern" (Van Engen 1992b, 53). It is "an entire constellation of beliefs, values and techniques . . . shared by the members of a given community" (Küng and Tracy 1989, 441-42). Thus a paradigm consists of "the total composite set of values, world-view, priorities, and knowledge which makes a person, a group of persons, or a culture look at reality in a certain way. A paradigm is a tool of observation, understanding and explanation" (Van Engen 1992b, 53).

Thus a trinitarian missiological paradigm, shaped by a biblical understanding of the Kingdom of God, would flow from the fact that the church's mission derives motivation, means, agency, and goals from the *missio Dei*, from God's trinitarian mission, through human agency, primarily by means of the church, directed toward the whole inhabited earth.[33] This larger viewpoint might help us understand the *breadth* of all the various issues that influence our missiological paradigm-construction and color our hermeneutic of text, community, and context—but it would also help us comprehend the *limits* of our praxis, the periphery beyond which we are no longer in touch with Jesus Christ, and therefore no longer participating in God's mission.

Limited

So, fourth, missiology is *limited*. The pyramid, taken as a whole, represents the boundary beyond which our missiological education gets so broad that it becomes meaningless. We know that missiology deals with a host of cognate disciplines. But we also are now aware that not everything in all those disciplines is missiology. To "give an answer to everyone who asks . . . for the hope that (we) have" (1 Pt 3:15, NIV) is mission. To study the phenomena of human religions is not. To use linguistics for the translation of the Scriptures and witness of our faith is mission. To only study languages is not. To seek to improve the way we do our accounting, business practices, administration and management in our mission organizations is related to missiology. But not all administrative and management theory is missiological. To seek new ways in which the church can be God's people in the cities of our world is mission. But not all sociology of urbanization is mission.

However, even here various mission theorists and practitioners will differ. Some will hold to a paradigm that is much wider than others. On the one hand, the scope of God's mission is as broad as we could possibly draw it. But on the other hand, the limits are more circumspectly defined by that which calls for conversion and new relationship to Jesus Christ. In the final analysis, Jesus Christ wants to "draw all men to him" (Jn 12:32) and does not "wish that any should perish" (2 Pt 3:9). That is at once the breadth and the limit of that which constitutes mission.

If we were to study Luke 4, for example, as a paradigmatic description of Jesus' mission from this point of view, we might find some very real hints as to how our missiological pyramid is both integrated and limited. Although Jesus' mission is as broad and large as Luke 4:18-19, yet it is circumscribed by that which is found in Luke 4:1-13. Jesus' mission will not include *only* feeding the hungry, or *only* political power, or *only* spectacle. There are limits beyond which Jesus, and therefore the church, cannot go. Yet within these limits, the *community* needs to be as creative as possible in its reading of the *text*, to bring to its *context* the full length and breadth, height and depth of the love of God in Jesus Christ (Eph 3).

SPECIALIZATION/INTEGRATION AND
THE MINIMAL COMPONENTS OF MISSION EDUCATION

As a member of the ICG/SWM faculty, one of the ways I am trying to live with the tension between specialization and integration is by searching for, and constantly modifying, a suitable definition of mission that seems to articulate most accurately the missiological pyramid I have described above. Such a definition must allow for both specialization and integration. As such, it must give expression to both the "church growth" as well as the "school of world mission" sides of the endeavor. So far, this is what I have come up with.

> Mission is the people of God
> Intentionally crossing barriers
> By any and all acceptable means,
> From church to nonchurch, faith to nonfaith,
> to proclaim in word and deed
> the coming of the Kingdom of God
> in Jesus Christ,
> through the churches' participation
> in God's mission of reconciling people
> to God, to themselves, to each other, and to the world,
> gathering them into the church
> and discipling them
> to become responsible members of Christ's church
> through repentance and faith in Jesus Christ
> by the work of the Holy Spirit
> with a view to the transformation of the world
> as a sign of the coming of the Kingdom of God
> in Jesus Christ our Lord.

This definition preserves the tension between specialization and integration and seeks to heighten the church growth activism that holds the pyramid together, while being clear about the limits of the paradigm. It is beyond the scope of this chapter to develop the shape this would take in terms of concrete curricular considerations. Briefly, I would suggest the following basic and essential components of a missiological education that is simultaneously specialized and integrative.

1. Biblical and theological reflection on God's mission.
2. Contextual analysis of God's world.
3. The church's reflection and practice of mission as God's people in context.
4. Understanding of the practice and results of church growth.
5. Holistic spiritual formation and insight.
6. Methodological and relational skills in integrational synthesis.
7. Missional action.

Another way to say this might be the following: The goal of missiological education for the twenty-first century at Fuller Seminary's ICG/SWM includes the integral growth and renewal of Christ's church and the transformation of God's world in a multitude of contexts in a biblically faithful manner.

And so—the tension persists and the process continues, in the power of the Holy Spirit.

Notes

1. Although dated, this portion of Verkuyl's *magnum opus* is an unequaled treasure trove of information about the discipline of missiology. Though we do not have room to deal with it in this chapter, another way of looking at the specialization/integration issue is to examine the people who have been involved in doing missiological teaching, reflection, administration, and praxis. Verkuyl's chapter "The History of Missiology during the Nineteenth and Twentieth Centuries" is an excellent survey in this regard, unparalleled in the field (Verkuyl 1978, 26-88).

2. Notice that the matter of independence of missiological education versus incorporation into the regular theological curriculum is a disciplinary variation of the specialization (thus independence) over against integration (thus incorporation) question.

3. One must remember that the predominant model of doing mission in Western Europe and (to a slightly lesser degree) in North America at the turn of the century was through mission agencies loosely associated with the churches, not through ecclesiastical structures as such. It would be natural, then, to assume that mission studies would also be carried out apart from the regular traditional track of theological education.

4. See, e.g., Myklebust 1959; Glazik 1968; Winter 1969a, 1979; Forman 1974; Beaver 1976; Hesselgrave 1978, 1979; Kinsler 1983, 1985; Hogg 1987; Soltau 1988; Conn 1983; Bosch 1982. One of the most helpful collections of essays along this line was the product of a mini-consultation on missions in theological education sponsored by the World Evangelical Fellowship, March 17-20, 1980, at High

Leigh Conference Centre. Gathered from a number of journals, the essays appeared together in Conn and Rowen 1984. In 1987 James Scherer gave an excellent overview entitled "Missiology as a Discipline and What it Includes" at the Annual Meeting of the Association of Professors of Mission, subsequently published in *Missiology* (Scherer 1987b). In that presentation he reminded folks about previous efforts to define the nature and scope of missiology. These include Myklebust 1955, 1957, 1961, Shenk 1987, Tippett 1973, 1974, along with Scherer's own earlier presentations on the subject 1971, 1985. One of the most recent discussions of this can be found in Bosch 1991, 489-98. See also "Inleiding: Wat Verstaan Wij Onder Missiologie" in Verstraelen 1988, 17-23.

5. Norman Thomas offered an excellent presentation on this issue to the Association of Professors of Mission (APM) in Chicago in June, 1989, entitled "Globalization and the Teaching of Mission"; it was subsequently published in *Missiology* (Thomas 1990). See also Neely 1993.

6. Please note in what follows that some missiologists work on defining *mission*, and then derive what they mean by the discipline of missiology, while others define *missiology* and then derive what they mean by mission. I do not have space here to evaluate the implications of either choice. Rather, I will assume that these missiologists in question want to be consistent, and that, in the final analysis, the two issues are too closely connected to make a difference in terms of our purpose here.

7. In this same article, Scherer quotes O. G. Myklebust as saying, "As I see it, the question, primarily and fundamentally, is not 'what missiology is,' but 'what mission is.' The present uncertainty is in no small degree accounted for by the failure of many missiologists to make the TEXT rather than the CONTEXT the point of orientation. Far too much attention, to mention just one example, is paid to religious pluralism and far too little to God's revelation and saving acts in Jesus as recorded in Holy Scripture" (Scherer 1987b).

8. Notice that I have not included in this discussion other definitions offered in the field that reduce missiology to purely descriptive research, data-gathering, limited history-writing, and purely theoretical reflection. Although these ways of defining missiology are clearly valid, they do not fit the case of the ICG/SWM that we are studying.

9. It is important to note the difference among these three in terms of the titles of their major works. Johannes Verkuyl's work is entitled *Contemporary Mission: An Introduction;* Alan Tippett's is called, *Introduction to Missiology*; but Donald McGavran's is *Understanding Church Growth.* A comparison of the three will show that they differ markedly in their approaches—primarily in relation to the specialization/integration dynamic. Interestingly, David Bosch's work is entitled, *Transforming Mission*—and one is hard pressed to find a concise definition of either *mission* or *missiology* in its 534 pages.

10. It is interesting to note here that a book published in Spanish that is essentially a development of Donald McGavran's and Peter Wagner's church growth theory was given the title *Misionología* (missiology), a matter that apparently brought no objection from either McGavran or Wagner (cf. Pate 1987).

11. This article was first presented verbally by Arthur Glasser to the American Society of Missiology in Chicago in June 1986.

12. For a history of the church growth movement, see, e.g., Van Engen 1981, 325-34; Rainer 1993, 19-72.

13. See Van Engen 1981, chap. 6, for an overview of this. During the late 1960s and 1970s McGavran debated not only the folks at the World Council of Churches, but also the evangelicals in North America, as well as with mission administrators and practitioners worldwide. In terms of church growth, he had a profound influence on the Southern Baptists and the Pentecostals, among others.

14. One thing that comes clear in Middleton's definitive biography of McGavran is this larger picture of McGavran as a missiologist of breadth, depth, insight, and integrational instincts (see Middleton 1990).

15. McGavran's missionary career in India, along with the impact of the Indian context on his missiology, also links him closely with Carey.

16. One of McGavran's early symposium volumes (1965) with contributions from his many friends contains a chapter written by Melvin Hodges on "Developing Basic Units of Indigenous Churches."

17. William Burkhalter wrote a doctoral dissertation ably demonstrating the close affinity of McGavran's missiology with that of Roland Allen (see Burkhalter 1984).

18. At the time of this writing, the ICG/SWM was offering the following concentrations, listed in alphabetical order: anthropology, Chinese studies, church growth, communications, contextualization, family in mission, general missiology, international development, Islamic studies, Jewish studies, Korean studies, leadership, research in missiology, spirituality and power ministry, theology of mission, translation, urban mission.

19. The three-arena nature of missiology is not original with me, or with Fuller's ICG/SWM. A number of others have highlighted something similar, particularly those who deal with contextualization from a missiological perspective (see, e.g., Nida 1972; Luzbetak 1963; Míguez-Bonino 1975; Coe 1976; Conn 1978, 1993a, 1993b; Conn and Rowen 1984; Glasser 1979; Kraft 1979, 1983; Kraft and Wisely 1979; Fleming 1980; Stott and Coote 1980; Hiebert 1978, 1987, 1993; Schreiter 1985; Padilla and Branson 1986; Tippett 1987; Shaw 1988; Gilliland 1989; Hesselgrave 1989; Sanneh 1989; Van Engen 1989; Dyrness 1990; Bevans 1992; and Jacobs 1993). This three-arena perspective draws theologically from a trinitarian view of mission as the *missio Dei* of the triune God, a view that is fast becoming a global consensus in theology of mission, although with some reservations as to the reshaping that the "missio Dei" concept received in ecumenical circles from 1965 to the 1980s (cf., e.g., Bosch 1980, 239-48; 1991 389-93; Newbigin 1978; Costas 1989, 71-87; and McGavran 1990, 20).

20. In relation to the *missio Dei*, see, e.g., Niles 1962; Vicedom 1965; John V. Taylor 1972; Verkuyl 1978, 163-204; and Stott 1979. For a fuller treatment of the hermeneutical issues involved here, see Van Engen 1993a, 27-36.

21. See, e.g., Arthur J. Brown 1907; Glover 1924, 1946; Wright 1952; Bavinck 1960; Gerald H. Anderson 1961; Boer 1961; Blauw 1962; Roland Allen 1962a, 1962b; De Ridder 1971; George Peters 1972; Costas 1974, 1982, 1989; Stott 1976; Newbigin 1978; Verkuyl 1978, chap. 4; Bosch 1978, 1991, 1993; Gilliland 1983; Van Rheenen 1983; Dyrness 1983; Senior and Stuhlmueller 1983; Hedlund 1985; Marc Spindler 1988; Gnanakan 1989; Glasser 1992; and Van Engen 1992a, 1993a. A combined bibliography drawn from these works would offer an excellent resource for examining the relation of Bible and mission.

22. Examples of some readily accessible works would include Bavinck 1977; Sundkler 1965; Verkuyl 1978; Padilla 1985; Scherer 1987a; Verstraelen 1988; Bosch 1980, 1991; Phillips and Coote 1993; and Van Engen, Gilliland, and Pierson 1993.

Clearly the most comprehensive work, which will be considered foundational for missiology for the next decade, is Bosch 1991.

23. See, e.g., Bassham 1979; Bosch 1980; Scherer 1987a, 1993a, 1993b; Glasser and McGavran 1983; Glasser 1985a; Utuk 1986; Stamoolis 1987; and Van Engen 1990.

24. See, e.g., McGavran 1972, 1984; McGavran (ed) 1972; Johnston 1974; Hoekstra 1979; Hedlund 1981; and Hesselgrave 1988. One of the most helpful recent compilations of such documents is Scherer and Bevans 1992.

25. This concept was at the center of the missiology of the 1989 meeting of the Commission on World Mission and Evangelism (CWME) at San Antonio, Texas (see, e.g., World Council of Churches 1989; Bosch 1992; Wilson 1990).

26. See, e.g., Robert McAfee Brown 1978, 50-51; Vidales 1975, 34-57; Spykman et al. 1988, xiv, 226-31; Schreiter 1985, 17, 91-93; Costas 1976, 8-9; Leonardo Boff and Clodovis Boff 1987, xxi-xxx, 8-9; Scott 1980, xv; Leonardo Boff 1979, 3; Ferm 1986, 15; Padilla 1985, 83; Chopp 1986, 36-37, 115-17, 120-21; Gutiérrez 1984a, 19-32; 1984b, vii-viii, 50-60.

27. Due to the venue of the conference from which this book emanated, I am assuming a strongly evangelical perspective that seeks, through the Holy Spirit, to be centered in a living, vibrant, personal relationship with Jesus Christ as the Son of God, about whose person, ministry, and work the gospels tell us, and about whom the apostles, Paul, and the early church testified. Clearly, once we loosen the hold on this Christology and move to a universalist position in relation to other religions, this center gets lost. If Jesus Christ is taken out of the center, missiology has no reason to exist.

28. For a more in-depth discussion of this issue, with supporting bibliographical comments, see Van Engen 1993a.

29. Orlando Costas was one of the most creative, integrative, and biblically focused praxeological missiologists in this regard. His concept of "integral church growth" has yet to permeate missiological and theological education as deeply as it needs to (see Costas 1974, 90-91; 1975, 68-70; 1979, 37-60; and 1992, 116-22).

30. What Karl Barth asked about the church must also be asked about our missiology. "How far does [the Church] correspond to its name? How far does it exist in a practical expression of its essence? How far is it in fact what it appears to be? How far does it fulfill the claim which it makes and the expectation which it arouses?" (1958, 641).

31. This well-known phrase can be found in many places (see, e.g., Neill, Anderson, and Goodin 1959, 81; Blauw 1962, 109; Van Engen 1993b).

32. See, e.g., Hempel 1965, 1966; Toulmin 1961, 1972; Barbour 1974, 1990; Kuhn 1962, 1977; Fetzer 1993a, 147-78, 1993b, Küng and Tracy 1989, 3-33; and Bosch 1991, 349-62.

33. However, one must be careful not to allow the *missio Dei* concept to take on the kind of deformation that it suffered in the missiology of the World Council of Churches from 1965 to 1985 (see, e.g., Scherer 1993a). What I have in mind here is much closer to what Georg Vicedom originally meant in *The Mission of God* (1965).

21

Moving Forward from Where We Are in Missiological Education

Edgar J. Elliston

Equipping God's people to accomplish the *missio Dei* in the twenty-first century will require more diversity and cooperation than has been known hitherto. As the opportunities are multiplying, the complexity of the task is also increasing, with new opposition. More of the same kinds of missiological education will put us further behind. The church needs new paradigms of missiological education freshly drawn from both the text and the contexts of ministry.

The other chapters of this book provide exposure to a wide range of contemporary perspectives in missiological education and to the discipline of missiology. Brief descriptions of the major Christian communities ranging from Roman Catholic, Eastern Orthodox, and Protestant to Pentecostal and Charismatic stretch our awareness of what is being done in missiological education. Views of and from vastly different regions and arenas of mission open vistas of opportunity and challenge for the church. The role of the behavioral sciences continues to challenge our contextual research and our interpretation of God's revelation. Hints to the many possible options for alternative delivery systems are presented with some criticism of the traditional and a proposal for a new way through decentralized partnerships. Together they present a renewed challenge to integrate the action of carrying out the *missio Dei* and to reflect about it in and from an educational viewpoint.

Edgar J. Elliston is associate dean for Academic Affairs and associate professor of Leadership in the Fuller School of World Mission. He served eighteen years with the Christian Missionary Fellowship in Ethiopia and Kenya.

This range of missiological concerns requires the whole church's attention for the equipping of the men and women who are committed to mission. No single congregation, agency, center, institute, college, seminary, or university can or should attempt to address all of the issues. No single theological or world perspective can expect to provide adequate discernment of either the text or context to complete God's mission. No single agency or research institution can address the range of actions to be taken or provide adequate reflection for the whole church. All of God's people are needed.

The other chapters depict significant diversity in addressing the basic educational questions: why, who, what, where, when, and how. This chapter gives more attention to these basic questions. When Andrew Walls responded to the request to reflect on designing a missiological education from scratch, he wisely said, "The first question must be about the people to whom it is addressed and the purpose for which it is designed."[1] His own odyssey illustrates the uniqueness of each person's equipping and the impossibility of "universalized" missiological education programs.

The rationale for designing curricula for missiological education should follow the same kind of sequence as in other education. One should begin with setting the purpose, selecting appropriate learning experiences and organizing them appropriately, and evaluating along the way and at the end to inform the essential curricular decisions. While this sequence, taken from Tyler's Rationale (Tyler 1949), provides a foundational curricular perspective for this chapter, Tyler's categories are not slavishly followed. They will be seen, however, in the curricular issues and in the organization of the recommendations.

While missiology is emerging as an academic discipline,[2] the purpose of missiological education is not just for the advancement of the discipline. It must equip men and women to lead others into the Kingdom of God, so they may become mature citizens of the Kingdom as they lead others also. Missiology provides a wide range of reflective and theoretical perspectives to assist in explaining both God's revelation and the phenomena we encounter, verifying our observations, and projecting reliable courses of action. God's servants in mission would be wise to learn these theoretical perspectives as very practical means to help achieve the mission to which God calls his people.

Missiological education necessarily addresses the development of all people to be able to cross socio-cultural, economic, spiritual, and other barriers with appropriate attitudes and spiritual maturity. Missiology primarily involves the communication of the gospel across the barriers that exist between the Kingdom of God and the kingdoms of this world, where issues of society, culture, language, world view, and diverse roles and status come into play. Wilbert Shenk argues, "Indeed, we should recognize that mission is always a cross-cultural movement—from the realm of the Kingdom into the world. Geography and culture are secondary to this fundamental fact."[3]

Missiological education addresses the equipping for and in this task. It also addresses the research and reflection about the task for the further equipping of others.

Missiological education may emerge from a single discipline, but more often is multi- or interdisciplinary. Theology, history, education, anthropology, sociology, linguistics, economics, geography, psychology, and political science all contribute to an understanding of God's revelation and of the world to which we have been commissioned as the people of God.

Excellence in missiological education should characteristically include rigor in terms of developing competence in theory and research and the development of commitment to the goal of mission. Gerald Anderson calls for rigorous research and writing in the classical missiological disciplines as a base for this education. In the same way, missiology sorely needs rigorous interdisciplinary and applied research.

Educational excellence occurs in the context of a holistic approach to education, including a focus on a person's character and relationship with God, knowledge, and skills. Effective missiological education demands a balanced focus on spiritual formation, ministry formation, and strategic formation[4] inputs (including cognitive and skill dimensions); ministry experience[5]; and dynamic reflection.[6]

Effective missiological education includes active participation of three major contributors: 1) the Holy Spirit, 2) the community in which one is to emerge, including one's instructors and followers; and 3) the emergent leader himself or herself.[7] The Holy Spirit superintends the whole process. The existing leaders and community provide the means for implementing the instruction by contextual preparation, selection of the emergent leaders, delivery of the instruction, discipline, encouragement, and recognition. The emergent leader's role consists primarily of trusting and obeying with the goal of becoming trustworthy and competent.

DISCIPLINARY FOUNDATIONS

Were one to rank the foundational disciplines for missiological education from the other authors in this text the order would be clear: biblical studies, theology, and behavioral sciences. These foundational disciplines provide bases for understanding the text and the ministry context both from which and into which the missionary is going. Mary Motte reminds us that the *"Dei Verbum*, the [Second Vatican] Council's *Dogmatic Constitution on Divine Revelation*, insisted upon the need for solid scriptural foundation for all those engaged in the proclamation of the gospel (nos. 21-25)."

Scripture provides the purpose, imperative, the substance of the message, values for the means, the criteria for evaluating the outcomes, examples of both effective and ineffective approaches, and criteria for distinguishing acceptable and unacceptable means of accomplishing the *missio Dei*. The beginning point of any missiological education then must be solidly biblical. All of missiology must be centered on what God has revealed leading to transformed lives characterized by faith and a missionary commitment.

However, as Paul Hiebert writes, "Theology is the daughter of mission, not its mother. Most of the theology in the New Testament was worked out in response to mission problems. . . . If we view theology in this light, missionaries need the help of theologians, and theologians would find their work relevant to everyday life."

Without a close integration in missiological education two dangers quickly surface. Hiebert describes them as "a theology divorced from human realities and a missiology that lacks theological foundations." Missiological education in the future must increasingly refocus on theology as the theological roots are seen in their missiological context. Wilbert Shenk describes the theological foundation for missiology,

> The Great Commission institutionalizes mission as the raison d'être, the controlling norm, of the church. To be a disciple of Jesus Christ and a member of his body is to live a missionary existence in the world. There is no doubt that this was how the earliest Christians understood their calling.

While an understanding of the text is essential, an understanding of the context is also necessary to interpret the text and to understand the people who are to receive it. Theology demands an understanding of the context. The behavioral sciences serve to assist in providing perspective and an understanding of the widely diverse contexts in which the communication of the gospel occurs.

Darrell Whiteman suggests that the behavioral sciences not only help in providing a perspective of understanding the ministry context, but they assist missiologists to understand their own contexts out of which they interpret Scripture. He suggests that the behavioral sciences also help clarify the "conversation between text and context, between gospel and culture, between the universal and the particular." Until both sides of the communication are

> dealt with, non-Christians will continue . . . to perceive Christianity as a foreign, Western enterprise. The relevance of the transforming power of Christ in their own life will escape them, and they will dismiss Christianity as something alien to them or of little consequence for their society.

To equip God's people for missiological ministry from the perspectives offered in this book, missiological educators must address several curricular variables. However, to design curricula the variables mentioned in this volume must be treated explicitly within the contexts where the missiological education is developed and delivered. Furthermore, in the formation of missiologists as agents of the Kingdom and as disciples reflecting on God's activity, one must remember that the primary superintendent and actor is the Holy Spirit. As missiological strategies are formulated, we must remember that the battle, its plan, and the outcome are the Lord's. We must be careful in our training not to discredit faith, commitment, and obedience through pride in academic excellence.

CURRICULAR VARIABLES IN MISSIOLOGICAL EDUCATION[8]

Curricular perspectives or values emerging from theology and the behavioral science-based understandings of the contexts provide the final layer of planning before the rubber meets the road in missiological education. The missiological curriculum is the process where the values, perspectives, and aims are brought to bear with the learners. These curricular perspectives require an ongoing process of decision-making to keep the educational process theologically sound and contextually appropriate. As any of the following variables change in the context—either the learning context or the context to be served—corresponding adjustments should be made with the other variables. In some ways it is like flying a thirteen-stringed kite. All need continuous attention, and one is in constant danger of becoming entangled in or entangling the lines.

Each of the following variables interacts with the others. As plans call for a change in one variable, all of the other variables should be brought into line with the change. The purpose, as the primary variable, provides the overall direction and intent. However, the immediate situation will determine the priorities of the remaining variables and the degree of influence each one will bring to bear. For example, if resources are limited, then the educational structures and delivery system will be affected. Selection of faculty and students will be affected. On the other hand, if the selection of a given group of people as students is a priority, then the delivery system, faculty selection, timing, costs, and venue will need to be adjusted. Or, again, if the venue serves as a primary priority, limitations may be placed on student selection, faculty recruitment, and cost containment.

Purpose

The purpose of missiological education[9] is to equip[10] the people of God[11] for mission. This equipping requires development in terms of cognition, skills, and spiritual formation. Effective missiological education will set the person who has been fully equipped on a path of both action and reflection. *Mission* here clearly refers to the *missio Dei*. Mary Motte, writing from a Roman Catholic perspective about the purpose of mission and missiological education, says, "the central meaning of mission is *a call to conversion*; it is a challenge to *transform culture*." Michael James Oleksa, from an Orthodox perspective, writes, "The initial goal of every successful Orthodox mission is to incarnate the gospel in a local language and culture, realizing that this task will require centuries to complete." From an evangelical perspective, Charles Van Engen writes,

> Mission is the people of God
> Intentionally crossing barriers
> By any and all acceptable means,
> From church to nonchurch, faith to nonfaith,
> to proclaim in word and deed
> the coming of the Kingdom of God
> in Jesus Christ,
> Through the churches' participation
> in God's mission of reconciling people
> to God, to themselves, to each other, and to the world,
> gathering them into the church
> and discipling them
> to become responsible members of Christ's church
> through repentance and faith in Jesus Christ
> by the work of the Holy Spirit
> with a view to the transformation of the world
> as a sign of the coming of the Kingdom of God
> in Jesus Christ, our Lord.

Learner Selection

The outcomes of missiological education depend more on the learners who are selected than any other variable. Questions of giftedness, calling, commitment, spiritual maturation, and life and ministry experience all come into the picture. To select the "right" people for missiological education one must first assess the expectations for being "thoroughly equipped" at the end of the educational process.

Through the preceding chapters several different kinds of people are identified as potential learners. If missiological education is to be broadly conceived, then the selection process must also be more broadly designed. Tite Tiénou questions learner selection, raising a much broader significance than his African focus, "Are the missiologists to be trained Africans or non-Africans?" Even among these chapters one almost reads a bias toward equipping the Western missiologist rather than the African, Asian, or Latin American. Who indeed will or should be taught? He poignantly raises another question bearing on learner selection, opening another arena of sensitive discussion, "Should we expect Africans to be consumers of mission or producers of mission and full participants in it?" Who *should* be taught? Samuel Escobar observes, "The key difference between a missionary and a missiologist is that while the missionary accomplishes the task that his or her call demands, the missiologist *also* reflects about the task in a *critical* and *systematic* way." Should we not select men and women who serve at every level who can and will reflect on the task in a *critical* and *systematic* way?

In addressing the question of selection Ralph D. Winter strongly argues that

> *missiological education for the lay person* is the best hope of rescu- ing our generation from a "Great Commission-less" Christianity . . . which is a deadly and widespread heresy within the Western Churches and . . . a fatal disease striking at the very root of the global Christian mission. . . . *Missiological education for the lay person* outranks the strategic importance of training of professional missionaries.

The key point is not

> whether lay people are being given the Bible or not, or seminary train- ing or not, since in fact most seminary students really are *lay people*. The key point is *which* lay people are able to get the necessary train- ing to be effective pastors and Christian leaders. Our seminaries are not teaching the wrong things. They may be teaching the wrong people. The awesome reality is that the *right people*, for the most part, are unable to gain access to the traditional institutional structure of the seminaries.

Who are the *right people* for missiological education? Are there Chris- tians who should not be equipped for their part in the *missio Dei*? Obvi- ously, not everyone should be accepted into any given missiological pro- gram. However, missiological education should undoubtedly be provided much more broadly.

Five Kinds of Missiologists

At least five different kinds of missiologists may be differentiated for the purpose of missiological education . The curriculum for each differs in specific goals and objectives, content, venue, cost, resources, faculty selec- tion, scope, timing, and delivery system, even though the purpose may re- main the same.

Each of the following kinds of missiologists will share a different mix of characteristics. A missiologist in terms of this chapter refers to a person who is committed to the study of, reflection about, and practice of Christian mission. The Kingdom needs several kinds of missiologists. These types of missiologists are unevenly distributed between the major variables of "study" and "practice." Many more practitioners are needed whose theoretical foundations may be less than theoreticians who make the study of the *missio Dei* their lifetime work. All, however, should reflect critically and systematically about the particular missional ministry to which they were called.

Briefly, Type 1 missiologists are practitioners who lead small groups where the sphere of influence is limited. They have the most contact with nonbelievers both in mono- and cross-cultural contacts. Nonprofessional lay missiologists are seldom formally educated for mission. In the New Testament they are the unnamed hundreds who were scattered abroad sharing the good news with their friends and relatives. They were the ones who first went to Judea, Samaria, the coastal plains, and Antioch. Hundreds of thousands of this kind of missiologist are needed in the church today, to send, support, and go in the making of disciples. These servants would likely move within their own cultures or, if they are bi-cultural, between their cultures.

Type 2 missiologists are also lay leaders, but they have typically had more nonformal instruction and more experience. They often supervise other lay workers as did the early deacons. Philip would have fit into this category. They are paraprofessionals and are seldom paid. Their sphere of influence is larger. Tens of thousands of this kind of missiologist are needed. This class of missiologist would often fit into what is described as nontraditional, "tent-making" or self-supporting missionaries. They often move across cultural boundaries and may have access among peoples who would be closed to the more "professional" missionary.

Type 3 missiologists have a still larger sphere of influence and often serve as short- or long-term missionaries. They typically have some formal education in missiology and may be paid or may be bi-vocational. They fit the traditional missionary role. They may serve in either generalist or specialized roles (for example, evangelism, church planting, teaching, development). They may or may not be ordained. Their influence, as with Type 1 and Type 2, is direct, face to face. They know the people they influence, and they deal with them directly.

Type 4 missiologists differ in their sphere of influence, which is much wider. Their influence typically is felt regionally. They may serve as mission administrators or team leaders. Their influence is indirect; that is, they may know who is being influenced, but they work with the missionaries and local national leaders or others who provide that influence.

Type 5 missiologists are even more distant from the people who are influenced. They typically have national or international influence. They influence through writing, teaching, mass media, or policy-making.

Each of these kinds of missiologists is called to influence others and reflect on that influence. Each one is crucial to the Kingdom and its functioning. However, the equipping that is required for each is different. The gifting required also differs. The distribution in terms of numbers of each type is different. The number of Type 1 personnel needed in mission vastly outnumbers the Type 5 personnel. Yet for every kind of missiologist theo-

logically and contextually appropriate missiological equipping/education
is required. Each requires a different balance of content, skill development,
attitudinal development, and ministry maturation.

Yet the selection for each kind of emerging missiologist requires a similar base. Each one must be called and gifted. The selection criteria should
follow the basic biblical guidelines of demonstrated faithfulness in ministry.[12] Winter correctly asserts, "The kind of leaders the Bible defines for the
church is not easily discernible at the time people in their early twenties
register in a seminary." He goes on to say, "It seems to me that unless seminaries make what they teach *accessible* to the full spectrum of believers, the
greatest leadership potential of the church cannot be harvested—nor can
the seminaries survive!"

Content

What should we teach? The content question is often the first question
raised, even before the "who" question. As noted above, many different
people are to be taught. What is to be taught will depend on who the learner
is and what the learner brings to the learning context in terms of giftedness,
calling, ministry experience, spiritual maturity, general and specialized education, and what the expectations are for the learner being thoroughly
equipped. The difference between the prerequisites and expectations comprise the required content.

How, when, and where the content is taught will shape the perception of
what the content is. Likewise, the content will be understood in terms of
who teaches. Given the preferred learning styles in much of the world today, the expression of the content should be considered in diverse terms
including story, parable, metaphor, drama, song, and art form alongside the
deductive propositional presentation. The diversity of God's self-revelation
in Scripture should be taken as a cue for the needed diversity in the expression of the content of missiological education.

Woodberry's focus on the *word*, the *church*, and the *world* as the basic
core issues for every missiologist is necessary, whether we are dealing
with a Type 1 or a Type 5 leader. Large missions such as Youth With a
Mission (YWAM) give their initial orientation to these three in the context of a strong focus on spiritual formation. YWAM equips many Type 1
and Type 2 leaders. While they may not be seen as missiologists, their
reflections provide the personal motivation and instruction for thousands
of churches across the globe to become involved in mission. On the other
end of the scale, at the Ph.D. level, these same issues remain, but in greater
depth and breadth.

Critical thinking and research need to be done in every realm of
missiological education and then translated appropriately for implementation. Every kind of missiologist needs to reflect critically in the midst of
missional action. Paul Hiebert identifies one of these critical areas,

We must reexamine the presuppositions behind our theories to determine the extent to which they are based on biblical assumptions, or
on secular scientific ones. . . . We must move from positivism and
instrumentalism to a critical realist epistemology. Modernity and its
offspring, colonialism, are built on a positivist epistemology . . . [that]
affirms that scientific knowledge is an accurate photograph of the
world, having a one-to-one correspondence with reality.

The instruction about conversion must go beyond the raising of hands or
the "making of decisions." As Hiebert says, "We must recognize that conversion must take place not only on the level of explicit beliefs, but also on
the level of world-view assumptions." Oleksa's multigenerational indigeni-
zing perspective needs to be a part of the content of our instruction.

Hiebert's call for breadth in instruction applies to every type of missiologist from the theoretical strategist to the front-line evangelist.

We must go beyond contextualization to an inculturation in which the
prophetic call of the gospel leads to personal and corporate transformation. Contextualization without transformation leads to Christ-pa-
ganism. Transformation without contextualization lacks evangelistic
outreach.

Part of the content must be the building of an awareness of history and
of current affairs which gives hope in the midst of suffering and opposition.
While one may disagree with Ralph Winter's statistics,[13] his perspective
about the relative growth of the church since the first century provides much
confidence in the midst of closed areas of mission where "creative access"
equipping and sending must occur. Now is the time, as Hiebert suggests,
that "we must move from a stress on the autonomy and independence of
national churches to interdependence and partnership in mission."

This new focus in partnership in mission is serving to usher in a new era
in missiological education, which must in part focus on postdenominational
missions. We live in a postmodern world, in which many missions are emerging that have little or no relevance to traditional denominational structures.
The Deeper Life Church in Nigeria, the Vision of the Future Church in
Argentina, the Hope of Bangkok Church in Thailand, and others like them
have been born outside the traditional denominational and mission structures. They comprise a significant growing edge of the church. Missiological
education needs to include the whole breadth of the church as new structures and forms are currently emerging.

Contemporary missiological content must, as L. Grant McClung, Jr. insists, include "the preeminence of Jesus and the presence of the Holy Spirit."
He continues, "Our training must follow the pedagogy and paradigm of the
Spirit in a Spirit-directed, Spirit-driven missiology that openly confesses
with Moses:

If your presence does not go with us, do not send us up from here. How will anyone know that you are pleased with me and with your people unless you go with us? What else will distinguish me and your people from all the other people on the face of the earth? (Ex 33:15-17).

In another vein, Tiénou writes of a liberating need in the content of missiological education in and for the Two-Thirds World,

What is urgently needed in Africa is missiological training that will liberate African Christians from perceiving themselves solely as re- cipients of mission. For it is increasingly difficult to hold these two convictions simultaneously: Africa should be a primary target of mission; African Christianity has remarkable vitality.

Ken R. Gnanakan in his relationship to the Asia Theological Association works with the content of theological and missiological education on a daily basis, and yet he writes that what is needed is "less theory, more praxis." He insists that it should be "faithful to the Bible," and in that way it will also be practical. He goes on to suggest that the missiological curriculum should be "holistic":

Holism refers to an interrelatedness. Missionary training must enrich the student in seeing the interrelatedness of all of life. When training has been holistic the missionary's whole approach to the ministry will be . . . to become part of the community and culture in such a way that . . . [the missionary] will not only display a sensitivity for the context, but will also be accepted by the hearers as part of that context.

While not all missiological education should be confined to seminary education, Gnanakan, Hiebert, and others all strongly contend that, as Gnanakan puts it,

Mission training must become part of seminary training. . . . Unless and until mission training is seen as part of overall seminary training, the division between mission and theology will itself continue to grow to damaging proportions.

The issue that Kennon L. Callahan made about the "mission" church (Callahan 1990) has yet to be realized by most seminaries and Bible colleges. We are no longer living in a Christian society (if we ever did). For pastors to be effective they must realize that they are serving in mission outposts. Part of the content of this missiological education is what Shenk and Gnanakan have called for as "intracultural" missiological education.

In our age of technology and the common triumphalism of the American, lessons from China need to be learned. Even as Tiénou raised the issue of suffering out of Africa, so also Dauermann raises the issue of suffering from the Jewish community. Missiological education must address the issue of suffering not in a triumphalistic way, but, as Dauermann suggests, through "compassional mission."

What must we teach? The whole counsel of God. We must also lay bare the circumstances —both spiritual and social—of the people who are yet to believe so that we may allow God's power to be employed through us to influence others toward the Kingdom. While not totally neglected in the other chapters, the spiritual context in which the *missio Dei* seeks to cross spiritual barriers does not receive prominent attention. One runs the risk in the study of missiology of employing the social sciences, which do not discern spiritual forces well, or working from Western theological paradigms, in which spiritual forces are minimized. The spiritual side of the *missio Dei* must be taught both in its theological fullness and in the communicational struggle for ultimate allegiance.

The social sciences serve an important function in missiology as they assist in the discernment of the social and cultural situations of the people to be served. However, because of pervasive Western rationalism, the danger to depend solely on the social sciences for discernment remains. It may be easy to explain complex spiritual phenomena using anthropological, sociological, or psychological theories while altogether missing the spiritual dimension.

In whatever we teach as content we must bring the learners to understand that it is only by God's power working through us that God's will can be done.

Costs

The cost of the missiological education must be borne in mind for every related constituency. Costs affect accessibility. The higher the cost, the less accessible the education will be to those people who need it most. Seminary and Bible college education is already out of reach for most of the lay people who would benefit from it the most both in the West and especially out of the West. A single master's level course at Fuller Theological Seminary or B.A. level course at Azusa Pacific University or Pacific Christian College is more than the annual salary of pastors in many countries.

Costs also influence one's perception of worth. A free missiological education is no more desirable than one which is out of reach. That which costs nothing is often perceived to be worth nothing. Costs must be commensurate with the perceived benefits and yet within the ability of the students and served constituency to pay.

And still, the cost of missiological education in its present forms simply excludes most of the leaders of churches worldwide. To design effective missiological education for the twenty-first century the cost simply has to be less for every level of missiologist.

Resources

Akhtar Hameed Khan, a noted Muslim scholar from Bangladesh, once counseled me about my projections about a people whom I considered poor. He said, "You need to look from their eyes."[14] I was thinking about the Turkana people in northwest Kenya, who are only now coming into a cash economy. They still largely function on a pastoral economy based on camels, goats, sheep, and occasionally cattle. By their dress, lifestyle, and general outward appearance I had concluded that they were poor because of having few resources. About five years later, when working with a missionary to establish a clinic in the region, I learned that he was correct in his counsel. The people were able out of their resources to establish a clinic, stock it, and provide community guidance for it. Poverty relates more often to the question of power than economics! (Christian 1993).

Available resources serve both to constrain and to enable the educational structure that is designed. If the resources are not sustainable or renewable from the community to be served, long-term difficulties will result. The question of what resources *ought* to be used should be asked more often. "Outside subsidies may be seen as useful for research and development, but provide a significant risk for ongoing program support" (Elliston and Kauffman 1993, 161).

The selection of resources should be constrained or guided by at least three key values:

1) The choice of resources should serve to meet the long term purpose. 2) The resources selected should serve to enhance local resources from the community being served rather than deplete or depress them. 3) The selection of resources should not move the community being served into a long term dependency on outsiders (Elliston and Kauffman 1993, 161).

Part of the design of missiological education should focus on the formation of resources for that education, whether finances, personnel, facilities, or research bases. One should not overlook the resources that are at hand in the community to be served. Those resources should be inventoried first to see how the educational structure can be designed. Local resources are critically important for the equipping of Types 1, 2, and 3 missiologists. Their sphere of influence is in the local community. To be effective, then, the local community must be engaged to empower these emerging leaders to have influence there. By engaging the local community in the educational process, appropriate resources are used and dependencies on outsiders diminish, freeing other resources to be used elsewhere. The use of local resources also builds ownership and local expectations enhancing the influence potential of the emerging leaders.

Timing

When should missiological education be provided? Questions about the learners' preferred learning style; career stage of development; and annual, monthly, weekly, and daily cycles need to be raised. The duration of each segment and of the whole program needs to be addressed in terms of the purpose and fit for the learners. The designer should ask, "How can the timing be adjusted to best accomplish the purpose, given the constraints of these other variables? (Elliston and Kauffman 1993, 159-60).

Missiological education requires flexibility. The range of different types of missiologists needing to be equipped requires a similar range of flexible options for timing. Some younger students may be able to study full time in a resident situation. Older, married, and fully employed learners may be able to give only an hour or two a week to structured learning experiences. Each type of missiologist requires a different set of timing constraints. To optimize effectiveness, timing issues should be designed for the convenience of the learner, not the institution, if the purpose is to be the primary guiding variable with the selection of the learner as a high priority.

Control

Tiénou asks whether the African will be the "consumer or the producer of mission." In part he is asking *who* will be in control? Will the old colonial structures remain intact? Will neo-colonial structures emerge? Will the thinking of the theological and the behavioral sciences be free to be African? Will the powers of economics and politics be African?

The exercise of control obviously involves the exercise of power. If part of the aim of missiological education is empowerment, it logically follows that the learners and the communities being served should increasingly participate in the control. Participation in decision-making provides a range of learning experiences that are difficult to simulate in the classroom. If missiological education is to emerge in and from a given community, whether the community is regional, ethnic, denominational, age, or gender related, that community must participate in its design, development, implementation, and evaluation.

Venue

Where should the education be provided? Obviously, if one is designing from the learners' perspective, it should be where it is accessible, where the learning will be optimal, and where the learners will be empowered most effectively to serve the community they are called to serve. Most frequently the venue is chosen for the sake of convenience for the institution to accommodate the faculty, have library access, and take advantage of institutional facilities.

However, in a time when venue paradigms are changing in business and other educational forms, theological and missiological education must also reconsider its venues. One may complete an accredited B.A. or M.B.A at home.[15] Businesses are increasingly using teleconferencing to link learners in several locations simultaneously. The new venue/time paradigm appears to be "wherever/whenever" (Barker 1992; Davis 1987; Tom Peters 1988; and Covey 1991). Now is the time for a new paradigm to appear because so many problems are occurring with the old one. As Barker observes, "Sooner or later, every paradigm begins to develop a very special set of problems that everyone in the field wants to be able to solve and no one has a clue as to how to do it" (Barker 1992, 39). This shift in venue and the related paradigmatic changes presents a significant risk for existing structures. Again, as Barker observes, "New paradigms put everyone practicing the old paradigm at great risk. The higher one's position, the greater the risk. The better you are at your paradigm, the more you have invested in it, the more you have to lose by changing paradigms" (1992, 69). He quips, "It is important not to mistake the edge of a rut for the horizon" (1992, 208).

Leaders always lead in a situation or context. To be effective they must be empowered in *that* context.[16] Their authority or right to use power comes from three sources: First, from God, who gives the right to use spiritual power. Second, from the people who have power over them and who *delegate* the right to use organizational or community resources for influence. Third, authority is *allocated* by one's followers; that is, they allocate the right to be influenced by the emerging leader in their situation. The emerging leader may use personal or organizational resources to influence. All of this process occurs in a context—a ministry context. One may lead in a school, but then he or she is a school leader. To lead in a community one must be empowered in that community. The venue for equipping or empowering should consider the ministry context if it is to be effective and efficient. One may be educated in one context, but will still have to be empowered in another.

Winter asserts,

> Off-campus education is also the only way the average post-secondary institution will survive in the increasingly "on the run" world in which we live. ... *Missiological education for the lay person* can best be achieved by off-campus education, and ... —believe it or not—the off-campus education of "lay people" is also the only way that the best selections can be made for the pastors/evangelists without whom the Christian movement cannot continue.

Flexibility with the venue of missiological education may be fostered in many ways, including shortened intensive courses, extension courses, distance learning through the use of mentoring, printed materials, video materials, interactive audio-video, interactive computer tutorials, computer conferencing, and teleconferencing. The media listed may be selected to fit the venue needs of the learner in ways which fit within the resources, timing constraints, and preferred learning styles of the learner. The learning venue always communicates cultural information. In fact, culture may be seen as a contextualized coping strategy for a given environment for a group of people (Ishino 1978). "The general principle is that the venue where the equipping is done should be as similar as possible to the projected ministry environment and the people to be served" (Elliston and Kauffman 1993, 161-62).

Delivery System

The delivery system provides the mechanism for conveying missiological education to the learners. LeRoy Ford describes it as the *means* of an administrative model which bring the curricular design and learners together to accomplish the objectives of the design and implement the instructional model (Ford 1991, 294).

When deciding about a delivery system, many possible options are open. The budding missiologist may turn to an individual for individualized mentoring outside any institution. On the other hand, church-based training in missiology, mission agency-based equipping, and other nonformal training programs are having a profound impact in missiological education. Mulholland pointed out that at one time in this century 40 percent of the North American missionaries were alumni of three Bible Institutes or Colleges (Columbia, Moody, and Prairie). Specialized institutes, collegiate programs, seminary programs, and university programs all serve important roles in the complex picture of missiological education delivery systems.

One needs to balance contextually *three basic modes* of education[17] to have an optimally effective delivery system. Depending on the balance among the three modes, a given model may be more appropriate for one type of missiologist than another. For example, the development of a Type 1 missiologist as described above normally would not require formal education.[18] However, for a Type 4 or 5 missiologist an extended formal education normally would be expected.

In addition to the basic mode of education, one needs to give attention to the *educational media and technologies* to be used. Basic governing principles of selection relate to the appropriateness of the media to the other variables, as noted in this chapter. For example, the media should be suitable for the learners' preferred learning style, available and accessible resources (people, instruction, finances, facilities, and time). The media should be appropriate for the faculty and institution. The cost/benefit ratio should be favorable (Kearsley 1993, 16.1-16.19). Some faculties and institutions are not prepared to develop or use interactive video, CD-ROM, teleconferencing, or computer conferencing. The media should contribute to the fulfillment of the purpose. If the building of community is important, individualized programmed instruction will likely be counter-productive without some complementary socializing efforts.

The design of or selection of a delivery system requires contextual adjustments as each of the other twelve curricular issues is addressed. A single approach to a delivery system is totally inappropriate in the diverse missiological community and world in which we are called to serve.

The delivery system serves as a significant formation influence on the learner. One should then look at the delivery system to see how the whole influences the learner. Normally, some diversity in the system is required to bring a wholesome balance in terms of formation.

The individual variables of the delivery system need to be tailored to the local context. Some of these variables include: 1) the balance between self-directed learning and teacher- or institution-directed learning, 2) the balance between extraction from the ministry setting and extension of the learning to it, and, 3) the focus on the dominant learning styles of the students.

Shenk's warning about technology must be applied to the delivery of missiological education.

> Modernity is the culture of scientific technology. . . . This means not only that we have developed more and more machines to do our work, but it also points to the fact that technique has come to pervade our lives. The ways we communicate and relate to others are shaped by technique. . . .
>
> On the one hand, we must reflect on the extent to which the church has understood the nature of modern culture and its impact on the human—individually and collectively. On the other hand, the church can ill afford to rely uncritically on technique in its witness. If technique leads to alienation, and the church bases its witness on technique, what reason do we have to believe that "witness" will not result in alienation rather than reconciliation with God and fellow humans?

Educational modes and media technologies must be considered in designing the delivery system. Additionally, one must ask who should design and who should participate in the delivery system. If the learners participate in the design, they will learn to design. If we seek to perpetuate colonial structures, an easy way to do that is to keep the learners out of the design loop.

If partnerships share the delivery system, the resource base will be extended, costs will be proportionally reduced, access will be increased to a much broader range of constituencies. However, if we enter into partnerships in delivery as suggested by Viggo Søgaard, our colonializing control will be lessened, our world view will likely be stretched, and even though ambiguity will be increased, God's purpose will be served. Søgaard states "Decentralized partnerships . . . could increase our ministry . . . maybe even a hundred times."

Now is the era of partnerships between dissimilar and similar partners in business and education. In the 1993 annual conference of the American Society for Training and Development held in Atlanta a whole series of seminars was offered about the formation of partnerships between higher education and non-educational institutions such as businesses. Late in 1992 the Western Association of Schools and Colleges (WASC) as the regional accrediting agency published a new set of standards for these kinds of partnerships. No single community can accomplish the task. Now is the time to establish partnerships among seminaries, colleges, universities, churches, relief and development agencies, missions, publishing companies, and in some cases, governments.

Søgaard writes,

> The biblical records challenge us to partnership and relationships. Unfortunately, Western individualism has caused much division in the life and ministry of the church. A partnership dedicated to missiological education will in itself be a testimony to the fellowship that exists among the servants of the Lord.

Finally, when considering a delivery system the system as a whole must be examined—not only the educational modes, media, and people or institutions involved, but the *support services* as well. The library, advising, admissions, finances, and other systems must all support the purpose.

Selection of Faculty

The selection of faculty must fit the other educational variables. A guiding principle is taken from Luke 6:40. Students fully taught will be *like* their teacher. Jesus spoke a true and fearsome thing in that brief statement. If we seek to develop a certain kind of person, then the teacher must first be that kind of person. I have a friend who has completed three postdoctoral fellowships, publishes widely, and participates regularly in both European and American conferences in his field. He teaches people who seek to be pastors. He has never pastored a church or been involved in a significant lay ministry. I wonder what his students will become. If the pattern of selecting faculty from Caucasian men continues, even though they may have the higher academic credentials, the diversity needed among the emerging missiologists will be threatened.

Birnbrauer identifies six variables to consider in instructor selection:

1. Composition of the trainee group;
2. Expectations of the trainees and sponsors;
3. Program length;
4. Culture of sponsoring organization;
5. Styles—of trainees and instructors;
6. Recursive—instructor's behavior must be a model (Birnbrauer 1993, 28.6-28.7).

If Type 1 missiologists are needed, they must be equipped by people who know what it is to be that kind of leader. They will probably be Type 2 or Type 3 missiologists themselves. Theologians do their best in equipping other theologians. If passionate missiologists are to be equipped, their teachers must demonstrate a similar passion.

A faculty attracts people of like passion, compassion, or commitment. If a given purpose is the priority, and certain kinds of people are desired as the graduates of a program, then the faculty selection process should have a good look at the purpose and proposed outcomes. If cultural, gender, and gift diversity is sought among the people to be equipped, then this kind of diversity must be found among the faculty. If a given set of commitments, attitudes, or skills is desired, faculty members with those commitments, attitudes, and skills are required.

Spiritual, Ministry, and Strategic Formation

A recurring and essential theme for missiological education is formation. L. Grant McClung, Jr. suggests that the formation of *passion* for God and his glory and passion for the lost is essential. Motte relates how spiritual formation has continued to be a critical part of the work of Catholic orders in order to develop "a lifestyle undergirded by a way of relating to God through Jesus Christ, and of relating to all human beings and creation within that relationship by the grace of the Holy Spirit."

Ken Gnanakan, taking up a critical Asian issue that rings true not only in the Christian faith but is emphasized in other religions as well, says,

Stress total formation. [While] God will continue to use all forms of attempts to accomplish his purposes, the most successful channels will always be men and women in tune with God. . . . [Shoki] Coe speaks in terms of "theological formation," "ministerial formation" and "life formation." . . .

Beyond skills and beyond techniques we must be in travail until the ministry of Christ is formed in each one, the ministry of which he himself spoke when he said, "I came not to be ministered unto but to minister" and "I am in your midst as one who serves—*ho diakonon*." We should be so caught up in that ministry that each one of us can say, "It is no longer I who work, but Christ who is working in me."

Samuel Escobar, writing from a Latin American perspective, echoes the same theme:

> Forming people for mission is an activity that should take place within the frame of a "person to person" relationship, which is fundamental as the environment for the educational process. No amount of academic excellence or doctrinal orthodoxy can substitute for this personalized dimension of the training for mission.

With this kind of emphasis on spiritual formation, one might be tempted to say this is all that must be done. Certainly one influences out of the kind of person one is. The formation of Christ within is critically important. However, Motte suggests that a focus on the spiritual alone is risky:

> [While spirituality has served as an] overarching framework for missionary formation and missionary education . . . in practice it leads to a certain downplaying of more formal missiological education. This results in an incapacity on the part of many missionaries to grasp the more subtle interplay between gospel and culture.

Spiritual, ministry, and strategic formation occur over the whole of a person's life. Clinton has demonstrated through significant research that formation is patterned and occurs in predictable ways over a lifetime.[19] The formation process includes learning experiences, one's response to these learning experiences, and time. Clinton calls these learning experiences "process items," because they serve as catalysts for the processing of formation. They are characterized by continuity, that is, for an individual certain kinds of experience tend to recur; sequence, that is, a progression is observable; and integration, that is, these processes fit together over a lifetime to form the person God can use effectively.

Spiritual formation or the process of spiritual maturation contributes to the development of a person's spiritual power base. This maturation process leads one to be more Christlike. Spiritual power forms the primary power base for Christian leaders. Spiritual formation also contributes to the formation of spiritual authority or the right to use God's power. "While spiritual formation is Spirit guided, existing leaders/trainers should be expected to encourage, facilitate, and expect it, both in the lives of the learners and in their own lives and ministries" (Elliston and Kauffman 1993, 167).

Effectiveness in ministry is based on character and one's relationship with God, not just on one's skill or knowledge. "Spiritual formation helps move one's ministry maturation process beyond a focus on skills and knowledge bases to a being base. Until the Lord has shaped the vessel, it will not serve His purpose" (ibid).

While several of the other authors noted the significance of spiritual formation, no one treated its significance in terms of the ministry context of the missiologist. The context is primarily a "spiritual" context in which spiritual power is the principal power issue at hand. Equipping men and women to wrestle with the "principalities and powers" using spiritual power must be at the heart of the purpose for spiritual formation. The danger of secularizing the missiologist at the very heart of the enterprise must be brought into focus. Spiritual formation is more than character formation. It must serve to equip the person to exercise spiritual power on the one hand and discern it on the other. If the missiologist is one who engages in the study of, reflection about, and practice of crossing barriers with the gospel of Jesus Christ, then spiritual formation must equip a person in this realm.

Spiritual formation does not occur automatically. It requires an active commitment on the part of the learner as well as those teaching. Instruction and the building of habits of personal and corporate spiritual disciplines help. The prime mover in the midst of the process is the Holy Spirit. Time for reflection and seeking the Lord's guidance is required along the way.

Community Building

The building of community is another essential part of missiological education for at least four reasons: 1) The commission was given to a community—the people of God—to accomplish; 2) effectiveness in mission requires working in community; 3) we are called to establish a community of believers; and, 4) the community of faith provides a hermeneutical community which aids in the interpretation of Scripture for the community. Any one of these reasons is adequate to justify our focus on community building as a part of missiological education. Shenk observes that "renewed understanding of the apostolic character of the church as embedded in the Great Commission" is required if we are to engage modern culture redemptively.

Mary Motte adds:

> There are not many examples of isolated missionaries, unattached from a community. Rather, the opposite is true. Missionary orders have grown up around outstanding persons who wanted to communicate the gospel message in a particular way or time, but always in relation to the church.

Missiological education, then, ought to give attention to two issues in its design. The first is the formation of a learning community in which the learners, faculty and others interact and encourage each other in learning and formation. The second is also important. As part of the curriculum, attention should be given to teaching the how and why of forming communities in other locations. Both the theological roots and understanding of the ministry contexts are essential for this intention.

Evaluation

Evaluation is not something to be included in the program and done if the budget and time allow for it at the end. Rather, evaluation may be seen as "the (1. Process) of (2. Delineating), (3. Obtaining), and (4. Providing) (5. Useful) (6. Information) for (7. Judging) (8. Decision alternatives)" (Stufflebeam 1973, 129).[20] Evaluation is always built on a set of criteria or values. Throughout the chapters in this book value issues have arisen many times. One only need reflect the number of times word like "must," "should," or "ought" have appeared.

Evaluation may inform decisions related to the setting of goals and objectives, the setting of structures, implementation, or recycling. In the design and implementation of missiological education all of these kinds of decisions will be required for each context. If evaluation is made a part of the planning, the decisions may be better informed.

KEY DEVELOPMENTAL ROLES

Throughout the process of developing missiologists three complementary roles must be recognized. Each one has been alluded to repeatedly up to this point. However, each one must be made explicit. The primary role in the development of a missiologist is the Spirit of God, who superintends the whole process. The Spirit works in and through the process of spiritual formation to form the person into Christlikeness. The Spirit is the one who calls, gifts, empowers, cleanses, sends, guides, prepares the context, and vindicates.[21]

The second role is that of the existing leaders in the community of faith. They provide the instruction, mentoring, examples, motivation, ministry assignments, hands-on discipline, and the "hands of the Holy Spirit" to mirror God's work. This role is the role of the missionary educator.

The third key role in the formation of a missiologist is the emerging missiologist himself or herself. Faithfulness and obedience, which build trustworthiness and competence, are required. While academic excellence may be an intermediate goal, trust and obedience are required to reach that goal.

CONCLUSIONS/RECOMMENDATIONS

In conclusion, we must do at least seven things to develop contextually appropriate and effective missiological education:
1. Develop our key values and clear conceptual framework based on Scripture and an understanding of the contexts from which and in which the learners will serve.

2. Set our educational priorities among the curricular variables described in this chapter. For example, we must, as Shenk says (referring to Kirk), "reorient the whole of theological education so that theology is informed by mission and mission is strengthened by theology."

3. Select appropriate learning experiences for the learners, sensitive to the expected outcomes and what they bring to the learning context.

4. Organize the learning experiences with appropriate continuity, sequence, and integration among the parts.

5. Deliver the learning with a system that uses an appropriate educational mode, with appropriate media, with the right people.

6. Evaluate the context to set appropriate goals, evaluate the resources available to set the appropriate structures, evaluate the implementation process to assure quality and evaluate the outcomes so the appropriate recycling decisions will be made (continuation, modification, or termination).

7. Recognize and affirm each of the key roles in the development of missiologists, including the Holy Spirit, existing missiologists in the community of faith, and emerging missiologists as they seek to trust and obey.

Notes

1. All subsequent quotations refer to statements made verbally by the participants during the conference from which this volume derives.

2. See Dressel and Marcus 1982 for a comprehensive description of the components of an academic discipline. Dressel suggests that an academic discipline will have its own component parts, including substantive, perceptual, and conceptual components, linguistic, mathematical, nondiscursive symbols, and technical language components, syntactical or organizing components, value components and conjunctive components which allow it to relate to other disciplines.

3. This chapter quotes the participants at the Missiological Education Conference. A quotation without a reference is from the participants.

4. J. Robert Clinton provides a set of useful definitions for spiritual formation, ministry formation, and strategic formation. He describes spiritual formation as "the development of the inner-life of a person of God so that the person experiences more of the life of Christ, reflects more Christ-like characteristics in personality and in everyday relationships, and increasingly knows the power and presence of Christ in ministry (Clinton 1989, 72). He describes ministry formation as "the development of ministry skills and knowledge, which are reflected by a leader's growth in experiential understanding of leadership concepts, growing sensitivity to God's purposes in terms of the leadership basal elements (leader, follower, and situation), identification and development of gifts and skills and their use with increasing effectiveness with followers, [and] ability to motivate followers toward beneficial changes which will harmonize with God's purposes" (ibid., 73). He goes on to describe strategic formation as "an overall ministry perspective, a ministry philosophy, which emerges from a lifetime of formational thrusts and interweaves lessons learned into an increasingly clear ministry framework that gives direction

and focus and ultimate purpose to a leader's life" (ibid., 74).

5. Ministry experience should be concurrent with the other learning in order to provide a realistic place for applying what is being taught. Ted Ward and Sam Rowan address this issue in a basal article (1972).

6. Dynamic reflection asks two kinds of questions: 1) How does what is being taught apply to my ministry? 2) From my ministry what should I be learning from the structured learning experiences? This reflective interchange should occur regularly and frequently—as often as weekly and no less frequently than bi-weekly.

7. The respective roles of the Holy Spirit, the existing leaders, and emerging leaders are developed more fully in Elliston 1993.

8. For a useful curricular design manual which is compatible with missiological issues see Ford 1991. He looks at the whole range of development from an institutional perspective to an individual lesson segment. See also Elliston and Kauffman 1993 for a more detailed development of this set of variables for an urban training context. See Elliston 1991 for a description of how these variables may be applied to relief and development workers. See also Simkins 1978.

9. "*Education*" is used consistently rather than *training* because *education* denotes a general preparation for unpredictable circumstances. *Training*, on the other hand, suggests specific orientation for a defined situation. A surgeon, for example, may be trained to do a specific procedure after having received a general medical education.

10. A very useful Greek concept, *katartizo*, lies behind the word, *equip*. See Delling 1979. The term used in Ephesians 6:11-12 and translated variously as "equip," "train," or "prepare" carries with it the idea of contextually outfitting, mending, or fitting together. It is the same word that Jesus used in Luke 6:40, when he suggested that when a disciple is fully taught (equipped, trained, perfected, outfitted), he will be like his master. A closely related word is used for the purpose of Scripture in 2 Timothy 3:15-16. Scripture is given so that a person may be thoroughly furnished or equipped for all good work.

11. The equipping should focus on women, men, families, and the corporate church. We are commissioned as God's people individually and corporately to accomplish his mission.

12. See a discussion of the biblical words used for selection of emerging leaders in Elliston 1993.

13. The number has dramatically moved from ninety-nine nonbelievers to one believer in 1430 A.D. to nine nonbelievers to one believer in 1993 (see Winter 1994, 3).

14. Akhtar Hameed Khan, personal interview, 1978.

15. Many universities are offering external programs ranging from the Open University in England to land-grant universities, such as the University of Oklahoma, and to smaller, private universities, such as the University of Phoenix in Phoenix, Arizona.

16. See Kanter 1983; Covey 1991; or Elliston 1993 for more complete descriptions of empowerment with personal, positional, and spiritual power. Basically, power is developed by its legitimized, disciplined, and recognized use.

17. Formal education normally refers to schooling. It is long term, centered in an institution, resource intensive, expensive, theory based and preparatory in nature. It is generally resistant to change. Nonformal education is normally short term, function oriented, and often associated with conferences, seminars and workshops.

It is planned, staffed, and budgeted, but is controlled by the market or the community it seeks to serve. Informal education is by definition unplanned. It is what occurs within the functioning of normal relationships. Informal education provides the most important dimension to a person's learning. A person learns world view, language, culture, and values informally. Informal education may be facilitated but not planned. When planned, it becomes nonformal education.

18. For a more complete treatment of the relation of educational modes to different kinds of leadership development see Elliston and Kauffman 1993 or Elliston 1993. See also Clinton 1988b.

19. This research is based on the review of more than three hundred published biographies of international church leaders and more than five hundred directed autobiographical studies of church leaders from about eighty countries. For a report of this research see Clinton 1988a, 1988b, 1989.

20. Key Terms:

Evaluation Process: The particular, continuing, and cyclical activity subsuming many methods and involving a number of steps or operations.

Delineating: Focusing information requirements to be served by evaluation through such steps as specifying, defining, and explicating.

Obtaining: Making available through such processes as collecting, organizing, and analyzing, and through such formal means as statistics and measurement.

Providing: Fitting together into systems or subsystems that best serve the needs or purposes of the evaluation.

Useful: Appropriate to predetermined criteria evolved through the interaction of the evaluator and the client.

Information: Descriptive or interpretive data about entities (tangible or intangible) and their relationships.

Judging: Assigning weights in accordance with a specified value framework, criteria derived therefrom, and information which relates criteria to each entity being judged.

Decision Alternatives: A set of optional responses to a specified decision question.

21. See the role of the Spirit in Kirkpatrick 1988.

PAUL PIERSON

Mission Educator Par Excellence

Paul Pierson: Mission Educator
Par Excellence

Dean Gilliland

Among the stories about how deans are selected, what happened at the School of World Mission in 1980 must be very special. The Search Committee had done its careful work and a "short list" was handed to us, the faculty of the School of World Mission, for final deliberation. One afternoon we met for what we hoped would result in a decision. Two names were before us. These persons were well known to us and to missiologists around the world. Either would bring marvelous gifts to the office of dean.

But we could not reach consensus. As discussion ground to a standstill, one of our number suggested the name of a person we did not know. He really couldn't tell us very much; the person was a Berkeley graduate with a Ph.D. from Princeton Seminary. We learned that he had been a missionary to Brazil and Portugal and, even as we deliberated, was the successful pastor of First Presbyterian Church in Fresno, California.

We shall always remember that serendipitous meeting. It was our introduction to Paul E. Pierson, who became the third dean of the School of World Mission. His coming was the beginning of a dynamic decade that brought solid growth and new directions. The combination of moment and need called for a special kind of dean and, unknown to us, God had been at work long before our process. What follows is a tribute to Paul Pierson, a dean who helped us better understand what mission and missiological education are all about.

Meetings, budgets, policies, public relations, curricular issues, and more long meetings—this is what deans are made of. Paul Pierson can talk eloquently about these things, but that would not be his real story. This mis-

---

Dean Gilliland served as a United Methodist missionary to Nigeria for twenty years. He began teaching at Fuller Theological Seminary in 1977, having served as principal of the Theological College of Northern Nigeria. He is currently professor of contextualized theology and African studies at Fuller's School of World Mission and president of the American Society of Missiology.

sion educator is pastor, missionary, teacher, and friend. Every act of "deaning," formal and informal, came from the authenticity of the person. Who he is accounts for his priorities and style. We want you to know Paul as we, his faculty, staff, and students, know him.

Our tribute involves four incontestable metaphors: "Dean of the Open Door," "Pastor and Encourager," "Innovative Networker," and "Historian for the Future." But first, we will briefly trace the journey that brought him to the School of World Mission.

HOW IT BEGAN

Paul Pierson was born in 1927 in Torrance, California, the third son of a strong Baptist family. He was reared with an interest in missions, a special gift of both his father and mother, who never forgot the missionary story while teaching Sunday School for many years. Growing up at home, Paul took care of the family gardens and livestock. During high school he worked in a steel mill and was able to save enough to pay for his first year at the University of California at Berkeley. As World War II was drawing to a close, college was interrupted for a year while he served in the navy.

Upon taking up his chemical engineering studies again at Berkeley, he came under the ministry of Robert Boyd Munger, well-known pastor of the First Presbyterian Church in that university town. Dr. Munger is remembered by all who know him as an inspired and effective promoter of missions. During Munger's ministry the Berkeley congregation sent out more missionaries than any other congregation of the Presbyterian Church in the U.S.A. This relationship with Dr. Munger profoundly influenced Paul to dedicate his own life for ministry and particularly missions.

The year 1950 was a momentous and transitional year. Paul married Rosemary Lucksinger, who was also a student at Berkeley, and soon after their marriage Paul entered Princeton Theological Seminary. Here he was challenged again by a gospel for all the world's peoples, especially through John A. MacKay and the German scholar Otto Piper. While he was coordinating weekend ministries of international students at the seminary, his vision for missions became even clearer. Their first child, Stephen, was born as Paul and Rosemary's seminary days came to an end in 1954.

THE MISSIONARY YEARS

After Paul served for one year as assistant pastor in Orange, New Jersey, the young family was commissioned to Brazil under the Presbyterian Board of Foreign Missions. The first year of missionary service was packed with experiences that would help prepare Rosemary and Paul for the lifetime work they anticipated. Vocationally, it was a year for learning Portuguese and, on the home side, a baby girl, Kathryn, was born.

With all the new cultural adjustments around them, Paul continued to read as much as possible. He told us frequently how he and a friend organized a study group around Donald McGavran's first major book, *The Bridges of God.* Controversial as the book was, it carried a prophetic message about church growth which, ten years later, was to become the hallmark of the new School of World Mission. It would not have occurred to Paul that God would lead him eventually to join McGavran and to take the school beyond what even the founder had dreamed.

Their first assignment after language school took the Piersons deep into Brazil to Corumbá on the border of Bolivia. Besides the small church in the town of Corumbá where Paul was pastor, he and local Christians evangelized in hard-to-reach places. The *pantanal* is the world's largest swamp area. Here, by boat, they ministered to groups of believers living on the small islands. A second audience involved the many people who lived in the dense forest that surrounded Corumbá. Paul and Rosemary had the joy of ministering to the members of those small churches, seeing the Christians grow and the churches multiply. He was able to lead two of the young men from these churches to enter seminary. The Piersons' second son, Stan, was born while they were in Corumbá.

By this time it was 1960 and the Piersons decided to take a study leave at Princeton, where Paul began his Ph.D. After a year they returned to Brazil, now a family of six, since David, their youngest, had joined them while at Princeton. Paul entered a new phase in the training of church leaders when he became professor at the Presbyterian Seminary of the North, in Recife. During the ten years at Recife, in addition to teaching, he served as dean and president. In this seminary environment Paul's openness and concern for people, especially students, helped facilitate the seminary's growth. There also were buildings to be built and budgets to be met.

PASTOR AT FRESNO

Leaving Brazil in 1970 marked another transitional year. After Paul completed the Ph.D. (*magna cum laude*), the family took up residence in Portugal in 1971. Paul taught at the Presbyterian Seminary in Lisbon until 1973. That year brought an end to his ministry in the Portuguese language, as he was called back to California. In 1973 the Pierson family moved to Fresno, where Paul served as pastor of the First Presbyterian Church until 1980.

If one thing could summarize those years at Fresno it would be the way Pastor Pierson led the church to see the big picture and how church members could be a part of it. His ministry was an eloquent declaration that the whole world needs a whole church that will work together. Coming out of the strain of the sixties, these were critical years for any local church in California, especially one in the city. However, Paul was greatly supported and followed by a dynamic group of people who were seeking to live out their faith with integrity and a high level of commitment to the Lord and to each other.

The Fresno church remembers Paul Pierson as one who is gifted at joining people together for ministry. He saw people with diverse gifts in his congregation. He saw how individuals could build personal relationships to accomplish things for the Lord. As one faithful member put it, "Paul helped us see that God is bigger than we thought. He showed us that our God is not just a Western God."

It is this blessing that the missionary family brought to Fresno. What Paul said about the world was credible because he had been out there in the world. He preached and counseled as one who was in direct touch with the world's people. His years in another culture helped him see the potential in people who were not always understood or fully accepted. He built bridges so that the church could form new relationships within the congregation and in the neighborhood. More people became involved in doing hands-on mission in their own city through such agencies as World Impact, while overseas visits brought exposure to world mission.

Paul Pierson helped the Fresno church understand what it was to be a "downtown church." He worked constantly and effectively to enable an urban church to remain strong. The traditional members were helped to appreciate and accept those who expressed their commitment in differing ways. The church demonstrated what it meant to be the family of God. The Piersons were able to bring a spirit of acceptance and innovation without alienating or fracturing the fellowship. This was due, in part, because they had lived in another culture.

Paul and Rosemary Pierson did not plan or even expect to leave Fresno, but the invitation to join the School of World Mission as dean would bring them, once again, into the work of missionaries to the world.

DEAN OF THE SCHOOL OF WORLD MISSION

We began this chapter by recalling how unusual it was to hire a dean the way we did. We had very little to go on. We were given a practical lesson on how God can reveal his mind to an institution. All that has been written up to this point is what we found out from others. We turn now to what we ourselves know about Paul Pierson. There is no lack of adequate information. The difficulty is how to cover in a few pages what is written so large and with such affection in our hearts.

Dean of the Open Door

During the Pierson years (1980-92) the outer area of the dean's office was designed in such a way that Paul's desk was in direct line with the open door. This was, in fact, an invitation. The unmistakable message was, "If

I'm visible to you, come in, the door is open." Sometimes this created a problem with the official scheduling of a day, but Nancy, Paul's assistant, knew how to handle this.

Making himself available was not something Paul figured out after coming to Fuller. Here was a missionary who had already been an educator, administrator, and pastor. What this open door meant was obvious: "All have a right to be heard, and anyone's problem is a real one." Entree to the dean was a leveling symbol. It made no difference if you were student, staff, or faculty. To the students this meant counsel and an ear to every kind of problem, from academic dreams to a need for funds. To staff it meant a confidential hearing of requests and encouragement. To faculty it meant listening to ideas, even the questionable ones, and freedom to pursue professional hopes. This faculty needed latitude, and that's what it got from Paul Pierson.

The open door meant the right of leaders from all churches to study at the School of World Mission and get equal and fair treatment. Denominations, such as his own Presbyterian Church, were important to his view of mission. But students from smaller and less-known churches of the world are also studying at Fuller, and all have freely benefited from Pierson's openness. If we had asked Paul who would qualify for his counsel, his answer would have been: "Whoever confesses Jesus as Savior and Lord and is committed to evangelizing the world can have my time."

An open door at Fuller Theological Seminary meant he would talk freely to the other two schools in this exciting, expanding, sometimes cumbersome institution. There is much to commend missions to theology and psychology, and Paul took initiatives with colleagues to find new ways of working together. The open door did mean taking some risks. But it was easier to talk about grand ideas and to test questionable waters and confront complaints with an open door.

To the very end of his life in 1990, Donald McGavran, the founder and first dean of the School of World Mission and Institute of Church Growth, would remind us that we are not living in the sunset of missions but in the *sunrise*. Paul Pierson embraced that metaphor with enthusiasm. Besides reminding us of the great opportunities for mission, he was a dean who said, "Come in, I want to talk to you about it."

Pastor and Encourager

The purpose of this tribute is to show the contributions Dean Pierson made to mission education. He came to the task in such a way that *people* were first, before any other agenda. Because the School of World Mission is a place where church leaders come from some seventy-five nations of the world, encouraging and affirming these students is probably the most important ministry a dean can have—at least Paul Pierson thought so. Nothing gave him more satisfaction than to have a warm relationship with these quality international leaders. Helping people comes naturally to him, but students have their special needs and they received his pastoral attention.

Paul is great with names. It took only one introduction for him to fix a name and face. It was easy to get information about students at faculty meetings because no one knew them better than the dean. He encouraged students to think highly of their gifts for ministry. Taking students with him to speak in churches was a regular thing. Students were greatly encouraged when the dean introduced them to congregations, whether large or small. His idea of pastoral care included finding funds for students, often very substantial funds. Many will remember how the dean found ways to keep their studies going. He could tap into resources that were unknown to most of us. It was routine for the faculty to hear from Paul about an unexpected contact made through his circles of friends in many places.

Paul's pastoral concerns reached into local churches, where he had a way of linking renewal with mission movements. He could show through his feel for history how churches and communities of Christians were reignited in their own faith by engaging in mission. In the early 1980s he attracted lay persons into a creative support group for the school. The *Partners*, as he called them, met on a regular basis, attended our SWM banquets, and experienced the joy of getting behind new projects with prayer and funds. This warm connection to church people was a natural expression of an incurable pastor who, as dean, had irrepressible good news to share about mission in today's world.

The faculty benefited from Paul's pastoral side. He bragged much about his faculty and advocated for us whether in seminary deliberations or in public contacts. He promoted cohesion. For example, Paul always led the weekly faculty hour of sharing and prayer in a sensitive pastoral way. Even though there is a purposeful commitment to unity among the faculty, we are, nevertheless, a diverse group, teaching in specialized fields, and practicing varied aspects of ministry. Dean Pierson, willingly, personally connected us to one another.

Innovative Networker

Probably all faculties have their standing jokes about each other. We have ours with Paul Pierson. It has to do with his inevitable, uncanny knowledge of people and recognition of names. These are usually names that no one else could ever know. He can narrate circumstances of meeting unlikely people so frequently that we would often ask ahead of time, "Paul, aren't you going to tell us that you know this person?" The humor was based on a well-known fact. Paul Pierson has wide-ranging contacts and, because he is so good at remembering friends, he uses this ability to the full advantage of the School. He is an intentional networker.

One has to know Fuller Theological Seminary to understand the intricacies of three semi-autonomous schools working together. There is much to negotiate when courses tend to overlap, even compete. The impact on admissions, curriculum, and budget makes demands every day on a dean. History shows how well Paul advocated for his school and the permanent benefits that resulted. He worked for more cooperation in recruitment and advising and went out of his way to get underfunded church leaders from the Two-Thirds World admitted. The value of the networking he did internally was recognized when he was asked to serve as interim provost for the seminary just as his deanship ended.

Paul's contributions to the Association of Theological Schools is a matter of record, serving and writing for the Globalization Task Force. It has always been important for him to be involved with mission organizations. He would say openly that he could not function in an academic setting without these connections, which kept him close to the mission scene. So he was active on boards such as the Latin America Mission and OC International during his years as dean. As part of his networking he kept close ties with foundations and funding agencies as consultant and resource person.

Paul did not forget the need for mission education in churches. His tenure as a pastor served him well in reaching out to local congregations. We have already mentioned how he visited churches week after week to stimulate mission thinking. He enthusiastically provided the way for a talented couple to offer courses in short-term missions, with a special training feature called "Discover the World." This program equips students to conduct seminars in local churches on the urgency for mission in today's world.

With his encouragement, the school became active in extension education to various centers in the Two-Thirds World. Korea was already underway, then Papua New Guinea began in the early 1980s, and, later, Nigeria. Along with this, faculty were encouraged to take their courses to international centers such as Australia, Kenya, Indonesia, Japan, and Singapore. Paul formed an Extension Committee, which has become a permanent feature of all planning.

It is here, in connection with Paul's networking, that we should mention the Ph.D. in Intercultural Studies, inaugurated in 1984. Paul saw this, the highest of our degrees, as the most appropriate way to serve international churches, primarily as a means of producing highly qualified teachers of missiology for training institutions worldwide.

Historian for the Future

Dean Pierson continues to make his solid contribution to teaching in the area of history of mission. He would say that all current thinking and action have precedents that must be understood and honored. This principle comes from the historian that he is. Still, Paul does not honor past events or facts standing by themselves. He rejects history when it becomes a recitation of moldy narratives. History is a tool, a means for understanding where we are now and how to gather wisdom for the future.

Beginning with his major course, *History of the Christian Movement*, his focus is on dynamic patterns, Spirit-charged personalities, and divine surprises. Paul Pierson is intrinsically respectful of students and colleagues who might seem, at first, to be rather ordinary. This is because of the way he reads history. We might even speak of the "Pierson Principle." It would be this: Renewal and great movements do not arise from the center but are more often born at the margins. Irregular, controversial, even rejected persons and their efforts have always been agents of change.

Responding to this as dean, Paul's orientation was forward. Many ideas, programs, initiatives, and additions had their start during his years. His look to the past positioned him firmly in the philosophy of the school. He was transparently loyal to Donald McGavran's vision. In the dean's office hangs a choice photograph of three deans—McGavran, Glasser, and Pierson. They are gathered closely around a table, pondering a large globe. Paul repeated many times the biblical phrase that McGavran used over and over again: *panta ta ethne* (Mt 28:19). This is a school that exists for "all the nations," and Paul would not let us forget that. But the big questions were always, "What can we do that we are not doing now?" and, "How can we do better what we are already doing?"

His clear insight into history made it possible for Paul to keep his perspective when risks had to be taken. One of the early tests of his deanship occurred in 1983 with what is commonly called "signs and wonders." The whole seminary felt the results of the introduction of a course that dealt with healing and miracles. Since this popular course was located in the School of World Mission and attracted large numbers of students, the new dean was under heavy pressure. He handled this in a way that worked out for the good of all constituent parts of the seminary. The "signs and wonders" event was the first among other programs that meant breaking new ground. Paul did not have to fully understand an idea before giving his support. He trusted his faculty and did not resist if he was convinced the Holy Spirit was leading.

Paul had plenty of new directions to deal with, because the faculty was never short on ideas. But he followed through in effective ways at both the conceptual and practical levels. The earliest additions were the leadership concentration and the Bible translation program. The leadership concentration, dating from 1981, required new funding for a faculty position and thinking through the curriculum in an integrative way. The Bible translation track, which offers both a master's and a doctorate in the field, is a one-of-a-kind program. It meant setting up a working relationship with Wycliffe Bible Translators for faculty and finding funds in a cooperative way. About the same time, Chinese studies was begun, offering a master's degree; it also required a new faculty appointment, the search for funds, and careful negotiations. Although a few courses in Islam had always been offered,

Pierson saw how critical Muslim studies had become, so he brought in an expert in the field and introduced Islam as a major discipline. Offerings in mission theology were more than doubled during Pierson's tenure by the addition of a new faculty person in this area. The multiple ways money was found when basically none was available are a testimony to Pierson's entrepreneurial talents.

More recently, still under Pierson's guidance, the Jewish studies program was successfully launched, bringing large numbers of Jewish students to the campus. Before he stepped down, Paul laid the foundation for an urban emphasis with new courses and began a search for faculty in this area. He has always been a strong supporter of women. He showed this by encouraging more courses for women and keeping the need for women faculty before us. One of the last projects undertaken by Dean Pierson was recognizing the massive Korean presence in SWM by arranging for Korean students to have their own Korean coordinator and strengthening ties with the Korean churches.

As a faculty, we are proud to know this teacher, pastor, administrator, and mission statesman. We celebrate a brother and colleague who is with us every day. If we were to end this in an appropriate way, we would commission Paul to a long vacation up in the Northwest salmon country. Nothing gives him greater pleasure than fishing and letting everyone know how big the catch was. He would like it most if he could have any or all of his family with him, especially Rosemary. He stretches some of his fish stories a little, at least we think so. This is to tell you, Paul, what a great catch we made when you joined us, and we have not stretched the story, not even a little.

CONCLUSION

Till the Final Book Is Opened
in the Final Circle

J. Dudley Woodberry

In his vision of the final circle made up of every tribe and nation, the Apostle John saw that the One "worthy to open the book" was the One "through whom all things were made," who fashioned us in the image of the Creator. As we reflect that image and are caught up in God's purpose "to make all things new," we in missiological education are called to discover new approaches by dealing with creative tensions, creative partnerships, and creative methodologies.

CREATIVE TENSIONS

We have compiled essays from different contexts: historical, ecumenical, regional, missiological, and future. Different perspectives and consequent tensions, therefore, are present in this volume by design. The challenge is to balance these perspectives and set priorities among them so that they do not result in a stagnating log jam but rather emanate in creative new forms. Here are some of the tensions that have emerged in these essays and the world in which we are called to serve.

Like all good religious education, missiological education has three goals—spiritual formation, graduate or undergraduate education, and ministry development. These involve, respectively, becoming, learning, and doing. Thus we face the challenge to keep in balance the inherent tensions among the spiritual, the academic, and the practical. Maintaining this balance will require guidance from missionaries and clergy, academics, and lay people. Likewise, schools will need to decide whether their calling is to train the masses of missionaries or educate the elite, the leaders and educators.

Certainly the content of missiological education must be concerned with the whole gospel, for the whole person, in the whole world. Consequently, it cannot be a single discipline beside others but must be interdisciplinary, involving both the traditional theological disciplines and the human sciences. Yet missiological education must avoid the danger of trying to do too many things at once. It must keep in mind its central focus—educating people to cross-cultural and other boundaries to evangelize and disciple the peoples of the world and form them into churches that love their neighbors, serve others, and multiply churches.

All balanced missiological education must involve the interaction of one's specialization with three core competencies—the word, the world, and the church. The *word* competency, centering on the theology of mission, provides the normative element. Missiologists must bring to the word the questions asked in other cultures and new contexts.

The *world* competency has fruitfully used tools from human sciences such as anthropology, sociology, and psychology. The world increasingly manifests poverty, population explosion, urbanization, environmental disasters, disease, racial and cultural diversity and tension, pluralism, secularization, and religious resurgence. In each situation the gospel is involved in present salvation and future hope.

The *church* competency centers on the lessons of the history of the expansion of the church and church growth principles, with concern for qualitative as well as quantitative growth. It also involves analysis and new understanding of what it means to be the church; what are the missiological directions of spirituality, and revival and church renewal; and what is involved in the relationship of churches with missions.

Other creative tensions involve the audience(s) for which students are preparing, since the world contains pre-modern, modern, and post-modern cultures. Then there are the questions concerning what is best taught at a base seminary or school and what can best be taught in extension sites and local churches where students interact with their current ministries. Finally, there is the creative tension of facilitating a continual humble learning posture of self-examination along with proclamation and positive service in the footsteps of the Master.

CREATIVE PARTNERSHIPS

The essays here collected represent a partnership between missiological educators who because of their agreement on the essentials of mission have been able to bring insights from their respective ecclesiastical, regional, and disciplinary perspectives that would be difficult if not impossible to gather from a more homogeneous group. The need for unity in life, worship, and witness certainly reflects Scripture (Jn 17:21) and may be seen in the pronouncements and experiences of repeated church and mission gatherings and movements such as the Edinburgh World Missionary Conference (1910), the World Council of Churches, Vatican II, the World Evangelical Fellowship, the Lausanne Movement, and A.D. 2000 and Beyond. Here we are looking specifically at possible symbiotic and synergistic partnerships in missiological education.

Despite the shifting demographics of Christians in the world, missiological educators in the West still have a significant role to play because of their established institutions, their libraries and technological resources, and the lessons they have learned through often painful errors of the past. Obviously, as the essays in this collection demonstrate, we need not only mission from every continent to every continent but mission educators from each continent to each continent. And we need not only multicultural and multiethnic mission teams around the world demonstrating the unity of Christ's body, but teams of multicultural and multiethnic mission educators around the world sharing the insights that have emerged throughout the globe. The danger is in confusing multicultural faculties with multicultural education. Recent experience has offered many examples of non-Western missiologists who have been as unable as their Western colleagues to divorce themselves from the Western educational cisterns from which they themselves have drunk. They have developed Western minds clothed in non-Western bodies.

Besides the partnership of persons from different cultures, we need the partnership of schools. In multi-school institutions, fields like urban studies need the expertise of persons and resources housed in schools of theology and psychology as well as schools of world mission. At Fuller these are being coordinated through an urban center. The cooperation with other Christian educational institutions and ministry agencies in the Los Angeles area are coordinated through the Consortium on Urban Leadership Development (COULD). Another area where the expertise of various schools can be pooled includes cross-cultural marriage and family ministries, where marriage and family therapists can join with missionary anthropologists and administrators in charge of missionary personnel. Still another area for cooperation would be study of the "demonic." Psychologists and psychiatrists can help to identify emotional and physical roots of multi-personality disorders. Cross-cultural missiologists might deal with the spiritual roots of demonic manifestations, and theologians might bring some biblical guidelines and balance.

The geographical demands of students in ministry and the financial and personal costs of relocation certainly call for the partnership of satellite educational centers that are related to a base school of world mission to service them and provide resources that cannot reasonably be replicated elsewhere. Maximizing of resources of personnel and libraries also encourages a partnership where different institutions specialize in specific fields, such as Islam.

Even within a field there is need for institutions to cooperate where personnel and resources are spread. In the medieval Middle East, which has provided the visual prototype for the present collection of essays, students and professors traveled from one center of learning to another to be exposed to different teachers and students. On this model, there are discussions about developing a program in Islam, where students or professors could travel so that students might study the Quran with Win Bijlefeld, professor emeritus of Hartford Seminary now living in Vermont; study Arab Islam with Harold Vogelaar at the Lutheran School of Theology in Chicago; study Indian Islam with Roland Miller at Luther Seminary in St. Paul, Minnesota; study African Islam with Lamin Sanneh at Yale; and study folk Islam, the Islamic resurgence, and Muslim evangelism with Dean Gilliland and myself at Fuller. Library resources might be provided through Hartford Seminary.

CREATIVE METHODOLOGIES

The last example, coupled with the needs and facilities that have been highlighted in this collection of essays, underscores the importance of developing creative methodologies for missiological education. The subtitle of this collection—*The Book, the Circle, and the Sandals*—reminds us that all effective methodologies must in some way provide for the interaction of theory, reflection, and experience. A glance back to the previous models of education for ministry may serve to inform us of their relative effectiveness in providing for the interaction of these necessary components.

The first form of ministry formation for Christian missionaries, practiced by our Lord and the Apostle Paul, was apprenticeship.[1] Here the theory, reflection, and experience were in constant interplay from locale to locale and along the way. Here becoming (spiritual formation), learning (education), and doing (ministry) were fused. The strength and weakness were preeminently dependent on the quality of the mentor. So basic is this model to the development of Christian character and ministry that it will need to be a major element in any effective models that are created. Distance learning through e-mail, for example, will be most effective if in some way it is combined with interaction with a mature leader in his or her context.

The second model of ministry formation for missionaries was the monastic order, both male and female. Here the nurturing was provided by the group, and the extent to which the interaction of theory, reflection, and experience took place was largely dependent on the nature of the group. The results in spiritual formation, scholarship, and missionary activity have been impressive. Yet vows of obedience by the members of the order are so basic to the model that, like the apprentice model, its strengths and weaknesses depend on the quality of the leaders.

The university model arose third and was almost exclusively knowledge based. Thus, for example, the *seminarium indicum* to educate missionaries for the East Indies was added to the University of Leiden in 1622. In universities the emphasis was on theory and reflection rather than experience, on learning rather than becoming spiritual or doing ministry. Learning was not only separated from mission in the world but even separated from the church. In this setting scholars could become professors of mission without significant missionary experience.

Self-standing seminaries were the fourth model. They borrowed from the apprenticeship model in that faculty often had a mentoring role if the faculty-student ratio allowed it, and students were required or encouraged to be involved in Christian ministry under the supervision of senior ministers. Like the monastic model, a community of students, faculty, and staff worshiped and had fellowship together. Self-standing seminaries borrowed from the university model in that instruction was primarily classroom based. Thus it provided for theory, reflection, and at least some experience, and facilitated spiritual formation, learning, and doing.

In this context, however, mission studies had to compete, often unsuccessfully, with other theological disciplines for a foothold in the curriculum. This problem was alleviated where seminaries spawned autonomous or semi-autonomous schools of world mission. By requiring at least three years of cross-cultural ministry experience as a prerequisite for entrance, the School of World Mission at Fuller was able in its early years to ensure the interaction of theory, reflection, and experience. But when a masters' program was added for pre-service students, the challenge of integrating experience arose, as in so many other schools. Likewise, as more courses in ministry skills are added, it is easy to focus on professional training rather than spiritual formation. And as increasing numbers of students commute to classes, the difficulty of providing for a worshiping community beyond the classroom increases.

Bible colleges and institutes have offered a fifth model of missionary education. As elaborated in Kenneth Mulholland's essay, they have been successful in integrating theory and experience, and fostering spiritual becoming, learning, and doing. As such, they have educated a significant percentage of the North American evangelical missionaries in this century. The quality of their education is influenced by their emphasis on accessibility to the masses and a significant percentage of skill-based courses.

A sixth model, coming from outside the Northern hemisphere, is theological education by extension (TEE). As Ralph Winter points out in his chapter, TEE was designed to integrate theory, reflection, and experience, uniting becoming, learning, and doing in an effort to educate leaders for their rapidly growing churches. Thus leaders were identified in the midst of their ministry. Professors went to clusters of students so the latter could continue to minister while enhancing their ministry potential. Mentoring relationships were established by senior leaders with emerging leaders.

A final church-based model of missionary education is developing in many new apostolic paradigm (or what some are calling postdenominational) megachurches around the world. Here prospective missionaries are trained in the ministries of the church, in classes in the church, and under the mentorship of senior pastors. This integrates theory and practice, and becoming, learning, and doing. The leaders, however, have skills that are adapted to modern and post-modern culture as formed in the West and often have little understanding of both the decontextualization and subsequent recontextualization necessary if Christian ministry is going to be relevant to other cultures.

The old models unadapted will not serve today's needs. The cost of Western residential education, the need for students to be in ministry, the increasing number of missionaries from the South and East, all militate against traditional Western residential training for the education of most of the world's missionaries. Furthermore, even the use of Western languages in missiological education communicates a Western world view that may not be relevant outside of some urban contexts.

On the other hand, technology greatly enhances the possibilities for new forms of education. CD-ROMs can store vast amounts of information, allowing for the multiplication of library resources. Silicon chips can process it, and telecommunications, interactive TV, and videos can all deliver it. Interaction can be provided by e-mail enriched by individual mentoring and community building on site. And experience can be provided as one remains in ministry. All these can continue for life-long development.

The best features of the historic models can be adopted and adapted. Various forms of apprenticeship can provide role models and accountability. The formation of communities of learners can provide for worship, fellowship, and accountability. The academic rigor of the university, the church connection of the seminary and church-based education, the accessibility and practical orientation of the Bible college, and the ministry enhancement in context of TEE all have their contribution to make to creative methodologies. As Viggo Søgaard points out, missiological education for the twenty-first century must develop methodologies that utilize creative partnerships where each institution or agency provides what its history, resources, expertise, and context offer, from which it is best able to contribute.

As God is pleased to utilize our faltering methodologies in bringing to completion his new creation, perhaps we shall hear the echo of those words uttered over the first creation, "It was very good." And leaving our earthly sandals at the door of heaven, we can join the circle of those from every tribe and nation as the Master Teacher opens the Book of Life.

Note

1. For a fuller treatment of this model and my subsequent five models I have borrowed freely from Van Engen 1994a. A longer version of this article was subsequently published as *Shifting Paradigms in Ministry Formation* (1994b). The longer version will also appear in Charles Van Engen, *Mission-on-the-Way: Issues in Mission Theology* (Grand Rapids: Baker, forthcoming).

Bibliography

Abraham, William J.
  1989   *The Logic of Evangelism.* Grand Rapids: Eerdmans.
Achebe, C.
  1989   "Conversation with Chinua Achebe." In *A World of Ideas* by Bill Moyers, 333-344. New York: Doubleday.
Acosta, Marcelo
  1991   "La adaptación transcultural al Islam." In *Ríos en la soledad.* Federico Bertuzzi, ed., 200-214. Santa Fe: Comibam.
Allen, Roland
  1962a *Missionary Methods: St. Paul's or Ours?* Grand Rapids: Eerdmans.
  1962b *The Spontaneous Expansion of the Church.* Grand Rapids: Eerdmans.
Allison, Norman E.
  1984   "Academic Preparation for the Missionary of the 1990s." Unpublished manuscript presented to the Advisory Council of the Division of Overseas Ministries of the Christian Missionary Alliance, March 12, 1984.
  1992   Personal letter to Kenneth Mulholland, August 24.
Amaladoss, Michael
  1990   "Mission from Vatican II into the Coming Decade." *Vidyajyoti Journal of Theological Reflection* 54(6):269-80.
  1992   "La mission comme prophetie." *Spiritus* 128:263-275.
Anderson, A.
  1990   "Pentecostal Pneumatology and African Power Concepts: Continuity or Change?" *Missionalia* 19(1):65-74.
Anderson, Gerald H.
  1988   "American Protestants in Pursuit of Mission: 1886-1986." *IBMR* 12(3):98-118.
  1991   "Mission Research, Writing, and Publishing: 1971-1991." *IBMR* 15(4):165-172.
Anderson, Gerald H., ed.
  1961   *The Theology of the Christian Mission.* New York: McGraw-Hill.
Anderson, Gerald H., and Thomas F. Stransky.
  1976   *Mission Trends No. 3: Third World Theologies.* Grand Rapids: Eerdmans.
Anderson, Ray S.
  1991   *The Praxis of Pentecost: Revisioning the Church's Life and Mission.* Pasadena: Fuller Theological Seminary. Republished as *Ministry on the Fire Line.*
  1993   *Ministry on the Fire Line.* Downers Grove: InterVarsity.
Anderson, Rufus
  1869   *Foreign Missions: Their Relations and Claims.* New York: Scribners.
Arias, Mortimer, and Alan Johnson
  1992   *The Great Commission: Biblical Models.* Nashville: Abingdon.

Armstrong, Regis, and Ignatius Brady
    1982   *Francis and Clare: The Complete Works*. New York/Ramsey/Toronto:
            Paulist Press.
Athyal, Saphir P.
    1992   Letters to Gerald H. Anderson, March 31, June 6, and September 15.
Autrey, C. E.
    1959   *Basic Evangelism*. Grand Rapids: Zondervan.
Azariah, V. S.
    1910   *World Missionary Conference 1910: The History and Records of the
            Conference*. Vol. I. Edinburgh: Oliphants, Anderson and Ferrier.
Barbour, Ian G.
    1974   *Myths, Models and Paradigms: A Comparative Study in Science and
            Religion*. New York: Harper & Row. (Reprinted by HarperSanFrancisco,
            1976.)
    1990   *Religion in an Age of Science*. New York: Harper & Row.
Barclay, William
    1953   *The Acts of the Apostles*. Philadelphia: Westminster.
Baritz, Loren
    1985   *Backfire: Vietnam—The Myths That Made Us Fight, the Illusions That
            Helped Us Lose, the Legacy That Haunts Us Today*. New York: Ballantine.
Barker, Joel
    1992   *Future Edge: Discovering the New Paradigms of Success*. New York:
            William Morrow.
Barrett, David B.
    1986   *World-Class Cities and World Evangelization*. Birmingham, AL: New
            Hope.
    1988   "The Twentieth-Century Pentecostal/Charismatic Renewal in the Holy
            Spirit, with Its Goal of World Evangelization." *IBMR* 12(3):119-129.
Barrett, David B., ed.
    1982   *World Christian Encyclopedia*. Nairobi and New York: Oxford Univer-
            sity Press.
Barth, Karl
    1958   *Church Dogmatics*. Edinburgh: T & T Clark.
Bassham, Rodger
    1979   *Mission Theology: 1948-1975 Years of Worldwide Creative Tension,
            Ecumenical, Evangelical and Roman Catholic*. Pasadena: William Carey
            Library.
Baur, John
    1994   *Two Thousand Years of Christianity in Africa: An African History 62-
            1992*. Nairobi, Kenya: Paulines.
Bavinck, J. H.
    1960   *An Introduction to the Science of Missions*. David H. Freeman, trans.
            Phillipsburg, NJ: Presbyterian and Reformed.
    1977   *An Introduction to the Science of Missions*. David H. Freeman, trans.
            Phillipsburg, NJ: Presbyterian and Reformed. (Originally published in
            1960.)
Beaver, R. Pierce.
    1976   "The American Protestant Theological Seminary and Missions: An His-
            torical Survey." *Missiology* 4(1):75-87.

Bediako, Kwame
  1992   *Urgent Questions concerning Christianity in Africa: Some Reflections on a Manifesto.* Unpublished paper.
Bellah, Robert N., et. al.
  1985   *Habits of the Heart: Individualism and Commitment in American Life.* Berkeley: University of California Press.
  1991   *The Good Society.* New York: A. A. Knopf.
Berger, Peter
  1990   "Foreword." In *Tongues of Fire: The Explosion of Protestantism in Latin America* by David Martin. Oxford, England and Cambridge, MA: Basil Blackwell.
Berkhof, Hendrikus
  1979   *Christian Faith: An Introduction to the Study of Faith.* Grand Rapids: Eerdmans.
Bernanos, Georges
  1937   *The Diary of a Country Priest.* New York: Macmillan.
Berney, James E., ed.
  1979   *You Can Tell the World.* Downers Grove: InterVarsity.
Bertuzzi, Federico
  1992   *El esfuerzo misionero en y desde America Latina.* Quito: CLADE III.
Bevans, Stephen B.
  1991   "Seeing Mission through Images." *Missiology* 19(1):56-57.
  1992   *Models of Contextual Theology.* Maryknoll, NY: Orbis Books.
Bevans, Stephen B., and James A. Scherer
  1992   "Mission Statements: How They Are Developed and What They Tell Us." *IBMR* 16(3):98-104.
Billy Graham Center
  1979   *An Evangelical Agenda: 1984 and Beyond.* Pasadena: William Carey Library.
Bird, Brian
  1990   "Reclaiming the Urban War Zones." *Christianity Today* (January 15):16-20.
Birnbrauer, Herman
  1993   "Identifying, Selecting, and Training Instructors." In *The ASTD Handbook of Instructional Technology.* George M. Piskurich, ed. New York: McGraw-Hill.
Blauw, Johannes
  1962   *The Missionary Nature of the Church.* Grand Rapids: Eerdmans.
Boer, Harry
  1961   *Pentecost and Missions.* Grand Rapids: Eerdmans.
Boff, Clodovis
  1987   *Theology and Praxis: Epistemological Foundations.* Maryknoll, NY: Orbis Books.
Boff, Leonardo
  1979   *Liberating Grace.* Maryknoll, NY: Orbis Books.
Boff, Leonardo, and Clodovis Boff
  1987   *Introducing Liberation Theology.* Maryknoll, NY: Orbis Books.

Bosch, David J.
  1978   "The Why and How of a True Biblical Foundation for Mission." In *Zending op Weg Naar De toekomst: Essays Aangeboden Aan Prof J. Verkuyl.* J. D. Gort, ed., 33-45. Kampen, The Netherlands: Kok.
  1980   *Witness to the World: The Christian Mission in Theological Perspective.* London: Marshall, Morgan and Scott.
  1982   "Theological Education in Missionary Perspective." *Missiology* 10(1):13-34.
  1983   "An Emerging Paradigm for Mission." *Missiology* 11(4):485-510.
  1984   "Missions in Theological Education." In *Missions and Theological Education in World Perspective.* Harvie Conn and Samuel Rowan, eds., xiv-xli. Farmington, MI: Associates of Urbanus.
  1986   "Toward a Hermeneutic for Biblical Studies and Mission." *Mission Studies* 3(2):65-79.
  1987   "Vision for Mission." *IRM* 76(301):8-15.
  1988   "Church Growth Missiology." *Missionalia* 16(1):13-24.
  1991   *Transforming Mission: Paradigm Shifts in Theology of Mission.* Maryknoll, NY: Orbis Books.
  1992   "Your Will Be Done? Critical Reflection on San Antonio." *Missionalia* 17(2):26-138.
  1993   "Reflections on Biblical Models of Mission." In *Toward the 21st Century in Christian Mission.* James M. Phillips and Robert T. Coote, eds., 175-192. Grand Rapids: Eerdmans.
Braaten, Carl E.
  1992   *No Other Gospel! Christianity among the World Religions.* Minneapolis: Fortress.
Brereton, Virginia Lieson
  1990   *Training God's Army: the American Bible School, 1880-1940.* Bloomington and Indianapolis, IN: Indiana University Press.
Brink, Paul
  1990   "Las Acacias Evangelical Pentecostal Church, Caracas, Venezuela." *Urban Mission* 7(3):46-50.
Brown, Arthur J.
  1907   *The Foreign Missionary: An Incarnation of a World Movement.* London: Revell.
Brown, Colin
  1968   *Philosophy and the Christian Faith.* Downers Grove: InterVarsity.
Brown, Robert McAfee
  1978   *Theology in a New Key: Responding to Liberation Themes.* Philadelphia: Westminster.
  1984   *Unexpected News: Reading the Bible with Third World Eyes.* Philadelphia: Westminster.
Bruce, F. F.
  1954   *The Book of Acts.* Grand Rapids: Eerdmans.
Brunner, Emil
  1931   *The Word and the World.* London: SCM.
Burgess, Stanley M., and Gary B. McGee, eds.
  1988   *Dictionary of Pentecostal and Charismatic Movements.* Grand Rapids: Zondervan.

Burkhalter, William
1984　*A Comparative Analysis of the Missiologies of Roland Allen and Donald Anderson McGavran.* Ph.D. dissertation, Southern Baptist Theological Seminary, Louisville, KY.

Burnham, Frederic B.
1989　*Postmodern Theology: Christian Faith in a Pluralist World.* San Francisco: Harper & Row.

Burrows, William R., ed.
1993　*Redemption and Dialogue: Reading* Redemptoris Missio *and* Dialogue and Proclamation. Maryknoll, NY: Orbis Books.

Bush, Luis
1990　"Getting to the Core of the Core—The 10/40 Window." *AD 2000 and Beyond,* September-October:4-8.

Callahan, Kennon L.
1990　*Effective Church Leadership: Building on the Twelve Keys.* New York: Harper & Row.

Cameron, Nigel, David Wright, Donald Meek, and David Lachman, eds.
1993　*A Dictionary of Scottish Church History and Theology.* Downers Grove: InterVarsity Press.

Carey, Willliam
1891　*An Inquiry into the Obligations of Christians to Use Means for the Conversion of the Heathens.* London: Hodder and Stoughton.

CELAM
1990　*Nueva Evangelización: Genesis y Lineas de un Proyecto Misionero.* Bogota: Consejo Episcopal Latinoamericano.

Chopp, Rebecca
1986　*The Praxis of Suffering: An Introduction of Liberation and Political Theologies.* Maryknoll, NY: Orbis Books.

Christian, Jayakumar
1993　"Analysis of Historical Responses to the Poor." Unpublished tutorial paper, School of World Mission, Fuller Theological Seminary.

Clinton, J. Robert
1988a　"Leadership Development Theory: Adapting Grounded Theory Research to Comparative Studies among High Level Leaders." Ph.D. dissertation, Fuller Theological Seminary.
1988b　*The Making of a Leader.* Colorado Springs: NavPress.
1989　*Leadership Emergence Theory: A Self-Study Manual for Analyzing the Development of a Christian Leader.* Altadena, CA: Barnabas Resources.

Coalter, Milton J.
1995　"Introduction." In *How Shall We Witness? Faithful Evangelism in a Reformed Tradition.* Milton J. Coalter and Virgil Cruz, eds., xiii-xx. Louisville: Westminster/John Knox Press.

Coe, Shoki
1976　"Contextualizing Theology." In *Mission Trends No. 3: Third World Theologies.* Gerald Anderson and Thomas Stransky, eds., 19-24. Grand Rapids: Eerdmans.

1988   "What Is Theological Education?" *Asia Journal of Theology* 2(2):546-547.

COMLA 3
1988   *America, llegó tu hora de ser Evangelizadora.* Bogota: Consejo Episcopal Latinoamericano.

Conn, Harvie M.
1978   "Contextualization: A New Dimension for Cross-Cultural Hermeneutics." *EMQ* 14(1):39-46.
1983   "The Missionary Task of Theology: A Love/Hate Relationship." *Westminster Theological Journal* 45:1-21.
1987   *A Clarified Vision for Urban Mission.* Grand Rapids: Zondervan.
1992   *Eternal Word and Changing Worlds: Theology, Anthropology, and Mission and Trialogue.* Phillipsburg, NJ: Presbyterian and Reformed. (Originally printed by Zondervan, Grand Rapids, 1984.)
1993a   "A Contextual Theology of Mission for the City." In *The Good News of the Kingdom: Mission Theology for the Third Millennium.* Charles Van Engen, Dean Gilliland, and Paul Pierson, eds., 96-106. Maryknoll, NY: Orbis Books.
1993b   "Urban Mission." In *Toward the 21st Century in Christian Mission.* James Phillips and Robert Coote, eds., 318-337. Grand Rapids: Eerdmans.

Conn, Harvie, M., ed.
1990   *Practical Theology and the Ministry of the Church, 1952-1984, Essays in Honor of Edmund Clowney.* Phillipsburg, NJ: Presbyterian and Reformed.

Conn, Harvie M., and Samuel F. Rowen, eds.
1984   *Missions and Theological Education in World Perspective.* Farmington, MI: Associates of Urbanus.

Cornoy, Martin
1974   *Seduction as Cultural Imperialism.* New York: David McCay.

Costas, Orlando E.
1974   *The Church and Its Mission: A Shattering Critique from the Third World.* Wheaton: Tyndale.
1975   *El Protestantismo en América Latina Hoy: Ensayos del Camino (1972-1974).* San José, Costa Rica: INDEF.
1976   *Theology of the Crossroads in Contemporary Latin America: Missiology in Mainline Protestantism, 1969-1974.* Amsterdam: Rodopi.
1979   *The Integrity of Mission: The Inner Life and Outreach of the Church.* New York: Harper & Row.
1982   *Christ Outside the Gate: Mission Beyond Christendom.* Maryknoll, NY: Orbis Books.
1989   *Liberating News: A Theology of Contextual Evangelization.* Grand Rapids: Eerdmans.
1992   "Dimensiones del Crecimiento Integral de la Iglesia." In *La Misión de la Iglesia: Una Visión Panorámica.* Valdir Steuernagel, ed., 109-122. San José, Costa Rica: Visión Mundial Internacional.

Costello, Gerald M.
1979   *Mission to Latin America.* Maryknoll, NY: Orbis Books.

Covey, Stephen
1991   *Principle Centered Leadership.* New York: Summit.

Cranfield, Charles
    1975-1979 *A Critical Exegetical Commentary on the Epistle to the Romans.* 2 vols. 6th ed. Edinburgh: Clark.
    1980   "Romans 9:30-10:4." *Interpretation: A Journal of Bible and Theology* 34:71-74.

Damen, Franz
    1987   "Las sectas: ¿avalancha o desafío?" *Cuarto Intermedio* 3 (Mayo):45-63.

Danker, William J., and Wi Jo Kang, eds.
    1971   *The Future of the Christian World Mission.* Grand Rapids: Eerdmans.

Davidson, Basil
    1992   *The Black Man's Burden.* New York: Times Books.

Davis, Stanley
    1987   *Future Perfect.* Reading, MA.: Addison-Wesley.

Dawson, John
    1989   *Taking Our Cities for God.* Altamonte Springs, FL: Creation House.
    1990   "Winning the Battle for Your Neighborhood." *Charisma and Christian Life* (April):47-61.

Dayton, Donald W., and F. Burton Nelson
    1974   "The Theological Seminary and the City." In *The Urban Mission.* Craig Ellison, ed. Grand Rapids: Eerdmans.

De Ridder, Richard
    1975   *Discipling the Nations.* Grand Rapids: Baker. (Originally published as *The Dispersion of the People of God,* Kampen, The Netherlands: Kok, 1971.)

Deford, Frank
    1976   "Religion in Sport." *Sports Illustrated* (April 19, 26, and May 3).

Deiros, Pablo
    1992   *Historia del cristianismo en América Latina.* Buenos Aires: FTL.

Dei Verbum
    1966   In *The Documents of Vatican II.* Walter M. Abbott, S.J., ed., 11-128. Piscataway, NJ: America Press.

Delling, Gerhard
    1979   "Artios/Katartidzo." In *Theological Dictionary of the New Testament.* Gerhard Kittel, ed. Geoffrey Bromiley, trans. Vol. a, 475-476. Grand Rapids: Eerdmans.

Deniel, R.
    1975   *Religions dans la ville: Croyances et changements à Abidjan.* Abidjan: INADES.

Dressel, Paul, and Dora Marcus
    1982   *On Teaching and Learning in College.* San Francisco: Jossey-Bass.

Duff, Alexander
    1866   *Foreign Missions: Being the Substance of an Address Delivered before the General Assembly of the Free Church of Scotland, on Friday Evening, June 1, 1866.* Edinburgh: Elliot.
    1868   "Evangelistic Theology." An inaugural address delivered in the Common Hall of the New College, Edinburgh, on Thursday, 7 November 1867. Edinburgh: Elliot.

Dussel, Enrique
  1981 *A History of the Church in Latin America: Colonialism to Liberation (1492-1979).* Alan Neely, trans. and rev. Grand Rapids: Eerdmans.
  1992 Letter to Gerald H. Anderson, June 25.
Dutt, R. C.
  1950 *The Economic History of India.* London: Routledge and Kegan Paul.
Dyrness, William A.
  1983 *Let the Earth Rejoice: A Biblical Theology of Holistic Mission.* Pasadena: Fuller Seminary Press.
  1990 *Learning about Theology from the Third World.* Grand Rapids: Zondervan.
Edwards, Jonathan
  1854 *The Works of President Edwards.* Vol. IV. New York: Leavitt, Trow and Co. (Originally published by Isaiah Thomas, Worcester, 1808-09.)
Elliston, Edgar J.
  1991 *Christian Relief and Development: Training Workers for Effective Ministry.* Dallas: Word.
  1993 *Home-Grown Leaders.* Pasadena: William Carey Library.
Elliston, Edgar J., and J. Timothy Kauffman
  1993 *Developing Leaders for Urban Ministries.* New York: Peter Lang.
Escobar, Samuel
  1987 "Recruitment of Students for Mission." *Missiology* 15(4):529-45.
  1991 "Evangelical Theology in Latin America: The Development of a Missiological Christology." *Missiology* 19(3):315-32.
  1992 "The Elements of Style in Crafting New International Mission Leaders" *EMQ* 28(1):6-15.
  1993 "The Whole Gospel for the Whole World from Latin America." *Transformation* 10(1):30-32.
Ferm, Dean William
  1986 *Third World Theologies: An Introductory Survey.* Maryknoll, NY: Orbis Books.
Fetzer, James H.
  1993a *Foundations of the Philosophy of Science: Recent Developments.* New York: Paragon House.
  1993b *Philosophy of Science.* New York: Paragon House.
Flannery, Austin, ed.
  1975 *Vatican Council II: The Conciliar and Post Conciliar Documents.* Northport, NY: Costello.
Fleming, Bruce
  1980 *Contextualization of Theology.* Pasadena: William Carey Library.
Ford, LeRoy
  1991 *A Curriculum Design Manual for Theological Education.* Nashville: Broadman.
Forman, Charles W.
  1974 "The Role of Mission Studies in Theological Education." In *Missions in Education, Proceedings: Twelfth Biennial Meeting of the Association of Professors of Mission*, 39ff. Chicago: Association Professors of Mission.

Fountain, Daniel E.
1989   *Health, the Bible and the Church.* Wheaton: BGC Monograph.
Francis of Assisi
        Canticle of Brother Sun.
Freytag, W.
1961   "Weltmissionskonferenzen." In *Reden und Aufsätze.* Teil II, 97-110.
        München: Kaiser Verlag.
Fritch, Thomas
1990   "It Started at the Dumpster." *Urban Mission* 7(5):54-57.
Frizen, Edwin L., Jr.
1992   *75 Years of IFMA (1917-1992): The Nondenominational Missions Move-
        ment.* Pasadena: William Carey Library.
Gaudium et Spes
1975   In *Vatican II: The Conciliar and Post-Conciliar Documents.* Vol. 1.
        Austin Flannery, ed., 903-1001. Northport, NY: Costello. (Originally
        written in 1965.)
Gensichen, Hans-Werner
1971   *Glaube für die Welt: Theologische Aspekte der Mission.* Gütersloh: Gerd
        Mohn.
Gibellini, Rosino, ed.
1975   *Frontiers in Theology of Latin America.* Maryknoll, NY: Orbis Books.
Giddens, Anthony
1990   *The Consequences of Modernity.* Stanford, CA: Stanford University
        Press.
Gilkey, Langdon
1987   "Plurality and Its Theological Implications." In *The Myth of Christian
        Uniqueness: Toward a Pluralistic Theology of Religions.* John Hick and
        Paul F. Knitter, eds. Maryknoll, NY: Orbis Books.
Gilliland, Dean
1983   *Pauline Theology and Mission Practice.* Grand Rapids: Baker.
Gilliland, Dean, ed.
1989   *The Word among Us: Contextualizing Theology for Mission Today.* Waco,
        TX: Word.
Glasser, Arthur
1979   "Help from an Unexpected Quarter or, the Old Testament and
        Contextualization." *Missiology* 7(4):403-409.
1985a   "The Evolution of Evangelical Mission Theology Since World War
        II." *IBMR* 9(1):9-13. (Reprinted in *Evangelical Review of Theology*
        11[1]:53-64; and in *Practical Theology and the Ministry of the
        Church, 1952-1984, Essays in Honor of Edmund Clowney,* Harvie
        Conn, ed. [Phillipsburg, NJ: Presbyterian and Reformed, 1990, 235-
        252]).
1985b   "Foreword." *The Third Force in Missions.* Paul A. Pomerville. Peabody,
        MA: Hendrickson.
1987   "Church Growth at Fuller." *Missiology* 14(4):401-420.
1992   *Kingdom and Mission: A Biblical Study of the Kingdom of God and the
        World Mission of His People.* Unpublished syllabus, School of World
        Mission, Fuller Theological Seminary.

Glasser, Arthur, and Donald McGavran
    1983   *Contemporary Theologies of Mission.* Grand Rapids: Eerdmans.
Glazik, Jozef
    1968   "The Meaning and the Place of Missiology Today." *IRM* 57 (Oct.):459-467.
    1971   "Missiology." In *Concise Dictionary for the Christian World Mission.* S. Neill, G. H. Anderson, and J. Goodwin, eds., 387-389. London: Lutterworth.
Glover, Robert
    1924   *The Progress of World-Wide Missions.* New York: Harper & Row.
    1946   *The Bible Basis of Mission.* Los Angeles: Bible House of Los Angeles.
Gnanakan, Ken R.
    1989   *Kingdom Concerns: A Biblical Exploration towards a Theology of Mission.* Bangalore: Theological Book Trust.
Gonzalez, Justo L.
    1970   *Historia de las misiones.* Buenos Aires: La Aurora.
Good, N. Sanford
    1992   Personal letter, September 9.
Gorski M. M., and P. Juan F.
    1985   *El Desarrollo Histórico de la Misionología en América Latina.* Doctoral dissertation, La Paz.
Gort, Jerald D.
    1980   "Contours of the Reformed Understanding of Christian Mission: An Attempt at Delineation." *OBMR* 4(4):156-160. (Also published in *Calvin Theological Journal* 15(1980):47-60.)
Greenway, Roger S.
    1973   *An Urban Strategy for Latin America.* Grand Rapids: Baker.
    1985   "Cities, Seminaries and Theological Education." *Urban Mission* 1 (September):3-6.
Greenway, Roger S., and Timothy Monsma
    1989   *Cities: Missions' New Frontier.* Grand Rapids: Baker.
Griffiths, B.
    1985   *Marriage of East and West: A Sequel to the Golden String.* London: Collins.
Grigg, Viv
    1990   *Companion to the Poor.* Monrovia, CA: MARC. (Originally published by Albatross, Sutherland, Australia, 1984.)
Guder, Darrell L.
    1995   "Locating a Reformed Theology of Evangelism in a Pluralistic World." In *How Shall We Witness? Faithful Evangelism in a Reformed Tradition.* Milton J. Coalter and Virgil Cruz, eds., 165-186. Louisville: Westminster/John Knox Press.
Gunton, Colin
    1985   *Enlightenment and Alienation.* Grand Rapids: Eerdmans.
Gutiérrez, Gustavo
    1984a   *The Power of the Poor in History.* Maryknoll, NY: Orbis Books.
    1984b   *We Drink from Our Own Wells.* Maryknoll, NY: Orbis Books.
Harvey, David
    1984   *The Condition of Post Modernity: An Enquiry into the Origins of Culture Change.* Cambridge: Basil Blackwell.

Hass, Aaron
  1990   *In the Shadow of the Holocaust: The Second Generation.* Ithaca, NY: Cornell University Press.
Hastings, Adrian
  1967   *Church and Mission in Modern Africa.* London: Burns & Oates.
  1973   *Christian Marriage in Africa.* London: SPCK.
  1977   *African Christianity.* New York: Seabury Press.
  1979   *A History of African Christianity, 1950-1975.* New York: Cambridge University Press.
  1992   "My Pilgrimage in Mission." *IBMR* 16(2):60-64.
  1995   *Oxford History of the Christian Church in Africa.* New York: Oxford University Press.
Hauser, A.
  1989   "Walter Arnold: The Man and His Theology." In *Proclaiming Christ in Christ's Way: Studies in Integral Evangelism.* V. Samuel and A. Hauser, eds. Oxford: Regnum.
Hayford, Jack
  1990   *A Passion for Fullness.* Dallas, TX: Word.
Hedlund, Roger E.
  1985   *The Mission of the Church in the World: A Biblical Theology.* Grand Rapids: Baker.
Hedlund, Roger E., ed.
  1981   *Roots of the Great Debate in Mission.* Madras: Evangelical Literature Service.
Hempel, Carl G.
  1965   *Aspects of Scientific Explanation.* New York: The Free Press.
  1966   *Philosophy of Natural Science.* Englewood Cliffs, NJ: Prentice-Hall.
Hesselgrave, David J.
  1988   *Today's Choices for Tomorrow's Mission: An Evangelical Perspective on Trends and Issues in Missions.* Grand Rapids: Zondervan.
  1989   *Contextualization.* Grand Rapids: Baker.
Hesselgrave, David J., ed.
  1978   *Theology and Mission.* Grand Rapids: Baker.
  1979   *New Horizons in World Mission.* Grand Rapids: Baker.
Hexham, Irving, and Karla Poewe-Hexham
  1990   "Charismatics and Apartheid." *Charisma and Christian Life* (May):62-70.
Hick, John, and Paul F. Knitter, eds.
  1987   *The Myth of Christian Uniqueness: Toward a Pluralistic Theology of Religions.* Maryknoll, NY: Orbis Books.
Hiebert, Paul G.
  1978   "Conversion, Culture and Cognitive Categories." *Gospel in Context* 1(4):24-29.
  1985a   *Anthropological Insights for Missionaries.* Grand Rapids: Baker.
  1985b   "Epistemological Foundations for Science and Theology." *Theological Students Fellowship Bulletin* (March):5-10.
  1985c   "The Missiological Implications of an Epistemological Shift." *Theological Students Fellowship Bulletin* (May-June):12-18.
  1987   "Critical Contextualization." *IBMR* 11(3):104-111.

1989 "Form and Meaning in Contextualization of the Gospel." In *The Word among Us: Contextualizing Theology for Mission Today*. Dean Gilliland, ed., 101-120. Waco, TX: Word.

1993 "Evangelism, Church, and Kingdom." In *The Good News of the Kingdom: Mission Theology for the Third Millennium*. Charles Van Engen, Dean Gilliland, and Paul Pierson, eds., 153-161. Maryknoll, NY: Orbis Books.

Hocking, William Ernest
1932 *Rethinking Missions: A Laymen's Inquiry after One Hundred Years*. New York: Harper and Brothers.

Hodges, Melvin L.
1965 "Developing Basic Units of Indigenous Churches." In *Church Growth and Christian Mission*. D. McGavran, ed., 111-130. Pasadena: William Carey Library.

Hoekstra, Harvey
1979 *The World Council of Churches and the Demise of Evangelism*. Wheaton: Tyndale.

Hoffman, Shirl J., ed.
1992 *Sport and Religion*. Champaign: Human Kinetics.

Hogg, William Richey
1952 *Ecumenical Foundations: A History of the International Missionary Council and Its Nineteenth Century Background*. New York: Harper.

1987 "The Teaching of Missiology: Some Reflections on the Historical and Current Scene." *Missiology* 15(4):487-506.

Hollenweger, Walter J., coordinator
1986 *IRM* 75(297-298).

Hopkins, Gerard Manley
1964 "God's Grandeur." In *Modern Religious Poems: A Contemporary Anthology*. Jacob Trapp, ed. New York/Evanston/London: Harper & Row.

Hunter, George G., III
1992 *How to Reach Secular People*. Nashville, TN: Abingdon.

International Bulletin of Missionary Research
1967 "Theological Education for Missions," (Issue Theme). *IBMR* 56:222ff.

Ishino, Iwao
1978 "Principles of Anthropology." Lecture notes, Michigan State University.

Isichei, Elizabeth
1995 *A History of Christianity in Africa: From Antiquity to the Present*. Grand Rapids: Eerdmans; London: SPCK.

Itioka, Neuza
1990 "Mission in the 1990s." *IBMR* 14(1):7-10.

1991 "Third World Missionary Training: Two Brazilian Models." *Internationalising Missionary Training*. David W. Taylor, ed., 111-120. Exeter: Paternoster.

Jacobs, Donald R.
1993 "Contextualization in Mission." In *Toward the 21st Century in Christian Mission*. James M. Phillips and Robert T. Coote, eds., 235-244. Grand Rapids: Eerdmans.

Jenkinson, W., and H. O'Sullivan, eds.
1991   *Trends in Mission: Toward the Third Millennium.* Maryknoll, NY: Orbis Books.

Jocz, Jakob
1981   *The Jewish People and Jesus Christ after Auschwitz.* Grand Rapids: Baker.

John Paul II
1990   *Redemptoris Missio: Encyclical Letter on the Permanent Validity of the Church's Missionary Mandate.* Washington, DC: United States Catholic Conference. (Also published in *Catholic International* 2[1991]:252-292.)
1991   "Encyclical Letter *Redemptoris Missio*: On the Permanent Validity of the Church's Missionary Mandate (Excerpts)." *IBMR* 15(2):50-52.

Johnston, Arthur P.
1974   *World Evangelism and the Word of God.* Minneapolis: Bethany.

Jones, Tracey K., Jr.
1986   "History's Lessons for Tomorrow's Mission." *IBMR* 10(2):50-53.

Jongeneel, J. A. B.
1986/1991   *Missiologie.* 2 vols. The Hague: Boekencentrum. (An English edition of Volume 1 was published by Peter Lang in 1992. Volume 2 is scheduled to appear in 1997.) *Missiologie* is also published as a single volume.
1991   Letter to Gerald H. Anderson, November 12.

Judd, Steven
1987   "The Seamy Side of Charity Revisited: American Catholic Contributions to Renewal in the Latin American Church." *Missiology* 15(2):3-14.

Junod, H. P.
1935   "Anthropology and Missionary Education." *IRM* 24(94):213-228.

Kallgren, Robert C.
1988   "Bible Colleges: Their Present Health and Possible Future." Doctoral dissertation, University of South Carolina.
1991   "The Invisible Colleges." *Christianity Today* (September 16):27-28.

Kane, J. Herbert
1978   *A Concise History of the Christian World Mission.* Grand Rapids: Baker.

Kanter, Rosabeth Moss
1983   *The Change Masters: Innovation for Productivity in the American Corporation.* New York: Simon and Schuster.

Kasdorf, Hans
1989   Review of *Lexikon missionstheologischer Grundbegriffe* (Müller and Sundermeier, eds.). *IBMR* 13(3):140.

Kearsley, Greg
1993   "Costs and Benefits of Technology-Based Instruction." In *The ASTD Handbook of Instructional Technology.* George M. Piskurich, ed. New York: McGraw-Hill.

Kinsler, F. Ross
1983   *Ministry by the People: Theological Education by Extension.* Maryknoll, NY: Orbis Books/Geneva: WCC.

1985   "Theological Education among the People: A Personal Pilgrimage."
        Theología: Seminario de Extension, Informative Bulletin 2:1-12.
Kirk, Andrew
1990   "Theology for the Sake of Mission." *Anvil* 7(1):23-36.
Kirkpatrick, John
1988   "A Theology of Servant Leadership." D.Miss. dissertation, Fuller Theo-
        logical Seminary.
Klaus, Byron D., Murray W. Dempster, and Douglas Peterson
1991   *Called and Empowered: Pentecostal Perspectives on Global Mission.*
        Peabody, MA: Hendrickson.
Knight, James
1992   "Coordination of Missiological Education and Research in the SVD
        Asia-Pacific Zone, Verbum." *Verbum SVD* 33(3).
Knitter, Paul. F.
1985   *No Other Name?* Maryknoll, NY: Orbis Books.
Kraft, Charles H.
1979   *Christianity in Culture: A Study in Dynamic Biblical Theologizing in
        Cross-Cultural Perspective.* Maryknoll, NY: Orbis Books.
1989   *Christianity with Power: Your Worldview and Your Experience of the
        Supernatural.* Ann Arbor, MI: Servant .
1991   *Communication Theory for Christian Witness.* Maryknoll, NY: Orbis
        Books. (Originally printed by Abingdon, 1983.)
Kraft, Charles H., and Tom Wisely, eds.
1979   *Readings in Dynamic Indigeneity.* Pasadena: William Carey Library.
Krass, Alfred C.
1982   *Evangelizing Neopagan North America.* Scottdale: Herald.
Kuhn, Thomas S.
1962   *The Structure of Scientific Revolutions.* Chicago: University of Chi-
        cago Press.
1970   *The Structure of Scientific Revolutions.* 2nd ed., enl. Chicago: Univer-
        sity of Chicago Press.
1977   *The Essential Tension: Selected Studies in Scientific Tradition and
        Change.* Chicago: University of Chicago Press.
Küng, Hans, and David Tracy, eds.
1989   *Paradigm Change in Theology: A Symposium for the Future.* New York:
        Crossroad.
Lakoff, George
1987   *Women, Fire, and Dangerous Things: What Categories Reveal about
        the Mind.* Chicago: University of Chicago Press.
Lang, J., and M. Motte, eds.
1982   *Mission in Dialogue.* Maryknoll, NY: Orbis Books.
Langerak, A.
1992   "Healing, Releasing, Proclaiming in a Cruciform World." *IRM*
        81(323):447-463.
Latourette, K. S.
1967   *History of the Expansion of Christianity.* 7 vols. Grand Rapids:
        Zondervan.
Laudin, Larry
1977   *Progress and Its Problems.* Berkeley: University of California Press.

Lausanne Consultation on Jewish Evangelism
1986   *World Evangelization* 13(42).
Lausanne Covenant on World Evangelization
1974   International Congress of World Evangelization, Lausanne, Switzerland, July 1974.
Lawson, Steven
1990   "Defeating Territorial Spirits." *Charisma and Christian Life* (April):47-61.
Laytner, Anson
1990   *Arguing with God: A Jewish Tradition*. Northvale, NY: Jason Aronson.
Legrand, Lucien
1986   "The Missionary Command of the Risen Christ." *Indian Theological Studies* 23(3):290-309.
Lewis, Donald M.
1995   *Blackwell Dictionary of Evangelical Biography: 1730-1860*. Oxford, England: Blackwell.
Lingenfelter, Sherwood
1992   *Transforming Culture: A Challenge for Christian Mission*. Grand Rapids: MI: Zondervan.
Lumen Gentium
1975   In *Vatican II: The Conciliar and Post Conciliar Documents*. Vol. 1. Austin Flannery, ed., 350-426. Northport, NY: Costello. (Originally written in 1964.)
Luzbetak, Louis
1963   *The Church and Cultures: New Perspectives on Missiological Anthropology*. Pasadena: William Carey Library. (Reprinted by William Carey Library, 1970, 1975; reprinted by Orbis Books, 1988.)
Marshall, I. Howard
1980   *The Acts of the Apostles*. Grand Rapids: Eerdmans.
Martin, Alvin, ed.
1974   *The Means of World Evangelization: Missiological Education at the Fuller School of World Mission*. Pasadena: William Carey Library.
Martin, David
1990   *Tongues of Fire: The Explosion of Protestantism in Latin America*. Oxford, England, and Cambridge, MA: Basil Blackwell.
Maust, John
1992   "Latin American Church Graduates from Evangelization Crash Course." *Pulse* (October 9):4.
May, Rollo
1969   *Love and Will*. New York: W. W. Norton.
Mayers, Marvin
1974   *Christianity Confronts Culture: A Strategy for Cross-Cultural Evangelism*. Grand Rapids: Zondervan.
Mbembe, A.
1988   *Afriques indociles*. Paris: Editions Karthala.
McClung, L. Grant, Jr.
1986   *Azusa Street and Beyond: Pentecostal Missions and Church Growth in the Twentieth Century*. South Plainfield, NJ: Bridge.
1990   "Mission in the 1990s." *IBMR* 14(4):152-157.

1991a "Forecasting the Future of Pentecostal/Charismatic Church Growth." *Global Church Growth* (October-December):4-6.

1991b "Interdependence in Global Pentecostalism." *World Pentecost* 28 (Spring):18-20.

1991c "The Pentecostal/Charismatic Contribution to World Evangelization." In *Mission in the Nineteen 90s.* Gerald H. Anderson, James M. Phillips, Robert T. Coote, eds. Grand Rapids: Eerdmans.

McCoy, John
1989 "Robbing Peter to Pay Paul: The Evangelical Tide." *Latinamerica Press* 21(24)(June 22).

McCurry, Don
1992 "Trouble in the Harvest Fields." *Intercede* (November).

McFadden, Robert D.
1992 "Five U.S. Nuns Shot Dead near Liberia Convent." *Pasadena Star News* (November 1):1.

McGavran, Donald A.
1955 *The Bridges of God: A Study in the Strategy of Missions.* New York: Friendship; London: World Dominion.

1972 *Eye of the Storm: The Great Debate in Mission.* Waco, TX: Word.

1977 *The Conciliar-Evangelical Debate: The Crucial Documents, 1964-1976.* Pasadena: William Carey Library.

1984 *Momentous Decisions in Missions Today.* Grand Rapids: Baker.

1988 *Effective Evangelism: A Theological Mandate.* Phillipsburg, NJ: Presbyterian and Reformed.

1990 *Understanding Church Growth.* Grand Rapids: Eerdmans.

McGavran, Donald A., ed.
1965 *Church Growth and Christian Mission.* Pasadena: William Carey Library.

1972 *Crucial Issues in Missions Tomorrow.* Chicago: Moody.

McGee, Gary B.
1986/1989 *This Gospel Shall Be Preached: A History and Theology of Assemblies of God Foreign Missions to 1959.* Vols. 1 and 2. Springfield, MO: Gospel Publishing.

McIntosh, G. Stewart
1989 "Acosta and *The De Procuranda Indorum Salute*—A Sixteenth Century Missionary Model with Twentieth Century Implications." *The M. R. Bulletin*, Tayport 3(2).

McKinney, Lois
1993 "Missionaries in the Twenty-First Century: Their Nature, Their Nuture, Their Mission." *Missiology* 21(1):55-64.

Menninger, Karl
1973/1978 *Whatever Became of Sin?* New York: Hawthorne/Bantam.

Menzies, William
1988 "Current Pentecostal Theology of the End Times." *The Pentecostal Minister* 8(3):9.

Michel, Otto
1983 "The Conclusion to Matthew's Gospel: A Contribution to the History of the Easter Message." In *The Interpretation of Matthew.* Graham Stanton, ed. Philadelphia: Fortress, 30-41. (German original, 1950.)

Middleton, Vernon J.
    1990   "The Development of a Missiologist: The Life and Thought of Donald Anderson McGavran, 1897 to 1965." Ph.D. dissertation, Fuller Theological Seminary.

Míguez-Bonino, José
    1975   *Doing Theology in a Revolutionary Situation*. Philadelphia: Fortress.

Missiology
    1991   "The Gospel and Our Culture." Theme issue of *Missiology* 19(4).

Moffett, Samuel H.
    1992   *A History of Christianity in Asia*. San Francisco: HarperSanFrancisco.

Moltmann, Jürgen
    1977   *The Church in the Power of the Spirit: A Contribution to Messianic Ecclesiology*. London: SCM.

Morrow, L.
    1992   "Africa: The Scramble for Existence." *Time* (September 7):40-46.

Mott, John R.
    1900   *The Evangelization of the World in This Generation*. New York: Student Volunteer Movement for Foreign Missions.

Motte, Mary
    1991   *To Be Hope and Joy: Witness Bearing a Glimpse of God*. Washington, DC: U.S. Catholic Mission Association.

Mouw, Richard J., and Sander Griffioen
    1993   *Pluralisms and Horizons*. Grand Rapids: Eerdmans.

Mraida, Carlos
    1992   "El papel de la enseñanza de misionología en la educación teológica en America Latina." Unpublished paper. Buenos Aires.

Mukherjee, Ramakrishna
    1958   *The Rise and Fall of the East India Company*. Berlin: Deutscher Verlager Wissenschiften.

Müller, Karl, and Theo Sundermeier, eds.
    1987   *Lexikon missionstheologischer Grundbegriffe*. Berlin: Reimer Verlag.

Munck, Johannes
    1967   *The Acts of the Apostles. The Anchor Bible*. Garden City, NY: Doubleday.

Myers, Bryant
    1992   "A Funny Thing Happened on the Way to Ecumenical-Evangelical Cooperation." *IRM* 81(323):397-407.

Myklebust, Olav Guttorm
    1955   *The Study of Missions in Theological Education*. Vol. 1. Oslo: Egede Instituttet.
    1957   *The Study of Missions in Theological Education*. Vol. 2. Oslo: Egede Instituttet.
    1959   "Integration or Independence? Some Reflections on the Status of the Study of Missions in the Theological Curriculum." In *Basileia: Tribute to Walter Freytag zum 60, Geburtstag*. J. Hermelink and H. J. Margull, eds., 330-340. (Second edition, Evang. Missionsverlag, Stuttgart, 1961.)

Narullah, Syed, and J. P. Naik
    1951   *A History of Education in India*. London: Macmillan.

N'Diaye, J. P.
  1979   "Le combat continue." *Jeune Afrique* 978 (March 10).
Neely, Alan
  1993   "The Teaching of Missions." In *Toward the 21st Century in Christian Mission*. James Phillips and Robert Coote, eds., 269-283. Grand Rapids: Eerdmans.
Nehru, Jawaharlal
  1990   *The Discovery of India*. London: Oxford University Press.
Neill, Stephen
  1959   *Creative Tension*. London: Edinburgh House.
  1964   The Bampton Lectures.
  1968   *The Church and Christian Union*. London: Oxford University Press.
  1970   "The History of Missions: An Academic Discipline." In *The Mission of the Church and the Propagation of the Faith*. G. J. Cuming, ed. London: Cambridge University Press.
  1984/1985 *A History of Christianity in India*. 2 vols. London: Cambridge University Press.
Neill, Stephen, Gerald H. Anderson, and John Goodwin, eds.
  1971   *Concise Dictionary of the Christian World Mission*. London: Lutterworth; Nashville: Abingdon.
Newbigin, Lesslie
  1978   *The Open Secret*. Grand Rapids: Eerdmans.
  1983   *The Other Side of 1984: Questions for the Churches*. Geneva: WCC.
  1986   *Foolishness To the Greeks: The Gospel and Western Culture*. Geneva: WCC.
  1987   "Can the West Be Converted?" *IBMR* 11(1):2-7.
  1989   *The Gospel in a Pluralist Society*. Grand Rapids: Eerdmans.
  1991   *Truth to Tell: The Gospel as Public Truth*. Grand Rapids: Eerdmans.
  1992a "The End of History." *The Gospel and Our Culture*, Newsletter No. 13 (summer):1-3.
  1992b "Woord Vooraf." *Nieuwsbrief Evangelie en Cultuur* 1 (July):1.
Nida, Eugene A.
  1954   *Customs and Cultures*. New York: Harper.
  1972   *Message and Mission*. Pasadena: William Carey Library. (Originally published by Harper & Row, New York, 1960.)
Niles, Daniel T.
  1962   *Upon the Earth: The Mission of the God and the Missionary Enterprise of the Churches*. London: Lutterworth.
Nottingham, W.
  1992   "Redeeming the Time." *IRM* 81(323):435-440.
Ogden, Schubert M.
  1992   *Is There Only One True Religion or Are There Many?* Dallas: Southern Methodist University Press.
Orr, J. Edwin
  1973   *The Flaming Tongue*. Chicago: Moody.
  1974   *The Fervent Prayer*. Chicago: Moody.
  1975   *The Eager Feet*. Chicago: Moody.

Padilla, C. René
    1980   "Hermeneutics and Culture—A Theological Perspective." In *Down to Earth: Studies in Christianity and Culture*. John R. W. Stott and Robert T. Coote, eds. Grand Rapids: Eerdmans.
    1985   *Mission between the Times: Essays on the Kingdom of God*. Grand Rapids: Eerdmans.
    1992   "Wholistic Mission: Evangelical and Ecumenical." *IRM* 81(323):381-382.
Padilla, C. René, and Mark Lau Branson, eds.
    1986   *Conflict and Context: Hermeneutics in the Americas*. Grand Rapids: Eerdmans.
Pate, Larry D.
    1987   *Misionología: nuestro cometido transcultural*. Miami: Editorial Vida.
    1989   *From Every People: A Handbook of Two-Thirds World Missions with Directory/Histories/Analysis*. Monrovia, CA: MARC.
    1991   "Pentecostal Missions from the Two-Thirds World." In *Called and Empowered: Pentecostal Perspectives on Global Missions*. Murray W. Dempster, Byron D. Klaus, and Douglas Peterson, eds., 242-258. Peabody, MA: Hendrickson.
Paul VI
    1975   *Evangelii Nuntiandi: Apostolic Exhortation on Evangelization in the Modern World*. Washington, DC: United States Catholic Conference.
Peers, E. Allison
    1969   *Ramond Lull*. New York: Burt Franklin.
Peters, George
    1972   *A Biblical Theology of Missions*. Chicago: Moody.
Peters, Tom
    1988   *Thriving on Chaos*. New York: Alfred A. Knopf.
Peterson, Stephen L.
    1991   "North American Library Resources for Mission Research." *IBMR* 15(4):155-64.
Pfister, L.
    1988   "The 'Failures' of James Legge's Fruitful Life for China." *Ching Feng* 31(4):246-271.
Philip, John
    1828   *Researches in South Africa*. 2 vols. London: James Duncan. (Reprinted in 1969 by Negro Universities Press, New York.)
Phillips, James M., and Robert T. Coote, eds.
    1993   *Toward the 21st Century in Christian Mission*. Grand Rapids: Eerdmans.
Poloma, Margaret M.
    1986   "Pentecostals and Politics in North and Central America." In *Prophetic Religions and Politics: Religion and the Political Order*. Vol. 1. Jeffrey K. Hadden and Anson Shupe, eds., 329-352. New York: Paragon House.
Pomerville, Paul A.
    1985   "Foreword." *The Third Force in Missions*, vii. Peabody, MA: Hendrickson.
Pope, Stephen
    1991   "Expressive Individualism and True Self-Love: A Thomistic Perspective." *Journal of Religion* 71(3):384-399.

Pousson, Edward K.
  1992   *Spreading the Flame: Charismatic Churches and Missions Today.* Grand Rapids: Zondervan.
Powell, Elsa R. de, et al.
  1992   "Evangelical Involvement in the Political Life of Latin America." *Transformation* 9(3):8-12.
Prien, Hans Jürgen
  1985   *La historia del cristianismo en América Latina.* Salamanca: Sígueme.
Proceedings of the Union Missionary Convention held in New York, May 4th and 5th, 1854.
  1854   New York: Taylor and Hogg.
Puebla Document
  1979/1980 Official translation in *Puebla and Beyond.* John Eagleson and Philip Scharper, eds. Maryknoll, NY: Orbis Books.
Race, A.
  1983   *Christians and Religious Pluralism: Patterns in the Christian Theology of Religions.* London: SCM.
Rainer, Thom S.
  1993   *The Book of Church Growth: History, Theology and Principles.* Nashville: Broadman.
Reddin, Opal L., ed.
  1989   *Power Encounter: A Pentecostal Perspective.* Springfield, MO: Central Bible College Press.
Report
  1992   "Report: Consultation on 'Partnership in Mission—What Structures?' Yaoundé, Cameroon, 15-20 Oct., 1991" *IRM* 81(323):467-471.
Rieff, Philip
  1966   *The Triumph of the Therapeutic.* New York: Harper & Row.
Ro, Bong Rin
  1987   *The Bible and Theology in Asia Today.* Bangalore: Asia Theological Association.
Ro, Bong Rin, and Ruth Eshenaur
  1984   *The Bible and Theology in Asian Contexts.* Taichung, Taiwan, ROC: Asia Theological Association.
Roberts, W. Dayton, and John A. Siewert, eds.
  1989   *Mission Handbook.* Monrovia, CA: MARC.
Rooy, Sidney H.
  1992   "Theological Education for Urban Mission." In *Discipling the City: A Comprehensive Approach to Urban Mission.* Roger S. Greenway, ed., 223-245. Grand Rapids: Baker.
Roseberry, R. S.
  1934   *The Niger Vision.* Harrisburg, PA: Christian Publications.
Rzepkowski, Horst
  1992   *Lexikon der Mission.* Graz and Vienna: Styria.
Sacks, Jonathan
  1992   *Crisis and Covenant: Jewish Thought after the Holocaust.* Manchester: Manchester University Press.
Sanneh, Lamin
  1989   *Translating the Message: The Missionary Impact on Culture.* Maryknoll, NY: Orbis Books.

Saracco, Norberto
1992   *El evangelio de poder*. Quito: CLADE III.
Scharpff, Paulus
1964   *History of Evangelism*. Grand Rapids: Eerdmans.
Scherer, James A.
1971   "Missions in Theological Education." In *The Future of the Christian World Mission*. William Danker and Wi Jo Kang, eds. Grand Rapids: Eerdmans.
1985   "The Future of Missiology as an Academic Discipline in Seminary Education: An Attempt at Reinterpretation and Clarification." *Missiology* 13:4 (October):445-460.
1987a   *Gospel, Church and Kingdom: Comparative Studies in World Mission Theology*. Minneapolis: Augsburg.
1987b   "Missiology as a Discipline and What It Includes." *Missiology* 15(4):507-522.
1993a   "Church, Kingdom, and Missio Dei: Lutheran and Orthodox Correctives to Recent Ecumenical Mission Theology." In *The Good News of the Kingdom: Mission Theology for the Third Millennium*. Charles Van Engen, Dean Gilliland, and Paul Pierson, eds., 82-88. Maryknoll, NY: Orbis Books.
1993b   "Mission Theology." In *Toward the 21st Century in Christian Mission*. James M. Phillips and Robert T. Coote, eds., 193-202. Grand Rapids: Eerdmans.
Scherer, James A., and Stephen B. Bevans, eds.
1992   *New Directions in Mission and Evangelization I: Basic Statements 1974-1991*. Maryknoll, NY: Orbis Books.
1994   *New Directions in Mission and Evangelization II: Theological Foundations*. Maryknoll, NY: Orbis Books.
Schreiter, Robert
1982   "The Bible and Mission: A Response to W. Brueggemann and B. Gaventa." *Missiology* 10(4):428-34.
1985   *Constructing Local Theologies*. Maryknoll, NY: Orbis Books.
Schultze, Quentin J.
1990   "The Great Transmission." In *Pentecostals from the Inside Out*. Harold B. Smith, ed., 93-104. Wheaton, IL: Victor.
Scott, Waldron
1980   *Bring Forth Justice: A Contemporary Perspective on Mission*. Grand Rapids: Eerdmans.
Senior, Donald, and Carroll Stuhlmueller
1983   *The Biblical Foundations for Mission*. Maryknoll, NY: Orbis Books.
Sepulveda, Juan
n.d.   "Reflections on the Pentecostal Contribution to the Mission of the Church in Latin America." Unpublished paper. James Beaty, trans. Cleveland, TN: Church of God School of Theology.
Sharpe, E. J.
1965   *Not to Destroy but to Fulfil: The Contribution of J. N. Farquhar to Protestant Missionary Thought in India before 1914*. Lund: Gleerup.
Shaull, Richard
1991   *The Reformation and Liberation Theology*. Louisville: Westminster/John Knox Press.

Shaw, R. Daniel
    1988   *Transculturation: The Cultural Factor in Translation and Other Com-
            munication Tasks.* Pasadena: William Carey Library.
Shenk, Wilbert R.
    1983   *Henry Venn—Missionary Statesman.* Maryknoll, NY: Orbis Books.
    1984   "The 'Great Century' Reconsidered." In *Anabaptism and Mission.*
            Wilbert R. Shenk, ed. Scottdale, PA: Herald.
    1987   *The American Society of Missiology 1972-87.* Elkhart, IN: The Ameri-
            can Society of Missiology.
    1992   "Reflections on the Modern Missionary Movement." *Mission Studies*
            17(1):62-78.
Shibley, David
    1989   *A Force in the Earth: The Charismatic Renewal and World Evangelism.*
            Altamonte Springs, FL: Creation House.
Sider, Ronald, ed.
    1988   "Words, Works and Wonders: Papers from an International Dialogue
            between the Pentecostal/Charismatic Renewal and Evangelical Social
            Action." *Transformation* 5(4).
Simkins, Tim
    1978   *Nonformal Education in Development.* Manchester, England: Univer-
            sity of Manchester Press.
Singh, D. V.
    1982   Foreword. In *From the Middle of the Sixteenth to the End of the Seven-
            teenth Century (1542-1700).* Joseph Thekkedath. Vol. 2 of *History of
            Christianity in India,* v-vi. Bangalore: Theological Publications in India.
Skarsaune, Oskar
    1991   *Incarnation: Myth or Fact?* St. Louis: Concordia.
Smith, A. Christopher
    1993   A Cumulative Index to the *International Review of Mission,* 1912-1990.
            Geneva: WCC.
Smith, Edwin W.
    1924   "Social Anthropology and Missionary Work." *International Review of
            Mission* 13(52):518-531.
Smith, George Adam
    1881   *The Life of Alexander Duff DD, LLD.* London: Hodder and Stoughton.
    1902   *The Life of Henry Drummond.* London: Hodder and Stoughton.
Smith, Thomas
    1883   *Alexander Duffy, DD, LLD.* London: Hodder and Stoughton.
Soltau, Addison P.
    1988   "The Mission Curriculum of the Future." *Mission Bulletin* (The Re-
            formed Ecumenical Synod) 8:3(August):1-17.
Solzhenitsyn, Aleksandr I.
    1972   *The Nobel Lecture on Literature.* New York: Harper & Row.
Spindler, M.
    1992   "Recensie van *Transforming Mission: Paradigm Shifts in Theology of
            Mission* door David J. Bosch." *Wereld en Zending,* 21.3:103-7.
Spindler, Marc R.
    1988   "Bijbelse fundering en oriëntatie van zending." In *Oecumenische inleiding
            in de missiologie: teksten en konteksten van het wereld-christendom.* F. J.
            Verstaelen, ed., 132-154. Kampen, The Netherlands: Kok.

Spittler, Russell P.
1990   "Maintaining Distinctives: The Future of Pentecostalism." *Pentecostals from the Inside Out*. Harold Smith, ed., 121-134. Wheaton, IL: Victor.

Springer, Kevin, ed.
1988   *Power Encounters among Christians in the Western World*. San Francisco: Harper & Row.

Spykman, Gordon, Guillermo Cook, Michael Dodson, Lance Grahn, Sidney Rooy, and John Stam
1988   *Let My People Live: Faith and Struggle in Central America*. Grand Rapids: Eerdmans.

Srinivas, M. N.
1963   *Social Change in Modern India*. Berkeley: University of California Press.

Stackhouse, Max L.
1989   "The Theological Challenge of Globalization." *The Christian Century* 106(15):468-471.

Stafford, Tim
1986   "The Father of Church Growth." *Christianity Today* (Feb. 21):19-23.

Stamoolis, James
1987   *Eastern Orthodox Mission Theology Today*. Maryknoll, NY: Orbis Books.

Steinfels, Peter
1992   "Shepherds or Wolves? Whatever, Flocks Grow." *The New York Times* (Oct. 27).

Stendahl, Krister
1976   "In No Other Name (Acts 4:5-12)." In *Christian Witness and the Jewish People*. A. Sovik, ed., 48-53. Geneva: Lutheran World Federation.

Steuernagel, Valdir R.
1992   *La Misión de la Iglesia: Una Visión Panorámica*. San José, Costa Rica: Visión Mundial Internacional.

Stott, John R. W.
1976   *Christian Mission in the Modern World*. Downers Grove: InterVarsity.
1979   "The Living God Is a Missionary God." In *You Can Tell the World*. James E. Berney, ed. Downers Grove: InterVarsity.
1981   "The Living God Is a Missionary God." In *Perspectives on the World Christian Movement: A Reader*. Ralph D. Winter and Stephen Hawthorne, eds., 10-18. Pasadena: William Carey Library.

Stott, John R. W., and Robert T. Coote, eds.
1979   *Gospel and Culture*. Pasadena: William Carey Library, .
1980   *Down to Earth: Studies in Christianity and Culture*. Grand Rapids: Eerdmans.

Stott, John R. W., and Basil Meeking
1986   *The Evangelical-Roman Catholic Dialogue on Mission 1977-1984*. Grand Rapids: Eerdmans.

Stronstad, Roger
1984   *The Charismatic Theology of St. Luke*. Peabody, MA: Hendrickson.

Student Volunteer Missionary Union
1900   *Students and the Missionary Problem*. Addresses delivered at the International Student Missionary Conference, London, January 2-6, 1900. London: Student Volunteer Missionary Union.

Stufflebeam, Daniel L.
    1973   "Educational Evaluation and Decision Making." In *Educational Evaluation: Theory and Practice*. Blaine R. Worthen and James R. Sanders, eds. Worthington, OH: Charles A. Jones.
Sundkler, Bengt
    1960   *The Christian Ministry in Africa*. London: SCM Press.
    1961   *Bantu Prophets in South Africa*. 2nd edition. London/New York: Oxford University Press.
    1965   *The World of Mission*. Grand Rapids: Eerdmans.
Sunquist, Scott W.
    1992   Letter to Gerald Anderson, April 29.
Sweazey, George E.
    1953   *Effective Evangelism*. New York: Harper and Brothers.
Sweetser, Eve E.
    1990   *From Etymology to Pragmatics: Metaphorical and Cultural Aspects of Semantic Structure*. Cambridge: Cambridge University Press.
Synan, Vinson
    1992   *The Spirit Said "Grow."* Monrovia, CA: MARC.
Taylor, John V.
    1972   *The Go-Between God: The Holy Spirit and the Christian Mission*. London: SCM.
Taylor, William David
    1991   *Internationalising Missionary Training*. Exeter, England: Paternoster.
Templeton, Charles B.
    1957   *Evangelism for Tomorrow*. New York: Harper and Brothers.
Thomas, Norman E.
    1989   "From Missions to Globalization: Teaching Missiology in North American Seminaries." *IBMR* 13(3):103-107.
    1990   "Globalization and the Teaching of Mission." *Missiology* 18(1):13-23.
Thomas, Owen C.
    1988   "The Challenge of Postmodernism." *Anglican Theological Review*. 62(2):209-219.
Tippett, Alan R.
    1973   "Missiology: 'For Such a Time as This.'" *Missiology* 1(1):15-22.
    1974   "Missiology, A New Discipline." In *The Means of World Evangelization: Missiological Education*. Alvin Martin, ed., 25-31. Pasadena: William Carey Library.
    1987   *Introduction to Missiology*. Pasadena: William Carey Library.
Tippett, Alan R., ed.
    1973   *God, Man and Church Growth*. Grand Rapids: Eerdmans.
Toffin, G.
    1990   "Le degré zéro de l'ethnologie." *L'Homme* 113 (janvier-mars):138-150.
Toulmin, Stephen
    1961   *Foresight and Understanding*. New York: Harper.
    1972   *Human Understanding: The Collective Use and Evolution of Concepts*. Princeton, NJ: Princeton University Press.
Tyler, Ralph
    1949   *Basic Principles of Curriculum and Instruction*. Chicago: University of Chicago Press.

Utuk, Efiong
    1986   "From Wheaton to Lausanne: The Road to Modification of Contempo-
             rary Evangelical Mission Theology." *Missiology* 14(2):205-219.

Van Beek, H.
    1992   "New Relationships in Mission—A Critical Evaluation." *IRM*
             81(323):417-434.

Van Engen, Charles
    1981   *The Growth of the True Church*. Amsterdam: Rodopi.
    1987   "Responses to James Scherer's Paper from Different Disciplinary Per-
             spectives: Systematic Theology." *Missiology* 15(4):524-552.
    1989   "The New Covenant: Knowing God in Context." In *The Word among
             Us: Contextualizing Theology for Mission Today*. Dean Gilliland, ed.,
             74-100. Waco, TX: Word.
    1990   "A Broadening Vision: Forty Years of Evangelical Theology of Mis-
             sion, 1946-1986." In *Earthen Vessels: American Evangelicals and For-
             eign Missions, 1880-1980*. Joel A. Carpenter and Wilbert R. Shenk,
             eds., 203-232. Grand Rapids: Eerdmans.
    1991   *God's Missionary People: Rethinking the Purpose of the Local Church*.
             Grand Rapids: Baker.
    1992a   "Biblical Foundations of Mission." Unpublished course syllabus. School
             of World Mission, Fuller Theological Seminary.
    1992b   "Theologizing in Mission." Unpublished course syllabus. School of
             World Mission, Fuller Theological Seminary.
    1993a   "The Relation of Bible and Mission in Mission Theology." In *The Good
             News of the Kingdom*. Charles Van Engen, Dean Gilliland, and Paul
             Pierson, eds., 27-36. Maryknoll, NY: Orbis Books.
    1993b   "When Everything is Mission, Nothing is Mission: The Dilemma of
             Ecumenical Mission Theology, 1930-1990." In "Contemporary The-
             ologies of Mission" (unpublished course syllabus) by C. Van Engen.
             Pasadena: Fuller Theological Seminary. Reprinted as "Conciliar Mis-
             sion Theology, 1930-1990." In *Mission on the Way: Issues in Mission
             Theology*. Grand Rapids: Baker, forthcoming.
    1994a   "Shifting Paradigms of Ministry Formation." *Perspectives* 9(8):15-17.
    1994b   *Shifting Paradigms in Ministry Formation*. Glendora, CA: self-published.

Van Engen, Charles, Dean S. Gilliland, and Paul Pierson, eds.
    1993   *The Good News of the Kingdom: Mission Theology for the Third Mil-
             lennium*. Maryknoll, NY: Orbis Books.

Van Rheenen, Gailyn
    1983   *Biblically Anchored Missions: Perspectives on Church Growth*. Austin,
             TX: Firm Foundation.

Vandervelde, George
    1993   "Koinonia Ecclesiology: An Ecumenical Breakthrough?" *One in Christ*
             29:126-142.

Verkuyl, Johannes
    1978   *Contemporary Missiology: An Introduction*. David Cooper, trans. Grand
             Rapids: Eerdmans.

Verstraelen, F. J., et al., eds.
    1988   *Oecumenische Inleiding in de Missiologie: Teksten en konteksten van
             het wereldchristendom*. Kampen, The Netherlands: Kok.
    1995   *Missiology: An Ecumenical Introduction*. Grand Rapids: Eerdmans.

Vicedom, Georg F.
   1965   *The Mission of God: An Introduction to a Theology of Mission.* A. A.
          Thiele and D. Higendorf, trans. (From the German original, Missio Dei
          [1957]). St. Louis, MO: Concordia.
Vidales, Raúl
   1975   "Methodological Issues in Liberation Theology." In *Frontiers in Theol-
          ogy of Latin America.* Rosino Gibellini, ed., 34-57. Maryknoll, NY:
          Orbis Books.
Wagner, C. Peter, and F. Douglas Pennoyer, eds.
   1990   *Wrestling with Dark Angels.* Ventura, CA: Regal Books.
Walls, Andrew F.
   1975   "The Nineteenth-Century Missionary as Scholar." In *Misjonskall og
          Forskerglede, Festskrift til professor Olav Guttorm Myklebust.* N. E.
          Bloch-Hoell, ed., 209-21. Oslo: Universitetsforlaget.
   1981   "'The Best Thinking of the Best Heathen': Humane Learning and the
          Missionary Movement." In *Religion and Humanism: Studies in Church
          History 17.* K. Robbins, ed., 341-352. Oxford: Blackwell.
   1988   "Missionary Societies and the Fortunate Subversion of the Church."
          The Evangelical Quarterly 60(2):141-55.
   1991   "Structural Problems in Mission Studies." *IBMR* 15(4):147-155.
   1993   A Cumulative Index to the *International Review of Mission*, 1912-1990.
          Geneva: WCC.
Ward, Ted, and Sam Rowan
   1972   "The Significance of the Extension Seminary." *EMQ* 9(1):17-27.
White, J. E.
   1992   "African-American Eyes." *Time* (September 7):52-53.
White, John
   1988   *When the Spirit Comes in Power: Signs and Wonders among God's
          People.* Downers Grove: InterVarsity.
Whiteman, Darrell
   1992   "The Legacy of Alan R. Tippett." *IBMR* 16(4):163-166.
Wilder, Robert P.
   1936   *The Great Commission—The Missionary Response of the SVM in North
          America and Europe: Some Personal Reminiscences.* London: Oliphants.
Williams, Don
   1989   *Signs, Wonders, and the Kingdom of God: A Biblical Guide for the
          Reluctant Skeptic.* Ann Arbor, MI: Servant.
Williams, Ron, ed.
   1990   *Foursquare World Advance 26(3).*
"Willowbank Declaration on the Christian Gospel and the Jewish People."
   1986   *World Evangelization 13(43).*
Wilson, Frederick, ed.
   1990   *The San Antonio Report—Your Will Be Done: Mission in Christ's Way.*
          Geneva: WCC.
Wink, Walter
   1992   "The Myth of Redemptive Violence." *Sojourners* 21(3):18-21,35.
Winter, Ralph D.
   1969a *Theological Education by Extension.* Pasadena: William Carey Library.

1969b "The Worldwide Problem." In *Theological Education by Extension.* Ralph Winter, 36-53. Pasadena: William Carey Library.

1979 "The Future of the Church: The Essential Components of World Evangelization." In *An Evangelical Agenda: 1984 and Beyond,* 135-163. Pasadena: William Carey Library.

1994 "The Growth of the Gospel." *Missions Frontiers* 16(1-2):3.

Winter, Ralph D., and Stephen Hawthorne, eds.

1981 *Perspectives on the World Christian Movement: A Reader.* Pasadena: William Carey Library.

Witmer, S. A.

1962 *The Bible College Story: Education with Dimension.* Manhasset, NY: Channel.

Woehr, Chris

1992 "The Horror of Being a Mexican Evangelical." *Christianity Today* (October 26):68-69.

Woodberry, J. Dudley, ed.

1989 *Muslims and Christians on the Emmaus Road.* Monrovia, CA: MARC.

World Council of Churches

1989 "Message from the World Conference on Mission and Evangelism, San Antonio, Texas." *IBMR* 13(3):130-132.

Wright, G. Ernest

1952 *God Who Acts: Biblical Theology as Recital.* London: SPC.

Zwemer, Samuel M.

1943 *Into All the World.* Grand Rapids: Zondervan.

Index

Acosta, Jose de, 110
AD 2000 and Beyond, 64, 272
Africa, training of missiologists for, 93-100
AIMS (Association of International Missions Services), 64
Al-Azhar Mosque, Chair of Islamic Studies, 189-91
Alaska, 86-90
Allen, Roland, 40, 217
Alliance Biblical Seminary, 115
Allison, Norman E., 46, 47, 51
Amaladoss, Michael, 81-82
American Association of Bible Colleges (AABC), 47, 48
American Society for Training and Development, 249
American Society of Missiology, 29, 213
Anderson, Gerald H., 30, 138
Anderson, Rufus, 40, 217
Anthropological Insights for Missionaries (Hiebert), 142
Anthropology, 98, 135, 137, 141-42
Arnold, Walter, 75
Asia Graduate School of Theology, 115
Asia, training missiologists for, 112-19
Asian Center for Theological Studies and Mission, 114
Asian Institute of Christian Communication, 201
Asian Missiological Graduate School, 114
Assembly of Latin American Bishops, 102
Association of International Missions Services (AIMS), 64
Association of Professors of Mission, 224
Association of Theological Schools (ATS), 210, 265; Asia Graduate School of Theology, 115; Seoul Declaration, 116-17
Athyal, Saphir P., 26-27
Aubry, Roger, 109

Avante, 105
Azariah, V.S., 11
Bantu Prophets in South Africa (Sundkler), 28
Baptists, 182
Barker, Joel, 246
Barrett, David B., 25
Barrington College, 46
Baur, John, 28
Bavinck, J.H., 217
Bediako, Kwame, 98
Behavioral sciences, 5, 98, 133-43
Berger, Peter, 63
Bernard, J.H., 17, 18
Bertuzzi, Federico, 108
Bevans, Stephen B., 30, 81
Bible, 48, 116-17, 180; Pentecostals and Charismatics, 61; *see also* Bible translation
Bible College Movement, 43, 44, 47; evangelical roots, 51
Bible colleges, 4, 43-53, 146, 275; accessibility, 45-46; brevity, 46; contextual nature of education, 49-50; curriculum, 50-51; definition and characteristics, 44-46; mastery of the Bible, 48; origins and historical development, 46-47; practical education, 49; seminaries and, 44-45; spiritual formation, 50; women, admission of, 45
Bible Institute Movement, 43, 46, 47, 52, 177
Bible Institute of Los Angeles, 170, 177
Bible institutes, 45, 275
Bible schools, 210; *see also* Bible colleges; Bible institutes
Bible translation, 5, 151-58, 266; computer literacy, 158; discourse structure, 152-53; management of project, 156-58; metaphors, 153-54; role of missiologist, 154-58; role of native speakers, 152-54; training the

304